RED DAWN OVER CHINA

FRANK DIKÖTTER

RED DAWN OVER CHINA

HOW COMMUNISM CONQUERED A QUARTER OF HUMANITY

BLOOMSBURY PUBLISHING
NEW YORK · LONDON · OXFORD · NEW DELHI · SYDNEY

BLOOMSBURY PUBLISHING
Bloomsbury Publishing Inc.
1359 Broadway, New York, NY 10018, USA
50 Bedford Square, London, WC1B 3DP, UK
Bloomsbury Publishing Ireland Limited,
29 Earlsfort Terrace, Dublin 2, D02 AY28, Ireland

BLOOMSBURY, BLOOMSBURY PUBLISHING, and the Diana logo are
trademarks of Bloomsbury Publishing Plc

First published in 2026 in Great Britain
Published in the United States 2026

Copyright © Frank Dikötter, 2026
Maps © Michael Athanson, 2026

All rights reserved. No part of this publication may be: i) reproduced or transmitted in any form, electronic or mechanical, including photocopying, recording, or by means of any information storage or retrieval system without prior permission in writing from the publishers; or ii) used or reproduced in any way for the training, development, or operation of artificial intelligence (AI) technologies, including generative AI technologies. The rights holders expressly reserve this publication from the text and data mining exception as per Article 4(3) of the Digital Single Market Directive (EU) 2019/790.

Bloomsbury Publishing Plc does not have any control over, or responsibility for, any third-party websites referred to or in this book. All internet addresses given in this book were correct at the time of going to press. The author and publisher regret any inconvenience caused if addresses have changed or sites have ceased to exist, but can accept no responsibility for any such changes.

Library of Congress Cataloging-in-Publication Data is available

ISBN: HB: 978-1-63973-397-2; EBOOK: 978-1-63973-399-6

2 4 6 8 10 9 7 5 3 1

Typeset by Newgen KnowledgeWorks Pvt. Ltd., Chennai, India
Printed in the United States by Lakeside Book Company

To find out more about our authors and books visit www.bloomsbury.com
and sign up for our newsletters.

Bloomsbury books may be purchased for business or promotional use. For information on bulk purchases please contact Macmillan Corporate and Premium Sales Department at specialmarkets@macmillan.com.

For product safety–related questions contact productsafety@bloomsbury.com.

For my parents,
Françoise Koolen and Gerard Dikötter

All warfare is deception.

— Sunzi (Sun Tzu)

Contents

Preface   xii

1. Incubation (1921–1926)   1
2. Fomenting Revolution (1926–1927)   39
3. Red Terror (1927–1931)   72
4. The Soviets (1931–1934)   103
5. Survival (1934–1936)   137
6. United Again (1936–1941)   171
7. Biding Time (1941–1945)   204
8. Civil War (1945–1949)   239

Notes   273
Select Bibliography   330
Acknowledgements   346
Image Credits   348
Index   349

Preface

Time grinds everything into dust: memories, people, objects, even buildings designed to last a thousand years. Until recently the vast majority of people left nothing behind but the clothes on their backs, yet even in our own digital age a search on the internet for a close friend or family member deceased only a few years ago may yield no more than a handful of pitiful results. We cannot conjure them back, even fleetingly, to ask the questions that matter so much to us now, nor can we travel back in time, if only to take the social pulse of a vanished era. We can, however, immerse ourselves in the record of the past, from oral interviews, personal letters or postcards tucked away in a folder to the sprawling archival deposits of state institutions. It is a deeply flawed, potentially all-consuming if not impossible enterprise, but it remains the best alternative to time travel.

In the case of China there is an added complication: the country was hermetically closed for decades after the Communist Party came to power in 1949, and even today access to primary sources, not least Party archives, remains haphazard at best. The Party controls history, not only its own but also that of its erstwhile rivals.

Despite these restrictions, a window into the past is offered as the result of a formidable enterprise undertaken by the Party itself between 1981 and 1989. The Central Party Archives, under the control of the Central Committee, working in collaboration with provincial archives from every corner of the country, produced well over 300 volumes containing original Party documents from 1923 to 1949. The volumes were printed in a limited edition with restricted circulation, meaning that they were intended for the eyes of senior Party members only. Yet even though they could not be purchased in bookshops or consulted in public libraries, they found their way across the border into Hong Kong.

At 400 to 600 pages per volume, the collection represents an unparalleled foundation for anyone wishing to unearth more about the history of the Communist Party. Yet, somewhat paradoxically, it has had only sporadic use by historians. The reason, perhaps, lies in another paradox: what becomes abundantly clear in one document after another is how marginal the Communist Party was in the history of China from its foundation in 1921 to the end of the Second World War in 1945. In Wuxi, the industrial city north of Shanghai where steam whistles and electric sirens alerted more than 100,000 workers to their shift, the Party had just twenty-five members in 1929. One may point to relentless and bloody repression, but even before the Communists were forced underground in April 1927 the province of Zhejiang, with a population of 20 million, had no more than 2,600 members (roughly one in 7,700 people).[1] Countless reports from other parts of the country complain of Party members rarely paying their dues, displaying little interest in ideology, attending few meetings and squandering local resources. Disciplined Marxist-Leninists they were not. Some Party branches existed merely on paper, as their representatives inflated numbers to claim more resources from the central authorities. Almost every European country, with the exception of Nazi Germany, boasted a larger number of Communists as a proportion of their overall population than any province in China. Even Portugal, despite ferocious repression under António de Oliveira Salazar, had some 25,000 members in 1934, or one person in 280, while in China before 1940 the figure was no more than one in 1,700, even if we accept the vastly inflated figures provided by the Comintern (the abbreviated term for Communist International, an organisation set up in 1919 in Moscow to promote worldwide revolution). This level was roughly equivalent to Communist membership in the United

States, a country not generally considered a leader in the world Communist movement. Finland, where the Party was illegal, boasted roughly 5,000 Communist Party members in 1935, equivalent to one in 700 people. Gansu province, a desperately poor part of the agrarian hinterland with 6.7 million inhabitants, ripe for revolution according to Marxist ideology, claimed 264 adherents in 1939, not even one per 25,000 people. After an internal purge of members viewed as insufficiently committed to the cause, membership in Gansu dropped to 143 by the end of the year. Only after 1945 did the Party begin to grow meaningfully.[2]

Primary sources from foreign observers confirm the trend. One United States military attaché, whose job it was to travel the country to assess the balance of military forces, pointed out in February 1934 that 'belief in a danger from communism in China is not warranted by the facts': the Party held less than 2 per cent of China, excluding Mongolia, Manchuria and Tibet. Among their possessions was the notorious Jiangxi Soviet, which issued its own stamps and currency, all bearing the image of Mao Zedong. The territory was poor, mountainous and unproductive, and therefore highly undesirable. 'Today not one large city, one port or one revenue producing area is under Communist control,' concluded the attaché.[3]

The marginal nature of communism would have been apparent to any newspaper reader in the republican era, a period of momentous change between the fall of the empire in 1911 and the advent of a Communist regime in 1949. Even key strategic moments were hardly frontline news, for instance the collapse in October 1934 of the Jiangxi Soviet after several campaigns of encirclement by the central government, forcing Mao and his followers to flee the region in a poorly organised retreat later referred to as the 'Long March'. One might suspect censorship, but the Nationalist government was pleased to announce its victorious entry into Ningdu, Mao's red capital, on page 3 of the newspapers.

The voluminous reports filed by foreign consular authorities from every region in the country confirm the liminal position of the Communist movement. Competing for attention were a great many other organisations, from secret societies to local gangs and bandit groups, many preying on local villagers, a few recruiting them into their ranks. Some became large enough to act as a shadow government, finding a compromise with local communities and protecting them from other bandits. All along, well before the fall of the empire, suppression campaigns were intermittently launched, although they invariably came at a cost to the local population. Henan province – always poorer than its neighbours – had more than 50,000 bandits in the early 1920s, although Hunan had fewer than 2,000.[4] As the consul general in Shanghai observed in 1920, local riots, mutinies of troops and looting of towns were events that chronically recurred in China.[5] There were also the constantly shifting relations and occasionally violent clashes between local, provincial and central armies in an enormous country that was still seeking central leadership by 1930. China, by then, was roughly the same size as Europe, with 500 million people. There were full-fledged foreign wars, with a Sino-Soviet war involving hundreds of thousands of soldiers in 1929, not to mention Japan's 1931 invasion of Manchuria, followed by continuous infringements until war was declared in 1937.

Yet little of this is reflected in the existing literature. Whether scholarly volumes or popular books on the history of modern China, the narrative is all too often dominated by the Communist Party. At times it seems like a fairy tale: the country is racked by an unholy alliance of 'imperialist powers' and 'reactionary forces', the Communists mobilise the 'peasants' by taking the land from the rich and distributing it to the poor, then they gradually unite the people in their fight against the Japanese invader and the fascist Nationalist Party, their arch-enemy led by Chiang Kai-shek. There is, no doubt, a great deal of variation, if not controversy, in this narrative, but at heart it follows the historical vision of the Chinese Communist Party.

The Communists did not wait until victory in 1949 to expunge the record and control the narrative. After they had wandered the south of the country in search of a new base for well over a year during the 'Long March', a mere 6,000 men and a few women arrived in northern Shaanxi in 1935. There they joined a roughly equivalent local force and established a new Red Army.[6] After careful vetting, Mao invited Edgar Snow, a young, idealistic reporter from Missouri, to come and interview him. Every detail of the encounter was dictated: 'Security, secrecy, warmth and red carpet'.[7] Snow spent several months at the Communist base, enthralled by the mythical version Mao offered of himself and his Party. A few months later, an article appeared in the *China Weekly Review* in Shanghai, introducing the mysterious leader of the Chinese Communist Party to the rest of the world. Snow presented a ragtag group of red soldiers entrenched deep in the hinterland as a more viable alternative to the central government with its 1.7 million troops. Mao was the leader-in-waiting in a war of resistance against the Japanese invader.[8] It was all hubris. *Red Star over China*, a book-length account of Mao and the Communist Party, followed a year later, becoming an instant bestseller, translated into many languages. The book made Mao into a household name and became the basis for all subsequent accounts of the rise of the Communist Party, and by implication of the history of modern China. It is, at heart, a romantic tale of Communists fighting in the hills for freedom, a David and Goliath story in which sympathy goes to the boy with the sling.

Since the Communist Party controls the past, everything unrelated or inimical to its success has been consigned to oblivion. While its own Party archives are replete with references to the Communist Youth League, a rival which was often far more popular, this organisation, tasked with recruiting young people, is rarely evoked by official historiography in any detail. A whole range of alternative voices, including a rich tradition of democratic thought and practice that ran throughout republican China, has been relegated to the shadows after 1949.[9] As in the story of David and Goliath, nobody remains standing except Mao, armed with ideological conviction, against Chiang Kai-shek, fascist leader of the corrupt and brutal machine of government. Huge chunks of history have been censored, are entirely unknown or remain untouched, and not just in the official historiography of the People's Republic. One can search the secondary literature in English in vain for a reference to the Sino-Soviet war of 1929, the largest military conflagration between China and a European power ever fought on Chinese soil. According to Michael Walker, who published a book on the topic in 2017, the list of historians of modern China who fail to mention the war in even a single sentence is 'both long and impressive'.[10] Similar comments could be made about many other key events, as we will see. As Robert Marquand points out, while history around the globe has been taken to task, queried, deconstructed and reconstructed, China's triumphal version of its past 'remains quaintly untouched', whether at home or abroad.[11]

There exists an abundance of primary material that can help us navigate the murky waters of the past. Besides the enormous collection of internally circulated Party documents mentioned above, one can consult the archives of the Nationalist Party, deposited on the outskirts of Taipei, as well as the personal records of Chiang Kai-shek. No study of the Communist movement in China can proceed without consulting the archival holdings of the Great Powers, not least Britain, France and the United States. In Shanghai, the famous Sûreté, or Special Branch, had more than two thousand staff, including special agents and translators. Part of their job was to keep tabs on Comintern agents, both local and foreign. Russian material is indispensable, including the holdings of the Comintern on China, made available in five volumes in Moscow between 1994 and 2007.[12]

What emerges from an evidence-based approach? The key word is violence, and a willingness to inflict it. Communism was never popular in China, no more so than in Finland or in the United States, and it was brought to the population at the barrel of a gun. The Communist Party was founded in 1921 with help from the Comintern, an organisation established by Moscow in 1919 to 'struggle by all available means, including armed force, for the overthrow of the international bourgeoisie'.[13]

The Comintern also had an interest in the Nationalist Party, a revolutionary organisation established under a different name in 1912 after the Qing dynasty had been overthrown by a loose coalition of military leaders. These soon fell out, each controlling a different part of the country. Moscow offered men, money and munitions, demanding in exchange that the Communists be allowed into their ranks. As the Nationalists set out to unify the country in a military campaign in 1926, the Communists in their midst encouraged mobs to loot and burn the property of wealthy merchants and landowners along the way. They also singled out foreigners as agents of imperialism, causing such havoc that Chiang Kai-shek was prompted to remove them from the ranks and end the alliance imposed by Stalin.

For years afterwards, the Communists left a trail of destruction, surviving on loot and ransom as they laid siege to towns, burning government buildings, killing so-called 'class enemies', seizing their property and distributing it to the troops. As the sources of plunder dried up and government forces came to the rescue, the Communists were forced to seek greener pastures elsewhere.

In 1930, the Communist Party began to change tack, attempting to hold territory in the hope of building up a conventional army. But they continually faced the same problem: how to abolish taxes and distribute the land in the name of communism while extracting enough revenue to feed their own troops. Time and again, they discovered that there was no magical surplus to be doled out. The result of land seizure was greater poverty for all, as farmers with even the slightest portion of wealth were forcibly dispossessed, scaring the others into hiding their assets and producing no more than the strict minimum required to survive. The Communists also carried out violent purges against an array of real or imagined enemies, whether villagers who spoke out against the regime's exactions or people suspected of fraternising with the enemy. These tactics all militated against any productive economy, not to mention belief in the cause.

By 1936, after having been forced to meander through inhospitable terrain for over a year, both the Communist forces and their cause were spent. Stalin, again, intervened, saving them from annihilation. After Japan declared war in July 1937, Moscow began providing crucial logistical help to the Nationalists, who were once more forced to tolerate an alliance with the Communists. Over the next few years the Japanese Army would do what the Communists were not in a position to accomplish, namely attack, destroy or displace government troops from all major cities along the coast. The Communists, on the other hand, remained safely ensconced in the hinterland, a poor, dusty and isolated mountain area on a loess plateau in Shaanxi province with a capital called Yan'an.

Violence was not merely incidental to the revolution. As Simon Schama observed of the French Revolution, violence was its engine from the very beginning, since revolutionaries undertake to demolish the old order. But a revolution is also based on a vision of a better future. The Communist Party made continual pledges and promises: landlords would be reined in, foreigners booted out, capitalists held to account. In 1940, Mao published a pamphlet entitled 'On New Democracy', portraying the Communist Party as a broad front striving to unite all 'revolutionary classes'. He promised a multi-party system, democratic freedoms and protection of private property. It was an entirely fictitious programme, but one that held broad popular appeal, as tens of thousands of students, teachers, artists, writers and journalists flocked to Yan'an in the following years. Soon after they arrived, the new recruits were forced to examine their own pasts and denounce each other. Thousands of suspects were locked up, investigated, tortured, purged and occasionally executed, even as the propaganda continued to beam a message of justice and equality for all.

By 1945 Mao had fabricated a formidable propaganda machine and a tightly controlled Party, as well as a sizeable army of red soldiers, although he controlled only a fraction of the country. Stalin once more lent a hand, sending close to a million troops across the Siberian border to march towards Korea, occupying the strategically and industrially vital area of Manchuria along the way. The Russians stayed until May 1946, locking out the central government of Chiang Kai-shek, quietly handing over the countryside to the Communists and helping Mao transform his guerrilla fighters into a formidable fighting machine.

Attrition gradually emerged as the key approach, as the Communists showed greater determination than the government, waging a pitiless war of fire, famine and sword. In May 1948 they began laying siege to cities in Manchuria, starving them into surrender. Changchun fell in October after 160,000 civilians had died of hunger in a six-month blockade. Villagers, recruited under duress, were hurled in increasingly large numbers against enemy troops in what were called human waves, a tactic that would leave the United Nations troops overwhelmed a few years later in the Korean War. Throughout the civil war, which lasted from 1945 to 1949, millions of refugees tried to escape, pouring into government-occupied territory and burdening already stretched services to breaking point. No one ever witnessed people fleeing towards Communist-controlled areas during the civil war. Cities began to topple like dominoes, their leaders fearful of the consequences of resistance against the war machine built up by the Communists. Chiang Kai-shek and his government fled to Taiwan, also known as Formosa. By the end of 1949, after a long and bloody military campaign, the People's Republic of China was finally proclaimed. The Communist Party referred to its conquest of the country as a 'Liberation'.

For generations, historians have interpreted this 'liberation' as a triumph of great social forces unleashed and harnessed by the Communists, who proposed a progressive vision more in tune with the spirit of the modern age.[14] In reality, the Chinese Communist Party, not least their Chairman, became more determined than their opponents in carrying out unrestricted warfare, devoid of any rules. They excelled in a very traditional pursuit of power, prevailing over their opponents through the amoral application of military strategy, including every ancient tactic prescribed by Sun Tzu and the other great strategists of the past: feign, lie, deceive, retreat, hit, run, sabotage; view everything as a means to achieving the end. And, when at long last in a position to attack, overwhelm the enemy in a war of relentless attrition. Most of all, believe in the cause.

I
Incubation
(1921–1926)

On the morning of 21 January 1793, Louis XVI, former King of France, heard his last mass, received the priest's blessing and was taken by carriage through the crowded streets of Paris to the Place de la Révolution, where a scaffold awaited him. After his hair had been cut and the collar removed from his shirt, he was tied to a plank, his head placed under the guillotine. Decapitation was swift, although by one account the blade did not sever the neck in one clean cut but sliced through the back of the skull and into the jaw. Charles-Henri Sanson, who had been his faithful servant as royal executioner since 1778, pulled the dripping head of his erstwhile master from the basket and showed it to an ecstatic crowd.[1] It was the culmination of a revolution that had started in 1789 with the storming of the Bastille, a state prison that stood as a symbol of the despotism of the ruling monarchy.

The coffin with the king's body, his head placed at his feet, was lowered into a pit covered with quicklime. With him was buried the notion of divine right. The revolutionaries held that power should be vested in the people, not in God. Since the people were sovereign, a related political principle was proclaimed, namely that the people should select their leader through suffrage. It was a notion that would unfold gradually in the nineteenth century, conquering much of the world in due course, as political orders invoking some sort of spiritual or otherworldly mandate came under attack. Much of the nineteenth century was to be an 'age of revolution', as tensions between autocracy and democracy played themselves out. In France, the home of revolution, Napoleon proclaimed himself emperor within a few years, ending the First French Republic. After his downfall in 1815, the monarchy was restored, although Charles X, in turn, was swept away by yet another revolution, this one in 1830. A further revolutionary wave swept over Europe in 1848 but ended in failure, although over the following decades the ruling monarchies were obliged to uphold some of the values of 1789, including limited suffrage and freedom of speech and assembly. France only became a republic in 1871, while it took the catastrophe of the First World War to bring down monarchies in Germany, Austria-Hungary and Russia.

Much of the colonial world was in thrall to the principles of the French Revolution. In Haiti, for instance, Toussaint Louverture transformed a slave rebellion into a popular movement for independence. Although he died in 1802, his large and well-disciplined army succeeded in crushing the French two years later, as the world's first black republic was proclaimed. A power struggle ensued, resulting in Haiti being divided into two halves. Former enslaved Haitians went to the north, where Henri Christophe, a former general who had fought under Toussaint Louverture, established a kingdom in 1811. In the following years he proclaimed himself Henri I, King of Haiti, and used forced labour to erect extravagant palaces and a string of fortresses. Henri I created his own nobility, designing coats of arms for his dukes, counts and barons. Slowly he descended into paranoia, seeing plots and conspiracies everywhere. He shot himself with a silver bullet at the age of fifty-three.

'Liberté, égalité, fraternité', translated as 'liberty, equality, fraternity', was adopted as the national motto in both France and Haiti. But what did equality mean? The revolutionaries in Paris had abolished slavery in 1793, only for Napoleon to restore the trade in 1802, spurring a wave of revolutionary violence in the Caribbean. Nor was equality extended to women: a popular sanction was meant to replace divine sanction, but in Paris the revolutionaries limited suffrage to men alone.

The moment that the revolutionaries proclaimed the principles of liberty and equality, emancipation became a key political goal for a wide range of different communities. People from all walks of life, whether women, Jews, enslaved people or serfs, clamoured for release from inferior political status. To these groups, labour activists, inspired by a philosopher named Karl Marx, added the workers. Marx himself, still a relatively obscure journalist aged forty-six, announced in the constitution of the International Working Men's Association (later called the First International), convened in London in 1864, that 'the emancipation of the working classes must be conquered by the working classes themselves; that the struggle for the emancipation of the working classes means not a struggle for class privileges and monopolies, but for equal rights and duties, and the abolition of all class rule.'[2] Marx referred to trade and commerce as a 'capitalist system', an intrinsically exploitative order in which one dominant class, termed the 'bourgeoisie', used its ownership of the means of production to exploit another class, namely the 'proletariat'. Marx envisioned a future in which, after an initial period dominated by the workers who would exercise their dictatorship to abolish private property, all class distinctions would gradually fade away and a socialist future of plenty for all would emerge.

One question that divided those fighting for labour rights was whether socialism could be achieved through reform alone, or whether revolution was required. It was a pressing issue, not least in Germany, where in 1878 Chancellor Otto von Bismarck banned political organisations intended to spread socialist principles. Paradoxically, the Social Democratic Party, fearing that a wave of strikes would provoke even more repression, renounced the more revolutionary aspect of their programme as soon as the anti-socialist laws were lifted in 1890. Trade unions and legislative reform, they believed, would lead to an expansion of social democracy, which over time would transform capitalism into socialism. Change, in other words, would come at the ballot box, not at the barricades. Social revolutionaries disagreed. As the

Marxist theorist Rosa Luxemburg spelled out in 1899 in a pamphlet entitled *Reform or Revolution*, only the revolutionary conquest of power by the proletariat could lead to the 'suppression of capitalism itself', whereas reform would just suppress its abuses.[3]

In Russia, where revolutionaries aimed to overthrow the Tsarist regime, a similar split appeared. The Mensheviks, a faction of the Russian Social Democratic Labour Party led by Julius Martov, favoured a large, inclusive organisation, one which would reach across the political spectrum and pursue legal methods and trade union work. The Bolsheviks, led by Vladimir Lenin, were hardline revolutionaries with little faith in either democracy or the working classes. While Marx had proposed that the workers should emancipate themselves, Lenin came up with a very different vision. Instead of waiting for the workers to gain class consciousness and overthrow capitalism, as Marx had suggested, a group of professional revolutionaries, tightly organised along strict military lines, would lead the revolution and establish a dictatorship of the proletariat to engineer the transition from capitalism to communism from above, ruthlessly eliminating all enemies of progress. 'But that is dictatorship you are advocating,' Leon Trotsky allegedly protested one day, to which Lenin replied, 'There is no other way.' Revolution, for the Bolsheviks, was war, violence its very foundation.[4]

***

Prior to 1926, the word 'communist' was not used when foreign authorities in the Shanghai International Settlement mentioned political activities inspired by Moscow. Bolshevism was spoken of instead.[5]

In October 1917, Lenin and the Bolsheviks had stormed the Winter Palace in St Petersburg, proclaiming a new government based on the 'dictatorship of the proletariat'. Inspired by 1789, they later referred to their seizure of power as a 'revolution'. The coup sent shockwaves through Europe and beyond. In one decree after another, the means of production, including land, banks, industry and transportation, were confiscated without compensation, handed over to 'the peasants and the workers'.

Church property was folded into the state. In February 1918 the new regime repudiated all sovereign debt and other financial obligations, expropriating the combined assets of foreign nations in Russia. International finance was stunned, Britain and France in particular losing tens of millions of pounds of investments.[6]

After the First World War ended in November 1918, a revolutionary wave unfolded across Europe as workers, after years of slaughter on the battlefield and regimentation on the factory floor, turned to industrial unrest. Inspired by Lenin, entire municipalities began flying the red flag, declaring themselves in favour of a dictatorship of the proletariat. In Italy, red was so common a colour that these were called the 'Red Years', with the Socialist Party growing to more than 200,000 members by 1920, and the General Confederation of Labour boasting over 2 million adherents. In Germany too, workers took to the streets, although the Social Democratic Party refused to hand over power to Soviet-inspired councils. Finland, a grand duchy of the now defunct Russian Empire, seeking to become an independent state, was torn apart in a civil war between Red Guards, led by the Social Democratic Party, and White Guards, supported by those opposed to socialism.[7]

No workers appeared on the streets in China. But when in April 1919 the victorious Allies at the Paris Peace Conference awarded to Japan rights to the former German concessions in Shandong province, protests erupted across the country. On May the Fourth, around 4,000 students gathered in front of Tiananmen, the front gate of the Imperial City in Beijing, calling for a boycott of Japanese goods. The movement rippled through the country, with chambers of commerce, student organisations and civil associations joining widespread strikes that by early June had paralysed parts of Shanghai, the commercial juggernaut on the southern estuary of the Yangtze River.

It was a nationalist outcry, and one aimed at imperialism in general. Its specific target was an obsolete institution known as the treaty port system, which had its origins in a small settlement in Canton (later known as Guangzhou), the only place the Qing dynasty had opened to foreign trade in 1759. As foreign demands for diplomatic representation, free trade and equal treatment began to mount, tensions came to a head during the first Sino-British War (1839–42), later remembered as the 'Opium War', when an imperial envoy called Lin Zexu, sent by the court to Canton to clamp down on a thriving black market, held foreign merchants and their families hostage in the settlement without charge or trial. Lin also publicly destroyed some 20,000 chests of imported opium, providing the spark for a conflict that would result in the Treaty of Nanjing in 1842. The treaty ceded a barren island called Hong Kong to Britain and opened five ports, including Shanghai, to foreign trade and residence. It was the beginning of the treaty port system, in which land known as a concession was leased to foreign powers, each country providing their own municipal services under the supervision of a consul. The system was designed to segregate foreigners from the rest of the population. In Shanghai, where mudflats along a mosquito-infested river were leased in perpetuity, the concession was called a settlement. The Qing, following a treaty concluded in the 1830s with traders from the Uzbek khanate of Kokand, also granted extraterritorial privileges to foreigners involved in criminal cases. They were exempt from the jurisdiction of local law and subject instead to the laws of their own country, in keeping with the empire's tradition of claiming sovereignty over people rather than tracts of land.[8]

The Great Powers, not least Britain, keen to ensure free trade and to control all points of access to the country, mercilessly expanded the treaty port system. Massive upheavals, notably a devastating civil war known as the Taiping Rebellion (1850–64), were leveraged to claim more enclaves on the coastline and along the great navigable rivers leading to a vast and underdeveloped hinterland. The so-called 'most-favoured-nation clause' ensured that any agreement negotiated by one country also applied to all others, creating a complex network of interlocking rights and privileges. The various powers stationed small garrisons in the concessions to protect foreign lives and property, with gunboats plying the coastal waters and inland rivers.

In 1898, in what was termed a scramble for spheres of influence, rivalry among the Great Powers worsened. Four years earlier, Japan had defeated the Qing and claimed the Liaodong Peninsula, at the extreme southern tip of Manchuria. It included Dalian, soon known as Dairen, as well as Port Arthur, a strategic harbour potentially controlling access to the Yellow River. The Japanese also occupied Taiwan and Korea, former vassals of the Qing Empire. Rattled by Japan's ambitions, France, Germany and Russia intervened, forcing the island nation to withdraw its troops from Liaodong. Russia immediately moved into the peninsula instead and began fortifying Port Arthur, which, unlike its Vladivostok naval base further north, did not freeze over during the winter. In 1898, Germany seized Jiaozhou Bay, centre of a large junk trade in Shandong, in retaliation for the murder of two of its missionaries. The Imperial German Navy began developing a naval base in the fishing village known as Qingdao. A few kilometres north of Qingdao, Britain demanded the port of Weihaiwei, backed by hills and guarded by rocky islands, while France obtained a concession on the south China coast at Guangzhou Bay.

At this point London sent an investigative mission to China, headed by Admiral Lord Charles Beresford. He advised against the dismemberment of the Qing Empire, as a unified China was worth more than control over a sphere of influence in a mere section of the country.[9]

The admiral returned by way of Washington, where Secretary of State John Hay in 1899 and 1900 proposed an 'Open Door' doctrine covering all of Asia. Hay supported the territorial and administrative integrity of China with equal access for all to any of the ports open to trade. Reactions from the Great Powers were evasive, and for the next half-century the geopolitics of China would be torn asunder by two divergent approaches: Britain, France and the United States were in favour of a united China, while Russia and Japan, which were arch-enemies, used the country as a bulwark against each other.

In 1904 the two went to war over Manchuria. To the surprise of international observers, Japan emerged victorious, sinking the Russian fleet at Port Arthur and crushing the enemy's troops at Mukden, later known as Shenyang. The lease of Port Arthur was signed over to Japan. Tokyo also took over the southern half of the Chinese Eastern Railway, built between 1897 and 1902 by the Russians as a concession from the Qing. The line ran through Manchuria, connecting Port Arthur to the Trans-Siberian Railway.

The Qing Empire, battered by foreign powers, undermined from within by revolutionaries clamouring for a republican government, collapsed in 1911. China became Asia's first republic, with an electorate of 40 million people voting for 30,000 electors, who in turn selected members of the National Assembly and the House of Representatives. But hopes for greater independence were dashed in the years that followed. As war broke out in Europe in the summer of 1914, Japan sided with the Allies against the Central Powers led by Germany and Austria-Hungary. Within months it had seized the German concession in Qingdao. China, in turn, issued a declaration of war against the Central Powers in August 1917, cancelling all extraterritorial privileges of Austria and Germany and seizing their concessions in Tianjin, the industrial and commercial giant in the north of the country. Beijing hoped that Tokyo would relinquish control over the former German concession, but in a series of secret agreements the Allies consented to Japan's permanent control of Shandong province. The Soviet authorities in 1917 disclosed the secret treaties in an effort to cast a shadow over the relations between what Moscow called the 'imperialist camp' and China. When two years later the Allies in Versailles, concerned that Tokyo might abstain from joining the newly created League of Nations, persisted in transferring German concessions to Japan, many in China felt betrayed, joining the May Fourth demonstrations.[10]

The May Fourth Movement was the centre of a broader movement of cultural renewal, triggered, again, by Japan after it had presented China with a series of humiliating demands in 1915. Participants were disillusioned with traditional values, not least those propounded by Confucius, the ancient sage who had lived 2,500 years earlier and now symbolised the old imperial order. They demanded that their country embrace the spirit of the modern age, including the principles of liberty and equality. Students and scholars debated a whole range of ideas from abroad, including democracy, universal suffrage, socialism, anarchy and every variety of individualism. Most of all, young people were receptive to 'Mr Science' and 'Mr Democracy', values that a prominent intellectual named Chen Duxiu proposed in a popular magazine called *New Youth* in 1915. Science and democracy became the two rallying cries of the May Fourth Movement.

Moscow dispatched several emissaries to China, charging them with spreading the gospel of revolution and recruiting local agents. Their efforts were piecemeal, especially before the foundation of the Comintern in March 1919, but decisive. Their chief target was students and professors.[11] In Beijing, early efforts can be traced back to A. A. Ivanov, who was attached to the Russian Legation at the time of the Bolshevik Revolution. He offered his services to the new regime, contacting local professors while lecturing part-time at Peking University. S. A. Polevoy, a sinologist who had previously worked at the Oriental Institute in Vladivostok, was also based at Peking University, and became a Bolshevik agent tasked with establishing contacts among influential thinkers. Ivanov and Polevoy befriended Li Dazhao, an imposing man with intense eyes under bushy eyebrows who assumed the directorship of the university's library in January 1918. Until his encounter with the two Russians, Li had been a supporter of liberal democracy. None of his writings before the autumn of 1918 betrayed much interest in Marxism. As he came to know the two agents, he began praising the Russian Revolution.[12] His article 'The Victory of Bolshevism' was published in November 1918: the defeat of German militarism, he wrote, 'was the victory of Bolshevism, the red flag, and the working class of the world'. He continued: 'The bells are ringing! The dawn of freedom is breaking! The world of the future will be the world of the Red Flag!'[13] Li was Moscow's first convert, and arguably China's most influential Communist. An obscure twenty-five-year-old called Mao Zedong, tall, lean and handsome, worked as an assistant in the library.

Soviet representatives also approached Hu Shi, a bespectacled philosopher educated at Cornell and Columbia who had returned to his country to lecture at Peking University. Hu would become a leading diplomat, as well as one of the country's most distinguished proponents of democracy. Since the young philosopher failed to turn up at the meeting, the Russians spoke to Chen Duxiu instead. Chen, by all accounts, would become the second most important Marxist.[14] With a small moustache, an obstinate forehead and eyes sparkling with intelligence, he was already acclaimed for his publications supporting the May Fourth Movement. He had been recruited as a dean at Peking University in January 1917, and later joined Li Dazhao's Marxist Research Society.

Soon after his encounter with Soviet agents in Beijing, Chen began to move away from the democratic values he had earlier espoused, turning his attention to Marxism. The May 1919 issue of *New Youth* was entirely devoted to the official creed from Moscow. Later that year Chen was briefly arrested and then expelled from Peking University for his extreme views. Once he arrived in Shanghai in February 1920, he kept close contact with Comintern envoys, convinced that 'nothing short of the establishment of a Soviet State will save China.'[15] As a British intelligence report noted, 'he has a number of doubtful Russian friends' and was in 'close touch with Bolshevik agents and particularly with Lizerovitch'. Jack Lizerovich was a Russian in direct contact with the Vladivostok Soviet. Chen also befriended Alexis F. Agariev, an agent based in the offices of *Shanghai Life*, a Russian outlet spreading the Bolshevik message under its editor-in-chief Gregory Semesheko from February 1920 onwards. Some thirty staff worked at the newspaper, most of them pro-Soviet Russians. Several were Soviet agents, including Lizerovich.[16] Substantial funds were available, as propaganda and finance worked hand in hand, thanks to a Russian cooperative society known as Centrosoyuz, or Central Soviet, also based in Shanghai. The Centrosoyuz was Moscow's Economic Bureau, in receipt of large sums of money from the Comintern. Agents from Chita, Beijing, Tianjin and Canton regularly visited the premises.[17]

A free school teaching Esperanto, opened by Vadim Stopany and Lu Shikai, was another outpost in Shanghai. When secretly interviewed, Lu admitted that his Russian colleague was working in the interests of Bolshevism. In February 1920, Stopany delivered a lecture in Esperanto to forty or fifty members of the Shipping and Godown Workers' Union, translated into Chinese by Lu Shikai.[18]

By now, Russian agents were active in several cities besides Beijing and Shanghai. Moscow was keen not only to recruit, but also to propagate its views. Rosta, the state news agency in Moscow, established branches in Beijing and Canton, while the Dalta Agency, the telegraphic agency of the Far Eastern Republic, gained a foothold in Vladivostok. They fed to newspapers in China information favourable to the revolution, portraying Soviet Russia as a new front that could blunt the hostile pressures of the imperialist camp, the best possible ally for China in its fight against the colonial powers.

Vladivostok, Chita and Tashkent also supplied a flood of revolutionary pamphlets, although soon printing presses were set up in Canton, Tianjin, Beijing and, above all, Shanghai, operating more or less clandestinely. As postal censors discovered, itinerant agents in the pay of Moscow were appointed to transmit these publications to every corner of the country. Abel Bonnard, a French missionary in Beijing, wrote in September 1920 that 'the Bolshevists are sparing no efforts. Their emissaries are well supplied with money and are working hard in every large town.'[19] By February 1921, a circular from the Ministry of the Interior demanded that severe measures be taken to restrict the spread of Bolshevism by agents from Moscow.[20] Most of these were Russian, but activists also arrived from other countries, convinced that Bolshevik principles would conquer the world. They could enter the country through its free ports, stay in foreign concessions and enjoy extraterritorial rights.[21]

The two most promising figures for the Bolsheviks, however, were not Li Dazhao or Chen Duxiu, but Sun Yat-sen and Chen Jiongming. Sun, in 1920, was already fifty-four years old, a meditative statesman with heavy brows, thinning front hair and a greying moustache. He was a household name, a revolutionary who had devoted his life to overthrowing the Qing. He had spent years in exile to raise funds for the cause, joining revolutionary Chinese students in Japan in 1905 to establish the Tongmenghui, the precursor of the Kuomintang, or Nationalist Party. When, on 10 October 1911, the military organised an uprising in Wuchang that led to the downfall of the dynasty, Sun was on the other side of the world. He returned to China, assembled his followers in Shanghai and proceeded to Nanjing, where he was elected the first provisional president of the newly founded Republic of China. Elected representatives of the government, however, were soon elbowed aside by the military commanders behind the 1911 revolution. Yuan Shikai, who controlled a large army, forced Sun to resign, dissolving parliament in 1913. Two years later Yuan attempted to restore the monarchy, proclaiming himself emperor, a move even his own supporters opposed. After only eighty-three days Yuan was forced to abdicate, dying in June 1916 of uraemia and chagrin.

Yuan's death left a fragmented political landscape, with provincial governors using their local armies to vie for power in ever-shifting alliances, ushering the country into a period that became known as the 'era of warlords'. An embittered Sun began to drift away from the liberal principles laid out in the country's provisional constitution of 1912. He wished the Nationalist Party, established in 1912 by merging the Tongmenghui with four other political groups, to become a centralised and disciplined party, marked by absolute obedience to its leader. He modified his vision of the revolution: instead of introducing a constitutional democracy, Party dictatorship would be imposed without a time limit to ensure order. Most of all, he demanded a military response to the political crisis: unity had to be achieved through an armed revolution against the country's warlords.[22]

In July 1917, with support from the local governor and members of parliament who had deserted Beijing, he established a new Republic of China in Canton, proclaiming himself president. The title of grand marshal soon followed, together with a plumed army cap, fringed epaulettes and military insignia across his braided uniform. But the decrees he issued were never effective beyond the confines of the Cement Works where he set up his office.[23]

In May 1918 Sun scurried back to Shanghai, where he drew closer to Chen Duxiu. He never lost touch with the Russian revolutionaries he had befriended in his earlier career, including Georgy Chicherin, the first people's commissar for foreign affairs in the Soviet government. In the summer of 1918, he sent a congratulatory telegram to Moscow on behalf of his government in Canton. 'The revolutionary parties of China and Russia should unite,' Sun wrote. Lenin, apparently, was moved. Chicherin responded, claiming in a letter that 'our victory is your victory, our defeat is your defeat.'[24] Sun may not have received the missive, but, despite strenuous denials, by 1919 he was in contact with the Bolshevik headquarters in Siberia and 'constantly visited by Bolshevik agents' in Shanghai, according to the police tasked with shadowing potential political agitators.[25]

In Canton, Sun had been welcomed by the municipal garrison under the command of Chen Jiongming. But the garrison was no match for the Guangdong provincial troops, with whom they clashed on several occasions. To protect his men, Chen took refuge beyond the provincial border in southern Fujian, where he welcomed Bolshevik agents, spending two days with a Korean Communist who described himself as a close follower of Lenin. Shortly afterwards, Chen sent a representative to meet A. S. Potapov, a major general in the Tsarist Army who had defected to the Bolsheviks and in December 1919 took up residence in Shanghai.[26] The Shanghai Intelligence Bureau described Sun Yat-sen and Chen Jiongming as 'the two outstanding features' in the progress made by Russian Bolshevism in 1920.[27]

One of Potapov's roles was to lay the groundwork for the arrival of Gregori Voitinsky, leader of a Comintern team sent to Shanghai in April 1920 to set up an East Asian secretariat.[28] Called the Shanghai Bureau, it was charged with conducting and financing revolutionary movements in China, Japan and Korea.

Its foundation coincided with a dramatic appeal by Moscow to the people of China. The Russian Revolution had sparked a brutal civil war, with the Red Army fighting a loose alliance of armed forces known as the White Army. In Siberia, the White Army was supported by Western powers as well as by China and Japan. All of them sent troops, France a token force of 500, Japan tens of thousands of men. The White Army at first succeeded in reducing the territorial orbit of the Russians, but Trotsky, the Bolsheviks' war commissar, implemented harsh measures to reverse the tide, including the use of barrier troops who shot soldiers trying to flee from the battle line. As Soviet armies marched east across the Urals, the Allied forces began to collapse.

On 26 March 1920, the moment red troops entered Siberia, Lev Karakhan, an Armenian-born Soviet diplomat with a wave of black hair and a neatly trimmed beard, transmitted a public telegram to Beijing via Irkutsk. The Karakhan Declaration offered to abolish all of Tsarist Russia's extraterritorial rights, treaties and indemnities encroaching on China's sovereign rights, and to return the Chinese Eastern Railway without compensation. The Red Army, Karakhan proclaimed, was marching east to bring 'liberation from the yoke of military force and foreign money' which, he continued, would stifle and enslave the 'masses of the Orient', at the head of which stood the Chinese people. Moscow was helping not just the workers and the peasants, but all the people of China, a message suppressed by the 'mercenary press of the Americans, Europeans and Japanese'. The announcement was pitched perfectly to appeal to nationalist sentiment. The contrast with the widely despised Treaty of Versailles could not have been greater.[29]

The Shanghai Bureau under Voitinsky, buoyed by the Karakhan Declaration, worked diligently towards revolution, to be coordinated across all of East Asia. Voitinsky met with a range of potential allies, including Li Dazhao, Chen Duxiu, Sun Yat-sen and Chen Jiongming as well as other future luminaries of the revolutionary movement. Chen Duxiu was charged with contacting provincial leaders. In Changsha he liaised with Mao Zedong, who set about organising a Communist group. But when, in October 1920, Sun Yat-sen and Chen Jiongming managed to recapture Canton, Chen Duxiu joined them as commissioner of education, a post he used to preach further revolution. The movement's centre of gravity shifted away from Shanghai. In the following months, assorted associations labelling themselves 'socialist' or 'communist' came into being in the southern capital. By April 1921, the French Sûreté even alleged that Chen Jiongming's 20,000 troops were being funded by Moscow.[30]

A range of publications, besides pamphlets distributed by Russian emissaries, helped spread the message. In Canton, the *Journal of Mutual Aid*, published under the auspices of Sun, now joined by his son Sun Fo, appeared in May 1921, introducing Karl Marx to its readers.[31] In Shanghai the *World of Workers*, published by Chen Duxiu, appeared in August 1920, followed a few months later by *The Workers* in Canton.[32]

After a year of preparatory work, the First Congress of the Korean Communist Party was held in Shanghai in May 1921. This had required great political skills in navigating turf battles, bridging ideological divides and dealing with factional infighting, and was followed by an initial meeting of the Japanese Communist Party. The formal launch of the Chinese Communist Party was delayed until July. The moment Voitinsky had left the country in January 1921, internal differences had surfaced over the nature of the Party and its ideology, while poorly coordinated local Communist groups had failed to unite into a single movement. Lenin sent Henk Sneevliet, alias Maring, a Dutch union leader with considerable experience in organising the revolutionary movement in Indonesia. Sneevliet discovered that he had to start from scratch. Again, the drive of Soviet emissaries proved decisive. But when, at long last, the First Congress convened in a classroom of the Bowen Girls' School in the French Concession on 23 July 1921, neither Li Dazhao nor Chen Duxiu attended. A dozen delegates were present, not counting Sneevliet and Vladimir Nikolsky, a representative of the Far Eastern Secretariat of the Comintern. Each delegate had received 100 yuan in travel expenses and a further 50 yuan for the return ticket, a tidy sum at the time. They represented fifty-three Party members from all of China. They squabbled over numerous issues, but on one subject were agreed: membership was small. The programme they adopted was harsh, including a call for the overthrow of the 'capitalist class' by the 'revolutionary army of the proletariat', the adoption of a 'dictatorship of the proletariat' to abolish all classes as well as private ownership of capital, and unity with the Comintern.[33]

Sneevliet, unimpressed, believed that the Chinese Communist Party had been founded prematurely. He had a point. As

G. C. Denham, the pre-eminent intelligence officer of the British Empire working on communism in East Asia, noted four days after the conclusion of the First Congress, 'the fulminations and promises by Trotsky and Lenin' had made very little impression in China so far.[34] Nationalism, not communism, was the rallying cry behind the May Fourth Movement.

The key to revolution, Sneevliet believed, lay not in Shanghai, where the Communist Party lived in isolation from the workers, but in Canton. The British authorities would have agreed. Communism had spread rapidly under Sun Yat-sen and Chen Jiongming, they observed, pointing out that its real significance 'lies in the fact that it is their leaders who control labour in Canton and the neighbouring ports'.[35] Arriving in the city in January 1922, Sneevliet witnessed a seamen's strike organised by the Nationalist Party, and was struck by its revolutionary potential. Some 300,000 workers took industrial action far beyond the confines of the city, up the coast to Shantou and south along the Pearl Delta to Hong Kong, where they forced the colonial authorities to declare martial law. The seamen prevailed, and a few months later the authorities were forced to meet several of their demands, including wage increases.

But the founding father of the Nationalist Party was not in Canton. Sun Yat-sen and Chen Jiongming had developed different ideas about the revolution and had clashed. Sun, driven by an overweening ambition to win full power, was set on a military expedition to conquer the country. Chen, on the other hand, inspired by the anarchist ideas of Pyotr Kropotkin, had transformed the districts under his control in southern Fujian into a benign version of Moscow, building roads, opening schools, even encouraging press freedom. Now he hoped to make all of Guangdong province into a model for others to emulate. The two leaders compromised, but as Sun tried in vain to set up a military government, he quickly encountered opposition from local trade unions and members of the provincial assembly. In February 1921, he had given a public speech in which, according to the French consul, he had declared that his goal was to 'install communism in China'. This caused widespread consternation, although his truncated parliament gave his proposal for a Northern Expedition the stamp of approval. He set off at the head of a weak contingent and soon found himself bogged down in Guilin, 500 kilometres north-west of Canton. Chen Jiongming opposed the use of military force and refused to continue to finance the expedition with provincial funds.

Sun, who had spent much of his career raising funds for the revolution, began to court foreign powers for financial support. In a *Manifesto to the Foreign Powers*, published on 5 May 1921, he presented himself as the sole legitimate president of the Republic of China, a true democrat who opposed the military commanders in control of the north. He asked that the Great Powers withdraw recognition from Beijing and accept Canton as the country's capital instead, allowing the customs revenue to flow to him. His manifesto was badly received. The American minister to Beijing, Charles R. Crane, half a year earlier, had already described Sun as an 'unscrupulous adventurer' with 'impractical and grandiose schemes' who showed 'great personal vanity'. Around the same time, the *New York Times* denounced him as a 'crafty and sordid opportunist'.[36] Great Britain was even more intransigent, the strike having demonstrated how a separatist government in Canton could undermine Hong Kong.

Before he arrived in Canton, Sneevliet spent nine days as Sun Yat-sen's guest in Guilin. They covered a wide range of topics, among them the reorganisation of the Nationalist Party, the need to establish a military academy, possible cooperation between the Communist Party and the Nationalist Party and an alliance with the Soviet Union. Sun was cautious, because embracing Russia inevitably meant further alienating Great Britain, a power with a commanding presence in China. But he and other officers were keen to hear more on military matters, not least on the Red Army.[37]

The already strained relations between Sun Yat-sen and Chen Jiongming degenerated further in the following months. On 1 June 1922, a furious Sun returned to Canton to strip Chen of all his functions. Instead Chen, who commanded respect as well as the balance of power, drove him out of town two weeks later.

Once again, Sun was a revolutionary in search of an army. He schemed, opening his residence in Shanghai to political leaders of every shade. He courted Wu Peifu, a powerful general who dominated much of the north, even as he parleyed with Wu's rival, Zhang Zuolin, the man in control of much of Manchuria. Keen to steer a potential ally to power, Adolph Joffe, Moscow's diplomat in Beijing in 1922, encouraged Sun in his negotiations and dangled the prospect of financial and military aid before him. But the Russians insisted on collaboration between the Communist Party and the Nationalist Party. At a Comintern meeting in July 1920, Lenin, realising that Bolshevism had little popular appeal beyond the shores of Europe, had changed tack and demanded that Communist parties worldwide join their nationalist counterparts in a United Front against imperialism. The new approach suited Sneevliet. Disappointed with the poor showing of communism in China and keen on a United Front, Sneevliet tirelessly promoted its advantages. A majority of party members including Chen Duxiu gradually came around to his views. The Second Congress of the Chinese Communist Party, held in July 1922, endorsed Lenin's emphasis on an alliance between the 'proletariat' and the 'bourgeoisie', as the Party officially joined the Comintern.

But which 'bourgeois' Party would be a viable partner for the Communists? To Sneevliet, who had witnessed how the strikers in Canton had brought an imperial power to its knees, the answer seemed clear. Further cajoling, goading and bargaining ensued, this time among leaders of both the Communist Party and the Nationalist Party. The idea provoked stiff opposition from the Communists and received no more than a lukewarm welcome from the Nationalists. Since the alliance would entail Communist Party members joining the ranks of the Nationalist Party, Sun Yat-sen insisted that new members pledge personal allegiance to him. Chen Duxiu, secretary general of the Party, denounced the Nationalists as a 'political party scrambling for power and profit'. Sneevliet also had to convince Moscow, where some leaders were suspicious of Sun Yat-sen's 'dictatorial habits' and critical of the Party's revolutionary potential. In Shanghai and in Moscow,

Sneevliet was the driving force behind a United Front. His vision would have long-lasting consequences.[38]

Membership of the Comintern came with conditions, twenty-one to be precise. The fourth read as follows: 'The duty of propagating Communist ideas includes the special obligation of forceful and systematic propaganda in the army. Where this agitation is interrupted by emergency laws it must be continued illegally. Refusal to carry out such work would be tantamount to a betrayal of revolutionary duty and would be incompatible with membership of the Communist International.' The fifth condition demanded 'systematic and methodical agitation' in the countryside: 'The working class will not be able to win if it does not have the backing of the rural proletariat and at least a part of the poorest peasants, and if it does not secure the neutrality of at least a part of the rest of the rural population through its policies.'[39]

In August 1922, at a further plenum of the Second Party Congress, the decision to call for individual members to join the Nationalists while retaining their Communist Party membership was passed. One month later, Li Dazhao and Chen Duxiu were among the first to join.

In Beijing, Ambassador Joffe was still trying to cut a deal with Wu Peifu. He disbursed funds freely, but was given the cold shoulder. The reason was clear: half a year after his resounding Declaration in March 1920, Karakhan had sent another missive, recommending that the Chinese Eastern Railway, owned by the now-defunct Tsarist regime, be handed over to the Soviet Union, that all anti-Soviet activities on Chinese soil should be repressed and that the Soviet occupation of Outer Mongolia be recognised – among other demands.[40] Negotiations proved disappointing, and ended when the Beijing government collapsed in December 1922. Joffe hastened to Shanghai, finding a more malleable ally in Sun Yat-sen, who had been spurned by Europe and the United States. A joint communiqué was published on 26 January 1923, providing the basis for cooperation between the Nationalists and the Soviet Union. The statement affirmed that neither signatory favoured a Communist or Soviet government for China 'because there do not exist here conditions for the successful establishment of either'. Sun acquiesced in Moscow's demand for Soviet troops in Outer Mongolia and did not challenge the return of the railway to the successors of the Tsarist regime. In exchange, the Bolsheviks promised Sun what he wanted most, namely an army.[41]

***

A base had to be secured for the army, meaning that Sun Yat-sen had to take back Canton from his erstwhile ally Chen Jiongming. His agents had been plotting with one of the armies posted along the border of Guangdong, a province inundated with small bands of warlord troops. Sun hired 40,000 mercenaries, mostly soldiers from Yunnan and Guangxi. Once they had captured the city and driven out Chen Jiongming, the youthful soldiers paraded through the streets, brandishing revolvers and guns, confiscating property and commandeering buildings. It was the final act in a local war that had lasted twelve months, bringing misery to the million or more inhabitants of Canton. While civil government was suspended, leading to the collapse of the sanitary system, the occupying forces encouraged gambling, since it produced much-needed revenue. The troops were estimated to cost some 20 million Chinese dollars a month.[42]

Since the funds raised locally were inadequate, in the following months the troops repeatedly pillaged the countryside, bringing an influx of paupers into Canton, with women carrying half-naked children forced to beg on the streets. Ordinary workers soon became disenchanted. They had welcomed the unions, but had to surrender a share of their income to finance Sun Yat-sen's projected expedition against the north. Unemployment surged as merchants, forced to advance funds, joined a surreptitious exodus. Once they became unemployed, people were press-ganged into service. 'It was a common sight to pass a hundred coolies lined up to be enrolled as unpaid carriers for lazy soldiers, if not to be sent to the front as "volunteer" companies', noted a foreign journalist. Temples and pagodas were auctioned off, with complete disregard for tradition: 'altogether some 848 public houses of worship, including 37 monasteries, 105 nunneries, and

706 temples in Canton City alone, were subject to confiscation together with their endowed properties, movable or unmovable, past as well as present.' Taxes were slapped on every conceivable transaction: export taxes, living taxes, transport taxes, even a tax on firewood which led to the withdrawal of such fuel from the city until it was repealed. Rice merchants no longer brought their goods to market, fearing that the army would confiscate the commodity without compensation. One visitor described the city's inhabitants as 'the most heavily taxed people on earth'. Trade was paralysed, but justice was swift. On the execution ground the condemned were hobbled out with shackled feet and arms tied, to be shot, occasionally bayoneted to death. A once prosperous city lay in ruins.[43]

A turning point came when Sun Yat-sen threatened to seize the customs house in Canton in September 1923. The loss of tariff revenues in Canton would have made it impossible for Treaty Powers to preserve the fiction of administrative integrity under the government in Beijing. Sun, always the opportunist, had been deliberately ambivalent about the Soviet Union, keen to raise funds from the other powers as well. A mere month after signing an agreement with the Soviet Union, he gave a speech at the University of Hong Kong, praising the crown colony's colonial administration and the English parliamentary system. After the Powers blocked his plans to take over the Canton customs, he fully embraced Soviet aid and advice.[44]

Aid from Moscow had already begun to arrive in May 1923, as Joffe offered 8,000 rifles, fifteen machine guns, four heavy guns and two armoured cars. It was a modest start, but the weapons came with 2 million Mexican dollars.[45]

Collaboration deepened, as missions were exchanged in September 1923. Canton sent a military team headed by Chiang Kai-shek, while Moscow ordered Mikhail Borodin to lead a contingent of Soviet advisors to Canton.

A young officer of medium height and slight build, with a trim moustache and flashing eyes, Chiang Kai-shek was thirty-six years old. He hailed from a small village in the seaboard province of Zhejiang, some 200 kilometres south of Shanghai. His father, a wine merchant, had died when Chiang was still a boy. His mother had raised sufficient funds to send him to a military academy near Beijing, where he showed such promise that he was sent to Japan for advanced military training at the age of eighteen. In Tokyo he was recruited by anti-Manchu revolutionaries and joined Sun Yat-sen's Tongmenghui in 1908. After meeting Sun two years later, he became his obstinate but loyal disciple. By the end of 1911, after the Wuchang uprising, he returned to China and joined the Nationalist Party. Over the following years he rose through the ranks, joining Sun in Canton in 1918. By the time he was sent to the Soviet Union, his master was chief of army, he chief of staff. Armed with letters addressed to Lenin, Trotsky and Chicherin, Chiang was warmly welcomed in Moscow. A great many meetings followed, although Chiang found time to study Russian and read *The Communist Manifesto* and other works by Marx. He even sang the *Internationale*, proclaiming his willingness 'to die in the struggle against imperialism and capitalism'.[46]

After several weeks, however, Chiang's hosts deserted him, drawn into the struggle between Stalin, General Secretary of the Communist Party, and what was called the Left Opposition, headed by Trotsky. Trotsky had placed his faith in a German October, instructing the Comintern to help German Communists seize power and launch a new wave of revolutions in Europe, which in turn would trigger a world revolution. In the Kremlin he had embraced and kissed Heinrich Brandler, the German Communist leader, a sign of how much hope he placed in the coming insurrection. The conviction that Germany would turn red prompted huge enthusiasm throughout the Soviet Union, with orators in theatres, schools and even circuses offering their vision of the Great Revolution's unstoppable march. The more sceptical Stalin raised sensible questions.[47]

The Comintern supervised the entire operation, with secret funds funnelled to paramilitary forces and revolutionary cells embedded within the trade unions. The revolution failed, not least because the Social Democratic Party supported the government. When reports of a crushing defeat reached Moscow, Trotsky's faith in an imminent world revolution was questioned, paving the way for Stalin's notion that socialism, at first, should be built in one country alone, namely the Soviet Union. Chiang was told that the provision of weapons and money would continue, but there were questions about Sun Yat-sen's plan for military unification. In a meeting with Trotsky, Chiang was told to focus instead on laying the groundwork for a broader movement of liberation, to take place in a distant future. Trotsky counselled 'patience'. Chiang was furious. Addressing a body of young Chinese students in Moscow, he warned them against 'lauding overmuch the works of foreign revolutionary leaders'.[48]

One day before Chiang's departure, the Comintern passed a resolution on China, critically examining the political principles of the Nationalist Party. It enjoined Sun Yat-sen to 'unleash the working class' and fully support the proletariat's political organisation, the Chinese Communist Party. The Nationalists were also urged to form a common front with the Soviet Union in the fight against imperialism. Again Chiang fumed, condemning the resolution in his diary as 'shallow and unrealistic' and complaining that 'they arrogantly place themselves at the very centre of the revolution'. He concluded that Moscow could not be trusted, since it had only one aim, 'namely to turn the Chinese Communist Party into an instrument for its own use'.[49]

Mikhail Borodin arrived in Canton in October 1923, where he was warmly welcomed by Sun Yat-sen, who 'made me sit with him and looked at me fixedly for several seconds'.[50] A tall, heavy man with a thick mane of black hair and a drooping moustache, he came with an impressive record. The son of emigrants, Borodin had joined the Bolsheviks at the age of nineteen, and had been compelled to flee to the United States in 1907 after being arrested for his revolutionary activities. After the October Revolution he returned to Russia, where he was assigned by the Comintern to help set up the Mexican Communist Party. So successful was his work as a revolutionary that he was assigned a similar mission in Scotland, although in Glasgow the authorities wasted no time in arresting and deporting him. After a few years of agitation in Turkey, Borodin was put on a train to China.

His first priority was to rebuild the Nationalist Party. In order to accomplish this mission, he had to gain Sun Yat-sen's trust. A mere month after he arrived, he took the lead in organising volunteer detachments to defend Canton against yet another attack by Chen Jiongming's troops. Sun viewed him as a saviour. Borodin began flattering Sun, praising his writings, hailing him as China's great hope in front of large audiences of students, workers and soldiers. Behind his back, Borodin was less complimentary, writing to his superiors in Moscow that he was 'very backward' and 'slow-minded', an 'enlightened little satrap' who 'considers himself the hero and the others the mob'.[51]

Borodin also cultivated other members of the Nationalist Party, explaining how they had to appeal to the masses, give land to the peasants and unite them under the colours of the Party in order to build up a stronger army. He worked tirelessly at creating a majority for the first Nationalist Party Congress, overcoming opposition from members of both the Nationalist and Communist parties. When they convened in January 1924, Borodin prevailed, as Communists were formally accepted into the ranks.[52]

There was intense infighting over every word in the manifesto issued by the congress. Wang Jingwei, a slight, handsome poet, gifted speaker and confidant of Sun Yat-sen, with decades of experience as a revolutionary, tried to substitute 'the people' wherever Borodin spoke of 'workers and peasants'. Borodin pressed hard. When concerns over antagonising the Great Powers arose, he pointed out that the imperialists were the enemies. He gave Sun a choice: join the oppressed of the world, or side with imperialism. 'Sun Yat-sen nodded his head and gave other signs of approval', Borodin recorded in his diary. In the final version, the manifesto condemned the 'economic oppression' of the country by imperialism, promising that the 'peasants and workers' would be 'liberated' in a 'revolutionary movement' led by the Nationalist Party. The Party was 'fighting for the peasants and the workers, which means that peasants and workers are fighting for themselves'.[53]

Sun and Borodin, at the conclusion of the congress, established a Central Executive Committee, handpicking every one of its members. Up to a quarter were Communist Party members, a percentage far out of proportion with their national membership. Li Dazhao was among them, as were Mao Zedong, Lin Zuhan, Zhang Guotao and Qu Qiubai, who would all become prominent in the Communist movement. The Communists headed two important departments, namely those charged with 'peasant affairs' and the organisation of the Party. Control of the Organisation Department, known as Orgburo in Russian, was essential in every Leninist organisation, since it was responsible for appointing Party members to all key positions and then supervising them.[54]

In order to train officers for the new revolutionary army, a military academy was established at Whampoa, situated on an island in the Pearl River some ten kilometres east of Canton. The academy, with a fort and military schools dating back to the 1870s, when China had first tried to modernise its army, was inaugurated in June 1924. It would become the nerve centre of the revolution.

Chiang Kai-shek was made commander, while Borodin designed the curriculum, patterned after the one developed by Trotsky for the Red Army. It placed political indoctrination above all else. Borodin taught every other day, alongside other unsalaried Russian teachers, giving lectures on the Russian revolution, imperialism, the world revolutionary movement, political economy, socialism and other subjects. A first batch of 574 resident cadets were recruited from various provinces, to take a course lasting six months, with Moscow paying most of the costs.[55]

The number of students assigned to propaganda work expanded rapidly, since the Soviets had devised a system under which political commissars were appointed at the highest level inside the army to ensure the loyalty of the officers and soldiers. Borodin selected Communist Party members for these positions, allowing revolutionaries like Zhou Enlai to take control of the political section at Whampoa. By the end of 1925 a report back to Moscow boasted how 'Communists are at the head of most political sections [in the army]; some even occupy posts as commanders.'[56]

Borodin pushed for more trade unions, financing them liberally with funds from Moscow. Liao Zhongkai, a Communist sympathiser close to Borodin, became director of union activity, setting up an office with a hammer and sickle flying above the door. The Profintern – the arm of the Comintern representing trade unions – came to Canton, setting up what one historian has described as a 'flood of new unions', one for every conceivable profession, from rickshaw pullers and cart pushers to bricklayers.[57]

On the same day that a National Labour Congress opened in Canton, Borodin presided over another project of his, namely the first Provincial Congress of Peasants. It was Borodin who first suggested that the land of absentee landowners be confiscated and redistributed to the poor. He was rebuffed by Sun, but persisted. The Peasant Affairs Department, established in February 1924, sent agitators to the countryside. For the most part these were Communist Party members, tutored in a Peasant Movement Training Institute by an overwhelmingly Communist faculty.[58]

Borodin had introduced the blueprints for a Leninist one-party state to Canton, including a centralised Party dictatorship, a politically indoctrinated army under the control of the Party and mass organisations to unite the 'workers and peasants'. In October 1924 came the Party's first major test. Merchants, already reeling from punitive taxes, had gone on strike in August. The head of the General Chamber of Commerce had ordered weapons abroad to arm a volunteer corps, comprising anywhere from 6,000 to 12,000 men. Charged with protecting private property and keeping public order, the volunteers were also deployed by the merchants to break strikes. They were a thorn in the side of the unions. Conflict with the Nationalist Party was brewing. When a Norwegian ship loaded with some 10,000 rifles and pistols and half a million cartridges arrived, Sun ordered his chief of staff to capture the shipment and store the weapons at the Whampoa Academy. Negotiations and expressions of goodwill followed on both sides, but the Soviets saw the incident as an opportunity to strike a blow at the right wing of the Nationalist Party. A Soviet vessel was dispatched, delivering some 18,000 guns and several artillery pieces on 8 October. Two days later, workers, students and soldiers controlled by the Communists paraded through the streets to mark the anniversary of the Wuchang Uprising in 1911, shouting revolutionary slogans. Whether or not the demonstration was a deliberate provocation remains unclear, but a skirmish occurred at the very moment when some of the seized weapons were being returned to the corpsmen on the waterfront. Both sides fired at random, then chased each other through the streets, resulting in some thirty dead or seriously wounded.[59]

Martial law was proclaimed. Chiang armed his troops. The showdown came on 15 October, later called Bloody Wednesday. The corpsmen were well organised and firmly entrenched in the rabbit warren of the city. After heavy fighting around barricades, the Nationalists began pouring kerosene in the gutters and setting fire to the city. Looting was widespread. By dawn the following day, fire and sword had reduced the city to a smouldering heap, with casualties counted in the many hundreds. Steamers from Canton to Hong Kong were crowded with refugees. But Sun had his victory.[60]

***

On 12 March 1925, aged fifty-nine, Sun Yat-sen died. He had travelled to Beijing to meet Feng Yuxiang, known abroad as the 'Christian General' for his alleged zeal in baptising his troops with a fire hose. Feng had dominated much of the north, and on 23 October 1924 had turned against his allies to seize control of Beijing. A few months later he called for a national reunification conference, which Sun attended.

By now the influence of the Soviet Union had spread far beyond Canton. Half a year earlier, on 31 May 1924, normal diplomatic relations had been established between China and the Soviet Union. The Tsarist Legation, a grand establishment housing the former empire's diplomats and their staff, was handed over to Lev Karakhan. The ambassador and his staff arrived in style, moving through the streets in a motorcade with horns sounding and flags flying the hammer and sickle. Red bunting was draped around the building's columns, while immense flags of the Soviet Union hung from windows, balconies and the flagpole.[61]

The treaty signed on 31 May was rich in promises. Article 5 stipulated that all mutually hostile propaganda should be suppressed. Both countries also agreed not to permit in their territories the activities or existence of any organisation whose aim was to use violence against the other government.[62]

From his new residence, Karakhan vociferously denounced imperialism, proclaiming that the Soviet Union alone among the Great Powers treated China as an equal nation with full sovereign rights. Even as he made the rounds trying to rally local students to the cause, he was secretly funnelling resources to the newly established consulates, where the offices of Soviet agents were now concentrated. In Shanghai, the Consular Building welcomed the Shanghai Agency of the Volunteer Fleet, the Far Eastern Bank, the Far Eastern Trade State Department and other agencies, leading to a marked revival of Bolshevist activities.[63]

In death as in life, Sun served the revolution, as the Soviets tried to capture his body. Lenin, the previous year, had been embalmed, his whitened, marble-like body displayed in a mausoleum. Karakhan wired Moscow for a similar glass catafalque, wishing to portray Sun as the Lenin of China, against the wishes of his family. A compromise was reached, as two funeral services were held in Beijing. After a Christian ceremony, his body was carried in a long procession to the city's Central Park, where he lay in state, a flaming red wreath placed before his bier by Karakhan.[64]

Much as they vied over his body, his entourage also fought for his last words. Sun left behind a testament which he had dictated to Wang Jingwei on his deathbed. Countersigned and authenticated by nine people, it was published on 11 March, on the eve of Sun's death. The same day a Letter of Farewell addressed to the Central Committee of the Soviet Union was circulated, prepared by Eugene Chen, the Canton foreign minister, and Borodin. It expressed Sun Yat-sen's wish that China and the Soviet Union 'walk hand in hand to victory in the great struggle for the liberation of the oppressed peoples of the world'. The unsigned letter was published in Moscow a few days later.[65]

In death, Sun Yat-sen was transformed into a saint, his testament becoming required reading in Nationalist Party ceremonies. Thousands of students, union leaders and politicians of different stripes paid their respects. The watershed, however, was not Sun's passing, but a riot in Shanghai a few months later during which a dozen people were killed.

Like the Legation in Beijing, the Soviet Consulate in Shanghai had marked its official opening with much fanfare, including a profusion of red emblems and electric lights. And like its counterpart in the capital, it had taken advantage of the opportunity to spread propaganda in schools and universities. Chief among these was Shanghai University, founded in 1922 with financial help from Canton by a veteran Nationalist called Yu Youren and directed by Qu Qiubai, a prominent Communist Party member. Chen Duxiu was its president. When the police searched the premises later that year, they found 'inflammatory anti-foreign articles', not least a hundred Russian volumes on socialist subjects. The dormitory walls were decorated with photos of Soviet leaders. On 8 February 1925 the university held a special commemorative service in honour of Lenin, with the acting consul general for the Soviet Union in attendance.[66]

When a few months later a worker named Gu Zhenghong was shot dead in a Japanese cotton mill, four students from Shanghai University began to mobilise the workers of the Nagai Wata Mills. Ironically, conditions in the mill were among the best, its owner a philanthropist who insisted that schools, crèches and other charitable institutions be provided for the welfare of all employees.[67] In the following weeks, labour unions rallied support for large-scale strikes that succeeded in bringing parts of the city to a standstill. The four students, however, were arrested and scheduled to appear in court on 30 May. That same day large groups of students took to the streets in a show of support, reading a telegram from Canton promising financial help for all strikers. Tempers flared, with scuffles between the protesters and the police leading to several arrests. But on a congested intersection near the Louza Police Station on Nanjing Road a crowd of pedestrians was pushed forward, making it difficult for those in front to retreat. Inspector Edward Everson, who defended the station's gate with Indian and Chinese police drawn up in a semi-circle, shouted a warning which could not be heard, then panicked and gave the order to shoot. In the ensuing stampede, several people were shot dead, others succumbing to their wounds in hospital. The following day outraged protesters rioted, attacking tramways and other symbols of municipal governance in the International Settlement. A general strike spread like wildfire on 2 June, affecting some 35,000 workers.[68]

The case highlighted the double standards inherent in extraterritoriality and the treaty port system. As the Student Association of Tsing Hua College eloquently put it on 6 June, 'however strong the provocation might have been, the principles of justice and right have been violated' in the shooting to death of unarmed citizens. An International Commission of Judges appointed to inquire into the incident agreed, concluding six months later that 'the foreigners in China have failed to take into account the principles of liberty and independence which they themselves have, by precept and example, spread abroad throughout China, concerning which the young and rising generation have been apt students.'[69]

Outrage grew at lightning speed. In Zhenjiang (alternatively romanised as Chinkiang), an important transportation hub on the intersection of the Yangtze River and the Grand Canal, students invaded the British Concession, manhandled the consul and looted his furniture and effects. Another outbreak took place in Jiujiang, further inland along the Yangtze, as protesters assaulted British and Japanese nationals. They also set fire to the Bank of Taiwan. In Hankou, a mob destroyed Japanese shops and attacked their owners. One was killed, his body 'stuffed down a drain from which it was with great difficulty extricated'. Then the students attempted to break into the British Concession and seize weapons from the armoury. After a fire hose had been turned on the crowd without effect, shots were fired in the air, also without result. As a last resort, the local volunteers inside the concession opened fire, killing eight and wounding several others.[70]

Borodin, more than anyone else, understood how ardent young students could be in their embrace of new ideals, and how easily they could be captured by a vision of a new society from which imperialism and capitalism would be banished. They were the new force, and he had cultivated them from the very beginning.

They fanned out to reach every part of the country. In Chongqing, as the French consul noted, a few local students had managed to whip up patriotic sentiment in early June, but only after the arrival of young agitators from Canton did the movement grow, as public speakers clamouring for a general strike could be found even in the 'smallest village'. On 4 July, the protesters ransacked foreign property and attacked government forces. Calm returned only after the mayor announced that rioters would be shot.[71]

From north to south, the country echoed with clamour against imperialism. The students, one astute observer reported, 'by yelling and by threatening to kill, burn, destroy are dominating everything, even officials'. 'What about justice for May 30th?' one young man asked rhetorically in a letter to the editor of a foreign magazine. 'Justice cannot be obtained by word of mouth, but only by an army and navy. In other words, Might is Right.' It was a conclusion that seemed inescapable to other earnest youngsters. Wang Fanxi, who was to devote his life to revolution, turned away from Hu Shi after May the Thirtieth to embrace Chen Duxiu instead.[72]

In Canton, however, the incident at first had little impact. Sun Yat-sen's death had left the city in a precarious state since the mercenaries he had hired in February 1923 had become increasingly concerned by the Nationalist Party's shift towards Moscow. On 6 June 1925 they staged an insurrection. It backfired badly, as the Nationalists responded with a force of 3,000 Whampoa cadets and local troops. A systematic hunt was organised after the insurgents surrendered a few days later, with a mob beating to death or throwing into the river hundreds of the soldiers who had pressed local people into forced service. Others had 'their heads smashed in or were disemboweled' by soldiers of Li Fook Lum, an ally of the Nationalists. The American consul estimated the number of dead at 1,500.[73]

It was a bloodbath, but one from which the Nationalists emerged victorious, finally in complete control of the city. At once they began to use the Shanghai shooting as propaganda to win popularity and further consolidate their position. On 20 June the labour unions under their command began a walkout, hoping to bring trade in Hong Kong to a halt in a repeat of the seamen's strike three years earlier. A monster demonstration against imperialism was planned. One day later information reached the Treaty Powers that students intended to make martyrs of themselves by attacking the concession on Shameen (spelt Shamian in modern romanisation), a small island with granite and brick colonial structures covered by bougainvillea, standing in the shade of giant banyan trees. The island, reclaimed from a swamp, was connected to the city by two bridges over a narrow canal filled with backwater from the Pearl River. It was immediately reinforced with barbed wire, sandbags and machine guns. On 23 June, the British consul general contacted the municipal government, warning against a provocation: 'I write in this serious strain so that it may not be said hereafter that brutal imperialist rifles wantonly massacred unoffending Chinese youth.'[74] At 2.30 in the afternoon, a procession of tens of thousands of demonstrators reached the road opposite Shameen. It seemed like an orderly parade, but then students and boy scouts began waving flags and banners, yelling slogans under the supervision of several agitators. Soldiers, led by mounted officers, began to take up positions under the verandas of shops lining the street. Suddenly a shot was fired on the Chinese side. The procession broke up in disorder, with people rushing for shelter. Two more shots followed, as well as what witnesses on the foreign side claimed was a 'heavy volley of rifle fire'. A French silk merchant was hit in the head and died instantly. British and French soldiers returned fire. An uneasy calm was restored only after twenty minutes. Over fifty demonstrators were killed by machine-gun fire sweeping across the two bridges, including twenty-three cadets and military personnel from the Whampoa Academy.[75]

The incident shocked the city, with tens of thousands taking to the streets to clamour for revenge. Shops were banned from selling foreign goods, while a boycott paralysed shipping between Canton and Hong Kong. Within a week the economy of the crown colony was paralysed, the harbour full of idle steamers. A flood of strikers arrived from Hong Kong, lodging in houses requisitioned by the municipal government. So infuriated was the population, according to a Soviet military expert, that 'one heedless word would have been sufficient to have this whole mass of several thousand rush upon Shameen.' The whole campaign greatly increased the prestige of the revolutionary government, isolating more moderate elements and cementing the united front between Nationalists and Communists.[76]

Several Russians proposed a military campaign against Hong Kong, as an 'open declaration of war against imperialism would swell the wave of the national-revolutionary movement in the country and lead to general open fighting against the foreigners'.[77] The idea was rejected, but hope of a revolution that would destabilise the imperialist camp was rekindled in Moscow. After Stalin had manoeuvred against Trotsky and the so-called Left Opposition, in 1925 he entered into an alliance with Nikolai Bukharin. Bukharin, the author of a widely read *ABC of Communism* and editor of *Pravda*, the Communist Party's official newspaper, was a theoretician in his own right, seeing imperialism as an economic system dependent on the international market, not least China. An anti-foreign movement in China, he believed, would create conditions in which the Europeans would be unable to trade, leading in turn to economic bankruptcy at home and consequently a violent revolution in the streets. It was a theory that gained credence as the boycott laid waste to Hong Kong.[78]

Help from Moscow increased. Borodin, who had set off with a handful of military advisers in 1923, had hundreds of agents under his command by the end of 1925. One detailed investigation listed the names of eighty-eight 'significant leaders of the highest rank of the Comintern', while by 1926 some 691 Russians were registered at the Soviet Consulate. 'Everywhere, and into the minutest cog in the political and military machines, Soviet influence has peacefully penetrated', reflected Ma Su, having served as Sun Yat-sen's personal representative in Washington.[79]

The flow went both ways, not least after a centre for training revolutionaries and agitators was opened in Moscow on 7 November 1925, coinciding with the anniversary of the October Revolution. Sun Yat-sen University, located near the Kremlin in a spacious building with a central hall decorated with crystal chandeliers and luxury fittings, welcomed a thousand students over the next two years. Even as ordinary Russians waited in long queues throughout the night in front of shops from which they hoped to obtain a small quota of meat, the students were well fed and clothed, with generous allowances offered by Moscow. Among the students who later made a name for themselves was Deng Xiaoping, nicknamed 'Little Cannon' for his short stature and aggressive demeanour. Many, however, were the sons and daughters of influential Nationalist Party members, including Chiang Ching-kuo, the fifteen-year-old son of Chiang Kai-shek.[80]

Borodin also distributed weapons lavishly. The value of the arms supplied to Canton in October and November 1925 was between 1 and 1.5 million rubles.[81]

Beyond Canton, Moscow had tried to gain an ally in the north, not least to protect the Chinese Eastern Railway in Manchuria. Moscow, so far, had managed to establish eight centres for Bolshevik propaganda in the region, all funded by Harbin, a city that had prospered after the Russians had selected it as the administrative hub for their railway concession in 1898. With wide, well-paved boulevards and imposing neoclassical buildings reminiscent of Paris, Harbin attracted tens of thousands of emigrants from the Tsarist Empire. Nationals from many other countries also worked in the industrial, banking and commercial enterprises that began to flourish with the arrival of the railway. But when the Nationalists and the Communists, with Comintern guidance, tried to organise a parade in the wake of the Shanghai incident, they failed. On 17 June 1925, dozens of agitators from Canton and Shanghai were taken into custody, as well as forty Russians and Koreans working on behalf of the Comintern. A wave of arrests followed in other cities in Manchuria.[82]

Moscow blamed Zhang Zuolin for the setback. A slim, diminutive man with finely chiselled features and delicate hands whose gentle manner hid a ruthless streak, Zhang had first gained fame fighting on the side of the Japanese during the Russo-Japanese War of 1904. By 1920 the marshal had emerged as the governor general of Manchuria, a strategic region coveted by both Russia and Japan. After Zhang clamped down on Bolshevik activities along the railway, the Soviet consul general in Harbin left for Moscow, reporting to his superiors how a sophisticated surveillance apparatus developed by the marshal with help from White Russians had made Communist propaganda impossible.[83]

Moscow found a counterweight in Feng Yuxiang. As Sun Yat-sen was lying on his deathbed, the Christian General began to eye his mantle, seeing himself as a suitable alternative to lead a campaign of national reunification. But weapons and ammunition were required. The Russians, on the other hand, were fearful that after Sun's death the Nationalist Party might reject communism. Even before Sun had breathed his last, they agreed to help Feng. In April, a group of twenty-nine military advisers arrived in Kalgan (known later as Zhangjiakou), a strategic gateway through the Great Wall on the road to Russia where the Christian General had established his headquarters. They were fully paid by Moscow, and helped train officers in the use of artillery, machine guns, cavalry and infantry. Workshops were converted into arsenals, churning out ammunition. Arms were delivered, including 27,000 rifles, ninety machine guns, cavalry saddles ('6 of them not complete') and three aircraft. But Feng resisted efforts by his advisers to implant political commissars and Communists in the army.[84]

Still, in January 1926, the Christian General was driven out of Beijing by his main rival, Zhang Zuolin. Feng stepped back in order to avoid further losses, and undertook a pilgrimage to the Soviet Union. By May he was in Moscow, where he visited Lenin's tomb and gave stirring speeches, assuring his audience that he was 'a son of a worker'. 'He fooled everyone,' one witness reported. Stalin promised more weapons, valued at 6 million gold rubles, by that August. 'Moscow supplied arms free of cost and also paid for the transportation of the supplies,' according to one specialist.[85]

By the summer of 1926, Moscow had successfully created entire armies in China, equipping, training and directing them by means of a huge staff, ready to do battle against the very government with which it had signed a treaty of recognition.

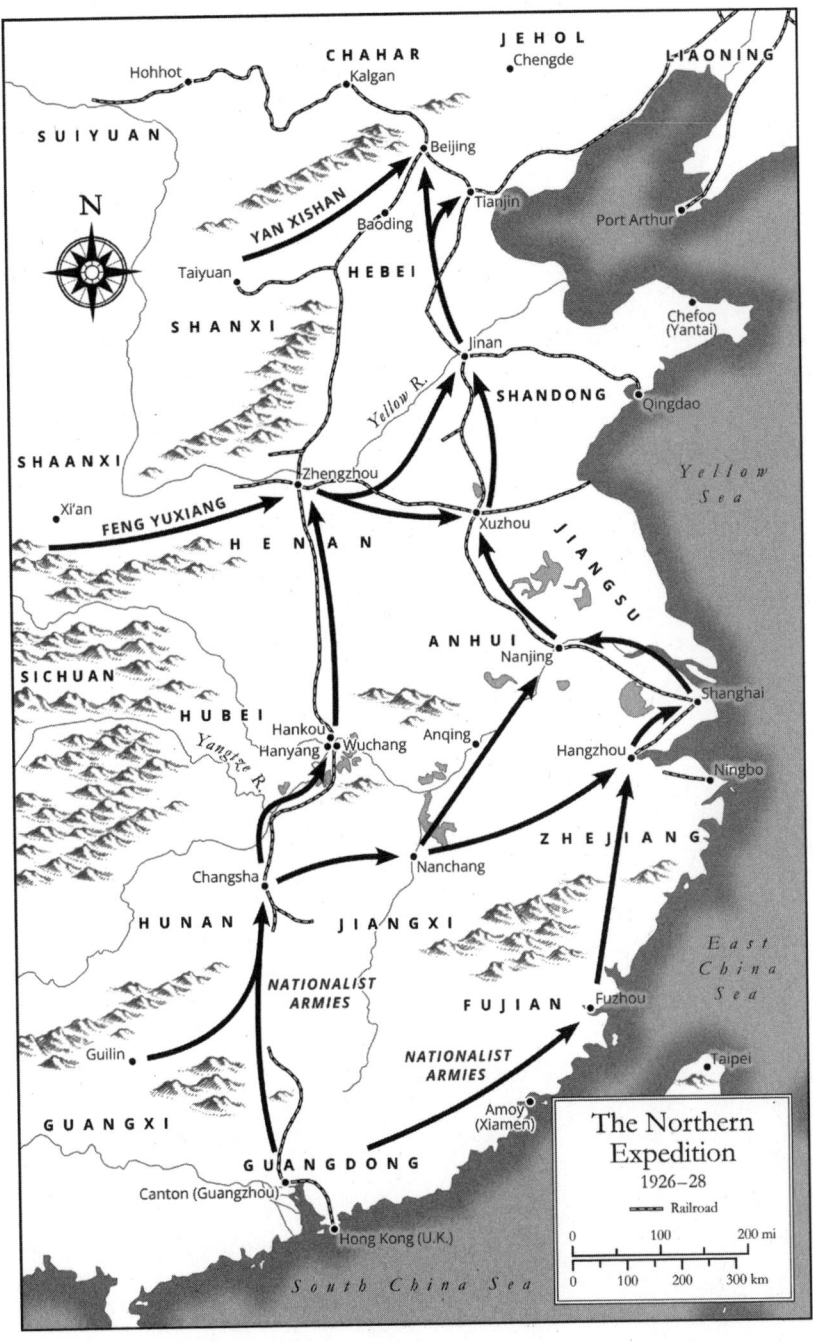

2
Fomenting Revolution (1926–1927)

By the end of 1925 the Communists had succeeded in taking control of virtually every political section in the Nationalist Army. 'Almost all the political work in the units is being done by them,' wrote Nikolai Kuibyshev, head of the Soviet advisers in South China, adding that 'some even occupy posts as commanders.' But in their haste to supply every division with a political commissar the Communists went too far. In a number of cases the troops they indoctrinated became so radical that they rebelled against their own officers, beating them or ignoring orders. In some units desertions were on the rise.[1]

Tensions between Nationalists and Communists, which had been simmering all along, came to the boil. 'The Communists are destroying our army,' claimed a faction of the Nationalist Party, formed at a gathering held in the Western Hills outside Beijing in November 1925.[2] They viewed the Communists as the cuckoo's egg in a sparrow's nest, and were determined to purge them. 'Strike the Communists from the Party Register!' they demanded in their manifesto. During their meeting, the group voted to terminate the contract of Mikhail Borodin, although in the absence of a quorum their decision was not binding. They also decided to censor Wang Jingwei and expel him for a period of six months. Wang, who had taken down Sun Yat-sen's testament, had benefited most from his master's death, but was seen as being too close to the Communists.³

Wang responded by convening a second Party congress in Canton in January 1926, promptly expelling all members of the Western Hills faction. It was a triumph of sorts, although it did not allay fears about Communist influence, least of all among the Whampoa cadets. A new Central Executive Committee, formed by Wang Jingwei during the congress, placed every strategically important government department in the hands of either the left wing of the Nationalist Party or a Communist, including such future stalwarts as Mao Zedong and Zhou Enlai. Borodin, for one, understood the danger, and tried to rein in the Communists, limiting their membership to one-third at most of any one committee.⁴

It was not enough. Kuibyshev himself, despite his report on the Communists, was part of the problem. An arrogant, self-important veteran with high connections in Moscow, he openly disdained Chiang Kai-shek and tried to place the Nationalist Army under his own control. He was close to Wang, who used him to undermine Chiang. In February, Nationalist Party members critical of forces on the left began to rally behind Chiang. A proud, ambitious but insecure man prone to abrupt decisions, Chiang himself feared being sidestepped. The Soviets, he wrote in his diary, 'suspect me, fool me'. He was deeply unhappy, prone to outbursts of uncontrolled anger. He tried to resign, then almost embarked on a trip to Moscow, only to be dissuaded at the last minute by his secretary, who suggested he make a stand.⁵

When, on the night of 18 March, the commander of the cruiser *Zhongshan*, flagship of the navy, allegedly received a phone call ordering him to move from Canton to Whampoa, Chiang feared that a coup was being attempted against him: 'I sensed that the zero hour of a Communist plot was at hand.' The commander was a Communist, and two days earlier a close ally had warned Chiang that something untoward was afoot. Chiang later explained that the plotters had planned to seize him the moment he boarded the ship and send him to Russia as a hostage.⁶ Although the course of events remains a mystery to this day, with some historians explaining the entire incident as a provocation engineered by Chiang himself, the outcome is clear: in the early hours of 20 March, Chiang declared martial law, ordered the captain arrested, disarmed the pickets who had thrived during the strike, and placed the Soviet advisers in protective custody. Communist Party members at Whampoa were also apprehended.[7]

Within days a compromise was reached. Moscow needed Chiang, much as Chiang needed Moscow. Both, no doubt, were biding their time. Kuibyshev was shipped off to Russia, while all political work inside the Nationalist Army was suspended. The power of the labour unions was curtailed, their members prohibited from forming armed squadrons.[8] In May, the Central Executive Committee agreed a further eight-point proposal, demanding a register of Chinese Communist Party members and prohibiting any member with dual party membership from heading a Nationalist Party or government department.[9] Wang Jingwei, humiliated, went into self-imposed exile. Borodin's wings were clipped. Chiang now reigned supreme. Vasily Blyukher, alias Galen, a gifted general who had been Chiang's trusted military adviser until he had returned to the Soviet Union for medical treatment in the summer of 1925, was recalled to Canton. Blyukher had helped Chiang crush the mercenary troops from Yunnan and Guangxi and unify Guangdong province.

Chiang could, at long last, begin the Northern Expedition so dear to his master Sun Yat-sen. Fiscal integrity had been brought to Canton by T. V. Soong, a slender young man who had worked at the International Banking Corporation in New York, resulting in considerable silver reserves which underwrote the military machine that was about to roll north. A mobilisation order was issued on 1 July. One week later, 100,000 men in brown uniforms began to march out of Canton. A motley crew of trained cadets, soldiers, young recruits, workers and peasants, they were divided into eight armies under Chiang's command. Accompanying the troops were hundreds of propagandists and agitators, some of them sent as vanguards along the line of march. They distributed pictures of Sun Yat-sen, put up posters denouncing the yoke of imperialism and called meetings, explaining how they came as liberators, not as conquerors. As Borodin stated: 'We paid as much attention to posters as to rifles.'[10]

A few days later Chiang's forces reached Changsha, the bustling capital of Hunan, set among rice fields in the middle of a fertile valley, and took the city without firing a shot. Even before they arrived, the local governor had resigned and fled to Wuhan. Encouraged, local Communists held a parade, then seized the governor's residence and turned it into their headquarters. When the Nationalist Army arrived, they were 'welcomed as heroes', with every shop flying the Communist flag. Student processions, lasting for hours on end, marched through the streets, proclaiming the virtues of communism. Trade unions were organised, with daily parades by the workers. The following months were relatively peaceful, although by October the city, as never before, was 'billed, placarded, circularised or snowed under showers of leaflets'.[11]

Throughout the province, posters went up and meetings were called the moment the troops entered a town or village. Unions were set up, branches of the Party opened, youth, students and women provided with their own organisations. The soldiers, by all accounts, were well behaved and well equipped, easily the best troops south of the Yangtze, the river dividing the country into two halves. The largest metropolis and chief port on the river was Wuhan. Some 800 kilometres to the west of Shanghai, it comprised three cities, including Hankou, a wealthy and cosmopolitan centre with foreign concessions sometimes referred to as the Chicago of the East, and Wuchang, where troops had overthrown the empire fifteen years earlier. Hanyang, on the right bank of the Han river opposite Hankou, was an arsenal city with the country's first modern iron- and steelworks. The Nationalists' main opponent was Wu Peifu, the general who controlled vast swathes of territory in the country, often in rivalry with Zhang Zuolin. Hankou and Hanyang were easily taken in early September, but the fighting for Wuchang, situated on undulating hills and surrounded by a crenellated wall, was ferocious. Chen Lifu, Chiang's personal secretary, remembered steering his horse through fields covered with dead bodies, the stench permeating the air: 'when my horse approached and moved its tail, the flies covering the dead scattered.' Wu Peifu only surrendered on 10 October, the anniversary of the Wuchang uprising. The attrition rate was high, but as the Northern Expedition proceeded the ranks of the Nationalists were replenished by local militia employed by government officials.[12]

Yet even as several armies battled for control of Wuhan, Chiang turned one column with his best troops east towards Nanchang, capital of Jiangxi province. The two-pronged attack was strategic, since without Nanchang and the treaty port of Jiujiang, further down the Yangtze, Wuhan could not be held. But Chiang also feared that Borodin might turn the labour unions in Wuhan against him. A bloody tide of battle ebbed and flowed around Nanchang for several months, reducing parts of the city and the surrounding villages to rubble. Sun Chuanfang, an ally of Wu Peifu, terrorised the local population with mass executions while his troops plundered the shops, some sending their loot home through the post. Only on 9 November, after Nationalist aircraft had dropped handbills warning that the city would be flattened, did Sun retreat. Jiujiang was captured the same week.[13]

The Nationalist victories took foreign observers by surprise. They also worried Borodin, as smouldering resentment began to develop into open jostling for power. Even as Chiang was still directing his troops outside Nanchang, Borodin began to regain the influence he had lost in March. He convened a Central Executive Committee of the Nationalist Party in Canton and packed it with Communist sympathisers. Its final programme honoured several demands made by the Communists, including a call for the formation of peasant self-defence units. In a calculated slight aimed at Chiang, the committee also sent a telegram to his rival Wang Jingwei requesting that he return. A few weeks later, a resolution was passed to move the site of the government from Canton to Hankou.[14]

One week before the departure of the first group of leaders to Hankou, Canton celebrated, declaring 7 November a holiday. The city was decked out with Soviet flags and portraits of Lenin and Sun Yat-sen. On outdoor stages, sketches of the key episodes of the Bolshevik Revolution were performed. In the evening, a banquet in honour of the Soviet delegates was held. After a long trek overland, first by train, then by palanquin, finally by boat, Borodin and his retinue arrived in Hankou in early December.[15]

The Northern Expedition had also startled Moscow. Bukharin, who earlier that year had become head of the Comintern, portrayed revolution in Asia as a necessary condition for revolution in Europe. As his organisation convened in November 1926, he announced that a Chinese revolution would deal a fatal blow to European capitalism, most of all to Britain. The Comintern's resolution specifically pointed out that 'The Chinese revolution is one of the most important and powerful factors which disturbs the structural stability of capitalism. During the last two years imperialism has suffered considerable reverses in China, the results of which will produce a considerable influence on the aggravation of the crisis of world capitalism.'[16]

Orders followed, instructing Soviet advisers to discredit opponents of revolution, stir up the population and organise agitation against imperialist powers. One letter of instruction, which only survived in a partially burned state, enjoined the advisers not to 'shrink from taking all and any measures including looting and mass... [acre?]' in order to 'provoke the intervention of foreign [troops?...]'. Moscow, in short, viewed revolution in China as auxiliary to its struggle with Europe.[17]

On 12 December, a five-hour mass meeting welcomed Borodin to Hankou. Standing next to him on the platform were Sun Yat-sen's widow and his son Sun Fo, as well as Eugene Chen, listening to speeches from labour leaders, merchants and students. Since the Nationalists had captured Wuhan, the workforce of the triple city had come under the control of some 260 labour unions. These were directed by the General Labour Union, an entity in turn under the thumb of the Political Bureau, the highest organ of the Communist Party. A succession of strikes followed, with disastrous results for trade and industry. Wages increased by an average of 50 per cent, followed by an even greater rise in the cost of living. Announcing that he intended to abolish paper money and foreign banknotes, Borodin called for a show of hands in favour of the revolution, which the crowd unanimously supported.[18]

Within a week of his arrival, Borodin, Madame Sun Yat-sen and Sun Fo addressed 3,500 delegates at a further meeting closely guarded by military pickets to advocate the 'overthrow of the British' and their supporters in Beijing. They called for a boycott of everything British, from the workers who unloaded their goods to the agents who exported their cargo.[19]

Tens of thousands of labourers employed in the mines, factories and processing plants went on strike. Led by students and radical agitators, they spent their days celebrating the revolution, making speeches or demonstrating in the streets. Marching students and workers carried banners with slogans such as 'Down with Capitalists and Imperialists', 'Support the World Revolution', 'Workers of the World, Unite'. Many insisted that the world could be transformed in a day. From press-packing plants preparing native products for foreign markets to the cotton-spinning and weaving mills, huge sectors of the city came to a standstill. The shipping industry, from junk traders plying the sprawling canals and lakes of central China to the powerful steamers navigating the Yangtze, was paralysed.[20]

Unemployment soared. The workers who had been encouraged to agitate against imperialism and capitalism now turned to the government for meal tickets. But the government could not find sufficient revenue, and consequently had to raise taxes, sparking further strikes, which in turn led to an exodus of silver, as merchants and well-to-do families began to desert the city. The government ordered that the homes and landed property of opponents to the revolution be confiscated. But no one was willing to buy, fearing that the government itself would be short-lived. The exchange rate for banknotes issued in Hankou weakened relative to those released in Shanghai or Beijing. More money was printed to buy rice for the hungry, leading to prohibitively high prices, not least for rice.[21]

In Hankou attacks on foreigners began on 3 January 1927. At yet another mass meeting, hundreds of thousands of striking workers were directed to the British Concession, storming the main buildings. The Union Jack of the British Consulate was hauled down, replaced by the Nationalist flag. Women and children were evacuated, with remaining foreigners mobbed. In the days following the demonstration against Britain, other nationalities including Americans and Japanese became virtual prisoners in their own homes. They, too, were forced to gather a few valuables and join the stream of refugees before their homes were looted.[22]

***

Among the demonstrators in Hankou were several peasant delegations from Hunan. One year earlier, following Sun Yat-sen's death, Borodin had tried to harness to the revolutionary cause the peasants in the countryside surrounding Canton. He had planned to divide the villagers into five classes, confiscating land from the rich for distribution to the poor. But he soon discovered that there were too few landlords from whom the land could be taken. Instead, his agents encouraged the poor to attack middling farmers, leading to a breakdown of the rural economy.[23]

Undeterred, one of Borodin's political advisers, appointed specifically to work on the 'peasant movement', had delivered talks at the Soviet mission in Canton, pointing out that the only hope for the Communists was to 'rely on the peasant masses', which would mean land distribution.[24]

In May 1924, Borodin had set up a Peasant Movement Training Institute in Canton, charged with producing activists to be sent to the villages to organise a peasant movement. In March 1926, Mao Zedong, still at thirty-two an earnest young man, was appointed as its head. Mao came from Hunan, where his family were frugal, middling farmers who had sent their son to the village school. Mao, who read voraciously in his Changsha high school, found Sun Yat-sen's writings so inspiring that he joined the revolution against the Qing. He enrolled at the local Normal School a few years later, publishing his first article in 1917 in *New Youth*, the popular magazine edited by Chen Duxiu. One of his professors, after accepting a position at Peking University, helped the young radical join him with a job in the library. In 1919 he returned to his home province, where several years of political activism attracted the attention of the local authorities, who issued a warrant for his arrest. Mao left for the safety of Canton, arriving in September 1925.

In December 1926, Mao was sent back to his home province to help steer the peasant revolution. Changsha, by then, was a changed city. One month earlier, to mark the Bolshevik Revolution on 7 November, 'Changsha [had] spread itself in the reddest rejoicing ever,' one observer noted, with a parade denouncing the twin evils of imperialism and capitalism. The civil authorities had unionised the entire population, from silversmiths and carpenters to postal employees. Villagers came from the countryside to take part.[25] They, too, had been organised into unions. But efforts to foment a peasant revolution backfired, as the most deprived villagers began looting the property of those who were better off. Anarchy reigned. As a report to Moscow pointed out, the peasant associations did not hesitate to shoot 'local tyrants and the gentry'. The result was that 'rich families flee and there is nobody left to pay the land tax. For the same reason there is no proper trade in grain and the prices are different everywhere, which has an influence on the rate of exchange. The merchants also close their shops in consequence of the demand for an increase in wages on the part of their employees.'[26]

The reason for the violence was always the same: there were few landlords from whom the land could be taken. The very term 'landlord' was an alien concept, imported from Russia via Japan in the late nineteenth century. Unlike Russia, China had no aristocracy living on vast estates cheek by jowl with impoverished peasants only recently emancipated from serfdom. It lacked feudal baronies or landed nobles who lorded it over a mass of immiserated peasants by virtue of a royal charter. No junkers, no squires, and nothing even vaguely equivalent to serfdom existed. As S. T. Tung, publisher of the *Chinese Farmer* with a doctoral degree in agriculture from Cornell University, put it, 'China has no "landlord class".'[27]

The land had for centuries been bought and sold through sophisticated contracts that were upheld in magistrates' courts. In some cases contracts even drew a distinction between the topsoil and the subsoil. Tenancy rights were also defined contractually, although the vast bulk of the land was in the hands of small owners. Trusts were set up by corporate entities to hold land, for instance temples, schools and, especially in the south, clans sharing a surname and organised around a common ancestor.

Village life varied enormously across China. In the north, where wheat was the staple, tightly packed villages were strewn across the dusty plains, with many farmers owning a small parcel of land. Further to the west, not least along the ancient silk road, tens of millions of people lived in caves hewn out of brittle earth on a loess plateau, which was sparsely planted with potatoes, maize and millet. These people of the dust stood in stark contrast to the farmers who cultivated the land along the fertile Yangtze valley, where rich deposits of silt left behind by a meandering network of lakes and rivers allowed them to produce several crops of rice a year. Further south, villagers often shared the same surname, with powerful lineages controlling the land and building ancestral halls, schools, granaries and community temples. Everywhere, huge disparities in wealth and power existed, and everywhere poor people were reduced to hiring out their labour, always running the risk of being abused by their employers. In the most backward places, the countryside was mired in fear and violence, with cycles of revenge and betrayal reaching across generations.

The main distinction, however, was not between 'peasant' and 'landlord', but between locals and outsiders. At best, the principal outsider was an official imposing a variety of taxes with a reasonably equitable hand; at worst he was a rapacious militarist plundering the countryside for revenue. Whatever the exact situation, there was one constant: in a crowded countryside where land had been freely alienable for centuries, there was simply too little to be confiscated and distributed to all and sundry without undermining the rural economy. No magic solution, least of all revolution, existed to solve in a single stroke the immensely complicated problems of the countryside. But plenty of paupers had nothing to lose, tramping the countryside in search of work, occasionally begging, sometimes recruited by bandits, often ready to join any and every cause. Many relished the opportunity to turn the world upside down, even for a day.

Moscow, with its rigid ideology based on class struggle, did not take this perspective, but did realise that widespread strikes by worker and labour unions could 'push the bourgeoisie, the merchants and the gentry into the arms of the imperialists'. The Politburo in Moscow, dominated by Stalin, ordered the Comintern to damp down the peasant movement, since 'the immediate outbreak of a civil war in the countryside, in the midst of a war with imperialism and its agents in China, could weaken the fighting capacity of the Nationalist Party.'[28]

Mao was the one assigned to rein in the movement in Hunan. On 20 December 1926, at a welcoming meeting in Changsha, he shared the stage in a local theatre with a Soviet representative of the Peasant International, addressing an enthusiastic crowd of 300. Mao gave a long and dull speech, counselling moderation: 'the time for us to overthrow the landlords has not yet come,' he said, adding that 'we must make some concession to them.' He supported a reduction in land rent instead, plus an increase in the wages of hired hands.[29]

For a month Mao inspected the countryside, gathering material for a report. What he found changed his mind. He discovered that the most despised people in the countryside controlled the peasant associations in what he termed the 'Movement of the Riff-Raff'. He applauded the way 'people with no place in society', trodden in the dirt, had taken power in their own hands, tying up the rich with a rope around their necks, crowning them with tall dunce caps and parading them through the villages. They swarmed into the houses of all those who opposed them, slaughtering their pigs and eating their grain. 'Those who used to rank lowest now rank above everybody else'; it was a campaign called 'turning things upside down'. Mao found their slogans attractive: 'Anyone who has land is a tyrant, and all gentry are bad.' They were now the masters, choosing their targets at random, striking down the wealthy and powerful, creating a reign of terror. A few were executed: 'the only effective way of suppressing the reactionaries is to execute at least one or two in each county who are guilty of the most heinous crimes.' So taken with the violence was Mao that he felt 'thrilled as never before'.[30]

Towards the end of his report, published in February 1927, Mao predicted that a hurricane would destroy the existing order: 'In a very short time, in China's central, southern and northern provinces, several hundred million peasants will rise like a mighty storm, like a hurricane, a force so swift and violent that no power, however great, will be able to hold it back. They will smash all the trammels that bind them and rush forward along the road to liberation. They will sweep all the imperialists, warlords, corrupt officials, local tyrants and evil gentry into their graves.'[31]

***

The strikes in Hankou prompted growing unease within the foreign community. Again, Moscow intervened. On 26 January 1927, Russian officials explained that in order to avoid joint intervention by foreign powers all revolutionary efforts must focus on a campaign aimed exclusively at British interests.[32]

Britain, Stalin and Bukharin believed, was the major capitalist power, and a collapse of its market abroad would result in workers rioting in its streets at home. But there was another reason why Moscow sought to turn the flames of nationalism against Britain alone. On 18 December 1926, Britain had taken the lead among the Great Powers by declaring to the world its willingness to 'negotiate on treaty revision and all other outstanding questions' as soon as a responsible Chinese government had been established. In his 'Christmas Memorandum', Foreign Secretary Austen Chamberlain offered to meet the 'legitimate aspirations of the Chinese people', including abolition of extraterritoriality, the relinquishing of all concessions and the granting of full tariff autonomy. After the crippling strikes against Hong Kong, the British government had realised that if it wished trade to continue it must take the initiative in negotiating the end of the very treaty port system it had for the better part of a century helped to develop. As Chamberlain later explained in an address to the China Society in London: 'In China more than anywhere else we are a nation of shopkeepers. We want to be able to trade with you and we see that the unity, strength and authority of your Government are things as necessary for our purpose as they are for yours.'[33]

The Christmas Memorandum was the result of years of skilful but persistent negotiation on the part of a team of experienced diplomats from the central government in Beijing who were keen to abolish extraterritoriality through reform rather than revolution. During the Washington Conference, convened in 1921–2 to prevent a dangerous arms race by imposing limits on naval expansion, the quiet diplomacy pursued by Alfred Sao-ke Sze and V. K. Wellington Koo had resulted in the withdrawal of Japan from Shandong and the retrocession of Weihaiwei from Great Britain. All major powers, including Japan, likewise undertook to respect the country's territorial integrity and to negotiate for the gradual elimination of the treaty port system. In the following years, Wellington Koo and others pressed further at a series of international conferences, including the Tariff Revision Conference in 1926, where the foreign powers consented to the beginning of tariff autonomy on 1 January 1929.[34]

Miles Lampson, British ambassador in Beijing, travelled to Hankou to seek terms with the revolutionary government, but on 3 January 1927 a mob seized the British Concession, prompting the evacuation of most foreigners. London resisted calls for armed intervention and proceeded with its offer of treaty revision, leading to an agreement on 19 February on the rendition of the Hankou and Jiujiang concessions.[35]

The rendition only intensified the anti-imperialist campaign, resulting in hundreds of foreigners scrambling to find their way to Shanghai, heavily protected by the Treaty Powers. In Liuyang, some fifty kilometres to the east of Changsha, the Wesleyan Mission had for months been subjected to constant harassment by a propaganda unit left in the wake of the Nationalist Sixth Army. In February, all foreigners were hounded out of the mission compound, pursued by lantern light and with threats of violence by a jeering mob down to the river, where they boarded a junk. In Nanxian, a mob broke into the China Inland Mission, smashed the doors, windows and seats of the chapel, wrecked the residence and stole all the furniture. Throughout the territories conquered by the Nationalists, Communist elements looted, burned or took over foreign institutions, using some of them 'as stables for horses, headquarters for soldiers'. Some churches were painted red. In early March, the Nationalists seized a steamer belonging to the Yangtze Rapid Steamship Company, a small shipping firm with a dozen vessels registered in Chicago. The ship, loaded with young agitators from Canton who had plastered it with anti-imperialist slogans, then toured the upper reaches of the river to urge a boycott against Britain. Hankou remained tense throughout, with Europeans and Americans pouring in from the interior to take ship for Shanghai. The violence repulsed Chiang Kai-shek, and on 10 February he issued a public order to protect foreign lives and property. To his diary he confided that 'the crimes committed [by the Communists] are greater than those of our enemies.'[36]

As the tide of war advanced, more towns and cities were emptied of foreigners. A turning point was Nanjing, the crown jewel of the Yangtze River where Sun Chuanfang had found refuge after his defeat in Nanchang. Allies of Wu Peifu sent troops from the north to help him defend the city and reinforce Shanghai, 300 kilometres downstream. Chiang sent some of his best generals in a two-pronged attack from Nanchang. Instead of making a stand, Sun left Nanjing almost undefended. Fearing the arrival of the Nationalists, on 23 March his soldiers began a chaotic retreat, trying to cross the river to return north. Although in the preceding days most foreigners had already been evacuated, a hundred remained in the city, many of them women and children. The first Nationalists began entering the city around midnight. The following morning armed bands of uniformed soldiers led by political commissars began systematically looting all foreign schools, hospitals and missions. John Williams, vice-president of Nanking University, was robbed of his watch and then shot dead. A young woman at the Presbyterian mission at first welcomed the troops from her window, but was then shot twice, although she survived. Another missionary only narrowly escaped death when the gun pointed at his head by a furious soldier misfired. Similar treatment was inflicted on members of the British

Consulate, where the harbour master and a second victim were killed outright, robbed and stripped of their clothing.[37]

'We are Bolshevists, we are proud of being Bolshevists, and we are going to act like Bolshevists,' one of the soldiers was overheard saying at the American consulate, where staff were forced to hand over their money and other valuables. 'Even stairways, window frames, doors and in short everything which could be torn out, were taken away,' wrote John Davis, the consul.[38]

Some thirteen buildings owned by Americans were torched. The Japanese consul, lying ill in bed, was shot twice but not killed. Simultaneously, troops on the bund along the river began to open fire on the foreign ships gathered to evacuate their nationals. 'All ships were hit countless times during the course of the morning,' resulting in one sailor being killed instantly by a bullet in the head. In the afternoon, after around fifty American nationals had succeeded in gathering on a hill near the river, American, British, French and Italian gunboats as well as destroyers opened a protective barrage of fire targeting the Nationalist positions. Landing forces helped the escapees scuttle across the lowlands towards the riverbank, where rowing boats took them to the warships. Thirty to forty Nationalist soldiers were reportedly killed in the crossfire.[39]

Many foreigners remained stranded in the city, although by several accounts the violence stopped from the moment foreign warships began to shell the city. Bugles were sounded, prompting the soldiers to cease their work of destruction.[40] While no conclusive evidence was ever produced, suspicion immediately turned towards Lin Zuhan, also known as Lin Boqu, an early follower of Sun Yat-sen who had joined the Chinese Communist Party in 1921. In March 1926, he became the political commissar for the Sixth Army, installing Communist Party and Communist Youth League members at every level to ensure that his troops were thoroughly indoctrinated. Chiang Kai-shek, for one, had little doubt who was behind the incident. Even as events were unfolding, he wrote in his diary that Wuhan and the Comintern had mobilised all their forces to topple him. The following day, on 25 March, he wrote that 'The Communist Party does this in order to get the foreign powers to intervene and destroy the success of the Nationalist revolution.' That same day he travelled to Nanjing to guarantee the safety of foreigners and their property.[41]

The Nanjing Incident, as it became known at the time, made headlines around the world. Hu Shi described it as 'the greatest crisis of the revolution', the latest in a series of 'deliberate anti-foreign moves' designed to provoke foreign powers and precipitate the 'imperialist war' that Bukharin and Stalin counted on to engulf their enemies. Hu Shi, who was in the United States at the time, could sense how public opinion, which had until then been sympathetic, 'changed overnight and turned against the revolutionary cause'.[42]

The foreign powers now wondered whether their nationals would be attacked in Shanghai. Unlike some of the smaller treaty ports, Shanghai was an international centre of trade and commerce harbouring 3 million people, including 50,000 foreigners. In the foreign enclaves, stretching nine kilometres along the waterfront, trolley cars ran through broad avenues, lined by attractive modern mansions, banks, hotels, clubs and parks. After a relatively quiet year in 1926, labour unions had become more active, inspired by reports on the benefits the new government in Hankou had brought the workers. They intended to undermine Sun Chuanfang, who controlled the Chinese city outside the International Settlement, and prepare for the arrival of the Nationalist Army. With the help of Soviet agents, the Communist-dominated General Labour Union armed a labour detachment of several hundred men. They also trained a further 5,000 pickets. They began a campaign of intimidation, resulting in more than ten strike breakers and others being gunned down as 'capitalist running dogs'. As a Comintern report phrased it, the 'red terror' had a 'sobering effect' on people opposed to the workers. The entire process was funded and supervised by Moscow, which provided 250 revolvers and 200 grenades. The aim, it was explained in a meeting attended by several Soviet agents, was to create an armed insurrection. 'We also strive to create an incident between the [local] troops and the foreign troops,' mainly by encouraging local soldiers to force their way into the International Settlement, 'with arms in hand'.[43]

Two days before the Nationalist troops arrived, Wang Shouhua, the Communist leader of the General Labour Union, launched an insurrection. Plainclothes gunmen and political activists, leading a motley crew of mill hands, factory workers, students and tram drivers, attacked police stations and seized their weapons. One police officer was shot through the head and left naked on the road by a furious mob. A general strike further paralysed the city, now controlled by the labour unions, which unleashed a spree of looting and burning, with 'great tracts of houses burnt down'. Thousands of people, 'a miserable stream of destitute families', sought refuge in the foreign-protected concessions.[44]

Bai Chongxi, chief of staff of the Northern Expedition, a Muslim general from Guangxi with a disciplinarian bent, known for undermining larger enemy forces with swift and decisive manoeuvres, arrived on 22 March 1927. Troops under Sun Chuanfang panicked, some trying to seek safety inside the Settlement, where they were rounded up and interned. Bai ordered his troops to end the strike, leading to pitched battles between his soldiers and the workers they tried to disarm. The general strike had, by now, claimed more than 300 lives, with over 1,500 shops and dwellings reduced to smoking shells. 'Men, women and children, weeping and moaning, were seen among the ruins, trying to scrape out a few belongings,' a journalist reported.[45]

A 'Worker's Supervisory Corps' of 3,000 members, some armed with rifles and Mausers, sprang into existence to take charge of public order. Concurrently, a 'provisional government' controlled by the labour unions was organised, heavily dominated by Communist Party members. Ignoring an order from Chiang Kai-shek to disperse, they proclaimed a Shanghai Commune which controlled the city. Bai Chongxi was reined in, as Chiang now feared that troops outside his control would decimate the strikers, giving Hankou a pretext to accuse him of a massacre and discredit him yet further. This meant that for the first time in its history Shanghai was under the indirect rule of a Communist Party.[46]

For several months Chiang had watched his rival Borodin strengthen the hand of the Communists. In December 1926

Borodin had called for a 'Joint Conference' to exercise 'supreme power' over the Nationalist Party, packing it with Communist Party members. In January 1927, after he had officially proclaimed Hankou the capital of Nationalist China, he began removing all restrictions the Central Executive Committee had imposed on Communist Party members in the previous May. The Politburo in Moscow supported all his moves, although they urged Borodin not to break the United Front. Chiang, eventually, was stripped of all his titles but that of Commander-in-Chief, or Generalissimo.[47]

On 26 March Chiang returned to Shanghai, where foreign powers, apprehensive of more revolutionary violence, were strengthening their naval forces, landing extra troops and organising a volunteer defence corps. After the Nanjing Incident, the exodus from the interior became a flood, with Europeans and Americans pouring into a crowded stronghold. They were not alone in seeking shelter beyond the reach of Hankou. All along the Yangtze, steamers were packed to the hilt with merchants and their families forced to leave their homes.

Towards the end of March open confrontations began to occur between the different factions of the Nationalist Party, namely members who favoured the Communists and those who opposed them. On 30 March in Hangzhou, 50,000 workers who called themselves the Hangzhou Labourers marched on the headquarters of the Communist-supported General Labour Union. Both sides clashed, resulting in numerous casualties. In Chongqing, a sprawling city in Sichuan province surrounded by mountains and criss-crossed by rivers, labour groups headed by agitators clashed with members of a more conservative body supported by Nationalist soldiers. More than a hundred were reportedly killed.[48]

Wang Jingwei, hoping to bridge the differences within the Nationalist Party, now stepped into the breach. During his exile abroad, Wang had met Stalin in Moscow, who had suggested sending him back to China to act as a popular counterweight to Chiang Kai-shek. Stalin feared that thanks to the Northern Expedition Chiang was becoming a national hero. Always keen to build bridges and gain allies, the Generalissimo himself had buried the hatchet and written to Wang, asking him to come out of retirement and take charge of Party affairs.[49]

Wang arrived in Shanghai on 1 April. That same day, Borodin dismissed Chiang as Commander-in-Chief.[50] On 2 April, the Central Supervisory Commission of the Nationalist Party gathered under Wu Zhihui, a veteran revolutionary and staunch opponent of the Communist Party, known as one of the Four Elders. Wu argued that the Communists, who were scheming against the Nationalist Party, were responsible for instigating the chaos prevailing in the Yangtze valley. 'A split with the Communist Party is inevitable,' Chiang wrote in his diary. Still he tried to rescue the situation, publicly praising Wang as 'one of the most loyal comrades in the Party'. After meeting him on 3 April, Chiang sent a circular telegram welcoming him as Chairman of the Party and enjoining all Party branches to unify under Wang's command.[51] But two days later Wang Jingwei and Chen Duxiu published a joint statement in the press. Proclaiming that no divergence in opinion existed between the Communists and the Nationalists, they called for a 'democratic dictatorship of all oppressed classes opposed to the counter-revolution'. The statement had an extraordinary effect. Chiang and other members of the Nationalist Party viewed it as a declaration of war. In an emotionally charged meeting, Wu Zhihui scolded Wang Jingwei to his face, accusing him of having 'thrown in his lot with the rebels'. Wang absconded the following day, boarding a ship heading upriver to Hankou.[52]

The central government in Beijing had followed closely the growing rift between the Nationalists and the Communists. One month earlier, the Russian steamer *Pamiat Lenina* had arrived in Nanjing, en route to Hankou with a group of Russians including Madame Borodin. Soldiers boarded the vessel and discovered trunks full of propaganda and secret instructions from Moscow hidden in the bunkers. The Russians were bundled off to Beijing, where Zhang Zuolin, a determined foe of Moscow, threatened them with execution. Zhang used the dossier seized from the Russians to announce on 3 April that Borodin was a Soviet agent, paid by Moscow to help the Nationalist Party wage war against

Beijing: 'The world should know that all officers of the Cantonese army were trained by Russians employed by Chiang Kai-shek in the Whampoa Academy at Canton.' 'I have Bolsheviks nearer still,' he continued. 'They share the control of the Chinese Eastern Railway. This is what I mean when I say I have Russia already in my house.'[53]

Keen to unearth more evidence of Soviet involvement in the country's domestic affairs, Wellington Koo requested that the foreign community allow his government to search the Soviet Embassy in Beijing's diplomatic quarter. In the early hours of 6 April, two small contingents of armed soldiers and police, accompanied by detectives with drawn revolvers, raided the premises. They emerged an hour later with several tonnes of incriminating documents, some partly damaged after the Russians locked inside the Embassy had tried to burn all the evidence. Soldiers had climbed up on the roof and poured buckets of water down the chimney. In this mass of soggy paper was further proof that Moscow had tried to overthrow the very government that it had recognised in the 1924 Sino-Soviet Treaty, an agreement that included a formal undertaking not to 'propagate Communistic doctrines' in China. Also dragged out of the premises were some sixty Chinese Communists, including Li Dazhao, who had sheltered inside after an arrest warrant had been issued against him.

The events were front-page news around the world. A selection of the seized material was passed on to foreign powers, including Great Britain. The evidence showed that Moscow had sent entire shiploads of arms and munitions to southern China to support a Communist revolution, together with political, economic and military advisers. Among the files were instructions from Moscow to spy and disrupt, as well as a ledger tallying all the payments made to promote revolution.[54]

The staggering extent of Moscow's involvement in revolutionary activities in China, including revelations of the magnitude of Russia's efforts to incite violence and seize British concessions along the Yangtze River, coming to light one year after the General Strike in Britain, prompted the British cabinet in London to order a similar search of Soviet premises. Suspecting that the trade delegation was used as a front for Soviet efforts to disseminate Communist ideas, foment social unrest and undermine the government, on 12 May 1927, the Metropolitan Police raided the offices of the All-Russian Co-operative Society (abbreviated as Arcos) in Golders Green. The documents they carted away were compromising enough to prompt Downing Street to break off diplomatic relations with Moscow. A few years earlier, the Anglo-Soviet Treaty had specifically stipulated that the Soviet Union would not use its international presence to subvert private enterprises and foreign governments. The Arcos affair, as it is commonly known, was a key moment in modern British history.[55]

The Beijing raid on the Soviet Embassy had comparably far-reaching consequences. Chiang Kai-shek was informed of the nature of the documents, including plans to eliminate him. One day after the raid, he began to plan a pre-emptive strike. On 7 April, he instructed his troops to protect all foreigners and their property. On 8 April, he ordered the Political Department closed, accusing its political commissars of being 'secret enemy agents' who had instigated widespread violence and chaos. The same day, the Nationalist Party released a declaration in the press demanding the immediate cessation of all Communist Party activities. Armed organisations such as labour unions and pickets were declared illegal if they refused to comply with orders issued by the army's headquarters.[56]

In the Shanghai Commune, the General Labour Union continued to impose its will, using armed pickets and gunmen dressed in black to intimidate or harass perceived opponents, including rickshaw pullers who failed to display their union membership badge properly. Encouraged by Wang Jingwei and Chen Duxiu's joint declaration of 5 April, the Communist Party came out in the open for the first time and 'spread itself in a blaze'. Violent clashes between soldiers and labour pickets, a force by now equivalent to two regiments, resumed on 7 April.[57]

On 12 April, Chiang ordered Bai Chongxi and Zhou Fengqi to disarm the pickets. In the early hours of the morning, at the short blast of a bugle and a single toot sounded from a siren aboard a warship in the harbour, Nationalist soldiers wearing white armbands began half a dozen simultaneous raids on buildings occupied by armed workers. These included the headquarters of the General Labour Union and the Pudong Third District Police Station, which armed gunmen had occupied for three weeks. Rifle and machine-gun fire echoed across the city for several hours. Some 500 workers inside the Fuzhou Guild, where a large quantity of weapons were hoarded, put up stiff resistance. But the strongest opposition came from the Commercial Press Club, where 300 to 400 armed pickets had taken refuge and returned fire, refusing to be dislodged. Several hours into the siege, heavy guns were brought in and trained on the building, at which point the defenders – unemployed seamen, former employees of the press, workers on strike – realised that their cause was lost and agreed to surrender. By the time the fighting abated, hundreds had been disarmed and arrested, with several dozen killed, the majority of these among the pickets. Twenty machine guns, 300 rifles, 200 Mauser pistols, 1 million rounds of ammunition, 7 cartloads of axes and 2,000 long-handled pikes were hauled from the premises.[58]

The raid came in the nick of time. For weeks the foreign powers had been pouring reinforcements into the International Settlement and the French Concession, including 40,000 marines and soldiers from Britain, the United States, Italy and Japan, as well as French Annamite troops from Indo-China. Britain alone had more than a dozen cruisers and destroyers in the area, deploying at all times at least four ships in the Huangpu River that ran along the Settlement. A perimeter with defensive checkpoints, some thirty kilometres in length and known as the Cordon, fenced off the foreign enclaves. In London, a whole series of strategic options were being considered in the aftermath of the Nanjing Incident, including the blocking of all crossings across the Yangtze to thwart the Northern Expedition. On 12 April, the British cabinet put its forces in Shanghai on standby. But once news of Chiang's intervention against the pickets reached London, Chamberlain stepped back from the brink, throwing his weight behind those cabinet members who opposed any military or naval action upriver.[59]

The General Labour Union was disarmed, but not subdued, holding a mass meeting on the afternoon of 12 April to denounce the arrests of the pickets. An enormous crowd attended, with numerous incendiary speeches but no further incidents. Later that day the union ordered yet another general strike for 13 April. Bai Chongxi, in control of the city, responded with a declaration of martial law.[60]

On 13 April over 100,000 people quit work in protest against the disarming of the union pickets. Despite heavy rain, at noon a huge rally was held in Zhabei, where most of the previous day's raids had taken place. As the parade approached the headquarters of General Zhou Fengqi, soldiers spotted marchers armed with iron rods, shouting 'Down with Chiang Kai-shek', 'Down with Reactionary Troops', 'Return Weapons to the Workers'. It was a breach of martial law, and they fired warning shots in the air. The crowd dispersed in a panic. Several side streets were blocked to prevent the demonstrators from entering the International Settlement. A volley was then fired at the crowd, although the situation was so confused that one journalist later reported that 'whether there are any casualties or not remains to be determined'. Another reporter saw dead bodies and wounded protesters on the ground, with blood staining the cobblestones. The *Shenbao*, Shanghai's leading newspaper, estimated that dozens had been injured, with a total of ten fatalities that day.[61]

After an in-depth investigation of the events of 12 and 13 April, the *China Times* on 18 April published a list of the names of 103 casualties, with forty-two deaths, including several passersby and twelve soldiers who had died in the raids. These figures corresponded to other estimates provided by local newspapers, both Chinese and foreign, although many dozens of victims were undoubtedly overlooked.[62]

On 14 April, Yang Hu and Chen Qun, two generals entrusted by Chiang Kai-shek with ensuring order in Shanghai, arrested over a thousand suspects, even as Bai Chongxi closed down the Shanghai Commune. At this stage, however, not even Yang and Chen were sure what to do with their prisoners. In a telegram sent to Chiang, they wondered: 'Will the Communist Party still be tolerated now? How should we deal with troublemakers?' The events in Shanghai were not, as popular lore would claim for decades to come, a massacre of thousands of revolutionaries, but a coup against the Communists.[63]

In the following months the suspects were interrogated, with dozens sentenced to death. One of them, Wang Shouhua, the Communist leader of the General Labour Union, was arrested, interrogated and executed by the military on 12 April. To this day, however, despite all the evidence to the contrary, historians of every stripe prefer a more lurid tale, one in which the victim was invited to dine at the home of a notorious gangster in the French Concession, who had Wang trussed in a burlap sack, bundled in a car, beaten and buried alive in a forest. Fantasy all too often trumps fact.[64]

In several other cities, the military also mounted raids against armed pickets. 'The modus operandi was to surround all suspected spots, open up a blast of machine gun and rifle fire, and then wait for developments,' noted one reporter.[65] In most cases there were few. In Hangzhou, Nanjing and Xiamen, the soldiers who took over the headquarters of labour unions encountered little resistance.[66]

In Canton, the Nationalist leaders in control of the city jumped the gun, proscribing all Communist activities as early as 9 April. On 15 April, Li Chai-sum (spelt Li Jishen many decades later), the local military commander, sent troops to disarm the pickets, arrest suspected Communists and occupy several strategic buildings, including labour unions. The entire operation resulted in fifty deaths, 200 casualties and 1,200 arrests. The British consul general wrote that 'the population manifested no sympathy with Communist prisoners.' He may have been biased, but the Communists themselves agreed, observing that the 'working classes' displayed very little concern. So spotty was attendance at a protest strike a week later that the government barely intervened.[67]

On 18 April, Chiang formally proclaimed Nanjing the capital of China. The Nationalist Party was now split, with two rival governments, one determined to exclude all Communists, the other committed to the United Front. On 28 April in Beijing, still the internationally recognised capital of the country, Zhang Zuolin ordered Li Dazhao and two dozen other Communists who had been seized at the Russian Embassy executed by strangulation, without any form of hearing or trial. It was a cruel display of power, all the more so as the executions were deliberately dragged out, each death taking about ten minutes.[68]

For a few weeks, Wuhan was celebrated as the 'Moscow of the East', as fellow travellers from all points of the compass flocked in to witness the unfolding of the next stage in the world revolution. They drowned the city in a flood of red, with parades, slogans, posters and meetings. The Comintern sent Earl Browder of the American Communist Party, Tom Mann of the British Communist Party and Jacques Doriot of the French Communist Party, stalwarts of the movement, to demonstrate support.[69] But underneath a scarlet surface power began to shift away from the Communists. The city was a wreck: cut off from the rest of the country, deprived of foreign business and paralysed by strikes, it was scarcely able to subsist. After Chiang Kai-shek clamped down on the pickets, money began to flow out towards Shanghai, seen as a safer destination, prompting Wuhan to impose a blockade on currency movements.

Wuhan staggered on for a few months, increasingly isolated as regional commanders throughout the south switched their allegiance to the Generalissimo. In Changsha, a city subordinate to Wuhan, the pickets were likewise disarmed, the unions ousted by the military.[70] Great hopes were now placed in Feng Yuxiang, the Christian General who had embraced Moscow in his search for weapons and munitions. In June, Feng used his newly equipped army to march across the north from his headquarters in Kalgan, entering Henan and taking its capital, the strategically important railway junction of Zhengzhou. Labour unions celebrated his arrival. 'From his army to the shirt on his back', one observer pointed out, Feng owed everything to the Russians. By holding on to the city, one through which all trains from the south had to pass on their way north, he could strike either at Wuhan or at Beijing. Feng became the key to the balance of power. Wuhan hoped he would defend them against Chiang Kai-shek, who had crossed the Yangtze days earlier and was keen to move on Beijing along the coast. But Chiang met Feng, conferring with him behind closed doors. Money may have changed hands, although the rumour cannot be verified. The outcome was a telegram in which Feng advised Borodin to return to Moscow, a fatal blow to the Communists in Wuhan. In a press conference, Feng appeared with a Nationalist Party emblem on his sleeve, explaining that he was joining the Generalissimo in the Northern Expedition.[71]

That same day, armed pickets in Wuhan gave up their weapons and deserted the General Labour Union headquarters, still occupied by the military. Even Young Pioneers, the Communist equivalent of the Boy Scouts, were ordered to return their sticks to headquarters. Eugene Chen, a slight, nervous man, remained defiant, declaring that 'We will take Nanjing within fifty days.' Two weeks later Borodin absconded in disgrace, followed by rapid decline in Soviet influence. On 15 July, the Nationalists in Wuhan severed their relations with the Communists. Wang Jingwei recognised Chiang Kai-shek. The next day one of the city's generals carried out a bloodless coup. Madame Sun Yat-sen and others quietly announced their retirement from politics, and left for Moscow.[72]

***

In Moscow, Stalin and the Left Opposition began blaming each other for the fiasco of the United Front. Trotsky and his temporary allies had distrusted the Nationalist Party as early as April 1926, and had opposed the Northern Expedition, arguing instead for a purely Communist programme to be carried out just by Communists. It was an improbable scheme, far removed from the reality on the ground, but one easily outdone by the even more fantastic delusions entertained by Karl Radek, erstwhile rector of Sun Yat-sen University. Radek argued that millions of armed workers should have occupied the International Settlement in order to destroy a main source of 'reaction' on which Chiang Kai-shek was said to have counted. In Hankou, he complained, the workers should have been armed with weapons from the

Hanyang arsenal to fight the dual forces of imperialism and capitalism. A genuine Red Guard should have been established, city and village soviets organised and the Nationalists swept away by the Communists. Stalin countered that without the Northern Expedition the 'revolutionary spirit' along the Yangtze valley would have remained dormant. He, too, vastly overestimated the potential of communism in China, but he had a point. The Communist Party had successfully used the Northern Expedition to set up trade unions and peasant associations in large parts of the south, spreading their propaganda far and wide. Membership, thanks to the United Front and generous backing from Moscow, had grown from a few hundred to 12,000 by the time the Northern Expedition began (the Nationalists boasted 350,000 members).[73] But while Stalin was more pragmatic than Trotsky, he too was steeped in Marxist ideology, believing that revolutionary forces merely required awakening to sweep away the old order. The reality was that the labour unions and peasant associations had been established at gunpoint, and dissolved the moment the military marched on or switched sides.[74]

Stalin changed tack, ordering the Communists to pull out of the Nationalist Army, establish an independent Red Army and set up a base in the south. He sent a fellow Georgian, Besso Lominadze, to help guide the operation. Lominadze, a tall man of barely thirty, arrived on 27 July 1927, officially relieving Borodin of his functions. At an emergency meeting two weeks later, Chen Duxiu, who had spoken out against the confiscation of land in the countryside, was conveniently made into a scapegoat, accused of having 'systematically paralysed the enthusiasm of the workers and peasants', thereby blocking their march towards liberation. Qu Qiubai, a young journalist who had worked as an assistant to Borodin and rapidly emerged as his right-hand man, became acting Chairman of the Party instead. Mao, a close ally of Qu, used the opportunity to point out that the way forward was to concentrate all efforts on military affairs, since political power had to be seized from the enemy: 'power grows from the barrel of a gun,' he famously opined. The statement came at an opportune moment, as Lominadze had arrived promising 15,000 rifles, 10 million cartridges, thirty machine guns and four mining weapons with 2,000 shells, the total valued at 1.1 million rubles, all to be shipped south from Vladivostok to a port the Communists would have to secure.[75]

Most of the troops that the Communists had been able to rescue from the collapse of the United Front belonged to Ye Ting and He Long, two disaffected generals formerly part of a fearsome 'Iron Army' under the command of Zhang Fakui. Their 20,000 soldiers were stationed around Nanchang, the capital of Jiangxi province. Zhou Enlai, having played a key role in organising the strikes in Shanghai, was now charged with overseeing the Party's military arm. Zhou, a shrewd, eloquent twenty-nine-year-old revolutionary of great practical ability, had spent several years as a young student in Japan, where he became an avid reader of *New Youth*. He returned home in 1919, at the height of the May Fourth Movement, and soon became involved in organising the boycott of Japanese goods. In Tianjin he was detained for six months for his political activities. He left the country, spending several years studying in France, where he joined a Chinese Communist Party cell. In 1924 he was summoned back, becoming the Whampoa Academy's chief political commissar as well as secretary of the Chinese Communist Party's provincial committee in Guangdong.

In July 1927, Zhou left Wuhan and booked a room in the Jiangxi Hotel in Nanchang, turning it into his headquarters. There he was joined by a small team of like-minded revolutionaries. Zhou was often described as diplomatic and pragmatic, although in Nanchang he was neither. Those who objected to his plans were angrily pushed aside, as Zhou insisted on gambling everything on a military insurrection. His troops took the city by storm on the morning of 1 August, easily prevailing over the local garrison. Zhou set up a Revolutionary Committee, which passed a flurry of decrees over the next two days. Then, as the Iron Army advanced towards the city, the Communists were forced to flee, although not, according to one account, without extracting some 300,000 dollars from the local Chamber of Commerce.[76]

The assault on Nanchang marked the effective birth of the Red Army, which the Central Committee now ordered to move towards Shantou (known at the time as Swatow), a major port in

Guangdong province where weapons could be delivered. As they trekked for weeks across the hilly landscape of Jiangxi, the troops tried to replenish their ranks by recruiting local bandits, but still suffered a high rate of attrition. The villagers they encountered, moreover, failed to rally spontaneously to the cause. On 8 September, the provincial Party committee ruled that the soldiers should henceforth march under the banner of the Communist Party. This meant that 'all evil landlords must be killed to prepare an uprising of the people in the province,' while 'a campaign of red terror must be carried out to destroy every single enemy.' It was a key turning point. As Zhang Guotao, one of the earliest adherents of the Chinese Communist Party and a key participant in the Nanchang uprising later remembered, the decision made by Lominadze, Qu Qiubai and others to pursue a pitiless 'burn and kill' policy only succeeded in 'dragging the Chinese Communist Party into terrorism'. The violence, in other words, came not in response to the exactions of their enemies but as a deliberate revolutionary strategy.[77]

Around 18 September, five Soviet agents disembarked in Shantou. On the evening of 23 September advance units of the Red Army arrived in the city port, unleashing chaos. 'An orgy of looting followed immediately,' one reporter observed. 'Everywhere were to be seen men carrying pieces of furniture or bundles of goods robbed from respectable houses,' the British consul noted.[78]

Prisoners were set free and shops closed. Several gangs of armed pickets, one carrying a banner of the Shantou General Labour Union, were seen dragging alleged enemies of the revolution, bound with ropes and chains, through the streets to be executed. The hammer and sickle appeared above the main entrance of the Seamen's Union, but not before some of its members were removed and replaced by more pliable elements. On arriving a few days later, Ye Ting restored order. Then, like every other occupying force in the country, whether bandit gangs or regular troops, he used his leverage to extort a large sum from the Chamber of Commerce. He demanded 400,000 dollars but apparently failed to collect more than 70,000.[79]

On 30 September the city awoke to find that the Red Army had fled overnight, only to be crushed ten kilometres outside the city walls by Nationalist troops allied to Li Chai-sum, the general in charge of Canton. Zhou Enlai and Ye Ting slipped away to Hong Kong, He Long to Shanghai.

Keen on a victory that might vindicate his China policy before the Fifteenth Congress of the Bolsheviks was due to assemble in Moscow in December, Stalin sent more agents and additional money. Heinz Neumann, a Comintern agent who had participated in the German October in 1923, landed in Shanghai where he met Besso Lominadze and collected a suitcase full of dollars to finance an uprising in Canton.[80]

Stalin, Lominadze, Qu Qiubai and others were convinced that the city harboured a proletarian base, ripe for rebellion. On 18 November, 700 workers from the General Labour Union, disbanded by Li Chai-sum months earlier, attacked the Waichow Club (Huizhou Club), which had once been their headquarters but was now occupied by their rivals, the Hong Kong Canton Strike Committee. 'With a shout the mob rushed towards the clubhouse,' stabbing several soldiers on guard. Four rioters were killed. Although they agreed to disperse when the police arrived, they had scored a victory. A few days later, the municipal government ceased to provide free board and lodging for the strikers who had started the boycott against Hong Kong in 1925. Disgruntled, and in many cases idle, they lit fires in no fewer than seventeen places, most of them the very buildings that had been converted into rice halls and dormitories for their exclusive use. In one case a blaze gutted twenty-one houses, five of them occupied by union offices, three restaurants and three brothels. To the Communist Party it looked as if the proletariat had the upper hand.[81]

Heinz Neumann, who had just arrived in Canton, joined Zhang Tailei, the key person in charge of organising the uprising. Zhang had worked as Henk Sneevliet's interpreter and accompanied Chiang Kai-shek to Moscow. Convinced that an army had to be crafted out of the paupers in the countryside to steer the Communist Party towards victory, in August 1927 he had rallied behind Qu Qiubai and Mao Zedong.

The uprising was planned for months, with the Central Committee under Qu Qiubai insisting that peasants join the uprising so that 'great numbers of landlords, local notables and government officials as well as all counter-revolutionaries' could be killed, and power permanently secured in Canton. On 26 November, Neumann and Zhang, with Ye Ting who had joined them from Hong Kong as commander-in-chief, judged the time to be right, sending out a message instructing all members to 'immediately prepare for an uprising'. 'The workers are extremely eager to seize power,' they continued, fixing the event for 13 December. After the police discovered two baskets with explosives on the evening of 9 December, the date was moved forward by two days. It seemed like an opportune moment, not least since the two rival powers in the province, Zhang Fakui and Li Chai-sum, were far away, sizing each other up across a battlefield in the hope of extending their territory. Only a police force of 3,000 was left to defend the city.[82]

A so-called Red Guard force of 2,000 armed workers and a cadet regiment of 1,200 soldiers attacked in the early hours of 11 December, overwhelming the city's General Police Headquarters, where several hundred prisoners were confined. These were released and supplied with weapons on condition that they join the Communists. A new government was instantly proclaimed, assuming the name of the 'Peasants', Workers' and Soldiers' Soviet Government'. It asked the workers to arise en masse and take control of the city, 'exterminate landlords and rich farmers', confiscate all land and wipe out all debts. All property owned by capitalists was to be confiscated, all houses of wealthy people to be converted into free lodging for workers. A young girl holding a rifle was heard haranguing a mob, advocating freedom to loot and freedom from debt. Recruits received a gun, twenty dollars and a red neckband or armband, but the effort failed to stir the population. Of the 290,000 workers organised in 125 labour unions, a mere 3,000 rallied to the red banner. After taking over all the police stations, the rebels gained control of the city garrison commander's headquarters, all communication buildings, the central bank, the post office and the railway station. People who resisted were shot in cold blood, with up to 300 police officers killed. The revolution rapidly turned into a looting expedition. Practically all police stations were ransacked, followed by several thousand shops and residences, with chairs, electric fans and household utensils lugged away by an armed crowd keen to acquire plunder. Wealthy shops were looted, some as many as eighteen times in a single night. Hatred between unions was rekindled, as the Red Guards led an assault on the General Labour Union, who weeks earlier had reclaimed the Waichow Club. The premises were torched, incinerating a hundred union members locked inside. Rebels tore through the retail business district, soaking sheets with petrol to set shops alight. The central bank was burned to the ground, although the vault remained intact. In total some forty-six streets were destroyed, tearing out the heart of the city, with flames jumping across buildings and roaring down narrow alleys, gutting over a thousand houses. In some cases the victims who tried to escape from the inferno were shot. These were random murders, but the Communists also had a list of class enemies to be eliminated. Fu Sinian, a patriot and prominent scholar who had taken a lead in establishing the Academia Sinica, the country's premier research institute, only managed to escape thanks to a secret informant. As the American vice consul put it, 'the much vaunted revolt of the proletariat turned out to be no more than a ghastly riot of looting, burning and killing.' On Shameen, gunboats as well as barbed wire and machine-gun nests kept the rebels at bay.[83]

The Iron Army under Zhang Fakui rushed to the city, arriving forty-eight hours after the uprising began. Li Fook Lum, whose troops had slaughtered Sun Yat-sen's mercenaries years earlier, also swung into action. Naval vessels began to ply the inner reach of the river, raking the bund with machine-gun fire.

The Communists offered little resistance, jettisoning their guns and trying to escape. They had identified each other by a red scarf or red tie, which they now discarded, although in many cases perspiration had caused the dye to leave a mark on their necks. Suspects were grabbed by the military, forced to their knees and summarily shot after their shirts had been torn away, at times to the applause of a crowd of onlookers. Execution squads patrolled the city, including members from rival unions, ferreting out supposed enemies and settling old scores with relentless zeal and cold ferocity. 'The members of this group which had not the slightest legal sanction, either in law or by custom, carried out executions whenever and wherever they willed,' causing the deaths of numerous innocent people. One thousand members of various unions were herded into a large theatre, then taken out in groups of forty to be shot, two rows at a time. To speed up the process, machine guns were used. The Russians, too, were rounded up, their shoes removed and their hands bound behind their backs, to be marched past the smouldering ruins. A dozen were shot, although the consul and his family were spared. One Russian who began to curse his captors and refused to kneel was bayoneted on the spot and shot ten times with a Luger pistol. In parts of the city bodies were piled in heaps on both sides of the street, some still quivering, to be hauled away on lorries and man-pulled carts. 'One picked one's way carefully around the corpses, skirted pools of blood, dodged overhanging electric wires, stepped over scattered bricks and passed trucks into which the police were directing coolies to throw the bodies of the executed,' one foreigner observed. Estimates varied, but most agreed that 2,000 to 3,000 suspects were executed, not including up to 600 people murdered by the insurgents.[84]

Nanjing acted swiftly, on the night of 14 December withdrawing recognition from all Soviet consuls and commercial agencies. In Wuhan, Russians were seen being marched off in their night attire, in some cases barefoot and roped together. Troops occupied the Consulate and proclaimed martial law, arresting hundreds of suspected Communists. Several dozen were executed in the following weeks, the prelude to what would become a heartless, unrelenting campaign against communism in the region. In Shanghai, a 'closed' sign in both Russian and English appeared on the door of the Consulate, with staff busy feeding secret documents into the furnaces in the basement. One hundred Russians were pronounced undesirable and given a week to leave the country. The Soviets, like the Chinese Communists, now had to go underground.[85]

3

Red Terror
(1927–1931)

The Canton uprising was supposed to be the spark that would ignite revolution, with peasants in the surrounding countryside rallying to the help of workers to transform the city into a scarlet stronghold. But as Ye Ting, who fled back to Hong Kong in the aftermath of the debacle, bitterly observed, 'The masses took no part in the insurrection. All shops were closed and the employees showed no desire to support us.' The villagers, too, had failed to show up in a timely manner when the hour of revolution struck. Among a string of proclamations, the Canton Soviet had appealed to 'all peasants to rise up strongly and confiscate all land, exterminate landlords and rich farmers and destroy all title deeds and promissory notes'. Again, a defeated Ye complained that 'the peasants did not help us.'[1]

A key to success, the Central Committee had surmised, were the peasants from the Hailufeng Soviet. The soviet consisted of Haifeng and Lufeng, two counties backed by a mountain chain overlooking the South China Sea. The region was plagued by bandits, who could easily retreat into the mountains, but who were lured back by the local riches, not least the region's abundant natural resources, including timber, fruit and rice, exported through the thriving port of Shanwei (known at the time as Swabue), half a day's sail from Hong Kong. Chen Jiongming hailed from the area, as did Peng Pai, son of a well-to-do landowner. Peng became enthralled by revolutionary ideals as a young student, and in 1917 went to study in Japan with Chen's financial backing. He returned in 1921 an ardent revolutionary, convinced that communism was the only future for his country. In Haifeng, where Chen Jiongming appointed him as county secretary of education, he advocated the abolition of private property and every other capitalist tool of oppression, including the law, the government and the state. A year later, he set up a peasant association, encouraging the villagers to claim the land and incinerate all title deeds. This was a step too far for Chen, who issued a warrant of arrest. Peng escaped to Canton, joining Sun Yat-sen and the Nationalist Party in 1924. There he became the first head of the Peasant Movement Training Institute, before being replaced by Mao Zedong in 1926.[2]

Peng Pai was one of the organisers of the Communist assault on Nanchang in August 1927. After the uprising had failed, the Central Committee had instructed the insurgents to prepare a peasant uprising in the countryside by 'killing all evil landlords' in a 'campaign of red terror'. This task Peng pursued diligently in Haifeng, having hacked his way south to his home town with a few hundred remnant troops. His reign of terror lasted only nine days, as he was easily defeated by Zhang Fakui. But he returned a month later, as Zhang had set off on the warpath again, busy confronting Li Chai-sum. This time Peng came with several thousand soldiers who had survived the onslaught on Ye Ting and He Long outside Shantou. In early November, this motley army took the county seats of Lufeng and Haifeng. Then they overwhelmed the local troops ensconced in Shanwei, the port in the bay area. A familiar scenario unfolded, with houses ransacked, two hundred people slaughtered and a further hundred kidnapped for ransom. Government troops dislodged them from the port a few days later, but Peng Pai by now was firmly entrenched in the countryside.[3]

A full campaign of terror swung into action, beginning with the mass murder of people denounced as landlords. On 7 November, to mark the anniversary of the October Revolution, in the presence of 6,000 people, nine victims were 'beheaded or disembowelled' in Haifeng, their remains left in the streets for dogs to eat. On 18 November, in a single day some fifty 'landlords' were killed, according to a report sent to the Central Committee. Peng Pai himself was no slacker, decapitating several victims himself; their heads hung from the platform where the executions took place.[4]

On 21 November, in front of a crowd of 50,000, Peng Pai inaugurated the Hailufeng Soviet, the first of its kind in China. Each of the 300 official delegates was enjoined to 'kill at least ten reactionaries' and lead the peasants to 'kill ten more', amounting to 6,000 altogether. 'But that is not enough since more will still be left behind,' Peng Pai decreed, so 'we must kill!' His logic was impeccable: 'If I do not kill today, tomorrow I will be killed, so it is better to kill a thousand innocents than to let a single guilty one escape.'[5]

As a rough guide to action, he suggested that the villagers should dispose of 40 per cent of the population. A list of twenty-eight classes of people to be exterminated was drawn up, including political opponents and those deemed socially undesirable, the incurably sick, prostitutes, priests, soothsayers, the blind, the lame and the elderly. A majority vote was required for revolutionary tribunals to redeem an accused person.[6]

The soviet was divided into districts and the districts into areas, each with an appointed executioner, responsible for a proper quota of heads every month. Harangues by revolutionaries were interspersed with public executions, conducted with no apparent pity. Ears and noses were cut off, eyes gouged, heads severed, bodies sliced and dismembered, alive or dead. A summary bullet in the back of the head was merciful. A common Communist principle which would endure all the way down to the 1970s was to make sure that every villager had blood on their hands. Once they were implicated in a crime, they were less eager to betray the cause. In one striking case, a village leader was paraded through the streets and compelled to kneel every few metres so that the assembled villagers could cut him with knives.[7]

The population was organised in groups according to age, with boys drafted into Young Pioneer units. They were asked to act as spies, informing on transgressors, including their own parents and the elderly. Young men aged twenty to thirty were drafted in the army, older ones prescribed other forms of service. People over the age of forty were considered a burden. Young girls and women were organised along similar lines, and trained in the use of weapons and propaganda.[8]

The soviet issued a string of other decrees, designed to establish a Communist society overnight. Land was confiscated, title deeds torched, even narrow strips of land between the fields, used to define ownership, ploughed over to erase all traces of private property. Shops with a capital of over $500 became public property, with many of their owners condemned and executed as capitalists after a committee had examined their accounts.[9]

Peng Pai never tried to rescue the Canton Soviet. Not only had the date of the uprising been moved forward by two days, but he was hemmed in by government troops. Throughout the terror, thousands of fugitives had managed to flee, either up north to Shantou or south to Canton and Hong Kong. With them came tales of dread and depredation. A week before the Canton uprising, one reporter noted that the stories streaming out of Hailufeng were 'so horrible that one hesitates to believe them', although, as he pointed out, they were confirmed by refugees. When Zhang Fakui suppressed the Canton Soviet, his justice was swift, pitiless and brutal, not least because of the horrors perpetrated in the Hailufeng Soviet. Zhang mirrored the very philosophy proposed by Peng: 'Today we must kill all Communists or they will kill us instead.'[10]

By the end of December one estimate put the death toll at 10,000, based on figures compiled for individual towns and villages where the body count was often in the hundreds, sometimes as high as 600 or 700.[11]

Only in January 1928 did the military authorities begin to send troops to the region. Not all soldiers were keen to fight, using their clout instead to extort money from the local chambers of commerce. Some went to restaurants, demanding to be served but refusing to pay. Guards had to be stationed to keep them under control. When they did attack the soviet, the fighting was so ferocious that towns changed hands several times, invariably reduced to ruins. Villagers who did not join the Communists in their retreat were regarded as traitors and reactionaries, and were massacred to the last man, woman and child on the return of soviet power. The result was that villagers dreaded the arrival of regular troops only slightly less than those of Peng Pai.[12] Throughout, the Communists demonstrated a quality they possessed in abundance, namely sheer, bloody determination.

Only towards the end of February did the tide turn, as Peng Pai and his followers were forced to retreat into the mountains. By then, the French consul in Canton was estimating that 25,000 people had perished under the iron hand of the Hailufeng Soviet. For months Peng continued to mount bloody raids, although eventually he was forced to flee to Shanghai, where in August 1929 he was betrayed, arrested, tortured and executed. The violence he had inflicted came back to haunt his descendants forty years later, when during the Cultural Revolution several of his relatives were killed in a local massacre that claimed 160 lives. In Shanwei his mother was imprisoned, his nephew pursued by a crowd who hacked off his head with a machete and hung it from the town gate. Peng Pai was fully rehabilitated in 1979, considered a martyr rather than a murderer.[13] In his home town of Haifeng, his bronze statue stands proudly on Red Square.

***

Peng was a pioneer, his soviet a blueprint for the future. But others, too, followed the Central Committee's injunction to form a Red Army, establish a base area and organise a campaign of red terror to usher the countryside into revolution. After the defeat in Nanchang, the Central Committee appointed Mao to a special South Hunan Committee and sent him back to his home province to organise an uprising, later called the Autumn Harvest Uprising. Months earlier Mao had predicted a hurricane, sweeping all the forces of reaction into their graves. Instead, on 21 May 1927, the reaction, headed by a general called Xu Kexiang, purged Changsha of its Communists. Nine months of misrule by the General Labour Union and its uniformed pickets had reduced the city to financial ruin, its public utilities wrecked, the post office, normally directly administered from Beijing, forced to remit its funds to the local government, which in turn issued inconvertible notes. In the surrounding countryside, the peasant associations had seized all the grain, sealed it in barns and fixed the price at a level considered fair to the poor. After the scheme had backfired, resulting in the impoverishment of all but the middlemen who bought up the rice to sell it elsewhere, the unions went further, declaring that no rice above a level required for immediate consumption should be sold. Xu Kexiang sent his troops to raid the General Labour Union, shooting more than a dozen pickets dead. Communist leaders vanished overnight. Gradually the Hankou–Changsha train service was resumed and steamers began to call at the port again, while the price of rice began to stabilise. Placards were taken down, parades ceased.[14]

Mao's insurrection began on 9 September, some fifty kilometres east of Changsha. 'As soon as the insurrection starts,' Mao wrote, 'every county will rise up at the same time.'[15] The slogans were, among others, 'Kill All Local Tyrants and Evil Gentry!', 'Confiscate Their Property!', 'Implement a Dictatorship of the Peasant Associations!' and 'Take the Land!' But the forces he had assembled numbered no more than a few thousand men, whom the local military easily crushed even before they reached Changsha. As the final report declared, 'the peasant masses did not rise at all.'[16] The Hunan Soviet lasted one day. The event was so insignificant that the press did not report it. For centuries, Hunan had been a battleground where fierce conflicts between warring factions were waged. Mao's grandly named Autumn Harvest Uprising did not even qualify as a skirmish. Mao absconded with 1,500 followers to Jinggangshan, a mountainous, inhospitable stronghold between Hunan and Jiangxi, long used as a sanctuary by rebels and bandits. Here he established an uneasy truce with two bandit leaders, trying to build up his forces. For his failure to organise a proper peasant uprising, Mao was later dismissed from all his Party positions.

But over the following months the unrest in Hunan continued. In Changsha, even as people prepared to celebrate the anniversary of the 1911 revolution on 10 October, the streets decorated with lanterns, someone in a crowd listening to a speech threw a bomb, injuring a dozen people. Communists were the prime suspects, but no one was brought to account.[17]

For several weeks, men and women were executed every day on the new motorway outside the city. The measures were stern but superficial, as leaders of the Communist movement remained at large. Changsha and the surrounding countryside were exhausted, having endured every possible terror. Despite the restoration of silver, an abundant harvest and cheap rice, 'the chief emotion in the minds of people is fear', one visitor recorded: fear of the Communists, fear of the local government, fear of neighbours. Thanks to the violence, in the countryside robbery and fraud flourished, perpetrated by thieves, bandits and blackmailers as well as the military. Bands of brigands, their ranks replenished by soldiers on the run, plundered, killed and held people to ransom. 'In the south of the province a young man has collected a force of more than 500 men,' the press reported, going from town to town to seize local magistrates and collect money from the local inhabitants.[18]

In November came the first warning that something altogether more sinister was afoot. At Liling, not far away from the region where Mao had tried to organise an uprising, another group of men went around looting and plundering, but this time in the name of communism. It was the beginning of a wave of revolutionary violence that would engulf south Hunan. Organised by the same South Hunan Committee that had sent Mao to Changsha, it aimed at seizing power in a South Hunan Uprising.[19]

Their man, this time, was not Mao Zedong but Zhu De, described by an admirer as a 'gentle, tender man when with his friends', but a 'grim, relentless fighter' when at war. Born in Sichuan in 1886, Zhu had pursued a military career, siding with the revolutionary forces in 1911. Like other commanders, he began to drift away from Beijing after Yuan Shikai's death in 1916, using his troops to claim territory in his home province. Zhu, a fervent reader of *New Youth*, had met Chen Duxiu in 1922, although Chen apparently gave him the cold shoulder. Zhu went on to study military science at Göttingen University in Germany, becoming a member of the

Chinese Communist Party with help from Zhou Enlai. After a year in Moscow, he was recalled in 1926 to join the Northern Expedition.[20]

Zhu was one of the insurgents in Nanchang in August 1927, assigned to lead a thousand soldiers. After they had been defeated outside Shantou, his men became isolated from the rest of the troops, who trickled down south towards Haifeng and Lufeng to join Peng Pai. Forced to retreat back north towards the Jiangxi border, Zhu spent the winter assembling his troops to conduct the South Hunan Uprising. On 12 January 1928, he led 4,000 troops on Yizhang, a prosperous city near the border separating Hunan from Guangdong, looting all shops and residences before reducing them to rubble. The rebels marched on to Pingshi, promptly looting, slaughtering and burning the city until no more than a third of all houses were left standing. They outdid their comrades in Canton, liquidating over 1,500 people in just three days, mainly merchants but also women and children. They vanished as quickly as they had appeared, but not before raising the red flag and proclaiming a soviet.[21]

Pingshi was supposed to be the spark that would ignite a peasant revolution, with Leiyang the centre of a new soviet. A city of about 500,000 inhabitants some fifty kilometres north of Pingshi, Leiyang was briefly abandoned in February by the local garrison, called on for duty elsewhere. Zhu De used the opportunity to occupy the city and proclaim a soviet. The usual procedures were followed, namely loot, kill and burn. Groups of insurgents wearing red belts, red ties and red leg wrappings went around the city, carrying off everything portable. The insurgents went about their jobs methodically, selecting the best buildings on every street and applying a mixture of powdered sulphur and kerosene before throwing a lighted flame. The fuel ensured that nothing but blackened ruins remained. Guards were posted outside, making sure that the people inside could not escape. Several hundred monks perished inside a temple set on fire after the doors had been bolted. In some places even the mat huts of paupers were burned down. To ensure that enemy troops could not find any lodgings, in March all houses along a seven-kilometre stretch of road leading to Leiyang were destroyed.[22]

The countryside outside Leiyang, including Anren, Chaling, Rucheng, Guiyang and Chenzhou, all within a day's march, also experienced a reign of terror. Everywhere a soviet was established, the land divided, class enemies killed and their houses burned. 'Kill, kill, kill the counter-revolutionaries! Burn, burn, burn down their nests!' Entire families were murdered. There were reports of people denounced as landlords who lost their eyes and ears before being left to roam the streets. The death toll is unknown, but in April a national newspaper summarised the damage in a headline: 'Thirty-Eight Counties Reduced to Ashes'. In Leiyang alone, by one estimate, 20,000 people had perished.[23]

The violence was so senseless that even those potentially sympathetic to the revolution turned away from the rebels. 'Why do you burn down houses everywhere? It makes life difficult for ordinary people. You could give the houses of corrupt officials and evil gentry to those in need, destroying them does not help anyone,' complained the brother of Huang Kecheng, one of the insurgents who would rise through the ranks to become chief of staff of the People's Liberation Army. In Chenzhou, 'the masses were upset', meaning that the people rebelled against the rebels, murdering the Party secretary and other leading Communist officials. Mao was another opponent of the red terror. Contacted by the South Hunan Committee, he dismissed the random violence as 'left opportunism', Marxist jargon for rash action undertaken in wilful ignorance of reality.[24]

Bai Chongxi was sent to drive out the Communists. His arrival in Leiyang in early March was part of a much larger mission. Since the Northern Expedition in 1926, several generals backed by large armies had been vying for control of the province, some paying lip service to Nanjing. The Communists were a minor affair, hardly reported in the press. On 11 March, Bai announced the conclusion of what was called the Hunan War, a feat he accomplished with little fighting by gradually incorporating local soldiers into his following as he marched through the province.[25]

Zhu and his remaining troops followed in Mao's tracks, heading for Jinggangshan. The two met in April, joining forces to create what was named the 'Fourth Red Army'. Instead of trying to create an uprising, they focused on consolidating their base area up in the mountains. But the local economy went bankrupt. Its impoverished inhabitants were barely able to feed themselves, let alone a growing army of bandits, vagrants and deserters. Mao and Zhu were forced to undertake raids in the surrounding valleys. Together, they went murdering, burning and looting. 'The life-style of the Fourth Red Army is itself very much marked by the habits of roving insurgents in the past,' Mao acknowledged.[26]

Their favourite targets were county towns, built like small fortresses with ramparts and a local garrison to protect the magistrate and his treasure. Yongxin, an ancient trading centre located along a river in a fertile valley a mere thirty kilometres north, was raided several times in June and July. Troops garrisoned the city, but the countryside to the south, between Yongxin and Jinggangshan, fell into the hands of the Communists. Opium had in the past enriched the district, and was favoured by Mao and Zhu, who reintroduced it. Even greater wealth beckoned further downriver in Ji'an, where the waters of the Gan River flowed towards Lake Poyang and merged with the Yangtze. Several times the city, with a large foreign presence, was on the verge of being captured.[27]

The Communists also roamed south, revisiting the very towns they had laid waste during the South Hunan Uprising. In July, long-suffering Chenzhou was taken once more, as were Yongxing (not to be confused with Yongxin) and Xingning. In August, Guidong and Rucheng were attacked. The procedure was always the same: take the weapons from the enemy, recruit their soldiers, loot the town, kill its leaders and burn all government buildings. In Xintian, by one estimate, 3,000 houses were destroyed, leaving 12,000 people wandering around homeless. For several kilometres around the city, all livestock used to plough the fields were driven away.[28]

In Guangdong too, there was a resurgence of the Communist movement in the countryside. Local insurgents captured and set alight Yangjiang, along the southern coast of Hong Kong, in the name of communism. Canton, where shops were being rebuilt between the gaunt brick walls of charred buildings, was on edge. Elsewhere in the province, too, the crimson standard seemed to be advancing. While the Hailufeng Soviet had been conclusively defeated, the Communists had managed to retain a foothold in the mountains of the hinterland. In August they were pressing on to Heyuan, a prosperous city along the East River. Just thirty kilometres to the north, bandits joined the Communists to endanger the city of Lianping. There were similar threats in other provinces, not least Hubei, where the Communists had become entrenched after the fall of the Wuhan government.[29]

Yet none of these red bands ever commanded more than 10,000 troops. Their forays were devastating for the local population, but amounted to little in a country where far larger forces were jockeying for power, with vast, powerful regional armies numbered in the hundreds of thousands, often coming to an understanding without a shot being fired, sometimes snarling at each other and lashing out, occasionally clashing in devastating wars which invariably drained blood and money from the local inhabitants.

Towards the end of August the Communists again began to attract the attention of Nanjing. In April 1928, having used the winter to reorganise his army and expand it into a force of more than a million men by incorporating large numbers of troops from regional governors who had pledged allegiance to Nanjing, Chiang Kai-shek had resumed the Northern Expedition. His aim was Beijing, still in the hands of Zhang Zuolin and his allies. The Nationalists pushed steadily northward along the railway, but in May encountered a major obstacle in Jinan, the capital of Shandong province. Japan had stationed troops in the city to protect its 1,800 nationals, and they soon clashed with Chiang's soldiers. The incident rapidly escalated into a full-fledged military confrontation, with a Japanese general deploying three-inch field guns, mortars, machine guns and bomber aircraft to lay waste to the old city where the Nationalists were holed up. The carnage that followed was an omen of things to come, with human flesh blasted by shrapnel and mangled bodies, including those of women and children, scattered on sidewalks, in doorways and along the main roads. Thousands were killed. The Generalissimo was obliged to seek a truce and apologise. The Jinan Incident was a turning point, as Chiang came to see Japan as a timeless foe. In his diary, he compared Jinan to Yangzhou, where in 1645, one year after they had founded the Qing dynasty, the Manchus had systematically slaughtered the local population for ten long days. 'We must never again forget the ancestral enmity between China and Japan,' he wrote. 'We must avenge this humiliation,' he continued, reflecting that revenge demanded careful, long-term preparation, both spiritual and organisational.[30]

By June four army groups had converged on Beijing, controlling the vital railway links south of the capital. Feng Yuxiang's troops had moved along the Hankou–Beijing railway and attacked Baoding, within striking distance of the capital. Zhang Zuolin viewed resistance as futile and decided to evacuate the capital, boarding a train to Manchuria. On the morning of 4 June his coach was blasted to pieces on the outskirts of Mukden (Shenyang) by bombs dropped from a railway bridge guarded by Japanese soldiers. It was, no doubt, the result of a plot meticulously executed the previous night by the Kwantung Army, a force under the control of the Imperial Japanese Army and established to defend the Japanese concessions in Manchuria.[31] Two days later, the Nationalist forces marched 'joyously' through the old gates of the capital, leaving an apprehensive foreign community unharmed. The northern coalition built around Zhang Zuolin rapidly unravelled. Zhang's son Zhang Xueliang, a slender, pale young man with a thick moustache and serious mien, took over, but decided to end the war and side with the Nationalists.

Within seven weeks the United States signed a new tariff treaty with Nanjing, now the sole recognised government in China, with other nations following suit. China, at long last, was united, at least in name, although tensions would remain for years to come, with the generals who had joined Chiang Kai-shek keen to preserve a measure of autonomy in their own regions. There would be endless haggling over issues of financial and military centralisation, with the constant threat of renewed civil war dangling over national unity. But the generals were united in their opposition to communism. On 23 August 1928, General He Yingqin, the army's chief of staff, announced to the press that since Beijing had been captured and the Northern Expedition had been completed the government had ordered troops to proceed to Jiangxi to deal with the 'disturbances created by the Communists under Zhu De and Mao Zedong'.[32]

Provincial troops from the south began to blockade Jinggangshan. Always a poet, Mao wrote defiantly:

> At the foot of the mountain, our flags and banners can be seen,
> At its peak our drums and bugle are heard to respond.
> The enemy troops besiege thousands strong,
> We stand alone and will not be moved.

Hemmed in, deprived of plunder, the local economy began to deteriorate even further. Months earlier, Mao had imposed a radical policy by confiscating all land, regardless of whether their owners were rich or poor. The land was controlled by the soviet, with villagers each allocated a plot according to their physical strength. They were compelled to work and pay taxes in kind, in effect meaning that any surplus not required to feed their families went to the soviet. In response, the villagers voted with their feet, leaving Jinggangshan in droves. Since those who remained were now tied to the land, effectively becoming bonded servants forced to work in the fields for the soviet, other economic activities fell by the wayside. These included sideline occupations that traditionally supplemented the income of the villagers, who used their spare time during the evenings or the slack season to produce paper umbrellas, cloth shoes, rattan chairs or twig baskets for the market. Due to 'unduly harsh treatment of the petty bourgeoisie', compounded by the blockade of Jinggangshan, the markets closed down, causing shortages in basic commodities. 'Necessities such as salt, cloth, and medicines are scarce and costly,' Mao explained. A few months later, the Party secretary of the Jinggangshan committee phrased it differently, noting that 'since the Red Army's sole income has been robbing the rich, and since so many mistakes have been made in land reform, with the petty bourgeoisie, rich peasants and small pedlars all treated as enemies, and since nobody has paid any attention to reconstruction or the economic crisis after all this vast destruction, the countryside is bankrupt, collapsing further by the day.'[33]

In December, Mao and Zhu were joined by Peng Dehuai, a simple soldier born and raised in Hunan who had risen through the ranks to become a colonel under the Nationalists in 1926. In May 1928 he defected to the Communists. A few months later, he took his remaining troops to Jinggangshan, attempting to rescue Mao from the blockade imposed by government forces. He found a mere 6,000 soldiers in straw sandals and summer clothes, shivering in the winter cold. The Communists had no option but to seek better pastures elsewhere.[34]

On 14 January 1929, they abandoned Jinggangshan. Pursued and repeatedly battled by government troops, they were forced to move south towards the border of Jiangxi and Hunan. Nowhere, Mao observed, did they find any popular support.[35] After several weeks, they set their eyes on the fertile and wealthy valleys along the Gan River. They trekked back north, leaving behind a trail of destruction which served the revolution by undermining the government. Ruijin, a mission station of the China Inland Mission, was 'looted clean and smashed up', according to local reports. In Ningdu the Communists first burned down the government premises and the telegraph office, then moved on to the German mission, smashing its doors and thoroughly plundering the place in three visits before bringing tins of kerosene and setting fire to the compound. The bugle was then blown to warn of the arrival of government troops.[36]

It was business as usual, but with a twist: on 22 January the Communists captured the Reverend Edward Young, an American missionary in the small town of Dayu. Zhu De himself gave the young man a fiery lecture, telling him to pay a ransom equivalent to US$10,000 or forfeit his life. George Schramm, a German missionary, was also discovered hiding with his family in an attic and approached by Zhu De, who spoke fluent German. Zhu offered him the position of army doctor. When Schramm refused, he, too, was abducted at gunpoint, together with his wife and five-year-old daughter. For days they were forced to march alongside the troops, until his wife and child were released. Weeks later, the two remaining prisoners managed to crawl away and hide in the middle of the night, making a run for it in the early hours of the morning.[37]

This episode marked the beginning of the systematic abduction of foreigners, which would only come to an end in April 1936 on express instructions from Moscow. By then, the number of foreigners kidnapped by Communists would have reached many dozens, with a few shot and several beheaded. Bandits, in the past, had occasionally kidnapped foreign nationals for ransom, a practice referred to as 'foreign tickets', but it was a perilous game, certain to attract the wrath of a central government committed to protecting foreign lives. For the Communists, it was not just a source of revenue, but also a means of propaganda. After arresting the Reverend Edward Young, Zhu De circulated an order proclaiming that the United States was an 'imperialist country which conspires with the reactionary Nationalist government and lends considerable sums of money to the latter to oppress Chinese labourers and peasants'. The United States responded by asking its nationals to leave south Jiangxi. With a single, bold act, the Communists now received the attention they craved, despite their insignificant numbers.[38]

Mao and Zhu continued to march through the countryside, testing, probing and attacking weak counties in the government's line of defence, moving with great celerity when confronted by regular troops. They learned guerrilla tactics, captured in neat prescriptions that would inspire rebels elsewhere for years to come: when the enemy advances, we retreat; he tires, we attack; he retreats, we follow in pursuit; we advance in waves; when pursued, we move in circles; we arouse the largest number of people in the shortest possible time. Guerrilla warfare, of course, had been practised since time immemorial, its doctrine dictated by common sense.[39] It boiled down to a simple principle, accurately captured by a French consul who saw that the guerrillas would simply move on when troops arrived: 'this game can last forever, as the number of bandits or Communists grows when they are joined by all sorts of malcontents and unfortunates to whom enrolment appears the only way out of future exactions.' The true strength of guerrilla warfare, however, lay elsewhere: all the partisans had to do was destroy, while those left behind had to rebuild. Mao and Zhu moved on when the pressure became too great, besieging county seats across the provincial border in south Fujian instead. In June they repeatedly battered Longyan, forcing the garrison to abandon the city, which was promptly plundered and burned. This brought the Communists within striking distance of the treaty port of Xiamen. When challenged by provincial forces, they fled back into Jiangxi. Nanchang, once Chiang Kai-shek's stronghold, was placed under semi-martial law in July, with armed soldiers parading the streets and officials no longer venturing outdoors without bodyguards.[40]

Moscow had followed reports on the Fourth Red Army with interest, deciding in January 1929 to explore ways of supporting them with advice and 'real help'. The timing was not fortuitous. In November 1927, the Left Opposition had disintegrated in Moscow, leaving Trotsky marginalised and easily crushed by Stalin. In January 1928 Trotsky was sent into exile to Kazakhstan, to be deported from the Soviet Union a year later.[41]

As soon as Trotsky had been dispatched, Stalin began implementing his rival's policies. Trotsky had warned against a 'new capitalist class' in the countryside, where villagers withheld grain from the cities. After grain supplies tumbled by a third in late 1927, threatening Moscow and Leningrad with starvation, Stalin sent procurement squads into the villages, ordering them to grab what they could at gunpoint. Those who resisted were persecuted as kulaks, a derogatory term meant to designate 'rich' farmers but used against anyone who opposed collectivisation. Bukharin, who had called on the peasants to 'Enrich Yourselves', in turn fell victim to Stalin in April 1929. Stalin began to see Mao and Zhu as fellow revolutionaries, praising them for 'dealing correctly' with the kulaks who so often played a 'counter-revolutionary role' in the Communist movement.[42]

Above all, the Soviet Union was about to go to war with China, and Stalin wanted Mao's support. Documents that had been seized in the raid on the Soviet Embassy in April 1927 indicated that Moscow was using the revenue generated by the Chinese Eastern Railway to finance the spread of communism in China. After diplomatic relations between Moscow and Beijing had been broken off later that year, the Russians continued to send large numbers of agents to Harbin and other cities inside the railway zone conceded to the Soviet Union. Zhang Xueliang, popularly known as the 'Young Marshal', continued the anti-Communist policy initiated by his father. In May 1929, he sent the police to raid a meeting of the Comintern in Harbin, arresting some forty Russians as well as Chinese Communists hailing from different parts of Manchuria. More documents were seized, again confirming that the railway was used as a conduit to propagate Bolshevist ideas.[43]

Zhang Xueliang took drastic measures, and on 10 July 1929 sent the police to commandeer the Chinese Eastern Railway's telegraph offices and stations. Soviet unions of railway workers were dissolved. Scores were arrested, including 174 Russians, some escorted under guard to the Siberian border to be expelled. They were replaced with Chinese personnel. The breach with Moscow could not have been wider.[44]

Lev Karakhan, the very man who years earlier had so magnanimously announced the return of the Chinese Eastern Railway without compensation only to renege on his promise, gave Beijing an ultimatum of three days, threatening to resort to all necessary means to protect Moscow's lawful rights. The Young Marshal did not respond.[45]

Stalin's answer was slow, but when it came on 6 August it was unequivocal. Vasily Blyukher, who had been Chiang Kai-shek's most trusted military adviser, was given command of an army assembled for the occasion, an overwhelming force of more than 150,000 troops. Two army groups smashed across the border, one from each end of the railway corridor, separated by 700 kilometres, moving along swiftly to hem in Zhang Xueliang's troops. Gunboats turned their turrets towards river cities that resisted. Artillery fire shattered entire towns, with aircraft dropping bombs without regard for civilian casualties. It was an awe-inspiring display of cold, calculated determination.[46]

The Young Marshal was forced to capitulate. The Generalissimo agreed to restore control over the railway to Russia, although Stalin at first rejected Nanjing's offer of peace. Only in November, after months of humiliation, did Moscow agree on the terms of surrender.

Stalin, as always, needed to degrade his enemy, but the protracted negotiations had another, more strategic purpose. As the Russians advanced along the railway, they systematically opened all the stores and granaries, distributing their contents to the local population.[47] It was a gesture designed to encourage insurrection. Stalin hoped that the population would rise and establish a revolutionary government in Manchuria. On 7 October he wrote to the official Soviet head of government Vyacheslav Molotov, pointing out that sending isolated detachments to Manchuria was not sufficient. Regiments headed by Chinese Communists had to be organised 'to stir up a rebellion among the Manchurian troops' and overthrow Zhang Xueliang: 'massacre the landowners, bring in the peasants, create soviets in the cities and towns, and so on'. Hunan was central to his plan, as he envisaged a two-pronged attack with guerrilla fighters launching a simultaneous assault on government troops throughout the south. Three days later, the Comintern section in China was instructed to 'strengthen and broaden the guerrilla movement, in particular in the districts controlled by Mao and in Manchuria'.[48]

It was yet another empty wish, as at this point the Chinese Communist Party numbered a little over 17,000 members. But weeks later Wall Street crashed. The financial crisis seemed to confirm Karl Marx's prediction that capitalism would collapse under the weight of its own contradictions. Stalin speculated that a 'high tide of revolutionary war' had at long last arrived. In December, as the effects of the financial crisis began to be felt around the world, the Central Committee in Shanghai demanded that all Party members combine armed insurrection in the countryside with uprisings in the cities. The ruling classes, it was explained, had been weakened by constant internecine war and were edging closer to complete collapse: all that was required for the regime to fall was a determined push from 'the raging tide of revolution'.[49]

This circular was probably drafted by Li Lisan, a tall man with an ostentatious manner and a penchant for issuing orders copied from his hero Stalin. In July 1928, Xiang Zhongfa had replaced Qu Qiubai as secretary general of the Party. The Russians had picked Xiang, one of the few who came from a working-class background, as their first proletarian to guide the Party in China. But Xiang was ill equipped to take the helm of a ship navigating in turbulent waters. Increasingly he relied on his right-hand man, Li Lisan, for all major decisions. Li now went a step further than his master in the Kremlin, believing that his troops could start a new phase in the world revolution.

In February 1930, Li pushed harder, writing in a circular that the entire country was in the grip of a crisis, with revolution around the corner. 'In the present revolutionary situation, it is obvious that one or several provinces can achieve victory first.' Wuhan and Changsha were manifest candidates.[50]

As always, there was money from Moscow. From February to September 1930, Moscow allocated the equivalent of US$140,000 to the Chinese Communist Party, although only US$78,000 were actually sent, equivalent to US$1.5 million in today's money.[51]

Mao, who was now acclaimed in Moscow and hailed repeatedly by *Pravda*, was buoyed.[52] He had been reluctant to risk his troops in the Autumn Harvest Uprising in September 1927, but now that he had moved centre stage he shared the Central Committee's revolutionary optimism. 'A single spark can set the prairie alight,' he wrote memorably on 5 January 1930.[53]

In preparation for the revolution, scattered troops throughout the south were reorganised into four army groups. The most powerful one was the First Army Group, under the command of Mao and Zhu, with a smaller Third Army Group under Peng Dehuai. A Second Army Group was organised under He Long, who had returned to his home province Hunan in 1928. A Fourth Army regrouped smaller forces north of the Yangtze River. Mao and Zhu assumed overall control of the Red Army.

Their plan was to attack Nanchang and Changsha separately, then regroup around Wuhan and take that city in a combined assault leading to victory along the entire Yangtze valley. 'Our red flag,' Mao wrote confidently, 'will fly throughout the entire world.'[54]

On the morning of 28 July 1930, as 20,000 troops under Peng Dehuai were massed outside Changsha, several hundred soldiers disguised as refugees emerged from hiding places inside the city and began to set fire to the government buildings and the main police station. Peng's main force entered unopposed, since the provincial governor had retreated to a nearby town leaving behind just four regiments of regular soldiers to defend the garrison. In their advance on the city, the Communists drove helpless farmers in front of them, their arms bound behind their backs. It was the first reported instance of a practice that would become common in the years to come. The garrison troops were unwilling to shoot the unarmed civilians. Once inside, Peng's troops separated into patrols of fifty to a hundred men each and began systematically to sack the city. First the houses of well-to-do people were looted, their belongings distributed to the local poor, then they were torched, their occupants murdered or held as hostages. Sometimes a notice was posted at the gate of a building, announcing that it was due for burning and inviting the poor to loot it prior to destruction. At first local ruffians joined the soldiers, but they soon sensed revulsion on the part of the population and began to fear future retribution. Churches were burned, prisons opened and several government officials beheaded. All the warehouses along the riverfront were destroyed, with a loss estimated at 3.8 million gold dollars. An estimated 1,500 to 2,000 people were slain, not counting those who were later reported missing. The post office was left untouched. Foreigners remained unharmed, having hastily boarded several warships anchored in the Xiang River. By 3 August, as the provincial governor returned with reinforcements, the soldiers had vanished as quickly as they had appeared, after securing a vast ransom from the Chamber of Commerce. Many city dwellers blamed the governor for having abandoned the city, although others praised his refusal to antagonise the Communists, believing that the occupation would only be of short duration.[55]

Heavy fighting followed outside Changsha in the ensuing days. Peng Dehuai had meticulously planned the assault, but had failed to consider how to withdraw. The governor surrounded the Communist forces and gave no quarter, leaving bodies strewn along the newly paved road outside the Liuyang gate. He also vigorously punished all those suspected of having assisted the rebels, reportedly executing some 1,800 suspects within five days.[56]

The Communists failed to keep Changsha. They displayed impressive tactics but poor strategy. It was a signature combination, one which came at great human cost and would prevail for decades to come.

As Peng Dehuai marched his troops towards Changsha, Mao and Zhu had approached Nanchang, which was to be taken in a closely coordinated attack. Mao later wrote that the city was too well guarded, prompting him to abandon the plan. Most contemporary reports, however, described the fall of Nanchang as imminent, since Mao's soldiers vastly outnumbered the defending garrison. Rather than attacking the city, a railway station across the Gan River was seized instead. A few shots were fired to commemorate the third anniversary of the Nanchang Uprising.[57]

Wuhan, too, was threatened, as He Long, commander of the Second Army Group, approached the city in July. He Long was a bandit, hailing from a poor family in Hunan, where he had become leader of a gang of outlaws at an early age. He joined the Nationalists during the Northern Expedition, only to betray them a year later, joining the Communists in the unsuccessful Nanchang Uprising. Even as a Communist he retained some of his former manners as a brigand chief, surrounding himself with a large retinue, including several cooks and four bearers to carry him in a sedan chair.[58]

After the unsuccessful Nanchang Uprising, in January 1928 Zhou Enlai sent him to the border region of Hunan and Hubei to continue the revolution. He Long's first target was Sangzhi, his native county up in the mountains on the northern edge of Hunan. Once local troops defeated the ragtag army of guerrilla fighters he had assembled, He was forced to seek refuge in Hefeng, an area of no man's land favoured by outlaws across the border in Hubei. The soviet he established quickly became locked in a vicious cycle of 'aimless burning and killing', according to one historian, as He Long fought fire with fire against local government attempts to dislodge him. In his native Sangzhi, 2,000 houses were torched and 300 families massacred in August 1929, or so the local magistrate explained. But He Long knew the country well, always evading capture. A few weeks later his band despoiled Cili, before crossing back into Hubei to capture the city of Badong on the Yangtze River.[59]

In early July 1930, the Second Army Group began laying siege to Shashi, an important commercial town on the Upper Yangtze situated 120 kilometres from Wuhan. Small market towns were invaded, with flames from burning villages seen at night. On the river down to Wuhan, the rebels removed all beacons, making navigation difficult in fog or at night. They used old muzzle loaders to bombard passing ships with grapeshot and nail. Wuhan normally had a population of 2 million, but now it took in a further 800,000 people compelled to evacuate a burning countryside and to take refuge inside its turreted walls. Rental prices soared by 50 per cent. As a result of guerrilla activities, the supply of rice required to feed the city was frequently cut off, prompting merchants to purchase food from Shanghai or Sichuan instead. Here too inflation was steep. At the end of July, panic seized the city, as the authorities proclaimed a state of martial law, stationing troops at all strategic points. Defences were bulked up with sandbags, machine guns installed at key intersections. Executions of people suspected of being Communists continued unabated.[60]

Eventually He Long was defeated, and chased from Shashi well before he reached Wuhan. In Changsha, Nanchang and Wuhan alike, the proletariat had refused to revolt. The dawn of revolution, it appeared, was not about to break, as Mao had predicted only a few months earlier.[61]

The very cities left paralysed by strikes a few years earlier had changed. Besides relentless repression of Communists, another factor was the willingness of employers to enter peaceful negotiations, leading to a steady decline in crippling strikes. In 1928 a code of industrial relations was promulgated, while the Nationalists encouraged new unions, leading to significant gains in wages and working conditions. By 1929 workers were the largest social group in the Nationalist Party, representing 29 per cent of its membership, a higher percentage of workers than could be found in the Communist ranks.[62]

Still, the Communists remained determined. Mao merged his army with Peng's badly battered troops. Together with He Long, one month later they once more tried to take Changsha, approaching the walled city from three different directions. By then, however, Chiang Kai-shek had sent one of his most competent and distinguished generals, He Yingqin, with fresh divisions from Nanjing. His precaution was prompted by Yan Xishan, governor of Shanxi, who ten days earlier had accused Chiang of abandoning the Yangtze valley to the Communists.

In 1911 Yan Xishan had led revolutionary forces against the Qing dynasty in Shanxi, only to claim the province as his own after Yuan Shikai's death, ruling virtually unopposed. He was seen as a moderniser, introducing hospitals and schools throughout the province. Such was his zeal for bringing Shanxi into the twentieth century that outsiders sometimes called him the 'Model Governor'. Yan joined the Northern Expedition and the march on Beijing, but in 1929 allied himself with the Christian General Feng Yuxiang and others in revolt against Nanjing. Even as his allies battled it out with the Generalissimo in what historians have called the 'Central Plains War', the Model Governor crossed the provincial border and led his troops straight to Shandong, claiming its capital Jinan in June 1930. Here he called for a national conference, aiming at nothing less than a new government with himself as president. Chiang decisively defeated his opponents, using his military clout to separate them and drive them back one by one on every front. It was a strategy he had mastered well: divide the opposition, force each side to the table through overwhelming military power and rule through a coalition. Once Feng had returned to the fold, Chiang turned his massive army against Yan, who fled to Beijing. When, on 18 September 1930, Zhang Xueliang also hoisted the Nationalist flag and swore allegiance to Nanjing, the country was formally unified, the so-called 'warlord era' a thing of the past.[63]

On 31 July, however, Yan Xishan and Wang Jingwei, the latter always an opportunist, had held a rump meeting of the Nationalist Party in Beijing, issuing a circular telegram urging the entire nation to 'Resist the Communists and Expel Chiang Kai-shek'. Even as the press was reporting that Peng Dehuai and his soldiers were looting Changsha, the two blamed the Generalissimo for withdrawing his troops from the Yangtze valley to fight in the Central Plains, leaving hundreds of kilometres of fertile farmlands undefended against Communist depredations. The accusation stung. On 5 August Chiang Kai-shek entrusted He Yingqin with 'suppressing banditry' in the three provinces of Hunan, Hubei and Jiangxi, equipping him with gunboats and aircraft, as well as troops, to do so.[64]

He Yingqin surrounded Changsha with entrenchments protected by barbed wire. Four aircraft strafed the enemy troops, forcing them into inhospitable terrain. In desperation, the Communists began commandeering buffaloes from the surrounding countryside, tying burning torches to their tails and driving them forward in the hope that they would break through the wire. Soldiers easily dispersed the poor animals with their guns. In early September, the government troops used the timeless principles of guerrilla warfare to lure the enemy deep into a trap on the outskirts of the city, where they were ambushed and mown down by machine guns. Mao, Zhu, Peng and He suffered a heavy defeat, with an estimated 4,000 killed and 5,000 taken prisoner.[65]

Their retreat was equally disastrous. With government troops in hot pursuit, He Long was forced all the way back to Hefeng, while Mao, Zhu and Peng found shelter in Donggu, a miserable yet impregnable town up in the mountains, close enough to the Yongxin county the Communists had dominated from their previous stronghold in Jinggangshan. Yet they were left undiscouraged. The Central Committee under Li Lisan, convinced that the dawn of revolution was at hand, insisted on yet another assault on Changsha. Mao opted for Ji'an instead, having long coveted the wealthy entrepôt along the Gan River.

Ji'an, a mere sixty kilometres from Jinggangshan, was an island in a sea of red, with Communists regularly controlling parts of the countryside before government troops chased them away in an endless game of cat and mouse. The walled city had easily repulsed earlier attacks, but on 4 October its garrison of 4,000 soldiers awoke to discover 30,000 soldiers massed outside. Among the red banners fluttering in the wind were ladders and bales of straw. The Communist strategy was invariably the same: climb the walls and claim the city. This time they succeeded, by sheer force of numbers and with the help of several field guns. By midnight their soldiers began filtering through the streets in small groups, shouting their battle cry: 'Kill, kill, kill!' They followed their usual routine: search every house, loot the wealthy, assemble the enemies of revolution, kill them in front of others, place straw and kerosene in all key buildings and torch them. According to several witnesses, for about a week over a hundred suspects were dispatched daily, sometimes shot, occasionally beheaded. Ransoms were levied, hostages taken. Eleven foreign nuns and missionaries, including a bishop, were captured in what headlines around the world announced as the largest haul since the notorious Lincheng incident in May 1923, when bandits had attacked and derailed a luxury Blue Express train between Shanghai and Beijing, taking 300 hostages, including twenty-five foreigners.[66]

Ji'an became a red capital for forty-five days. He Yingqin sent a special division, battling the Communists and liberating the city on 18 November. One week earlier, many of the hostages, including nine of the foreigners, had already been marched ninety kilometres south of Ji'an towards the Communist redoubt of Donggu, transformed into a fortress with soldiers billeted in the surrounding villages, far inside inhospitable land. When a Nationalist division tried to encircle the area, they were lured deep into a trap in Longgang, a narrow plain surrounded by hills. Instead of gunning them down, the Communists recruited the soldiers and killed off their officers. A few weeks later Lieutenant-General Zhang Huizan, commander of the division, was tortured in a denunciation meeting, with villagers taking turns to cut his flesh and peel his skin. Mao celebrated his demise with a poem. Zhang's severed head was placed in a bamboo cage and sent down the Gan River to Ji'an, where it was retrieved and forwarded to Nanjing. His death came as a personal blow to Chiang Kai-shek.[67]

Mao, having earlier sustained a crushing defeat outside Changsha, was at long last vindicated. On 22 December, at a meeting of all the Party leaders in their Jiangxi base, he insisted on a new approach in fighting the government troops: 'lure the enemy deep into Red areas,' and 'adopt the tactics of protracted war,' meaning that the enemy must be trapped in the mountains, harassed, shot at from all sides at night and cut off from firewood, grain, oil and salt, with big posters propagating the benefits of switching sides.[68]

Mao had his critics. As one might expect in any political organisation, even a closed one, there were differences of opinion on tactics, disagreements over strategy and occasionally disputes about ideology, not to mention personality clashes, endless chicanery and naked or more covert manoeuvring for power. By all accounts, Mao excelled at the latter, never missing an opportunity to consolidate his position when negotiating the complex political currents coming from Shanghai and Moscow. In the summer of 1929 he had succeeded, with the help of a young man named Lin Biao, in blocking Zhu De, claiming overall leadership of the Fourth Army. Mao had cultivated Lin, a gifted but resentful young field commander trained at the Whampoa Academy, although equally Lin had done his utmost to pit Mao against Zhu. Zhu had grumbled, complaining that he was 'merely a toy in Mao's hands', devoid of any power, leading an outraged Peng Dehuai to call Zhu a coward, advising him to fight. But Zhu accepted his subjugation. As the Russians noted, 'Party activists are dissatisfied with Mao because he is apparently a military dictator, never convenes a meeting and issues all orders himself.'[69]

He faced further challenges, not least from the local Party leader Li Wenlin, who had welcomed Mao and Zhu to Jiangxi in

February 1929. Tensions soon surfaced. Li, another graduate of the Whampoa Academy, knew the province well and viewed Mao's tactics with suspicion. One year later, Mao placed his brother-in-law, Liu Shiqi, in charge of a campaign designed to purge the ranks. As in all terrorist organisations, members lived in fear of spies, sleepers, provocateurs, double-dealers or renegades who might worm their way into the ranks. Since there were always members who were fickle and could switch sides, not to mention those who failed to keep up with a constantly changing Party line, there was always good reason to scrutinise membership. But all too often this was just a pretext for eliminating rivals. 'The Party organisation is unsound, shallow and lax,' and consequently prone to penetration by enemy forces, Liu Shiqi reported to the Central Committee in May 1930. 'Rich peasants', 'landlords' and 'AB elements', the last named after an Anti-Bolshevik group allegedly organised by the Nationalists, had infiltrated the Party at every level, with several of them serving as Party secretaries. In reality, the AB group did not exist, but it was a perfect cover for persecution of local cadres loyal to Li Wenlin. Scores of alleged AB members were subsequently ferreted out, their leaders put to death, as an impatient Liu threatened anyone who disobeyed him with execution. Cadres found wanting were promptly shot, resulting in more than a thousand deaths. 'It is not that we killed the wrong people,' an investigation later commented, 'but rather that the executions were too harsh.' But in August, as Mao was far away trying to seize Changsha, Li Wenlin and his followers outflanked an isolated Liu, forcing him to scurry off to Shanghai.[70]

Mao, on his way back to Jiangxi in October, wrote that a 'majority of the leading organs' were filled with AB elements and 'rich peasants', requiring a thorough purge. One month later, the Comintern, keen on a hard line against landowners, instructed the Central Committee to make Mao chairman of the Revolutionary Military Council, the supreme military authority.[71]

Li Wenlin was one of the first people Mao placed under arrest in late November. The relationship between the two had deteriorated further as Li knew from experience that Mao's tactic of 'luring the enemy in deep' would devastate the area, prompting troops to desert. Li was quickly charged with being an AB element. Hundreds of his followers were likewise arrested and tortured, forced to provide names of accomplices. They, too, were arrested and tortured. 'The interrogations relied wholly on torture, there was no attempt to patiently interpret the suspect's statements or corroborate them with collateral evidence,' a report later admitted. 'No torture method was too outlandish,' its author continued, including 'nailing the hands of suspects to the table' or 'inserting the heated end of a rifle inside their rectums'.[72]

In December, when the witch-hunt was taken to Li Wenlin's stronghold in Futian, a political commissar rebelled, leading a small detachment of 400 soldiers to arrest the team of interrogators. He was backed by several thousand troops and their officers, who denounced Mao as a 'dictator' and executed one hundred of his followers to make their point. Mao, in turn, condemned them as counter-revolutionaries. Zhu De and Peng Dehuai sided with Mao, seeing the rebellion as further evidence of an AB plot to undermine the Party. Even as the Central Committee in Shanghai began to investigate, the purge broadened, now including the rebels and their every single potential ally. Thousands more were apprehended and subjected to torture. The suspects, having duly confessed, were often executed at night, away from the crowds, sometimes up to sixty in a single batch. A simple end was a blessing, as some of the more reviled victims were 'disembowelled or had their hearts scooped out', their bodies left uncollected. The same principle always applied: 'better kill a hundred innocent people than let a guilty one escape.' By the lowest estimate at least 2,000 people were slaughtered, with one report stating that AB elements were killed 'by the thousands and tens of thousands'.[73]

Purges were intrinsic to a utopian vision of radical transformation, one which could only be brought about by a Party purified of all corrupt elements. In Guangdong, among the remnants of the Hailufeng Soviet dwelling in the mountains near the East River, a similar massacre took place in 1930–1, as imaginary AB elements were blamed for having contaminated the troops. Suspects were tortured until they confessed, often executed without trial once they had provided the names of their fictitious accomplices. Gu Dacun, their leader, admitted that up to a thousand victims were put to death, eventually prompting the dissolution of the local army itself. Gu himself was later taken into custody as an AB suspect, although his life was spared.[74]

On 19 February 1931, the Politburo in Shanghai noted 'some excesses in his actions', but fully supported Mao in his 'struggle with class enemies'.[75]

Li Lisan had, by then, been repudiated by Moscow, with Pavel Mif sent instead in October 1930 to direct the revolution. A mediocre but ambitious young man, Mif had taken over Sun Yat-sen University in Moscow from a disgraced Radek in 1927. He wasted no time in uncovering alleged 'Trotskyists', the term used to discredit real or alleged opponents of Stalin, with more than 200 students sent for interrogation to the infamous Lubyanka, headquarters of the secret police in Moscow. Many were dispatched straight to labour camps in Siberia, with only ten recanting and allowed to return to China. Two more managed to escape. At Sun Yat-sen University, Mif relied on a handful of students who could speak fluent Russian. His favourite was Wang Ming (Chen Shaoyu), a shrewd, eager young man with a talent for flattery. Wang ingratiated himself with Stalin, who demanded that the Comintern undergo a process of 'Bolshevisation', code for Stalinism as opposed to Trotskyism. Wang accordingly wrote a pamphlet entitled *The Struggle for Bolshevisation of the Chinese Communist Party*. He and his followers, later known as the '28 Bolsheviks' for their loyalty to Stalin, were sent back to Shanghai in 1929. After Pavel Mif had engineered Li Lisan's removal in January 1931, they emerged from the wings, snatching power for themselves with Wang Ming elevated to the Standing Committee.[76]

Pavel Mif returned to Moscow in April 1931, believing that the Chinese Communist Party was in good hands. But on 24 April the Party's spymaster, Gu Shunzhang, was arrested. He headed the Central Special Branch, responsible for espionage and security, and had detailed knowledge of hundreds of individual cases in a vicious underground war of double-dealing, kidnapping and murder. Gu defected to the enemy, telling them everything he knew. Raids were carried out across the country, with thousands arrested. In Shanghai alone 259 members were apprehended in the International Settlement (thirty-three were executed). These included Xiang Zhongfa, still the nominal secretary general of the Party. He, too, tried to switch sides, but on 24 June 1931 nonetheless received a bullet in the head.[77]

Gu Shunzhang also paid a heavy price. Over the following months no fewer than sixteen bodies, members of his extended family, including his wife, his father-in-law and his mother-in-law, were disinterred in various parts of the International Settlement and the French Concession. Zhou Enlai had personally ordered their extermination. 'In each case the victims were strangled and buried without coffins, generally face downwards, a mode of burial considered particularly repugnant,' an observer with close knowledge of the case revealed. Regular reprisal killings would continue to rock the city for well over a year, not least the disposal of a couple whom a Communist agent chopped up and dissolved in acid.[78]

One of the raids in Shanghai targeted the Pacific Secretariat of the Profintern, the abbreviation for the Comintern's Red International of Labour Unions. In June 1931 the Special Branch of the Shanghai Municipal Police arrested its director, who went by the name of Hilaire Noulens, and seized three steel boxes with incriminating evidence. So complex was the string of aliases under which Noulens operated that it took more than sixty years for his real identity to come to light. Jakob Rudnik was a Ukrainian-born agent of the Comintern's secretive Liaison Department, the intelligence branch responsible for working with underground organisations in carrying out subversive activities. He and his wife were entrusted with overseeing huge financial transactions for East Asia through a sophisticated courier system, disbursing a sum equivalent to US$7 million in today's values. Among the documentation were cipher messages from Moscow, intelligence reports on work in the military and interviews with leaders of the Chinese Communist Party.[79]

Although a great deal of the information was kept secret, the case made international headlines. Moscow initiated a show of support, bankrolling a worldwide campaign in favour of the Noulens run by Wilhelm Münzenberg, a leading propagandist of the Communist Party of Germany. Supporters included Albert Einstein, Clara Zetkin, Maxim Gorki, Agnes Smedley, Madame Sun Yat-sen and Edgar Snow. The Noulens received the death penalty, although the sentence was commuted to life imprisonment. They would be released in 1937.[80]

Even as the underground organisation in Shanghai was being battered, a campaign to extirpate the Communists was unfolding in Jiangxi. Progress, at first, was slow. Conventional warfare was bound to fail, as regular troops were ill prepared for chasing lightly equipped guerrilla fighters across the dense forests and high mountains of a province stretching 600 kilometres from north to south and 500 kilometres from east to west. In July, Chiang Kai-shek took personal command, establishing his headquarters in Nanchang to direct 300,000 troops. The Nationalists managed to reclaim several Communist strongholds, including Ningdu, a walled city in south Jiangxi. Success was costly, as the town was flattened, with aircraft dropping some 120 bombs weighing seventy kilos apiece. By September, as the government regained control of large areas of territory, the Communists were forced to move further south, close to the border with Fujian province. They left behind a distressed landscape. The 'protracted war' vaunted by the Communists was, in effect, a scorched-earth tactic, imposing huge costs on the local villagers, who were forced to hide their supplies and take to the mountains. 'We saw no people, the houses were cleaned out as if by floods, there was no food, no woks, no pots,' a Nationalist commander later recalled. Not surprisingly, substantial numbers of poor villagers rallied to the government's cause and helped their troops. Others fled, with 100,000 refugees awaiting help, food and shelter in the city of Ganzhou alone.[81]

The territories controlled by the Communists began to shrink. By September, exhausted and hemmed in by the Nationalists, their funding from Shanghai cut off, it appeared that the Chinese Communist Party was about to collapse.

4
The Soviets
(1931–1934)

When Zhang Xueliang had raised the Nationalist flag on 18 September 1930, Japan interpreted his act of allegiance to Chiang Kai-shek as an unforgivable affront. By August 1931, the leaders of the Kwantung Army, quartered in Port Arthur, were preparing for military action, outspoken in their intention to expel the Young Marshal from the region. The railway zone under their control was a scene of feverish activity, with long lines of military trains loaded with food and munitions, field guns covered by canvas and bales of hay for the cavalry, moving up and down the South Manchuria Railway. Japan, under the settlement reached after the 1904 Russo-Japanese War, was allowed a maximum of 15,000 troops in Manchuria, but by one estimate 40,000 troops were scattered from Port Arthur up to Changchun, and from Mukden down to the north bank of the Yalu River, which separated Manchuria from Korea, also occupied by Japan.[1]

The Russians, not least by the manner in which they had used a minor skirmish along the Chinese Eastern Railway in 1929 to launch a full-fledged invasion of Manchuria, were an inspiration to Japan. Impressed by the ease with which the Soviet Army had prevailed, Japanese officers copied their approach and concocted an incident along a stretch of railway in Mukden. On the night of 18 September 1931, precisely one year after Zhang Xueliang had signed up to Nanjing, the Kwantung Army used a small amount of dynamite to damage rail lines near Mukden. They immediately cried sabotage and rushed troops to the spot. The Mukden Incident was the pretext to invade all of Manchuria.

Japan's timing was opportune, in more than one way. The United States was in the midst of a depression, Britain was leaving the gold standard after speculative attacks on the pound, while in Austria the failure of the country's largest bank caused the collapse of the stock market, in turn threatening the financial system of Europe. The Kwantung Army, within weeks, swiftly occupied all major cities from Port Arthur up to Shenyang and Changchun. In the name of peace and order, the railways, communications, the mint, all banks and the press were brought under their control. Even as soldiers fanned out along the railways, a counterflow could be observed, with a stampede of wealthy families moving south of the Great Wall to Beijing, loaded with bundles of jade, jewellery and paintings. Zhang, weak and emaciated from a bout of typhoid fever, offered no resistance, acutely aware of Japan's overwhelming military superiority. In December, his troops evacuated Manchuria, passing through the small town of Shanhaiguan, where the Great Wall plunges into the sea.[2]

Chiang Kai-shek rushed back to Nanjing, but did not declare war on Japan. He, too, viewed resistance against an efficient, modern military machine as futile. His government was already overwhelmed by a devastating flood in Hubei and Hunan, as vast sheets of muddy water stretched inland as far as the eye could see, transforming the entire Yangtze valley into a grey, tideless, inland sea. The harvest, food stocks, cattle and people were all swept away. Occasional dots protruded from the water surface, with desperate villagers clinging on to dykes, eventually forced to let go as exhaustion took hold. Half of the native city in Hankou disappeared under water, except for the upper floors of a few modern buildings. Everywhere the flood bore human bodies along with dead dogs, donkeys and horses, but also dysentery, cholera and typhoid. Across Wuhan, a city frequently flooded by heavy rain during the hot and stifling summer, with two major rivers meeting each other in a basin studded with lakes, an estimated 1,000 people died each day. Even in Nanjing, where government officials scrambled to extend help to 30 million homeless and destitute people, parts of the capital were inundated for months, its back waters 'thick with corpses'. In the freezing cold, before government offices, stood thousands of students who had poured into the city from all over the country, shouting slogans that demanded 'War with Japan!', 'Fight with Japan!' They stormed the offices of C. T. Wang, the foreign minister who had so successfully won unconditional tariff autonomy in 1928.[3]

Nanjing preferred to turn towards the Great Powers and the League of Nations. Japan, some twelve years earlier, had agreed to join the League as one of the four permanent members on its council, in exchange for its continued control of several concessions in Shandong. The League Council, on 30 September 1931, passed a resolution noting Japan's intention of withdrawing its troops as soon as possible. Foreign powers also attempted to contain Japan, urging Tokyo to refrain from attacking Jinzhou, an industrial centre located between Mukden and Beijing. Tokyo solemnly pledged to respect the city, only to bombard it in November. Further diplomatic notes were exchanged, with the League Council offering more words as well as a commission of inquiry. By early February 1932, Japan had completed the military conquest of Manchuria when gaunt and tired troops, clad in furs to protect them against the bitter cold, marched into Harbin. Manchuria, with its vast plains of black, fertile soil rich in coal and minerals, surrounded by densely forested mountains, was worth the fight. Besides its natural resources, Manchuria was a captive market of 30 million potential buyers. Most of all, Japan coveted the region as a buffer state against Russia.[4]

In January 1932 a second front opened in Shanghai, a city which had become the centre of an anti-Japanese boycott. Students, young merchants and apprentice clerks, among others, enlisted as pickets, in effect taking over the city, systematically examining the stock of each shop and riffling through the baggage of all incoming passengers at the railway stations. Some offending goods were seized and burned in the streets. None of the activists attacked any Japanese-owned shops, although strikes brought many Japanese mills and factories to the verge of bankruptcy. On 18 January a group of Japanese monks left the concession, stopped in front of a local towel factory and began chanting the Japanese national anthem. A riot ensued, with one monk dying in the fray, providing the pretext the Japanese military attaché was hoping for.

On 28 January, several companies of marines were sent across the International Settlement into Zhabei, the heavily industrialised district where workers lived in densely packed, redbrick terraced houses. They were an easy target for Chinese sharpshooters. Japan responded with a combined naval and aerial bombardment of the unarmed civilians of Zhabei, to the outrage of most of the world. Instead of suing for peace, Chiang Kai-shek sent the Nineteenth Route Army, which fought against overwhelming odds with a determination that surprised most observers, none more so than Japan. Soon more than half of Japan's standing army was in China. The deaths on both sides reached tens of thousands. Zhabei was reduced to ashes, 'smashed, ripped and gutted'. On 3 March, a ceasefire was negotiated, with an armistice concluded in May 1932.[5]

***

On 7 November 1931, the anniversary of the October Revolution, Mao Zedong proclaimed the Chinese Soviet Republic, also known as the Jiangxi Soviet. Three months earlier, four government divisions had attacked its capital Ruijin, only to withdraw following the Mukden Incident.[6]

Ruijin, surrounded by steep mountains, in the midst of an inhospitable frontier region straddling the border of Jiangxi and Fujian, became the nerve centre not only of the Jiangxi Soviet but also nominally of several other base areas in China, the main ones being located in Fujian, Hunan, Hubei, Anhui and later Sichuan. They would endure for three years, though even at their height they would cover no more than a combined 150,000 square kilometres, equivalent to 2 per cent of the country's territory. In terms of relative size, this was comparable to the state of Washington in the United States or La Paz Department in Bolivia on the South American continent.[7]

Since Ruijin was a ruined city, bombed by the Nationalists, all soviet institutions were established in a barricaded zone far from the centre. An ancestral hall was converted into government headquarters, air-raid shelters were dug, an airfield built and a vast area, called 'Peng Pai Square', cleared for military reviews. Above the main entrance of the ancestral hall were two big red silk banners embroidered with the hammer and sickle, one for the Soviet Union, one for the Communist Party. On 7 November, the founding of the red state was celebrated with parades, speeches and songs, the day ending with the delegates standing up to sing the Internationale.[8]

The levers of power, however, no longer rested with Mao. After the Party's underground network had been destroyed in Shanghai, the Central Committee moved to Ruijin. Its Politburo was dominated by Zhou Enlai and a young man called Bo Gu, who formally replaced Xiang Zhongfa as Party secretary in September 1931. A gangly, bookish man sixteen years younger than Mao, Bo had never fought in battle, but came armed with dogma. A faithful follower of Stalin, he had been trained in Moscow in the use of the Party machine.[9] His patron Wang Ming, recalled to the Soviet Union in September 1931 to assist Pavel Mif, backed him unfailingly. Communications between Ruijin and Moscow took place by radio, controlled by Zhou Enlai at one end and Wang Ming at the other.

The Politburo, dominated by the 'Bolsheviks', hung on every word from their master in Moscow. Moscow dictated a harsh approach towards 'landlords' and 'rich peasants'. As Pavel Mif stated, 'the first and fundamental task' of the Chinese Communist Party was to see that 'the agrarian revolution does not become a kulak revolution', with 'rich peasants' managing to win control of the organs of power in the soviets. In the Jiangxi Soviet, 'landlords' and their dependants were banned from owning land altogether, while 'rich peasants' were allocated marginal plots with poor soil. Since anyone could potentially be denounced as a 'landlord' or a 'rich peasant', and since the land in parts of the soviet had been distributed on 'countless occasions', no one felt secure. Grain output plummeted, as the villagers merely farmed sufficient food to meet their own needs. In normal market conditions, determined by supply and demand, the value of their agricultural output would have increased, but the Party capped prices.[10]

Prices of daily necessities, on the other hand, increased. Before the foundation of the soviet, a shirt and a pair of trousers cost 1.8 yuan, which by 1933 had almost doubled to 3.4 yuan. Commodities such as salt and oil experienced such rampant inflation that by 1933 consumption had plummeted by 80 per cent. Trade was in the doldrums. 'The main reason is that in the past, as we began our struggle, we randomly burned down cities and the Red Army did not observe discipline, so most of the towns and cities inside the soviet have already been ruined,' a political commissar noted. Their shops destroyed, treated as class enemies, merchants could barely operate. 'We are poor, we cannot buy anything, everything today is too expensive,' the villagers complained. To bridge the gap and make ends meet, many turned away from their fields and tried to trade in oil, salt and other commodities. Others quietly took to the roads, with deserted fields appearing along the border of the soviet as early as March 1932.[11]

Before the establishment of a soviet, the main source of revenue for the Communists had been plunder and ransom. The guerrilla fighters would enter a village, confiscate the assets of those deemed to be enemies of the revolution, boldly proclaim the abolition of all taxes and move on. But now they actually needed to tax their own population, even though the main source of revenue, namely the assets of well-to-do people, was already exhausted. At first the funds required for the government to function were simply taken from the population, 'first from local tyrants, then from the gentry, landlords and rich peasants, then from middle peasants and finally from every poor peasant who had no more than a handful of money'. Once taxes had been imposed, they rapidly multiplied, since the dwindling resources of their subjects could never meet the needs of an expanding government. Some of these taxes 'are easily mistaken by the people for the exorbitant levies of the past', one report suggested. Since taxes and surtaxes were inadequate, the government organised 'gift teams' to solicit free contributions and voluntary donations, 'for instance noodles, sweet potatoes, vegetables, fruit, pork, chicken and duck eggs, straw sandals and money'.[12]

Compounding the situation was the insistence of the soviet on 'total independence' from the surrounding territories. This included printing soviet currency with the likeness of Lenin on various denominations. Unfortunately, this paper money was not welcome, least of all outside the soviet. 'In many places banknotes are not valued and even turned down,' a report pointed out in 1933. Since the currency was not respected, prices were 'surreptitiously raised', among other 'heinous plots and schemes of the counter-revolution within and without to sabotage the revolution'. A black market appeared, barter spread, with goods traded for other goods. People refused to surrender or trade in the old currency at exchange stations or local banks. It took further laws, followed by additional government agents, to enforce the use of the red currency, including 'execution by shooting'.[13]

Trade with the outside world was a lifeline, revived somewhat belatedly in January 1934. Ruijin had a reputation for producing fine tobacco, which was earmarked for export. Grain, timber and camphor were sold to replenish the government coffers. Tungsten, a rare metal of extreme hardness, was found in abundance in south Jiangxi, contributing almost half of the world's output, with exports to the United States, France and Germany. Thousands of villagers were sent down the mines to work in dire conditions, extracting more than 4,000 tonnes over a three-year period. All of these commodities were smuggled across the soviet border, with a thriving parallel trade in currency. A deal was even struck with Chen Jitang, who became governor of Guangdong in 1931. Chen was a moderniser, paving streets, establishing schools and building factories, all of which required money. He agreed to take the tungsten in exchange for salt and other necessities.[14]

The entire economy suffered from the economic blockade imposed by government troops. But even without these restrictions commodities tended to leave rather than enter the soviet. Besides harsh taxation and arbitrary confiscation, the fastest way to ensure that wealth drained away from the region was the paper money printed in Ruijin. Growing shortages of essentials contributed to the outflow.[15]

An impecunious government soon imposed war bonds on its impoverished population. Minor amounts were issued in August and in December 1932, followed by a much larger batch of 3 million yuan in August 1933, maturing in seven years. Though few people expected the regime to last that long, villagers had little choice but to commit themselves. The bonds were evenly distributed among the counties, which handed down a quota to each town, which in turn evenly imposed them on their villages. When spendthrift villagers still refused, more mass meetings were held, followed by more house visits to recalcitrant elements. Months later, in some areas, the cadres forced purchasers to return the bonds, depriving them of both the principal and the interest.[16]

Throughout, the villagers were subjected to mass meetings, with attendance compulsory. On average, they took up five days every month. Regular show trials took place during which 'landlords' or 'rich peasants' were executed. The purge against supposed AB elements abated, but never disappeared, with more show trials and more executions. At all times, anyone refusing to obey soviet directives risked accusations of being a counter-revolutionary.[17]

Labour, much like the economy, was primarily geared towards the needs of the war machine. Men aged forty or below were recruited into the army or press-ganged as conscript labour. 'The villagers do not wish to join the Red Army, the soviet uses ropes to capture them,' one report claimed. In the town of Changnang, 320 men were recruited from a local population of 1,784, meaning, in effect, that most work was left to women and the elderly. In Caixi, another town investigated by the Communists, some 485 of the 554 men aged between sixteen and fifty-five were enrolled in the Red Army, leaving men to perform just 11 per cent of all work in the fields. Everywhere, by 1933, shortages if not conditions of outright famine were becoming apparent.[18]

The Red Army had 70,000 uniformed soldiers, who were paid in full, but also a Red Guard Army of as many as 100,000 men, poorly armed and untrained conscripts, without uniforms, aged from fifteen to twenty, and used more often than not as cannon fodder, sent in to harass the enemy's flanks or to precede the regular soldiers and be slaughtered. No amount of recruitment could ever satisfy the army's insatiable need for red soldiers or red guards alike. Even after establishing their Soviet Republic, the Communists never abandoned the idea that cities could be seized and an 'initial victory of the revolution' secured in 'one or more provinces'. Apparently oblivious of past disasters, in January 1932 the Central Committee urged attacks on Nanchang, Fuzhou or Ji'an. The plan was abandoned in favour of a softer target, namely Ganzhou. Mao and Zhu objected, but they were in the minority. On four occasions in 1932 Ganzhou was assaulted. In March, the city was 'bombarded by such objects as they [the Communists] had', before they began digging underneath the city gates to place explosives. Once a gap had been created, the soldiers rushed forward, only to find themselves trapped in a narrow funnel, to be mown down by machine guns. Still they rushed forward. Even after the arrival of relief troops the Communist attacks continued.[19]

Smaller towns were also targeted, for one simple reason: with its population terrorised and an economy in freefall, the regime was compelled to maraud outside its territory. Repeatedly the Red Army went on forays into the neighbouring province of Fujian, retreating with food, salt, munitions and fruit. 'There seems to be no finality possible under present conditions,' one journalist pointed out, since the Communists would lose one battle only to dart off to another, 'sweeping the countryside clean as they go'. Once they had acquired sufficient food, they retired to the soviet, only to break out again when hunger spoke. Since the government troops could not always be everywhere, the advantage was on the side of the guerrilla fighters.[20]

Widespread destruction of infrastructure was part of the Communists' strategy. When they could, for instance in Xinfeng in May 1930, they tore down the parapets and burned the gates that protected a county seat, lessening the cost of a future strike. Within the soviet too, the ancient walls that surrounded market towns were levelled. Not only were they symbols of a feudal order to be erased, but towns had to offer unimpeded access to the Red

Army. Similarly, while much of the country was busily building modern roads, the Communists tore these up. The guerrilla fighters walked along paths though valleys and mountains, while roads could invite invasion by government troops. As the journalist Gerald Yorke observed in 1933, roads ceased at the exact point where one entered the red state.[21]

Efforts were made to provide the soviet with the accoutrements of a modern state. All newspapers were banned, replaced by the Party's own publications, mainly *Red China* and *Struggle*, each with a circulation running from 27,000 to 40,000. The mint was essential, as was an arsenal and a military academy. Existing schools were taken over and new ones established, with 3,000 Lenin primary schools catering for children. A Karl Marx University was founded. On paper, in an elaborate world tirelessly built by slogan and proclamation, women were liberated and sent to school. 'Anyone who comes to visit our soviet areas will immediately find this to be a brand new world of freedom and light,' the opposite of the 'dark hells' prevailing outside the Jiangxi Soviet. Hospitals, in the midst of continuous warfare, were essential, although the leadership itself relied mainly on a former missionary hospital in Dingzhou, dismantled and transported to Ruijin in 1933. The reality was that the demands of permanent warfare drained all human and material resources, with education, health standards and even basic necessities like food, shelter and clothing deemed to be temporarily dispensable, at least until the future of the revolution had been secured. The end, always beckoning ahead like a lodestar, justified all means.[22]

***

The Jiangxi Soviet was controlled by the First Red Army, with two other armies dominating important soviets elsewhere. In Hunan and West Hubei, He Long presided over the Second Red Army. The Fourth Red Army was located in the Dabie Mountains east of Wuhan, on the border of Hubei, Henan and Anhui. Besides the three soviets, there were also a few pockets in Guangdong, not least along the East River and on Hainan Island, but these disintegrated by the end of 1931, under pressure from the new provincial governor Chen Jitang.[23]

When shining a spotlight on the soviets, it is easy to overlook the fact that huge chunks of territory housed barely any Communists. In Shaanxi province, where Mao and his acolytes would arrive after an arduous trek several years later, in September 1927 the Party numbered 2,177 members in a population of 12 million people. By 1930, the provincial committee was described as 'non-operational'. Two years later, when 2,000 guerrillas trekked for hundreds of kilometres through the province, they did not find a single village with a Communist Party member. A 'cradle of revolution' it was not.[24]

In Henan, a densely populated province with fertile floodplains all along the Yellow River, the provincial Party committee reported a grand total of 155 members in April 1930. The situation did not improve. One year later, the committee pointed out that 'at this point in time the most pressing organisational issue in the province is the absence of even a single functional Party branch.' Nothing the Party did had 'any influence on the population', except for a dozen guerrilla fighters in Linying who 'kidnapped people like bandits'. In neighbouring province Hebei, hugging both Tianjin and Beijing, the Party hardly functioned, with most activities abandoned in much of the countryside. As to Tianjin proper, the commercial rival of Shanghai with millions of factory workers, in 1932 'the municipal Party committee did not distribute a single leaflet, put up a single slogan or send out any propaganda material to any factory, workshop or dormitory.'[25]

In Zhejiang, a wealthy maritime province far removed from inland Shaanxi, the campaign to suppress the Chinese Communist Party resulted in a decrease from 2,600 to 1,563 members in the months following April 1927, with several hundred lingering in prison, not counting defections. The vast majority were released in 1928. By 1932 the Party had waned to the point where both the 'proletariat' and the 'peasantry' considered the Communists to be no more than brigands. In all Shandong by 1932 the Party boasted fewer than twenty women, most of them students. 'We are poorly organised,' the provincial committee tersely concluded.[26]

The reality was that the Party only thrived where it managed to create conditions of extreme distress, first through plunder and depredation, then by attracting further depredation on the part of the government troops sent to suppress them. The Nationalists themselves had planted the seeds of this violence, not least during the Northern Expedition undertaken with the Communists before April 1927. One such region was Wuhan and the surrounding countryside in Hubei, where Borodin had reigned supreme. Everywhere in 1926 trains with specially equipped coaches for the use of young men and women had arrived, distributing posters, shouting slogans, organising parades and establishing a political bureau with a labour union, a student union and a peasant association in every town and hamlet. The more entrenched they were, the more militant and radical they became, and in turn the more violent the reaction from the victims of revolution once the troops moved on or switched sides. After 15 July 1927, when the Nationalists in Wuhan recognised Chiang Kai-shek and his capital Nanjing, relations with the Communists were severed. But it was not until the departure of all Russians later that year that executions were cranked up. In the week after Nanjing broke with Moscow on 14 December, the Wuhan cities of Hankou, Wuchang and Hanyang, fearing a coup on the lines of the one mounted by the Communists in Canton, killed dozens of suspected Party members. Arrests and executions continued daily during the following months, not least when refugees brought news of the ruin of Leiyang and other cities in Hunan. Towards the end of March the *North-China Herald* counted fifty-six executions in six days in Hankou alone. The provincial Party committee itself reckoned that between 5 March and 25 April 1928, an average of six people a day were executed in Wuhan.[27]

Violence escalated to even greater levels in the countryside, with revolutionary and government forces resorting to ever more drastic means of suppression, trapped in a cycle of murder and arson. Even before Wuhan turned against the Communists, Wu Peifu, the northern general who had used the city as a stronghold before his defeat in October 1926, cracked down on peasant associations whenever possible. Later, in the absence of government troops, the local magistrates hired bandits to eliminate the Communists, much as the Communists recruited bandits. Bandits used bandit methods, summarily beheading, disembowelling, burning to death or otherwise disposing of suspected Communist leaders.[28]

In the following years, as He Long rampaged through Hunan and Hubei, trying to impose communism by fire and sword, entire counties were bloodied. He Long, like Mao Zedong and Zhu De, was eventually forced to retreat into the mountains, establishing a soviet in Hefeng on 13 January 1929 with only a thousand followers. Over the following three years, the soviet gradually extended its reach to Cili, Shimen, Badong, Enshi and other counties, all the way down into the plains as far as the Red Lake district to the east, and along the Yangtze River between Changsha and Wuhan.

He Long's prime concern was survival, which meant recruiting more soldiers. A bandit himself, he had little hesitation in enlisting more bandits in his ranks, including self-defence units recruited to fight off revenue collectors and sworn brotherhoods rampant in the region. As in the Jiangxi Soviet, local men were pressed into service, with quotas set so high that by 1931 even the physically unfit were enrolled. Throughout, families could be seen knocking on the doors of the soviet government to demand the return of their menfolk. They highlighted a problem that bedevilled every soviet: 'No one will tend to the fields once they are enlisted!' they complained. In large sections of the countryside – Jianli, Shishou, Huarong, Mianyang – grain production collapsed even as recruitment jumped.[29]

Land distribution was designed to liberate labour, but did not proceed as planned. Before long, it was not just 'landlords' and 'rich peasants' who were condemned as counter-revolutionaries, but even those described as 'middle peasants'. In Jianli, as elsewhere, a 'rich peasant' was defined as a man 'whose annual income exceeded his expenditure', a 'middle peasant' as one whose annual income merely sufficed to meet the expenses of his family, and a 'poor peasant' as one whose income was inadequate, forcing him to sell his labour to support his family. Since in Jianli county 'middle peasants' made up 80 per cent of all farmers, many voted with their feet. Those deemed to be 'landlords' were occasionally hung up and tortured into revealing where they had hidden their wealth. Everywhere men were drafted into the army or set to work, while women were enrolled in special units, washing and mending clothes or making shoes for the troops. Many fields were left neglected.[30]

In 1930 the soviet attempted to create an entirely self-sufficient economy. Villagers were forbidden to sell their produce on the market, and were required to deliver it instead to special 'transport stations', earmarked to oversee all commercial exchanges between the 'red' and the 'white' zones. Credit notes were printed and imposed at gunpoint. The villagers still refused to use them, resulting in panic buying of all essentials, not least salt, coal and oil. Every yuan printed by the soviet was supposed to be equivalent to a yuan printed outside the soviet, but by 1932 the black-market exchange rate was 1 to 10. The soviet tried to raise funds by imposing a whole range of taxes and surtaxes, including 'mutual assistance fees', 'Communist endorsement fees' and even 'sock and shoe fees'. Bonds were sold, forced on the population, but with a twist: in some places the certificates were never handed out and instead were sold multiple times. By late 1932 the soviet resorted to holding people for ransom, sometimes a dozen at a time per district. 'The judicial department has become a kidnapping centre,' it was observed. Those dissatisfied with the state of affairs were 'accused of being counter-revolutionaries and were tortured and imprisoned', in the words of Deng Zhongxia, political commissar of He Long's Second Red Army. As in any area under Communist control, there were no half measures: people either joined the cause or were seen to oppose it.[31]

Collective shops were set up, selling a variety of goods at a discount when compared to ordinary shops. Party members and local cadres were the main users. 'They came and took but did not pay,' according to one report, even as ordinary villagers had to join long queues, sometimes for days on end. When all the supplies were gone, the collective shops purchased goods from the ordinary shops instead, causing an even greater deficit as well as inflation. 'As a result many necessities like salt, sugar, paper, cloth, tools and even grain are lacking.' All the collectives were bailed out and closed after a season. Party members turned to ordinary shops instead, using their status to buy on credit although few ever settled their bills.³²

Regular forays were carried out into the surrounding regions to patch up a faltering economy. In some adjoining areas, every single kernel of grain or piece of clothing was captured. Even ordinary people were allowed to undertake raiding expeditions, meaning that villagers were encouraged to fight other villagers. 'We sent our peasants to white areas, we stole their resources, it was a mistake, we were like colonisers,' one report revealed. Since the Communists, by their own admission, 'used to burn and kill everything in the white zones', the result, in parts of the soviet, was a desolate borderland that exacerbated the inhibition of trade.³³

The devastating flood of the summer of 1931 further undermined the soviet. The muddy, deadly water was the same everywhere, but its effects varied considerably. No one fled into the red zone, but out came a steady stream of bedraggled refugees, including not just ordinary men, women and children but also more than half of all Party members, with membership tumbling from 30,000 to 13,000. The entire area around the Red Lake, with soviet structures established on its many islands, had to be abandoned in 1932, prompting the inhabitants to return to their half-empty villages with the help of the Flood Relief Commission.³⁴

The Central Committee sent to the rescue Xia Xi, one of the 'Bolsheviks' from Moscow who had accompanied Wang Ming back to Shanghai in 1929. Wang Ming now hoped to impose tighter control over the Hunan and West Hubei Soviet. Xia, a sinister-looking man, saw enemies of the Party everywhere, apparently believing that he himself was the only true Bolshevik. Only a thorough purge, he thought, could save the soviet from perdition. AB elements were lurking everywhere, as well as a whole array of other counter-revolutionaries, chief among them Trotskyists. In a fearsome purge, Xia Xi managed to eliminate a great many. 'A shocking number of Communist Party and Youth League members were executed,' one Communist Party member later claimed. Xiao Ke, a general who would join He

Long a few years later, estimated that the purge decimated the ranks of the army, which decreased from 20,000 to about 4,000. 'We arrest randomly, we torture randomly and we kill randomly,' a report declared at the time. The result, the report concluded, was a population cowed in perpetual fear. By 1933, He Long had to retreat all the way back to Sangzhi, the home county that had been his base years earlier.[35]

***

The Fourth Red Army could be found in the Dabie Mountains just fifty kilometres north-east of Wuhan. The region straddled the three provinces of Hubei, Henan and Anhui. At the heart of what was called the Hubei–Henan–Anhui Soviet was Macheng, a county seat located amid lush green hills leading to densely forested mountains. The main route across the mountain range was up north from Macheng to the Huai River valley in Henan along a number of imposing passes.

In Macheng the seeds of the soviet were planted in 1925 by a young revolutionary called Dong Biwu. A native of the neighbouring town of Huang'an, Dong had joined Sun Yat-sen's Tongmenghui, the predecessor of the Nationalist Party, and participated in the 1911 revolution in Wuchang before converting to communism while living in Shanghai in 1919–20. He returned to Hubei in 1921 to set up a local cell, attracting dozens of young recruits in Macheng. They propagated the faith, running bookshops or publishing newspapers for cover. Several years later, advance agents of the Nationalist Party arrived to set up labour unions and peasant associations in the region. In the winter of 1926–7, spurred on by the young radicals, members of the peasant associations began attacking local dignitaries, beheading them in huge denunciation meetings. After the failure of the Nanchang Uprising in August 1927, small batches of rebels began to arrive in the region, succeeding in taking Huang'an and establishing a temporary soviet in November that year. They proceeded to kill roughly a thousand of their enemies, burn the houses and confiscate the assets of the wealthy, but after a few weeks superior government troops defeated them.[36]

For several years ragged bands of guerrilla fighters roamed the region, establishing a base camp before ferocious repression forced them to move further up the mountains. Like Communists elsewhere, they staged a series of uprisings, plundering for survival, ransoming the wealthy, executing local notables, occasionally wiping out entire enemy villages. And like Communists elsewhere, they became locked in an endless cycle of revenge, battling for control with local militia or government troops. The result, in large swathes of territory stretching across several counties, was 'economic destruction, in particular in red zones, on a truly dreadful scale', as one report put it. In Huang'an, their erstwhile possession, 'counter-revolutionaries came and burned, revolutionaries came and burned in turn, resulting in some three-quarters of all houses having recently been torched, with entire villages reduced to rubble.' The villagers 'would not even erect a straw hut, as they feared that it might be burned down again within days'. Several families sometimes huddled together in the charred remains of a single home. A few months later, in December 1929, another report phrased it somewhat differently: 'The Party killed people mindlessly. Over the past two years, it burned many houses and killed a great many people who were not landlords ... Some Party members committed adultery, causing discontent among the population.'[37]

Besides misery, the Communists also left a message of change through revolution, as well as underground members of their organisation, laying the foundation for the soviet established in February 1930. Yet even by this time they had fewer than 2,000 followers. These were local bandits and disbanded soldiers, although most were recruited through personal ties, whether fellow clan members or family friends, creating strong social links throughout the region. Few cadres had even a cursory knowledge of Marxism. Many, indeed, were illiterate, with some members believing that 'Soviet' was the name of an important yet mysterious Party leader.[38]

The soviet fared poorly. In 1930 the land was distributed, but the plots were so small that productivity immediately plummeted. The villagers lacked motivation, and always for the same reason: they knew that the surplus they produced would be confiscated.

There was another factor, common to all regions administered by Communists: 'They were afraid of being classified as rich peasants. They were not willing to produce more. Whenever they saw other farmers working, they would ask them, "are you trying to become a rich peasant?"' A 'rich peasant', according to the soviet, was a cultivator who actually managed to earn some money, however small the amount. The villagers not only squirrelled away the little cash they had in hidden places, but also abandoned parts of the harvest. 'The farmers became lazy.' Arable land lay fallow, even as the population went hungry. The cadres lorded it over their subjects, refusing to till the land themselves. 'It was like serfdom in feudal times,' Zeng Zhongsheng, the new leader appointed in September 1930, commented.[39]

In April 1931, Wang Ming sent Zhang Guotao to the soviet, hoping to bring it into line. Zhang found 20,000 troops and a population of 1.8 million people in the midst of widespread food shortages. In June, one report pointed out that thousands of people had nothing to eat, with several starving to death, one hanging himself in desperation. The economy was bankrupt: the men had been recruited in large numbers by the Fourth Red Army, while the remaining villagers had been pressed into some kind of service, women making socks and mending shoes for the soldiers, children busy standing guard. The soviet, unable to run the local economy, relied on raids instead. But after the surrounding countryside had been repeatedly pillaged, no 'landlords' were left to plunder, forcing the raiding troops to seize provisions from poor people. As one report suggested, 'it caused the villagers to oppose us in the white areas.' Some of the problems the soviet encountered were caused by a large-scale campaign of encirclement, launched later by the government troops in November 1931, but Zhang concluded that the main reason for the setbacks 'seemed to lie in the inherent shortcomings of the soviet movement'.[40]

The solution lay in a thorough purge of the leadership. It rolled over the soviet like a tidal wave, sweeping away anyone accused of working for the enemy. In a familiar scenario, suspects were interrogated, tortured and pressed into revealing the names of others. How many were executed is unclear. In his memoirs published some thirty years later, Zhang claimed that 600 people were arrested, a hundred purged and forty shot. He was being somewhat disingenuous. The report he himself sent to the Central Committee in November 1931 proudly announced that 2,500 AB elements, enemy agents, spies, hoodlums, gangsters, mutineers, landlords, rich peasants and other counter-revolutionaries hiding inside the ranks had been 'eliminated', including 700 Party members. Zhang was the political commissar of the Fourth Red Army. Its commander, Xu Xiangqian, a short, thin and quiet man, later recalled in his memoirs that in just three months in 1931, up to 2,500 people had been physically eliminated from the army. Xu backed Zhang, even though he later admitted that the majority of those purged were 'able, experienced warriors, leaders with close links to the masses'. Not until 1937 would he find out that his own wife had been denounced, tortured and killed as a 'reorganisationist'. 'Arrests and executions were all done without any evidence, on the basis of confessions alone.'[41]

The purge weakened the army, yet continued even as government troops were surrounding the soviet. By August 1932, Zhang Guotao and Xu Xiangqian decided to flee the area, taking the Fourth Red Army on a three-month-long march to Sichuan province, a thousand kilometres to the west.

The population they left behind had a pitiful fate. By 1933, as government troops continued to enforce a blockade, the villagers were reduced to eating tree leaves. Many died of hunger, although not all waited for starvation to take hold, escaping to white zones instead. Government officials and missionaries who visited the area found 'uninhabited villages, half-burnt houses, fields lying uncultivated' with whole sections of the population wiped out. The soviet finally collapsed in 1934, its remaining guerrilla fighters slaughtered.[42]

***

'To go to Sichuan is as hard as to go to Heaven,' Li Bai once wrote. The poet lived in the eighth century, but his proverbial line was still invoked in the 1930s. The province, as large as France, was surrounded by mountains. The fastest route was along the

Yangtze, although even with the advent of modern steamship services the voyage from Shanghai to Chongqing, Sichuan's capital, took longer than crossing the Pacific Ocean.[43]

The military leaders relished the province's isolation, determined to keep their realm independent of the central authorities, whether in Beijing or Nanjing. They were also keen to stave off communism, repressing its followers mercilessly. In 1927, the province harboured no more than 600 Communist Party members. Like so many other Communists the country over, they were unable to envisage any form of political action other than that prescribed by Moscow: 'we should immediately lead the peasants in an armed rebellion to confiscate the land and slaughter all local landlords,' the provincial committee trumpeted in October 1927. A few months later they realised that in this predominantly agricultural province of 48 million souls there were too few 'peasants' willing to join the Party to start even a modest uprising. By 1931, after a series of failed insurrections, membership lingered at just 1,500.[44]

Zhang and Xu arrived in north Sichuan with 20,000 followers in early November 1932, establishing a foothold along the border with Shaanxi. They were dressed in rags, without shoes or socks, with shreds of cloth wrapped around their feet, resembling an army of beggars. The timing was fortunate, as two of the provincial generals were at war with each other. Liu Wenhui, who regarded Chengdu as his personal domain, was isolated by a coalition built by his main enemy, Liu Xiang, headquartered in Chongqing. Although the province was accustomed to civil war, the fighting was ferocious, not least since Liu Xiang had a fleet of planes and made a practice of 'dropping 240-pound incendiary bombs on the towns and cities held by his enemies'. The Fourth Red Army used the civil war to capture Tongjiang, Bazhong, Bazhou and Nanjiang, the wealthiest counties in the region. Much of this conquest took place without a shot fired, as local soldiers and county officials simply ran away. The situation looked promising, with rapid progress being made. The Communists, for once, relied on the power of the word instead of the sword to win over the population. The soldiers behaved, paying for the food they took from the thriving markets and shops stocked to the hilt with native goods. 'Propaganda is their main reliance and plenty of information and literature is being scattered informing the people of the blessing of Communism,' the *North-China Herald* reported favourably. In Bazhong, Zhang Guotao himself recalled, 'endless streams of people' read the public notices they posted. They delivered public lectures on the benefits of a soviet regime. Even the well-to-do at first welcomed the abolition of exorbitant taxes and the stern measures taken against opium. The army also positioned itself strategically throughout the region, hoping to attract the disaffected. Deserters, tramps, riff-raff and 'sundry brigand bands', according to the French consul, joined in huge numbers, inflating the troops to 45,000.[45]

The Central Committee in Ruijin was unimpressed, denouncing their march out of Hunan as 'escapism' and demanding the imposition of a soviet. Warfare soon resumed, as Tian Songyao, the regional satrap charged with eliminating the Communists, reclaimed several county seats. In Tongjiang, recaptured in turn from Tian by the Fourth Red Army in January 1933, the church and other buildings were wrecked, and local officials killed or held for ransom. In Bazhou, a town which changed hands several times, the Communists wrecked the post office, confiscated the grain and killed all draught animals, leaving the place strewn with dead bodies. In a mulberry grove near a mission compound, thirty-six pits were found in which hundreds of human corpses had been unceremoniously dumped. To finance the upkeep of its troops, the Fourth Red Army began to sell the very opium it had at first prohibited. Other tried-and-tested means of raising money were used, including the ransoming of local notables and wealthy merchants. Well-to-do people were arrested indiscriminately, their goods confiscated, their wives and daughters taken away, their property burned to the ground. A few were shot as 'bourgeois parasites' or 'vermin'. As early as March, Liu Xiang, the key player in the province, reported to Chiang Kai-shek that 'since they kill randomly, they have lost the support of the people.'[46]

In pursuit of economic self-sufficiency, the soviet issued its own currency and imposed price controls. A copper mint was established in Tongjiang, capital of the soviet. Besides coins, copper notes were also circulated, made of cloth or paper. The rate was set at thirty coppers for a silver dollar, but faith in the notes declined rapidly, as people from all walks of life began to sell rice, wheat and cloth in exchange for silver dollars, which they hid. After a year the value of the copper notes had fallen to about 250 to the dollar. Capital fled, all the way to Shanghai.[47]

Soon enough, market towns were drained of goods and people. Shortages spread. The Communists undermined trade once they began to tear up all the roads around every town they controlled. Salt became so rare that the dirt floors in old salt shops were dug up. Men were forced to join the army, which consumed the food, of which much smaller amounts were produced in the fields since only women were left to cultivate them. Funds for agriculture were lacking, with capital mobilised to wage a defensive war. Tools for production, consequently, became scarce. While the rich were subjected to deprivations, the poor appeared less zealous than initially expected. As in every soviet, cooperatives were established to remedy the scarcity of labour, capital and tools, with entire villages divided into 'land cultivation corps', composed in the main of women. But to the local cultivator, whether male or female, collective farming all too often meant work that benefited someone else. Many fields stood empty. The main activity of any government, in the past or under the soviet, was to collect tax. Previously, the local authorities had only a dim notion of how much land was cultivated and what the fields actually yielded. Villagers were expert at concealing strips of land, withholding part of their harvest or otherwise short-changing the tax collector. But under the Communists there was nowhere to hide. Specially appointed commissioners made detailed records not just of all land holdings but of all the members of each household as well as the quantities of chickens, sheep, cattle, pigs, dogs, tools and furniture.[48]

By late 1934, in the words of Zhang Guotao, the soviet and the region around it had become a 'lemon with all the juice squeezed out'. The ravages of war had depleted the soviet of food and supplies. Famine was looming, meaning that 'the army might have to contend with the people for food.'⁴⁹

***

In Ruijin, the Jiangxi Soviet faced a similar predicament. Bo Gu, the bookish young man who in September 1931 had become Party secretary, had pushed Mao aside. In a conference at Ningdu in October 1932, Bo Gu and his 'Bolshevik' followers on the Central Committee had taken Mao's military approach to task, not least over his reluctance to seize Ganzhou. This was not the first time that Mao had preferred to preserve and nurture his troops rather than launch them in a doomed assault on a city solely to please the masters in Moscow. For his 'opportunist line' and 'hesitation' in 'capturing major cities', he was sent on sick leave, losing his grip over the First Red Army. Zhou Enlai replaced him as political commissar.⁵⁰

In February 1933, Mao was moved instead to land reform. Bo Gu and the 'Bolsheviks' had pursued an even harsher policy towards so-called 'rich peasants' than Mao himself, but now they wished the movement to be widened yet further, including a class analysis of every villager. After the Mukden Incident in September 1931, the government troops had withdrawn, allowing the Communists to establish their Jiangxi Soviet. Provincial forces had continued to battle the First Red Army, but after an eighteen-month interval troops organised by the central government returned. They had repulsed both He Long and Zhang Guotao in central China, and in January 1933 they began to close in on the Jiangxi Soviet. By launching a renewed campaign of land redistribution, Bo Gu and his acolytes hoped to discover more land and squeeze yet more property out of the population to finance the war effort. In the process, 'secret counter-revolutionary organisations' as well as previously overlooked 'remnant feudal forces' could be swept away, the ranks cleansed once and for all.⁵¹

In February 1933, He Yingqin, once again in charge of fighting the First Red Army, assembled a force of 400,000 men. In Fujian, the Nineteenth Route Army, which had so stubbornly fought the Japanese in Shanghai, defeated Communist remnants in the province and forced them back across the border into Jiangxi. Troops from Guangdong were also ready to suppress the Communists, waiting for mobilisation. But again Japan came to the rescue. For several weeks, troops from the Kwantung Army had been taking up positions in Jehol, a province rich in coal and other minerals running along the Great Wall from the east of Mongolia to the Bohai Sea at Shanhaiguan. They complained that Zhang Xueliang, the Young Marshal, had stationed his troops in the area. When on 9 February the League of Nations demanded that Japan clarify its intentions, Tokyo retorted that the province was an integral part of Manchuria. On 18 February, the Young Marshal pledged never to give up Jehol, but a few days later, as four Japanese columns began smashing through the province, his troops melted away. On 24 February, a stunned international conclave watched in silence as the Japanese delegation walked out of the assembly hall in Geneva, withdrawing from the League. After a sickly, bed-ridden Zhang Xueliang resigned, He Yingqin was ordered to leave his headquarters in Nanchang and take charge of the Young Marshal's troops. The Japanese, who had made their way down the narrow mountain passes onto the plains of north China, were just twenty kilometres from Beijing and less than fifty from Tianjin. 'The thunder of their artillery could be heard in both of those great cities,' one journalist reported. He Yingqin placed seven army groups totalling a quarter of a million troops all along the key passes of the Great Wall, hoping to stabilise the situation without expanding the battlefield. In May, Chiang Kai-shek had little alternative but to sign a truce in Tanggu, a small port at the mouth of the Hai River outside Tianjin, but not before his representatives were made to wait for hours in the broiling sun before the Japanese Consulate. The truce demilitarised huge swathes of the north.[52]

Land redistribution in the Jiangxi Soviet continued unabated, with a call in June 1933 to 'root out' all 'landlords' and 'rich peasants' who had been wrongly classified as merely 'middle' or even 'poor peasants'. The campaign was merciless, not least since 'rich peasants' were accused of hiding the grain, becoming scapegoats for an unfolding famine. In parts of the soviet, ordinary villagers were reduced to eating tree leaves and grass roots, while even Red Army soldiers suffered from a 'serious shortage of grain'. In the following months, some 14,600 families were reclassified, even though many were households of very modest means. But the soviet received its windfall, measured in grain, property and land. The forfeits and fines squeezed from these families alone amounted to more than 600,000 dollars.[53]

It was a stop-gap measure, and one that came with unintended consequences. Chief among these, as Mao himself pointed out, was the dispossession of 'rich peasants' as well as 'the tendency to violate the interests of the middle peasants', with attacks on ordinary households so harsh that some fled to the mountains in 'terror'. It was the beginning of the gradual collapse of the soviet, caused by increasingly large numbers of people either fleeing into neighbouring areas or turning against the regime.[54]

Against this background, Chiang Kai-shek began yet another campaign of suppression in September 1933, his fifth to date. But this time he changed tack, recognising that the bayonet alone could not defeat ideas. One year earlier, he had suggested that policy should be 'three parts military and seven parts politics'. By this he meant modernisation. An extensive road network was built, including highways of tamped earth with a top layer of gravel, kept in good repair by dedicated teams, up to one man for every kilometre of road. Engineers of the China International Famine Relief Commission completed some of the major thoroughfares. A railway was under construction. Telephone lines were erected right up to the areas near the red state. The local militia were reorganised, partially armed and placed under the control of their magistrates. Higher up the ladder, Chiang installed trusted governors in the key provinces, not least Jiangxi, run by Xiong Shihui, a small, alert man keen on reform.[55]

Chiang's military strategy changed. Instead of chasing guerrilla bands across vast mountainous expanses, his troops began to build blockhouses of red or grey stone around the soviet, one for every village with 200 families or more. These were usually unmanned, although a few came with a wing to house a couple of soldiers, others with an overhanging crow's nest. All were encircled by a trench, with a curved roof and an inscribed tablet over the door. Towns had their city walls reconditioned, with further forts, trenches and entanglements on the outskirts. In Nanchang, where the city wall had been converted into a wide boulevard, a new rampart was built from scratch. German military advisers were recruited to help implement the scheme and complete it efficiently.[56]

Chiang was also betting on education, decreeing that twelve special schools be opened in each of the sixty-three counties under government control in Jiangxi. Three 'normal schools for rural education' opened in the province, with a fourth on the books. Two hundred of its graduates dispensed advice to the villagers. Reformatories for captured or repentant Communists were built. In Nanchang, 5,000 inmates were divided into three categories, each wearing a different badge: soldiers who had crossed over (purple badge), prisoners of war (green badge) and political prisoners (red badge). The schools and reformatories, like the roads and the blockhouses, were to extend gradually into red areas as soon as ground was recovered. Mutual aid societies were encouraged, with 1,800 appearing after the Flood Relief Commission loaned them 590,000 dollars in 1931 to purchase food, cattle, tools and seed. The provincial authorities set up a further 300. Cooperative credit societies, too, were established, with low interest rates for members. A stable grain market – possibly statecraft's most enduring challenge since time immemorial – was pursued under the auspices of a Bureau of Food Control, providing the province with the information required to enter the market as a purchaser and either raise or stabilise prices, buying, transporting and storing in government warehouses before selling again.[57]

Most of these schemes took time and could hardly be expected to solve within a single season problems accumulated over centuries. But the villagers did receive instant relief by the change in how they were required to pay their taxes: the much reviled tax collectors were eliminated, with dues paid directly to the magistrate. Though less dramatic than the burning of all title deeds and mortgages by the Communists, this approach had its appeal for those familiar with the usual consequences following the advent of a soviet form of government.[58]

The most important change, arguably, was in the soldiers themselves. The quickest and most foolproof method of turning entire villages against the government was to billet troops permanently on them, as they mercilessly conscripted, taxed, extorted and generally abused the local population, creating the ideal conditions of extreme distress in which communism or other forms of organised rebellion thrived. When a detachment of government troops surrendered, sometimes the soldiers were not even recruited by the Red Army but given a dollar or two, for they were less valuable as allies than as parasites living on the surrounding country. After the Nineteenth Route Army had defeated the Communists in large parts of Fujian, they imposed taxes so heavy and oppressive that whole communities deserted their villages. In 1933, the British consul in Fuzhou opined that the poor were better off under the Communists. But he also observed that this was not the case for districts under direct government control. Their troops were tidy and well equipped, some with a steel helmet, others with a straw hat, each carrying a face towel, a trenching tool, ammunition in a cloth belt, a mess tin and a mug. Where previously villagers had been press-ganged and marched to the front under escort, they now received regular pay, were treated well and were generally disciplined. Rice depots, as well as the new roads, helped ensure that troops had to depend less on foraging for food. Most of all, Special Movement Corps (*biedongdui*), called 'Einsatzgruppen' by their German advisers, acted as Chiang Kai-shek's eyes in every district, reporting any irregularity, abuse of power, failure to fight, disloyalty or oppression of villagers directly to him.[59]

The new approach was time-consuming but effective. On the one hand, the cordon began choking off the soviet; on the other, local rehabilitation projects attempted to decrease the ranks of malcontents. But the defeat of the Jiangxi Soviet, by October 1934, was ultimately of the Chinese Communist Party's own making. Since the encirclement made outflanking operations and other tactical manoeuvres impossible, the First Red Army was placed on the defensive. Guerrilla warfare was no longer an option, since the Nationalists moved slowly, consolidating new advances with more fortifications and trenches. Instead, the First Red Army undertook a series of frontal attacks on fortified towns. Encouraged by its Comintern advisers, it began to defend strategically unimportant towns, portraying surrender as politically unacceptable. 'Cities captured from the enemy must be held, the surrounding areas must be fortified and the local population enrolled to defend them,' Moscow instructed in March 1934. Three months later, the main Comintern agent in Shanghai reported back to Moscow, describing the losses resulting from continuous positional warfare without adequate supplies as 'enormous'. In defending the city of Guangchang alone, the Red Army lost a fifth of its troops.[60]

Even before Chiang Kai-shek's blockhouse operations had begun in October 1933, some 80 per cent of all men had been forcibly recruited, leaving a rural economy in freefall and a population on the edge of starvation. Relentless campaigns to squeeze ever more resources from the population followed, carried out under threat of violence. In March 1934, the renewed land distribution undertaken by Mao was judged inadequate, with a further campaign launched to identify even more hidden opponents of the regime. Leaders now called for a Red Terror, 'because only a reign of Red Terror can possibly stop or paralyse the counter-revolutionary activities of the landlords and rich peasants'. On 23 May, the soviet announced that in every war zone 'all landlords and rich peasants who engage in counter-revolutionary activities must be arrested and executed on the spot.' Soldiers, on capturing a city, were enjoined to use Red Terror and 'kill those who spread rumours and cause trouble, kill those who work as spies for the enemy, kill those who sabotage the revolution, kill those who lead others to defect!' But even outside areas where war operations were in progress, a wave of terror led to the wrongful execution of 'rich farmers'. The abuse was so extreme that one month later Zhang Wentian, premier of the Jiangxi Soviet, was forced to intervene. Some 'wavering elements in our Party have become utterly confused', he announced on 28 June, using the terror not only 'to deal with the counter-revolutionary landlords and rich peasants, but also to use it against all landlords and rich peasants'. The outcome of these measures, Zhang pointed out, was 'panic among the masses', since everyone could be deemed a suspect.[61]

Soldiers deserted, convicts escaped, villagers fled. As early as December 1933, desertion had become so common that culprits were ordered to be shot on the spot if they ran away with their guns. Ringleaders of entire squads, platoons or companies that deserted en masse were to be tried in public and shot. Those who assisted deserters by forging an official seal or travel pass were also to be executed. In May 1934, young boys aged six and above were asked to join the ranks of the Red Army and 'sacrifice their blood' in defence of the Jiangxi Soviet. But, despite a desperate search for recruits and stringent rules against desertion, ever growing numbers of soldiers crossed over to the enemy. Some of the boy scouts themselves took to the mountains. 'Having been repeatedly defeated by government forces on the battlefield and having found the people who used to be with them now siding with the government, the Communists in Jiangxi and Fujian have been disheartened and consider their cause a lost one,' reported the *China Press* after interviewing many of the rank and file who had absconded.[62]

Bands of migratory victims, many having lost family members and property, took to the forests and mountains. Desperate for food and weapons, they ambushed and attacked Communist soldiers by night. In parts of the soviet, thousands of young men joined millennial secret societies, for instance the Big Sword Society, that were also turning against the Communists. In July 1934, near Ganzhou, local cadres took the lead in shepherding entire villages across the border into government-controlled territory. On one occasion twenty such escapees were lured back by the Communists with promises of better treatment, only to end up in prison, serving as a deterrent to others. Incidents of mass flight were common, even in areas far removed from the border, according to a Communist report. As Cao Boyi, the foremost historian of the Jiangxi Soviet, wrote more than half a century ago, the government's blockhouse strategy provided the villagers with an opportunity to escape safely, turning a trickle of desertions into a flood, ultimately leading to the collapse of the soviet.[63]

In June, government forces began to advance in two columns towards Ruijin. They moved slowly, taking several months to reach their target, as the Communists fought for every bit of ground, destroying bridges and torching abandoned towns. In November, at long last, the troops entered the city. It was deserted, since the Communists had forced its inhabitants to evacuate under threat of death. The soldiers found the wreckage of a six-year effort to establish a Chinese Soviet Republic, with burned villages, devastated temples and deserted farms. Hundreds of bodies were strewn around, including women and children, wild dogs nibbling at body parts. Tingzhou, not far away from Ruijin, presented the same scene of desolation, with ruined shops, charred buildings and empty fields. In Ningdu, a city to which the Communists had retreated just weeks before its fall, women and old men made up the local population. A Confucian temple, used as an execution ground, was heavily pitted with bullet holes. The ground in a graveyard was littered with skulls and remains of people hastily decapitated by the fleeing rebels. Some five kilometres from the city, they also found a natural rock fortress rising high above the surrounding valley. Here, more than 500 people had taken refuge, fighting off a siege mounted by the Communists. Exhausted, the defenders had been forced to yield after a stubborn thirteen months, with the 300 survivors paraded through the streets of Ningdu before being beheaded.[64]

Mass graves were discovered across the soviet. In Toubeizhen, a small town east of Guangchang, a burial site with 5,000 corpses was found. Thousands more were located in pits scattered around Ningdu. Locals stumbled upon a thousand decomposed corpses along a river, most of them washed up on the banks or buried in the sand. One cable sent to Nanjing mentioned that the retreating Communists had massacred up to 10,000 civilians in the countryside surrounding Ji'an, including Fengxi, Anyuan and Wucun. Estimates of the total death toll were advanced, including a high of 1 million, but none were very convincing, not least because the area occupied by the Communists was always shifting, villagers as well as soldiers often died in raids carried out beyond the soviet, and no one had kept track of how many local people had escaped and never returned. But one figure was based on carefully computed numbers: of an original population of 5.6 million, only 4.3 million remained, indicating the loss of 1.3 million people.[65]

5
Survival
(1934–1936)

While searching for surviving documents in the liberated areas of Jiangxi, time and again the government authorities came across the writings of a foreign leader, namely Li De. Luo Zhuoying, one of the generals who had led the march on Ruijin, expressed his admiration for the 'brilliant mind' sent by Moscow who had so masterfully analysed every stage of the campaign and even predicted the government troops' most recent operations. Otto Braun, who assumed the name of Li De, had arrived in the Jiangxi Soviet in September 1933, to become the main military adviser charged with implementing instructions from Moscow. Born near Munich, Braun had joined the Communist movement at an early age, participating in an uprising that led to the establishment of the ill-fated Bavarian Soviet Republic in 1919. He landed in prison on several occasions, charged in 1928 with high treason. He escaped to the Soviet Union, where the Comintern sent him to China.[1]

A tall man with blue eyes peering through large, round eyeglasses, Otto Braun had studied at the Frunze Military Academy in Moscow, and admitted being rigid in issuing orders, which he dispensed liberally on a broad range of subjects, from the military to the economy. He was also prone to ignoring the views of others, including Zhou Enlai. In May 1934, preparations for a breakthrough from the area had been set in motion, but in August Zhou began to propose the wholesale evacuation of the soviet, including all its installations, instead of the temporary retreat planned by Braun. This implied a much larger and more cumbersome operation, with non-combat troops moving alongside fighting units to carry large quantities of equipment and war materiel. Bo Gu had envisaged a more mobile force with a residual base left behind in Ruijin. Zhou's views prevailed, and a date was set for October. On the 16th the Red Army attacked a weak spot in the fortified perimeter near Yudu, some forty kilometres to the west of Ruijin. They encountered very little resistance. A force of about 75,000 to 81,000 men broke through, including 60,000 combat troops. Among them were fifty women, mainly the wives of top leaders, segregated in a special unit. All other women were left behind, 'and unfortunately afterward many were killed'. The men were divided into two groups. The first was the command column, with all the key leaders and staff troops; the second comprised support services, including a field hospital and a reserve division, also transporting hundreds of bundles of propaganda leaflets, silver and gold in kerosene tins, and arsenal machinery. Each person had individual rations meant to last for about two weeks. Soldiers carried the leaders, including Mao, in sedan chairs.[2]

The operation had been meticulously prepared over many months, in top secrecy, with Otto Braun, Zhou Enlai and Bo Gu in charge. Mao did not learn of the evacuation plan until October. But the scheme suffered from one major flaw: the triumvirate had no clear destination in mind. The initial idea was to link up with He Long in the Hubei area, or join Zhang Guotao, who had retreated to Sichuan, but concrete information about both was sparse. Military intelligence, however, indicated that a triangle existed on the borders of Guangxi, Hunan and Guizhou which was relatively free of enemy fortifications. It helped that Chen Jitang, the governor of Guangdong who had agreed to buy the soviet's tungsten, was willing to extend his trade agreement to include a ceasefire and right of way for the Red Army. Chen, one might surmise, calculated that if the Communists were to move towards Hunan, Guangxi, Guizhou and Sichuan, they would burden his rivals, among them Chiang Kai-shek, while keeping clear of his own province.[3]

The Red Army successfully broke through a series of fortified rings, trekking west for several weeks along the Hunan and Guangxi borders, through precipitous gorges and over mountain passes, much of it uncharted terrain. The troops moved slowly, not least the support column, with thousands of carriers lugging along bulky equipment, including office furniture and a printing press, meant to help build a new soviet behind enemy lines. They trudged along by night to avoid detection, further impeding progress. As the weeks passed, the heavy furniture, printing machines and even Party documents were dumped, some of them buried, while the reserves and the porters began to abscond. Special units were established to prevent the marchers from escaping, with the authority to execute culprits if they would not stop, but to little avail. 'Today over one hundred soldiers dropped behind on the march,' one commissar noted in his diary. The strategy was to feign illness, straggle and then hide in a village. In one army of 10,000 for which specific figures are available, more than 4,000 men deserted within the first six weeks. One thousand were caught, including 857 who were subsequently executed. Standard procedure was for a deserter to confess in front of the assembled troops, kneel and be shot in the head.[4]

The Red Army encountered their first disaster near the Xiang River in the north-west of Guangxi province. By then, desertion had reduced the troops from 81,000 to about 64,000. The Xiang had its source just north of Guilin, capital of Guangxi province, flowing past the hills and paddy fields of Hunan, straight through the capital Changsha, to disgorge its muddy waters into Lake Dongting. It was the chief means of transportation for the province until the advent of the railway. Chiang Kai-shek's troops were in pursuit, moving in parallel towards the river. The Red Army planned to cross at Quanzhou, a walled city where the Canton–Hankou railway began following the river north. The whole area had been transformed into an extensive fortress, with a vast system of trenches and forts with stone walls up to a metre thick.

Reporting posts were everywhere. An enemy brigade, moreover, had arrived first and occupied Quanzhou. Reinforcements were on the way, with provincial troops hurrying along the motor road from Guilin, including infantry, light artillery, a machine-gun corps, cavalry and soldiers pushing and pulling wheelbarrows. Instead of bypassing the town, Mao demanded a battle. The Military Council was split, with Zhu De casting the decisive vote in favour of an attack.[5]

Even as the Communists bickered over the plan, the provincial troops approached both their flanks and ambushed them, mercilessly hammering their positions for three days and three nights, causing thousands of casualties. The battle provided cover for the remaining Communist forces to cross the river on improvised pontoons twenty kilometres further south, even as they were strafed by enemy aircraft. By the time the Red Army emerged on the other side, their numbers had been reduced to about 35,000. The *South China Morning Post*, in what remains the most probable estimate, ventured that the Communists suffered 10,000 men killed and 6,000 taken prisoner. Large numbers also succumbed to cold and hunger, abandoned by their comrades along the way. In Jieshou alone, the local authorities tried to care for 3,000 of these 'human derelicts', although their condition was such that a dozen died every night.[6]

It should have been relatively easy for the vast armies assembled by the central government to mop up the remaining forces, but Chiang changed tack. Throughout, he had viewed the Communists as an impediment to his vision of a sovereign and united nation. But now he realised that he could drive their remnant forces through the last provinces in the south which still resisted the writ from Nanjing, using them as a pretext to send government troops in pursuit and occupy their territory. He told his secretary Chen Bulei: 'Sichuan, Guizhou, Yunnan: each one of these three provinces is an enemy. If the Communists enter Guizhou we can just follow them, it is a better strategy than using the troops to conquer the place. Sichuan and Yunnan will have to welcome us if only to save themselves.'[7]

The government troops moved strategically, positioning themselves in such a way that the Red Army advanced slowly but surely into the province of Guizhou along overland routes, plundering every village through which they passed. Once they had entered Guizhou, the provincial troops from Guangxi abandoned the chase. In Guizhou the Communists looted and partly torched the walled city of Liping on 15 December. 'From all reports it would seem that the bulk of the Red Army is being disturbed but little by the rearguard actions that are taking place at various intervals along the way,' a bemused journalist from the *North-China Herald* observed. The Communists continued to head west, although their final destination was still undecided. Otto Braun suggested joining He Long's Second Red Army, even though radio contact with the group had been lost. Instead, Mao preferred staying in Guizhou. Zhou Enlai agreed, shifting his allegiance for the first time towards Mao. They settled on Zunyi, 300 kilometres from Liping, a destination easily reached within a few weeks, with abundant supplies captured from rich trading centres along the way.[8]

The main obstacle to Zunyi was the Wu River, narrow and torrential, moving in a broad arc north-east through the mountainous terrain of central Guizhou as it was joined by numerous tributaries before merging with the Yangtze River near Chongqing. The Wu was famed for its narrow junks, designed to navigate the sharp corners of the river on its lower waters. The provincial troops guarding it were badly armed and poorly trained, with little incentive to fight. 'We literally drove them away before us,' Otto Braun remembered. It took two days to build bamboo bridges to cross the river. Zunyi sat in a small valley, gateway to the fertile plains leading to Chongqing. The city, conquered on 7 January 1935, had enormous stores of food and textiles, which were promptly plundered, although they were still insufficient to accommodate the needs of the Red Army. Villages in the vicinity were ransacked as well. The Communists stayed only two weeks, although propaganda teams were formed, mass meetings held, committees established and even land reform started.[9]

Mao used the break to convene a meeting of the Politburo. Since leaving the soviet he had been busy manoeuvring for support against Otto Braun, Bo Gu and the other 'Bolsheviks', even though in principle an enlarged session could not be held without the presence of members from the other base areas, above all Zhang Guotao and He Long. Forty people assembled, all of them given the right to vote, although only a dozen were actual Politburo members. At Ningdu, in October 1928, Mao's grip on the Red Army had been broken; at Zunyi in January 1935 he reclaimed it. Most participants listened in silence as Mao laid into his opponents, castigating them for 'right opportunism'. His most vocal supporter was Lin Biao, 'who cultivated an especially rude tone'. The outcome was that Bo Gu was ousted as general secretary of the Party, replaced by Zhang Wentian, an ideal candidate since he was one of the so-called 'Bolsheviks' but had also formed a close bond with Mao during the march. Mao removed Zhou Enlai as de facto commander-in-chief and claimed the position for himself. A 'resolution' was passed, although it was not minuted and was never mentioned again until the dissolution of the Comintern in 1943. It was, in effect, a carefully calculated coup.[10]

Zunyi was abandoned on 19 January. The plan was now to move north and cross the Yangtze into Sichuan in order to join the Fourth Red Army. But enemy forces sealed off the whole of the Yangtze River. Mao, keen to score a victory as new leader, confronted the enemy at Tucheng. Even as his troops were dealt a resounding defeat, he refused to withdraw. 'They broke through us, captured a hilltop, and cut our corps into several segments,' one survivor recalled. 'They poured bullets down on us. It was terrible, we didn't have a chance. We kept retreating towards the town. The shooting only stopped at nightfall.' In Chongqing, a relieved population poured into the streets to celebrate as a central government representative announced that the Communists in Guizhou were a spent force. Licking their wounds, the Communists wandered the countryside for several weeks, then turned back and reoccupied Zunyi. The once thriving city presented a desolate sight, its shops standing empty, homes plundered and boarded up, with shredded posters acclaiming the revolution fluttering in the wind. A new plan was ratified, namely to march towards the south of Guizhou and then veer back up north through Yunnan to find a crossing point across the upper reaches of the Yangtze.[11]

While the Communists were still roaming the countryside, central government troops marched into Guiyang, the capital of Guizhou located south of Zunyi. They investigated the administration of Wang Jialie, the provincial governor, who was widely despised for oppressing the local population with exorbitant taxes. Wang, known as the 'King of Guizhou', a man who 'is out for nothing but his own interests', resigned on 8 April. Chiang Kai-shek, among a series of measures taken to lift the province out of its misery, personally ordered a one-year suspension of the land tax.[12]

In Sichuan, too, the central government began to play a much larger role. The province was easily the worst governed of China, divided into different garrison areas that were often at war with each other. Already in February 1933, Chiang Kai-shek had ordered Zhang Qun, former mayor of Shanghai, to take over the provincial administration and create a coalition between the six local armies battling each other, with the aim of uniting them against the Communists. Liu Xiang, whose troops were based in Chongqing, was politically more astute than his rivals and promised to cooperate with central government troops in suppressing the Communist forces. In February 1935, the Generalissimo personally moved from Nanchang to Chongqing to supervise operations against the Communists in neighbouring Guizhou. The streets were decorated with red lanterns in his honour. His troops behaved well, and were welcomed by a population alarmed at the prospect of an invasion by the Communists. Their predatory behaviour, it seemed, was a blessing in disguise. Chiang Kai-shek wasted no time. The entire provincial administration was reorganised under his direct supervision. Liu Xiang was appointed provincial governor. Soon afterwards, Liu dutifully issued a manifesto lightening the tax burden. In April, Tian Songyao, who had mercilessly exploited his own population even as he fought Zhang Guotao, was summarily dismissed, to be court-martialled at a later date.[13]

In March, the Communists again left Zunyi behind, setting off on their journey to Sichuan via Yunnan. But time and again they encountered government troops, who prevented them from moving westward. For the best part of two months, they tramped around in huge circles, occasionally engaging in a few skirmishes, but more often than not avoiding their opponents. Otto Braun considered that the whole enterprise 'degenerated into outright flight', as the Communists followed zigzag routes with endless forward and backward marches and diversionary movements. The aimless wandering was later described as a clever ploy to confuse the enemy, but the initiative clearly lay with the government troops. Chiang had learned important lessons in fighting the guerrillas, not least the futility of sending formal troops to pursue lightly equipped adversaries who travelled by night through inhospitable, densely covered terrain, often enduring the cold winter rain. Guizhou had hundreds of square kilometres of small, conical hills enveloped by mist. It was Chiang who applied the principles of guerrilla warfare, making sure that troops were always on his enemy's heels, blocking access to easy terrain and much needed supplies, hoping to tire them out. Unlike his opponents, he had a clear strategy: 'ingenuity in varying tactics depends on mother wit', meaning that traditional warfare must be discarded in favour of adapting to the terrain. Attrition rather than confrontation was the goal. The Communists were exhausted, with disease, hunger and desertion cutting large swathes through the troops. 'They run as we rest,' the Generalissimo pointed out, until 'in the end they collapse altogether.'[14]

The Communists themselves became confused by the endless marching, chasing, feigning and running. One radio operator wondered why they had crossed the same river and passed through the same villages so many times. Mao's greatest critic was Lin Biao, who became so frustrated that he wrote to the Military Council to complain about his mentor: 'This will wear down the troops, is it appropriate to lead like this?'[15]

On several occasions they were badly battered. In early April in Xifeng, where the population panicked and took to the roads when the Communists approached, they sustained heavy casualties. A few weeks later, 2,000 dispirited men with their weapons were captured in Longli county, twenty-five kilometres north of Guiyang. 'They showed a broken morale and offered no resistance.' Members of the Red Cross who followed in the path of the Communists reportedly found several badly wounded soldiers, unable to move and 'groaning in filled graves'.[16]

Towards the end of the month, hundreds more were killed in furious fighting as the marchers broke through a cordon to cross the border into Yunnan. By now, the troops had been reduced to about 22,000 soldiers, according to the Party's own General Headquarters. 'Virtually all the fatalities had been caused by the march itself or unintended but forced battles,' or so Otto Braun opined. On 24 April, they finally entered Yunnan province, making their way rapidly north past Kunming, the capital reinforced by hastily constructed loopholed walls of mud and brick, sandbags and barbed wire, machine guns and trenches. They took the county seat of Wuding instead, releasing all prisoners, ransacking the place, destroying municipal records and eliminating officials and all the wealthy notables they could find. But reports that the wife and eight children of the magistrate had had their throats cut were found to be inaccurate. The marauders reached the Jinsha River marking the frontier with Sichuan around 1 May. The provincial governor had demanded that all the boats on the river be destroyed, and all dwellings on the south bank burned. His orders were not followed, even though a few vessels here and there were filled with stones and sunk. The soldiers felled trees to build floating bridges over the turbulent river, allowing 15,000 followers to cross.[17]

Once in Sichuan, the Communists besieged Huili, a strategic city on the provincial border with high, impregnable walls surrounded by a moat. The commander in charge was as ruthless as the Communists, and burned all houses in the vicinity to deprive them of supplies. Scouting planes dropped bombs, although it took much longer for government reinforcements to arrive. They surrounded the Communists, giving the defenders an opportunity to make a series of charges, with ferocious hand-to-hand fighting. It was a resounding defeat for the Red Army, which sustained enormous losses and was compelled to withdraw. Peng Dehuai now rallied behind Lin Biao in taking Mao to task for his disastrous military leadership. His stance cost him dearly, as he was denounced as a 'right opportunist' and forced to make a self-criticism.[18]

Ahead lay forbidding highlands inhabited by the Lolo, guerrilla fighters who waged a relentless war against government troops. Given their common enemy, a treaty was easily concluded, granting the Red Army food and safe passage. Sichuan was emerging from the winter, with fields of rapeseed in blossom, intermingled with white magnolia and cherry blossom. The melting snow from the Himalayas turned rivers into raging torrents. The troops hoped to cross the Dadu River near Shimian, but found the ferry destroyed and the east bank sealed off by government troops. The main forces decided to move a hundred kilometres further north towards Luding, the site of an eighteenth-century suspension bridge which had been part of an ancient imperial road connecting Lhasa, the capital of Tibet, to Chengdu.[19]

The crossing of the Luding bridge on 29 May 1935 must be one of the most celebrated battles in the Chinese revolution. Countless propaganda films have been churned out depicting a squad of soldiers bravely crawling across the hundred-metre span of iron chains from which all wooden boards had been removed, hanging perilously above the rushing waters far below, even as enemy guns sprayed them with bullets. They inched forward, with several soldiers hit by bullets and tumbling to their deaths, until their opponents panicked and tried to set fire to the few remaining planks. The enemy fled in terror as determined soldiers stood up and ran the last few metres through the flames, their clothes and eyebrows singed by fire.[20]

In 1997, the Sichuan-born historian Chang Jung visited the site and interviewed a sprightly ninety-three-year-old. A Catholic, like many locals in the area in the 1930s, she remembered that the Communists had borrowed her doors and those of neighbours to put on the bridge, but did not recall the soldiers coming under any fire at all. Chang Jung concluded that the real story of the battle was not quite that she had been told. For this and other critical comments, a small but vociferous army of sinologists roundly condemned her, as did the formidable Party machine in the People's Republic. She was never again invited to an academic conference.[21]

In 2004, Sun Shuyun set out to retrace the Long March and interviewed a tall, broad-shouldered blacksmith who had also helped lend the doors of his home. He explained that the guards on the other side had old weapons that could barely be fired and fled the moment the Red Army approached. 'There wasn't really much of a battle,' he said. Sun too concluded that the real story of the battle was not quite that she had been told. No sinologist uttered a word.[22]

Still, legitimate doubts remain over the value of two interviews conducted sixty years after the events took place. But locals were not the only witnesses. The region was largely evangelised by French priests, many working in isolated hamlets, some seldom speaking their mother tongue except when they travelled to meet each other. They sent regular reports to their Consulate in Chengdu, a number of which have been preserved in the National Archives in Nantes. One such was written by Father Valentin, who devoted his life to the local inhabitants of Luding. He watched as the Communists arrived on 29 May. 'Not a shot was fired at them,' he declared in his account of the events. It took six days for an estimated 20,000 soldiers and a few hundred women to pass through the town. No one fell off the bridge, no one set fire to it and no one died in crossfire. 'They ransacked everything on their way and burned down a good part of the market at Luding,' he commented. In Lengqi, a few kilometres up the road, they confiscated all the grain they could lay their hands on, and proceeded to strip the local leper hospital of all its possessions, including books, beds, food, medical instruments and medicine. Georges Bechamp, the consul who read all incoming reports, noted that wherever the Communists went they acted as 'absolute masters' of the premises, encouraging the local riff-raff to join them in plundering the property of those considered to be better off. Spotter planes saw houses on fire when the Communists were forced by approaching troops to move on. But before they ran off they tried to destroy the bridge, managing to cut all but four of the eighteen chains that held together 'the finest bridge in China and the wonder of foreign engineers'. Half a year later the bridge was under repair at an estimated cost of 120,000 dollars.[23]

The region was controlled by Liu Wenhui, the general ousted from Chengdu in 1933, and it was he who had probably ordered his men to evacuate Luding. Liu was a master of the skirmish, keen to preserve his troops by avoiding all conflict yet careful not to provoke the ire of Chiang Kai-shek. He was hardly alone in viewing the Communists as a plague to be passed on as quickly as possible to neighbouring rivals. The longer they stayed, the higher the price to pay, not least since the Red Army was constantly trying to replenish its ranks. Locals encouraged to participate in the looting had no option but to join, either as porters or as soldiers. In some villages every young man was recruited, voluntarily or not. In Party parlance, this was termed 'draining the pond to catch the fish'. When villagers went into hiding, Red Pioneers were sent to find them and force them to attend a village meeting on pain of death. After a defector or two had been shot in the head in front of the assembled villagers, they meekly signed up their sons.[24]

Outside Luding, central government troops blocked the Communists' attempt to move eastward, forcing them to continue further north into even more inhospitable highland, this time dominated by Tibetans. There were no roads, only narrow paths though treacherous moors, vast primeval forests, torrents spanned by bamboo bridges and mountain passes four or five thousand metres above sea level. Spring seemed to recede, as temperatures plunged to freezing point at night. The Communists, used to plundering the countryside for supplies, discovered that the locals would drive their livestock away to hide in the forests and mountains. In a world turned upside down, they were the ones to practise guerrilla warfare on the Communists, ambushing isolated groups and straddlers. 'More and more, our route was lined with the bodies of the slain, frozen or simply exhausted,' Otto Braun wrote. They all had lice. Bleeding dysentery was rife, while typhus made an appearance. Chiang Kai-shek's strategy was paying off.[25]

Towards the middle of June, the Communists managed to capture the small town of Tianquan. News reached them that the Fourth Red Army under Zhang Guotao and Xu Xiangqian was on its way towards Mougong, a small town with a highway to Chengdu. Panic began to spread in Chengdu, where it was feared that the two armies might combine and descend upon the city, located in a vast plain bordered by a semicircle of steep mountains. The First Red Army arrived in Mougong a week later, finding a lama settlement abandoned by the locals. A few days later they were contacted by envoys from Zhang Guotao, and trekked to the Lianghekou district. What they discovered astonished them: the Fourth Red Army was twice the size of their own army, their soldiers well fed and warmly dressed, with ample supplies to spare.[26]

***

In November 1934 Zhang Guotao had begun to prepare for a retreat from his soviet around Tongjiang. He had followed the First Red Army's every move, believing that they were headed for western Sichuan. The moment he realised that Mao and Zhu had managed to cross into Yunnan province, he and his followers set off towards the Mougong area, some 500 kilometres to the west as the crow flies. The easiest route would have been down the highlands into the plains all the way to Chengdu, and then back up into the mountains. But even crossing the Jialing, a deep and wide river with rapids raging past cliffs and precipices, was an unusual military challenge, with provincial troops strategically deployed along the west bank. The river cut the province into two halves, east and west, rushing down the mountains before widening into a broad navigable estuary that meandered down to Chongqing, where it joined the Yangtze.[27]

The Fourth Red Army opted to cross at Cangxi, building many dozens of makeshift rafts that were carried over the mountains. In April 1935 they took the provincial troops by surprise, building a pontoon, seizing local vessels and crossing in the middle of the night. Panic now seized Chengdu, with several hundred foreigners evacuating in motor cars, joined by thousands of locals streaming south towards Chongqing. Chiang rushed five of his own divisions into the province to protect the city. The Communists had no alternative but to trek around the plain through difficult mountain terrain, passing through Jiange and Jiangyou before claiming a temporary capital in the small city of Beichuan towards the end of May. Beichuan, in a valley surrounded by high peaks with twisting, steep roads hewn out of rocky cliffs, was also poor, dominated by minority people with their own headmen, lamas and chieftains. Decades of communism after 1949 would do little to alleviate the poverty, and in 2008 a devastating earthquake wiped the place off the map altogether.[28]

Having realised that the Chinese Central Soviet had ceased to function since the First Red Army had left Jiangxi, Zhang Guotao decided to establish a North-west Federation in Beichuan instead. Taxes were abolished, rents reduced and opium prohibited. But to survive he and his followers had to adapt to local customs, not the reverse. Throughout, ferocious fighting took place with government troops. Bombers targeted Communist positions near their temporary capital, inflicting heavy casualties. In June 1935 they set out for Mougong, passing through highlands dominated by Tibetans.[29]

The meeting at Lianghekou went badly. Zhu De admired the Fourth Red Army, admitting that his own force 'used to be a giant, but now all the muscles are gone, there is only a skeleton left'. But Mao Zedong was suspicious of a charismatic, confident rival who could steal his thunder. The North-west Federation seemed like a direct challenge for leadership. In a whispering campaign, Zhang Guotao was accused of 'opportunism' and 'political backwardness'. Zhang, in turn, questioned the validity of the decisions reached at Zunyi, not least the manner in which Mao had been coopted on to the Politburo. They also differed over the strategy to be pursued. Both leaders wanted to move as closely as possible to the border with the Soviet Union, realising that without financial and military assistance from Moscow, they could not survive. Zhang's goal was to make his way to Xinjiang through Qinghai province. But the First Red Army, already exhausted by ten months of relentless marches, were reluctant to tramp over frozen passes, through a high moorland and across the stony deserts and salt plains of Central Asia. A compromise was reached, as the troops were divided into two columns that would advance separately towards Gansu, where Mao would veer east along the ancient silk road towards Shaanxi, while Zhang would go west towards Xinjiang. North of Mougong, both columns found a land scrubbed of food. Alerted to their arrival, the locals had abandoned towns and farms, hidden or carried away their provisions and driven off their livestock. Zhang ended up trapped in a remote corner where he had to fight the Tibetans for survival. 'The resistance of the Tibetans made us feel ashamed,' Zhang later admitted.[30]

But it was the right column under Mao which encountered the most difficult terrain, as the mountains led into a high plateau at 4,000 metres above sea level. 'A deceptive green cover hid a black viscous swamp, which sucked in anyone who broke through the thin crust or strayed from the narrow path.' Cold rain turned into sleet at night, when soldiers huddled together in a desolate landscape devoid of even a shrub as far as the eye could see. Some of them never woke up. Conditions eased up after a week, but the march to Gansu was equally arduous, with mountain peaks alternating with barren precipices, storming rivers spanned by suspension bridges, all these natural barriers dotted here and there with garrisoned towns that had to be assaulted, often at great cost, or somehow circumvented. In Gansu the marchers encountered advance troops of Hu Zongnan, a Whampoa graduate and fearsome general who had earlier blocked their way on the Sichuan plateau. There were skirmishes rather than battles. By the end of September, the First Red Army approached the area of Minxian in south Gansu, a mere hundred kilometres south of the capital Lanzhou on the Yellow River, not far from an enormous loess plateau to the east, formed by sediments of yellow, porous dust deposited by the wind over the centuries. The loess hills straddling the border between eastern Gansu and northern Shaanxi, described by a traveller in 1913 as 'a nest of plunderers lost in the wilderness', had for centuries provided refuge for bandit gangs. Missionaries began to leave their stations for Lanzhou.[31]

In Gansu members of a local Pioneer Corps under the command of Xu Haidong and Liu Zhidan approached the First Red Army, briefing the troops and helping them navigate their way through Gansu towards Shaanxi. As the mountains began to recede and the troops entered loess country, cave dwellings replaced houses while food became scarcer due to the partially calcified soil. Roads eroded quickly and often sunk below the surface, with the wooden wheels of ox and donkey carts pulverising the brittle earth. In October, some 6,000 survivors of the Long March arrived in Wayaobao, a small mining town near Yan'an in north Shaanxi.

Chiang Kai-shek had used the Communists to impose a measure of unity on the more dysfunctional southern provinces, sending central troops to Guizhou and Sichuan. Hu Zongnan, who blocked the way for the Communists to Xinjiang, was about to enter Lanzhou, transforming how Gansu province was run. There was another component to the pursuit of the Communists through vast stretches of inhospitable land: the Generalissimo knew that the main enemy was Japan, but could hardly train his troops openly in preparation for war with a militarily superior enemy who had troops deployed across Manchuria. As one astute military attaché from the United States remarked, the anti-Communist campaign not only kept a vast army of men occupied, but also provided training for the troops, much as Mexican Border service did for the National Guard just before the entry of the United States into the First World War. Noted the British military attaché in Nanjing in June 1936, reports about activities against Communists 'to a very large extent are intended to cover Chiang Kai-shek's military preparations against the possibility of war with Japan'. A Japanese naval attaché expressed a similar thought, observing that Chiang Kai-shek 'used the Communist menace as an excuse for training his troops in actual warfare'.[32]

Japan was conscious of the danger. What Tokyo feared most was an alliance between Nanjing and Moscow. On 17 December

1932, almost exactly five years to the day after Chiang Kai-shek had expelled all Soviet consuls and commercial agencies, diplomatic relations between the Soviet Union and China had resumed. This was the logical outcome of Japan's invasion of Manchuria, not least when followed by resounding inaction on the part of the League of Nations. On the other hand, the moment the Kwantung Army arrived in Harbin, the two rivals suddenly shared a border stretching well over 2,000 kilometres. Between 1 March 1932, when Japan turned Manchuria into the puppet state of Manchukuo, using the last Qing emperor Pu Yi as a figurehead, and 30 November 1935, Tokyo denounced 255 illegal acts and incidents along the Manchu–Soviet border, including thirty aircraft intrusions. Across the Amur River in Vladivostok, ancient fortifications were being bulked up, with a steady stream of planes and submarines spotted in the port. The local population was wretched, but grain arrived regularly by ship from Argentina and Australia to feed 5,000 marines.[33]

In the summer of 1935, Chiang Kai-shek was forced to make yet another concession to Japan. In a secret agreement between He Yingqin and Yoshijirō Umezu, commander-in-chief of the Kwantung Army, all troops and organisations seen to be inimical to Japan were forced out of Hebei and Chahar provinces. Rumours initiated by the Japanese news agency in Tokyo, given full prominence by papers in Shanghai, began to circulate, alleging that the Generalissimo had reached an understanding with the Communists and that Nationalist Party leaders were openly urging an alliance with the Soviet Union in order to counter Japan. Major General Kenji Doihara, director of the Special Service Division of the Kwantung Army, began to discuss measures to prevent Communist penetration into Chahar. By October, as the Chinese Communists arrived in Wayaobao, they were 600 kilometres away.[34]

***

Behind the allegations of a secret deal between Chiang Kai-shek and the Communists was the escape of the Second Red Army under He Long. In 1933, government troops had driven He and what remained of his battered forces all the way back to Hefeng. He Long was joined by Xiao Ke, a debonair young man who led an army group out of Jiangxi in August 1934 to explore possible escape routes from the Central Soviet. In Guizhou, on the very border with Sichuan, Hunan and Hubei, He Long and Xiao Ke established a new soviet, which survived for about a year. Their approach followed a well-established routine: the wealthy were executed, debts abolished, land redistributed. A villager who tilled his own land was tolerated, but one who had others working in his field denounced as a 'landlord'. Executions were held on stages decorated with flags and artificial flowers. The crowd, soon used to the ritual, passed its verdict on cue, as with one voice. When they shouted 'kill', the condemned turned deathly pale, to be led away and executed. Prisoners were routinely tortured. Those who died of starvation, abuse or illness were carried away and buried without a coffin, 'as one would bury a dog', according to Rudolf Bosshardt, a Swiss missionary who was held for ransom and travelled with the troops for a year. At one point executions became almost a daily affair, as men tightly bound and stripped to the waist were led away, their clothes usually appropriated by the executioners.[35]

Dayong was the capital of the soviet. Fierce fighting broke out in March 1935, forcing the Communists to evacuate the soviet and head back all the way to Sangzhi, He Long's region of birth. Before leaving Dayong, the Communists killed several thousand people, leaving their bodies to rot. 'A pond outside the West Gate was full of corpses which were being devoured by dogs,' wrote British army officer K. E. F. Millar, sent on a mission to negotiate the release of the foreign hostages held by He Long. The local inhabitants, he added admiringly, were a plucky crew, first deprived of everything by He Long, then left to face starvation caused by the Nationalists who requisitioned the food to feed their troops. Dayong was not the only place left in ruins. Everywhere agricultural land in a zone of about ten kilometres outside the erstwhile Communist base had been abandoned, devoid of any vegetables. Beyond the red base, the fields looked tidy, brimming with beans and peas. 'The contrast was marked,' commented

Bosshardt. Along the road out of the soviet, three volunteers sent to negotiate the release of the missionaries 'saw the bodies of many who had been shot and beheaded'. 'The condition of the whole district was terrifying,' they further observed.[36]

By October 1935, He and Xiao had sustained a series of military defeats at the hands of a formidable array of provincial and government troops. Their supplies exhausted, fearful of being surrounded, they decided to pull up stakes. In November, near their erstwhile capital of Dayong, the Communists managed to break through a defensive perimeter and cross the Lishui River, followed by the even more formidable Yuan River which separated the northern, more mountainous areas from the rest of Hunan. There was little fighting, as government and provincial troops shepherded them in the required direction, namely south. The general in charge of stemming the Communist tide received two demerits from the chairman of Hunan province. He Long and Xiao Ke divided their troops into two columns. Their sally south through the province was spectacular, with the main force occupying cities including Anhua and Xinhua in rapid succession. Since the region was rich in silver and pewter mines, and the workers refused to accept paper notes, the government had to keep a large supply of silver dollars on hand to meet their payrolls. The Second Red Army, estimated at 15,000 men, captured much of this money, and may possibly have used it to buy safe passage, raising further suspicions over the central government's determination to eliminate the Communists. Both columns then swung westward to occupy Xupu, where they tore down all government posters and replaced them with their own propaganda before proceeding to loot shops and wealthy residences. Throughout the town, soldiers could be seen carrying baskets and boxes full of confiscated articles, not least clothing and shoes.[37]

For a few days, Changsha lived in fear of an invasion, but it soon became clear that the Second Red Army intended to follow the same circuitous route around Sichuan taken by Mao and Zhu one year earlier. The marchers moved at great speed, entering Guizhou above Tongren. All the central provinces were now free of Communists. Chiang increased his grip on Hunan, much as he had strengthened his hold over Sichuan and Guizhou. Guiyang, unlike the previous year, was well prepared, with Guangxi troops supplementing the central government forces. In January 1936 they inflicted a severe defeat on the Communists, at the exact same spot in Longli where Mao had lost several thousand soldiers the previous April. He Long was forced to move on to the Yunnan border near Zhaotong. In Yunnan his men were repeatedly compelled to fight, sustaining heavy casualties. They trekked north, crossing the Jinsha River near Lijiang and moving upstream through Tibet, occasionally taking a town, resting and resuming their march. Hundreds perished of hunger on high passes and along barren wastelands. By June, the marchers poured into the Batang valley before turning east towards Ganzi in Sichuan.[38]

The circling movement they had made was even bigger than the one followed by the First Red Army. They united with Zhang Guotao, whose move out of Sichuan towards Gansu had been cut short by the arrival of winter and the strategic positioning of central troops. In October 1935, even as the First Red Army reached Shaanxi province, Zhang had set up an alternative Central Committee, denouncing Mao Zedong, Zhou Enlai and other leaders for having 'violated the spirit of the Party' and undermined the unity of the Red Army. There were now two Red Armies, two Military Councils and two Central Committees.[39]

Moscow intervened, sending Lin Biao's uncle with a message of unity. Lin Yuying, who arrived in northern Shaanxi in November 1935, dispatched a telegram to Zhang, explaining that following the rise of Adolf Hitler in 1933 members of the Seventh Comintern Congress had passed a new policy of opposition to fascism. It meant that all forces in China should bury their differences and come together in a United Front opposing Japan. Lin knew Zhang, the two having worked together as far back as 1922. Zhang responded with a long list of grievances against Mao. A flurry of cables followed, but a stubborn Zhang refused to budge. Only after Zhang Wentian invoked the full authority of Stalin did he finally come to terms. 'We had to lure him out of his cave, one step at a time,' Zhang Wentian later recalled.[40]

In August 1936 Zhang Guotao and He Long arrived in Gansu, determined to rejoin the First Red Army in Shaanxi province. But this time the Communists encountered stiff opposition. Their men, who for months had survived on a daily diet of barley, were keen on better food and attempted to take Minxian. Even though they greatly outnumbered the garrison troops inside the walled city, they were unable to prevail. An ill-conceived siege lasting five weeks ensued, with planes from the provincial army coming to the rescue by dropping ammunition and medical supplies. The Communists sustained great losses and were finally driven on, only for central government troops to cut them to pieces as they tried to cross a tributary of the Yellow River near Qingyuan. Not until 2 December 1936 did a chastened Zhang Guotao finally arrive in Shaanxi with 10,000 men. He had lost well over half of his army since meeting up with Mao near Mougong more than a year earlier. The combined forces of the First, Second and Fourth Red Armies were formally united again. To mark the occasion, in a special ceremony in the new capital Bao'an, covered with bright posters and red flags, the Long March was formally declared over.[41]

***

One year earlier, Mao, always the demagogue, had turned a disastrous, headlong escape into a feat not seen since the mythical figure of Pangu had separated heaven and earth. 'We say that the Long March is unprecedented in the annals of history, that the Long March is a manifesto, a propaganda team, a seeding machine.' He continued: 'The Long March has announced to some 200 million people in eleven provinces that the road of the Red Army is their only road to liberation.'[42]

But as the Communists themselves admitted a few years later, they had been almost entirely wiped out: the losses in their organisation were estimated at 'one hundred per cent in Nationalist areas and 90 per cent in the Soviet areas and the Red Army'. Party membership fell to 40,000 during the Long March, roughly one member for every 11,000 people.[43]

The Communists, in short, had roughly the same popular appeal as an obscure religious sect or minor secret society. Their message of a 'proletarian uprising' against 'capitalism', despite fifteen years of relentless agitation funded by Moscow, had failed to find much of a reception among the workers in any of the country's many towns and cities. Calls for land distribution had a certain appeal in the countryside, although the Party's reputation, after years of depredation if not outright terror, was such that most villagers viewed the arrival of the Red Army with dread. Ordinary farmers did not need a doctoral dissertation in economics to realise that they would have to work much harder for less income in order to feed the soldiers. And for those who did seek academic credentials, there was the survey of farmers carried out by a University of Nanking team led by the American economist John L. Buck. From 1929 to 1933, they studied 168 villages distributed over twenty-two provinces, collecting vast amounts of information on every aspect of the lives of more than 16,000 households. *Land Utilization in China* scrupulously noted the many regional differences in the countryside, but the overall image that emerged from the study did not point to the existence of vast inequalities. Over half of all farmers were owners, many were part-owners and fewer than 6 per cent were tenants. Most farms were relatively small, and very few were more than twice the average size. Tenants were not generally much poorer than owners, since only fertile land could be rented out. A majority of villagers supplemented their incomes with handicrafts and other forms of non-agricultural employment which produced roughly one-sixth of their incomes. One-third of all the cultivators surveyed were unaware of any adverse factors in agriculture. None blamed expensive credit, exploitative merchants or land tenure. Few of them viewed warfare as a significant cause of famine, although they identified drought and flood as a major source, followed by insects, frost and wind. This was not precisely a countryside seething with revolutionary fervour.[44]

There was, of course, the Chinese Communist Party's opposition to imperialism, but beyond shrill condemnations and the systematic destruction of missionary property, including orphanages and hospitals, this amounted to rather little, especially when compared with the relentless pressure the central government exerted on foreign powers to liquidate the treaty port system and extraterritoriality. By 1933, a string of foreign concessions had been relinquished, while in June 1931 the unconditional surrender of the foreign enclaves and extraterritoriality in Tianjin after five years and Shanghai after ten years had been agreed. 'Thus was brought to an end, by fortuitous intervention of other events, the story of the National Government's campaign for the abolition of foreign extraterritorial rights, the citadel of "Unequal Treaties",' concluded the British ambassador Miles Lampson in 1933. In September 1930, the much decried indemnity funds obtained by the foreign powers in compensation for the damage caused by the Boxer Rebellion, an uprising that had culminated in a siege of the foreign legations in Beijing in 1900, were remitted in full to the central government, to be used for education, railway building and public works.[45]

Cities, and large swathes of the countryside, were being pushed into the modern age, one step at a time. Even as the Communists promised to create a new world overnight, provincial and central governments were undertaking a colossal modernisation programme, often with the financial and technical assistance of foreign countries. In terms of education, the Rockefeller Foundation alone spent US$37 million in China between 1913 and 1933, a sum which was topped only by the US$117 million the foundation spent in the United States. All over the country, new roads were being energetically and enthusiastically built, 'roads which are levelling the walls and entirely changing the face of old Chinese cities, roads running along the banks of rivers, winding in and out of villages, even climbing over mountain passes'. By 1933 the railway system covered more than 10,000 kilometres, transporting 45 million passengers annually. A building frenzy was transforming cities small and large alike, as walls were torn down, moats levelled, swamps filled, highways constructed and bridges built. Public parks, libraries, museums, schools and hospitals were slowly superseding the common landmarks of imperial towns, whether memorial arches, temples, drum towers, guildhalls, teahouses or pawnshops. Canton, in 1933, was a long way from the Communist occupation of 1927, its charred houses torn down and replaced by new roads, buildings and civic improvements, including the obligatory Sun Yat-sen Memorial Hall. Further north, Nanjing was entirely rebuilt, with libraries, power plants, electric lights, flour mills, soap factories, asphalted roads, neon lights, telegraph and telephone installations, modern schools, colleges, hospitals and hotels. These cities were not exceptions. The statistical secretary of the British Embassy wrote in 1932 that 'nearly every large city and even many villages are now lit by electricity; modern gravitation water supplies are gradually being provided; almost all cities have telephone systems, with many automatic exchanges, and almost all provinces have extensive long-distance telephone services.'[46]

If there was one overwhelming threat to the country, it was Japan. Yet the Chinese Communist Party, fixated on Chiang Kai-shek, hardly ever mentioned the island nation. The Long March was later explained as an attempt by the Communists to get closer to the territories occupied by the Kwantung Army, but the country which had invaded all of the north was not brought up even once at the Zunyi conference in January 1935. The decision to move towards Shaanxi was only taken several months later, on the basis that the province was closer to the Soviet Union, from which financial and military assistance was imperative if the Party was to survive.[47]

Stalin yet again came to the rescue, offering his hapless followers in China a lifeline. One year after the Japanese delegates had marched out of the League of Nations, Moscow had embraced Geneva, fearful of the rise of Nazi Germany. Maxim Litvinov, in charge of foreign affairs from 1930 onwards, supported a policy of collective security with Western democracies against Hitler. Stalin, fully aware of the degree to which Britain was fundamentally hostile to the Soviet Union, was doubtful, but acquiesced, given the lack of any viable alternatives. In any event, standard Marxist-Leninist tactics prescribed seeking an alliance with an inveterate enemy, one who could always be isolated and destroyed at a later stage. Once Japan began expanding its control over north China, a joint march on Moscow by the two most determined anti-Communist powers, namely Germany and

Japan, became a distinct possibility. Following endless border disputes, by July 1935 the Comintern openly referred to Tokyo as a 'fascist enemy'.[48]

The answer was a United Front against fascism. Georgi Dimitrov, concluding the Seventh Comintern Congress on 13 August 1935, called for the 'working class' to unite into a 'popular front against fascism'. Social democrats, previously derided as 'social fascists', were suddenly welcomed as allies. 'Bourgeois democracy', Dimitrov explained, was actually a form of bourgeois dictatorship which was preferable to a more fascist kind of bourgeois dictatorship. Stalin began to encourage Communist parties around the world to seek a united front with those in power instead of trying to overthrow them. The drum of world revolution fell silent, replaced by strident calls for unity against fascism. In several countries, including France and Spain, popular front governments were formed in 1936.[49]

Wang Ming, the Chinese Communist Party's key man in Moscow, wasted no time in launching an 'Appeal to All Compatriots', drafted on 1 August 1935 and published a few months later, urging his fellow citizens to rise up and unite in the fight against Japan. But Chiang Kai-shek and several other leaders were explicitly excluded as 'traitors'. None of this reached any of the Chinese Communists, who were all wandering in the wilderness, divided into two rival Central Committees and hurling insults at each other. But when Lin Yuying arrived in Wayaobao in November 1935 bearing the same message, Mao immediately understood its significance. A United Front against Japan finally provided the Communist Party with a message that was popular and was backed with a promise of more funding from Moscow. Students across China, even in the midst of the 1931 flood, had clamoured for war, seemingly unconscious of the huge military imbalance between the two powers and the fact that their country had yet to develop a strong sense of national unity under a central government. For several years, 'national salvation' groups had appeared in most cities, holding 'indignation demonstrations', issuing circular telegrams, manifestos and appeals and generally urging the population to rise against Japan. Agitation increased in 1935 after Japan made new claims over Hebei and Chahar provinces. In December 5,000 students in Beijing, called Beiping since the national capital had moved to Nanjing, went on strike, demanding that the government send soldiers from all parts of the country to fight the enemy.[50]

Almost overnight, the Chinese Communist Party changed its tone. On 1 January 1936, Mao embraced the United Front, explaining to his colleagues that the Comintern now viewed the Chinese Communist Party as 'the greatest Bolshevik Party outside the Soviet Union': the recognition was bound to result in massive military assistance, or so he surmised. A few weeks later, Mao began to undermine Chiang's loose coalition of provincial armies by cultivating Zhang Xueliang. When the Young Marshal had withdrawn his men from Manchuria in December 1931, Chiang entrusted him with suppressing the Communists in Hebei. In the summer of 1935, after the Kwantung Army in a secret agreement had demanded the withdrawal from north China of all units hostile to Japan, Zhang's troops had had to retreat still further, ordered by the Generalissimo to go to Gansu and Shaanxi province, where the Communists were anticipated to arrive via Sichuan.[51]

By now, the 130,000 former Manchurian soldiers were far from home and disgruntled. Accompanying the troops were several hundred students and teachers, who had joined them after the Japanese had closed their schools in Manchuria. Zhang Xueliang's income depended on the mines and lands and forests of Manchuria, which the Kwantung Army had seized, and soon he found himself forced to depend on Nanjing for funds, leaving his troops poorly paid, and his schools and headquarters in dire straits. A few of his officers wished to return to their homeland to fight the Japanese, not the Communists. Some of the soldiers and students were easy prey for Communist propaganda. So were the 40,000 provincial troops in Shaanxi under General Yang Hucheng, who were also underpaid and under the supervision of the Young Marshal.[52]

On 28 November 1935, the Young Marshal himself had made a secret trip to Nanjing to court the Russian ambassador, Dimitri

Bogomolov. He did not ask for military support, but indicated that he was one of the younger Nationalist Party leaders who fully understood the importance of close relations with the Soviet Union. He assured the ambassador that, in any war between Tokyo and Moscow, China would side with the Soviet Union. Two months later, on 20 January 1936, Mao instructed his envoy Li Kenong to open negotiations with the Young Marshal, offering a united front against Japan and Chiang Kai-shek. The Young Marshal, Mao was told the following day, 'expressed his willingness to work towards founding a government of national salvation', while there was no lack of soldiers in his army who were favourably inclined towards the Communists. But more meetings revealed that Zhang Xueliang, while eager to fight Japan, did not want to oppose his boss in Nanjing.[53]

On 9 April Zhou Enlai was sent instead, spending a night in Yan'an, thrashing out a compromise with the Young Marshal. Zhang, assigned to suppress the Communists, actually agreed to let the Red Army move about the region freely, although he refused to countermand the Generalissimo's orders publicly. At midnight that same day, Mao circulated a cable suggesting that the Communist Party advocate unity among the people and a 'cessation of the civil war' against Chiang Kai-shek. Eventually, the time when it would be 'possible and practical' to 'order Chiang's suppression' would come, but support from 'more people and more armies' was required first.[54]

Mao, after arriving in Wayaobao in October 1935, had found the region mired in extreme poverty, its inhabitants barely able to scrape a living. His troops roamed the province, but scope for plunder was limited. Having exhausted all local resources, by the end of February his men had crossed the frozen river separating Shaanxi from Shanxi to the west, and occupied seven counties only a hundred kilometres away from Yan Xishan's model capital in Taiyuan. They did so in the guise of a United Front, loudly proclaiming their determination to fight 'Japanese imperialism and Chinese rascals and treasonous thieves', including Yan Xishan. The Chinese Communist Party, so they proclaimed, was ready to work together with all anti-Japanese compatriots, and ready to abandon class struggle. The usual slogans favouring land distribution were dropped. Zhang Xueliang could easily have chased and crushed them, but refused to do so. Even before the secret agreement of 9 April, underground agents were active among his troops, circulating 'Appeals to the Officers and Soldiers of the North-eastern Army' and other propaganda material.[55]

Yan Xishan proclaimed martial law in Taiyuan and sent his family to Beiping. Yan, like some of his erstwhile peers in Guizhou and Sichuan, was reluctant to invite Chiang Kai-shek's troops into his domain, fearful of a quiet takeover from Nanjing. As a United States military attaché named Joseph Stilwell phrased it, the Model Governor was 'frantic for fear he will get too much help'. On the other hand, a large Communist presence openly defying Japan in a province adjacent to Jehol might prompt an even more crippling intervention from the Kwantung Army. Some observers even believed that Mao was deliberately rattling the cage to provoke a Japanese attack, precipitating the war he so craved. After the Model Governor's own provincial troops proved unequal to the task, for the first time in his twenty-five years of iron rule over the province, he reluctantly appealed for help to the central government. By early May, the Communists, with their wounded, their grain supplies and their looted treasure, were herded across the Yellow River back into north Shaanxi, where they faced no opposition from Zhang Xueliang's troops. Martial law was lifted in Taiyuan. Yan Xishan dutifully resigned, only for his resignation to be refused. The Model Governor had to be treated gently, for fear that he might suddenly accept terms from the Japanese.[56]

Yet even as Mao sought to entice away the very general tasked with his suppression, Stalin kept the door to Chiang Kai-shek open. Negotiations over a non-aggression pact, potential military assistance and a mutual assistance treaty had been underway since the resumption of diplomatic relations in December 1932. Facing a common enemy, Moscow and Nanjing needed each other, although both tried to impose their own terms. Stalin dangled a promise of military aid, while Chiang Kai-shek played off Moscow against Berlin and Tokyo, both keen on an anti-Comintern

Pact. While Wang Ming's August 1935 declaration had excluded Chiang Kai-shek as a 'traitor' from any form of United Front, Stalin was attempting to force the Generalissimo to reach some sort of agreement with the Chinese Communist Party.

Chiang, by contrast, tried to delay, hoping in due course to annihilate the Communists. On 19 October 1935, a week after just 6,000 marchers under Mao had turned up in Wayaobao, Chiang met the Russian ambassador Bogomolov in Nanjing. He hinted that Japan was offering a military alliance, although he had no intention of accepting it. A few weeks later, at the Nationalists' Fifth Party Congress, more pro-Japan figures were promoted. Shortly afterwards, Bogomolov was informed that Moscow had agreed in principle to sell weapons to Nanjing. But help depended on Chiang entering negotiations with the Communists. As Litvinov pointed out, there had to be some assurance that the weapons would actually be used against Japan, not the Communists. In January 1936, Chiang asked his representative in Moscow, Deng Wenyi, to meet Wang Ming. On the table was a United Front, including weapons, ammunition and rations for the Communists. But in exchange the Generalissimo insisted that the soviet be disbanded and the Red Army integrated into the central government troops.[57]

Contacts between the Nationalists and the Communists continued over the following months, but the talks stalled. Chiang was a stubborn man, unwilling to give way on the principle that the only recognised government was in Nanjing, not in Wayaobao. Mao was just as determined to keep his troops out of the clutches of the central government.

But Chiang played his hand better. Mao's foray into Shanxi had lasted three months and had ended in a military fiasco. Instead of a principled fight against Japan, it had come across as yet another looting expedition, resulting in the defeat of the new United Front policy. Against expectations, it had not resulted in a wave of popular support around the country. The Generalissimo, on the other hand, established a much firmer foothold in Shanxi province, close to the territories controlled by Japan. When, over the summer, Chen Jitang in Guangdong attempted to detach himself from Nanjing by declaring himself commander-in-chief of an anti-Japanese expedition, his troops did not follow their leader. After Li Zongren, head of neighbouring Guangxi province, proposed to help by placing his provincial army at Chen Jitang's disposal, the entire Cantonese Air Force took off in some sixty planes, defecting to Nanjing. There was simply no appetite left for yet another regional war. Chen Jitang fled abroad, while Li Zongren was offered a new position in Nanjing, where Chiang could keep watch on him. By the summer of 1936, in the words of Joseph Stilwell, the military attaché who would emerge as one of the most important players in China during the Second World War, 'China is more nearly united than she has ever been before and this has been accomplished without the civil war that would have given Japan a chance to push her program in the North.'[58]

In July 1936, one year after the Comintern had trumpeted its new United Front policy, not even a simulacrum of unity with the recognised government had been achieved. When Guangdong and Guangxi had rebelled, before several journalists Mao had praised their 'bold and independent' spirit of resistance and their refusal to 'become traitors and slaves without a country' by joining Chiang Kai-shek. It was 'not only natural but also necessary', he added, that certain leaders within the Nationalist Party wanted to 'split away from Nanjing'.[59]

The Young Marshal, speaking to Bogomolov again on 24 July 1936, took exactly the opposite position, pointing out to the Soviet ambassador that, given Japan's military might, national unity above all was required. Zhang Xueliang dismissed the rebellion in the south as a mere distraction. Again he expressed his admiration for the Soviet Union, not least its Red Army. Not once did he mention the Chinese Communist Party.[60]

Even as negotiations between Nanjing and Moscow stalled, relations with Berlin flourished. Trade boomed, as Germany, for the first time, sold more than Britain to China. Besides goods, including industrial equipment and armaments, experts also arrived in ever greater numbers. The Generalissimo had long used German military advisers, including in 1927 Colonel Max Bauer, Erich Ludendorff's right-hand man in the First World War, and later Hans von Seeckt, the former head of the Reichswehr, until he was recalled by Hitler in March 1935. Alexander von Falkenhausen, already in China since April 1934, took over, continuing to whip Chiang Kai-shek's troops into fighting trim. In July 1936, a barter agreement for 100 million marks was signed, with tungsten and other raw materials heading for Germany in exchange for munitions. But Chiang tried to keep an even balance, repeatedly asking Moscow to send back Vasily Blyukher, the very man who had built up his Whampoa Academy before leading the Sino-Soviet War in 1929.[61]

Since Mao was the odd man out, standing in the way of a United Front, Moscow intervened. Writing on 27 July 1936, with Stalin's blessing, Dimitrov offered some 'urgent advice', condemning the declaration in support of the rebels in the south as 'incorrect'. It was a 'political mistake', he judged, to place Chiang Kai-shek in the same category as the Japanese occupiers, all the more so since fighting both Japan and Nanjing simultaneously was a pipe dream. An olive branch must be extended to Nanjing 'immediately'.[62]

On 25 August the Chinese Communist Party offered a complete turnabout, appealing in an open letter to 'the glorious history of cooperation between our two parties during the last great revolution'. The Communists proposed to become part of a national defence government and promised that the Red Army would submit to the command of a centralised military headquarters. They appeared magnanimous, self-sacrificing and intensely patriotic. It was not all hot air: Pan Hannian, the main negotiator between the Communists and the Nationalists, was told that the new policy, henceforth, was to 'work with Chiang and resist Japan'. After Pan Hannian entered into more talks with Nanjing, Chen Lifu, one of the Generalissimo's most trusted lieutenants, told him that the Chinese Communist Party would have to end its policy of sabotage, cease the forcible confiscation of land, abolish all existing soviets and remove the name and insignia of the Red Army, to be subject to control by the government's Military Council. Chen did not harbour high hopes. 'They had never kept their promises, and deception was their strong point,' he complained.[63]

Naturally the Communists agreed. By now Chiang was ready to consolidate the entire north-west, much as he had whipped the south and south-west into shape. In June, after the Communists had been chased out of Shanxi, units of the central government had taken Wayaobao, routing the Red Army and seizing a large quantity of military supplies. The Communists had been forced to flee to Bao'an, a small town with most of its houses standing in ruins, deserted by its inhabitants after a series of calamities. The leadership had to live in loess caves by the foothills, and turned it into their capital half a year later. On 25 August, the same day on which the Communists affirmed their desire for a united front in an open letter to the nation, Mao appealed to Moscow for military assistance in order to fund a new offensive in Ningxia, a sliver of a province between Gansu and Mongolia. The Communists counted on aircraft and heavy artillery, but received nothing, as Stalin feared that his help would scupper negotiations with Chiang for a United Front.[64]

The Communists soldiered on nonetheless, but in October were dealt yet another devastating blow. In Weizhou, a mere sixty kilometres inside Ningxia, the Muslim inhabitants were so determined to defend their city that they used stones, hoes, spades and other improvised weapons to repulse the invaders. When the Communists decided to negotiate instead, making ample promises to the city elders, their overtures were spurned. Provincial troops came to the rescue, resulting in bloody clashes with heavy casualties on both sides. Hu Zongnan, in charge of the central government troops in the area, recovered all the major cities and cornered the Communists on the west bank of the Yellow River. On 18 October the Communists began pleading with him for a United Front, to no avail. One week later, forty-six Communist leaders headed by Mao Zedong and Zhu De sent an appeal to Chiang and the other generals in the north-west, requesting an immediate halt to the offensive and the formation of a United Front instead. In his diary, Chiang wrote that 'whether they are sincere or not, they are puppets of the Comintern who will sacrifice the Chinese people.'[65]

Even as they faced annihilation, the Communists scored a major publicity coup when Edgar Snow, a young reporter from

Missouri, published a series of interviews with Mao in the *China Weekly Review* on 14 and 21 November. Mao, introduced as the 'Chairman of the Chinese Central Soviet Government', presented himself as the leader of an alternative state who had magnanimously acceded to all of Nanjing's demands, provided that Chiang agreed on 'waging war, decisively and finally, against Japanese aggression'. He promised that the Red Army would not utilise a war 'in an opportunist way'. He argued that, if the Communists controlled just three or four more provinces, they could summon to war a greater and more effective force than Nanjing's entire army. Mao posed as a democrat, noting that despite severe repression the students nationwide had organised themselves politically. 'When the masses are given economic, social and political freedom, their strength will be intensified a hundred times,' he prophesied.[66]

Increasingly, the message of a United Front began to gain popularity, partly because the Communists could pose as the more enlightened and determined party. Students and intellectuals, in particular, seemed swayed by the idea. 'For all their scholarship [they] would seem never to have heard of the Trojan horse,' commented the British ambassador.[67]

Mao demanded immediate war, but no commander could allow an outsider to decide on the timing and manner of military engagement. Chiang, like every other observer with a basic knowledge of the military balance between the forces, knew that time was required to unite the country and modernise the army. He had pursued both goals in a steadfast manner, and was about to bring the strategically vital north-west back into the fold. For months, he had also been busy preparing for what could only be an eventual war with Japan. From the Yellow River south to the Yangtze, several east–west and north–south sections of the railway lines were being fortified. Great dugouts, built of cement and reinforced steel, were being completed in strategically placed cities, designed to serve as shelters for the civilian population and storage depots for grain, munitions, fuel oil and petrol. In anticipation of an invasion by Japan, China had bought a fleet of aircraft, estimated at 750 by 1936, with a system of defence lines spreading like a fan, including advance, intermediate and base airfields. Chiang had also been buying naval mines from abroad, and was secretly converting many of his ships into minelayers. The purchase of war equipment accelerated, not least via Nazi Germany. Chiang was criss-crossing the country, each tour attempting to draw the country closer together.[68]

The north-west was the weak link, and the Generalissimo was keen to oversee what would be the sixth and final campaign against the Communists. In October he personally moved to Luoyang, an ancient Buddhist capital 400 kilometres to the east of Xi'an, in much the same way that he had taken up residence in Chongqing several years earlier. He made Zhang Xueliang and Yang Hucheng responsible for carrying out the task. But Zhang objected, repeatedly pleading in favour of a United Front. A headstrong Chiang brushed his concerns aside. The Young Marshal complained to a close adviser that Chiang had a 'head like a stone' and refused to listen. 'My men won't fight the Communists,' he said. Chiang, in turn, confided to his diary that Zhang 'wants to fight the Japanese, but does not want to annihilate the Communists, because he does not have the determination to last even five minutes'. The Young Marshal also turned to Yang Hucheng, described by a close observer as 'one of the most unscrupulous bandit-generals left over from the early days of the republic'. Yang was from Shaanxi, and viewed the province as his own preserve. When asked for advice, he volunteered a far more radical idea than simple appeals for unity: 'Wait for Generalissimo Chiang's visit to Xi'an. We can hold the emperor hostage and demand submission of all feudal princes in the realm.'[69]

6

United Again
(1936–1941)

Chiang Kai-shek arrived in Xi'an on 4 December 1936, taking up residence at a hot spring nestled in a scenic hill some twenty kilometres out of town. Xi'an, like so many other provincial capitals, had transformed itself over the years, lit by electricity with shops presenting a blaze of light in the evening. Broad, well-paved roads had been driven through all parts of the city, carts and hand trucks having to replace their iron-rimmed wheels with rubber tyres instead. Heavy snow fell on the city over the following days, saving the winter crop that had withered from a prolonged drought. The farmers rejoiced, but students were up in arms. One month earlier, Mongolian soldiers backed by the Japanese had invaded the windswept plains of Suiyuan, a province between Shanxi and Manchuria. Troops from the central government had successfully defended their territory, inflicting heavy casualties on the enemy. Their victory resulted in a stiffening of popular opposition to Japan. Strike fever spread from Shanghai to Qingdao, targeting Japanese enterprises. On 3 December, a thousand Japanese marines in full war kit landed in Qingdao, occupying strategic positions throughout the city port. Their mission was to protect Japanese lives and property after 36,000 workers went on strike in the textile mills.[1]

At first stunned by the Qingdao invasion, Chiang became even more determined to achieve national unity and eliminate the Communist threat in the north-west. He was fully aware of the danger presented by the Young Marshal's troops, who were widely reported to have fraternised with the enemy. On 5 December, he spoke on the importance of the suppression campaign to the assembled officers of Zhang Xueliang and Yang Hucheng, only to alienate them further with his uncompromising stance. More quarrels with the Young Marshal followed two days later. On 9 December, Chiang Kai-shek summoned General Jiang Dingwen, one of his most trusted henchmen, instructing him to assume command of the campaign instead. The Young Marshal, in effect, ceased to have control over his troops, with the more disaffected units to be transferred and replaced. Resentment spread among the ranks. The same day several thousand students organised a National Salvation parade, determined to present Chiang with a petition demanding resistance against Japan. The Young Marshal personally intervened to help disperse the crowd and avoid bloodshed, although several demonstrators were wounded in the ensuing mêlée.[2]

Zhang, never a strong character, appeared carried away by the atmosphere prevailing in Xi'an, as the city was hit the following day by swirling rumours that Nanjing had signed a pact with Japan to fight the Red Army. Adding fuel to the fire, on 10 December Mao declared in a cable to Zhang that he refused to demobilise even a single red soldier in negotiations over a United Front. On the evening of 11 December, the Young Marshal assembled his most loyal officers and ordered the arrest of Chiang Kai-shek. Next morning, as Chiang heard shots being fired by the mutineers, he scaled a wall and tried to escape from his compound. He was found barefoot in a moat at the bottom of the hills, clad only in a thin gown covering his sleeping suit, his back badly injured. Even before Chiang was escorted to Yang Hucheng's residence and placed under arrest, Mao received a telegram from the Young Marshal's headquarters, announcing that 'the emperor is being taken hostage.'[3]

That same morning Yang Hucheng dispatched his troops to key intersections in Xi'an, arresting the provincial governor and

Chen Duxiu, leading figure in the May Fourth Movement and co-founder of the Chinese Communist Party.

Li Dazhao, leading scholar, political activist and co-founder of the Chinese Communist Party, circa 1920.

Henk Sneevliet, Dutch revolutionary and Comintern agent who was in 1921 instrumental in founding the Chinese Communist Party, circa 1933.

Sun Yat-sen (right), founder of the Nationalist Party, and his disciple Chiang Kai-shek, circa 1924.

Sun Yat-sen with his wife, Soong Ching-ling, in the winter of 1924.

Wang Jingwei, Nationalist Party leader and rival of Chiang Kai-shek, 1910s.

Mikhail Borodin, Comintern agent picked by Stalin to lead the revolution in China, 1925.

Manchurian leader Zhang Xueliang (left), nicknamed the Young Marshal, posing with Chiang Kai-shek, circa 1930.

Otto Braun, German revolutionary and Comintern agent sent to China in 1933 to guide the Chinese Communist Party.

Bo Gu, leader of the Chinese Communist Party from 1931 to 1935.

Mao Zedong (left) with Zhu De, military strategist and co-founder of the Chinese Red Army, circa 1938.

Mao Zedong, as pictured on the influential book *Red Star over China*, published by Edgar Snow in 1937.

Wang Ming, Soviet-trained leader of the Chinese Communist Party and rival of Mao Zedong, circa 1938.

Mao Zedong (right) with Zhang Guotao, a rival Communist leader who defected to the Nationalists in 1938.

Zhou Enlai, political commissar and chief negotiator of the Chinese Communist Party, 1930s.

Mao Zedong (left) with Kang Sheng, in charge of internal security at Yan'an, early 1940s.

Mao Zedong (right) with Patrick Hurley and Chiang Kai-shek in Chongqing, 1945.

General George C. Marshall, pictured with Chiang Kai-shek and his wife, Soong Mei-ling, after arriving in China as special ambassador to China in 1945.

Yan Xishan, provincial governor of Shanxi from 1911 to 1949.

his wife plus a string of other dignitaries, including Generals Jiang Wending and Chen Cheng. Later that day the mutineers sent a circular cable with eight demands, including a more democratic form of government, an end to the civil war, the release of all political prisoners and the convening of a conference on national salvation.[4]

The coup came as a complete surprise in Bao'an, and caused great excitement. Mao laughed with joy, acclaiming Chiang's arrest as 'revolutionary'. He sent a cable to Wang Ming in Moscow suggesting a 'public trial by the people', hoping to see the Generalissimo executed. Zhu De objected, saying that, even before Moscow was informed, 'the first thing to do is to kill Chiang'. In their cabled response to Zhang, Mao Zedong and Zhou Enlai recommended that he use his most trusted guards to avoid corruption, further suggesting that 'in case of an emergency his execution would be the best option.' Mao ordered his troops to take up positions around Xi'an, putting his army at the disposal of the Young Marshal. Tongguan, opposite a hill around which the Yellow River bent sharply towards the east, had obvious military importance, for it commanded the approach to Xi'an from both Nanjing and Beiping.[5]

Chiang Kai-shek, even under duress, had greater foresight than any of the Communist leaders in Bao'an. He knew that Moscow would never condone the coup, since Japan might use it as a pretext to launch a full-fledged war. On 14 December, *Pravda* denounced the developments in Xi'an as a scheme instigated by pro-Japanese elements, followed by a similar condemnation by *Izvestia* on 15 December. The editorials reflected Stalin's position. Around midnight on the 14th, the irate leader had phoned Georgi Dimitrov to ask him point-blank if he had sanctioned the events taking place in China. 'This is the greatest gift that one could offer Japan,' he remonstrated. He then enquired if Wang Ming, who wished to send a telegram instructing the Communists to kill Chiang Kai-shek, was a 'provocateur'.[6]

One of the 'pro-Japanese elements' the Soviet editorials had highlighted was Wang Jingwei, Chiang Kai-shek's most likely successor, who had toured Japan earlier that year and was then in Germany, recuperating in a spa following an attempt on his life, and apparently cultivating Herr Hitler. Wang hurried back to China a week later.[7]

On 16 December, the Comintern sent a directive to the Chinese Communist Party, denouncing the Young Marshal's actions and ordering them to 'seek a peaceful solution'. The cable came like a bucket of cold water. Mao and his acolytes had got ahead of themselves, recommending on 14 December that Zhang Xueliang launch a purge of all pro-Chiang elements among the troops and 'create a spirit of fighting to the death', joining the Red Army in taking on all enemy troops. One day later, even as central government units were advancing towards Xi'an, Mao suggested striking at the 'enemy's head' by taking their combined forces on a huge strategic detour to assault the capital of Nanjing itself. It was yet another castle in the air, aimed at implicating the Young Marshal even further and provoking a war between Xi'an and Nanjing. Zhou Enlai arrived in Xi'an on 17 December, ensuring there was a direct link between the Young Marshal and Mao.[8]

Mao withheld information about the Moscow cable from both Zhou and Zhang until the evening of 20 December. Since he could not hide instructions from the Comintern any longer, he changed tactics. Always the master stirrer, he instructed Zhou Enlai on 21 December to circulate a rumour that He Yingqin, the general placed in charge of all military operations in Nanjing, was in cahoots with Japan, plotting to have the Generalissimo killed by pushing for a military campaign against Xi'an. The accusation was without substance, but spread widely, later to become the standard interpretation in the People's Republic. But no such plot existed. He Yingqin, believing that a combination of military pressure and diplomacy was needed to secure the release of the Generalissimo, realised that he must deploy loyal troops near Xi'an so that negotiations could be opened from a position of strength.[9]

The Young Marshal himself began to have doubts about his plan, and anxiously awaited directions from the Comintern. The editorials in Moscow condemning him as an agent in Tokyo's pay did not augur well. Once Zhang realised that the Communists had double-crossed him, Chiang Kai-shek became his only hope. Two days after the coup, the Australian journalist William Henry Donald, Chiang Kai-shek's trusted adviser, who by a happy coincidence had also been a mentor to the Young Marshal years earlier, arrived in Xi'an. A wan and ill Chiang was moved to more comfortable quarters, but remained embittered. As Donald observed, Chiang was 'a Gibraltar of stubbornness', and that very stubbornness 'cemented the plinth on which he stood', preventing a breakdown in his character. He refused to yield. The Generalissimo's assessment of the overall balance of power was accurate: Stalin had disowned Zhang, and Mao was using Zhang while Yang and Zhang were drifting apart. Editorials published around the country clamoured for Chiang's release. Hu Shi, a democrat who was highly critical of the severe constraints on basic freedoms imposed by the central government, captured the public mood when he published a piece entitled 'Zhang Xueliang's Betrayal', condemning the Chinese Communist Party: 'last year the Chinese Communist Party promoted a so-called "United Front", but the betrayal at Xi'an very clearly tells us that such a "United Front" is entirely impossible.'[10]

Zhang Xueliang seemed contrite, conscious of the error of his ways. Donald had brought along Chiang Kai-shek's diary, handing it over to the Young Marshal. He read a few pages and said slowly: 'I see. Chiang all along has been preparing for war against Japan. I'm beginning to see him in a new light.' But Zhang had very little leeway. The city was controlled by Yang Hucheng, the outskirts by the Communists, their armies silent but menacing. Chiang knew that the Communists were the crux of the problem, but refused to meet Zhou Enlai, the man charged with solving the crisis for Moscow. On 20 December, the former finance minister T. V. Soong (known as T.V.), who years earlier had served as Canton's commissioner of finance, also travelled to Xi'an. His sister Soong Mei-ling, or Madame Chiang, had sent him to secure the release of her husband. Chiang entrusted T.V. with speaking to Zhou three days later, together with Madame Chiang who by then had also joined her husband. Chiang repeated the demands he had made during earlier negotiations with Pan

Hannian, including the abolition of the Soviet Government of China. But he agreed that no central government troops would be stationed in Shaanxi or Gansu, while the Young Marshal would retain overall command in the region. This appeared to satisfy the mutineers, although the terms provoked outrage among their officers. On 24 December, even as preparations were being made for Chiang Kai-shek's return to Nanjing on Christmas Day, Yang Hucheng had a violent altercation with the Young Marshal: 'you started the coup and without securing anything you are allowing the Generalissimo to go,' he said, adding that Chiang would 'surely cut off their heads'.[11]

Communist lore, widespread and enduring, has portrayed Zhou Enlai as the suave player whose wit and repartee in a meeting on the evening of 24 December with his erstwhile Whampoa Academy boss brought the incident to a close. But there was no such meeting. When Zhou Enlai was taken to Chiang's quarters that evening, the Generalissimo brushed him off, telling him that 'if you have anything to say, you can speak to Xueliang.' On Christmas Day, as peace parleys continued, a desperate Zhou Enlai approached T.V., saying that 'the Chinese Communist Party has no demands towards Chiang Kai-shek, but I hope Chiang Kai-shek can tell me face to face that he will no longer suppress the Communists, that would suffice.' Chiang Kai-shek refused, explaining that the goals of national unity and a unified army command were supreme. 'But if in future you no longer sabotage our national unity, follow our orders and accept a unified command, not only will I no longer suppress you, I will treat your troops without discrimination.' Zhou agreed to these conditions, yet still tried to extract a last-minute concession from T. V. Soong, namely the 'rights of the people to express themselves freely' and the 'gradual release of the political prisoners'. T.V. said he would do his best, urging Zhou to talk to Yang. After Chiang had called both Zhang and Yang, telling them that although their methods were rebellious he pardoned them for their act, he was free to go. Later that afternoon, Chiang, Donald, T.V. and Madame Chiang, together with their retinue, squeezed themselves into three cars and left for the airfield, accompanied by the Young Marshal, who placed himself under voluntary house arrest.[12]

***

A wave of joy swept the country. In Nanjing the Generalissimo was 'carried through the streets in a tumultuous ovation'. Parades were held in Shanghai, with firecrackers going off till late into the night. Students demonstrated around the clock in Beiping, having unanimously condemned the coup and demanded the release of Chiang Kai-shek. 'Never since the signing of the Armistice which ended World War I had I seen such jubilance on the part of any great populace,' one journalist wrote. The Generalissimo's personal prestige was vastly enhanced, the country more united than ever. But the opportunity to eliminate the Communists was gone. As Chiang phrased it in his diary, 'the achievements obtained over ten years have been ruined in a single day.' Had it not been for the Young Marshal's attempted coup, Generals Jiang Dingwen and Hu Zongnan would have finished off the Communists, either cornering them or pushing them across the border into Mongolia. This would have meant continued military support from Germany, without incurring the wrath of Japan. As one military historian put it, 'had German influence been given more time to work and spread in China, the Japanese might have met a far different foe.'[13]

In Xi'an, the triangular alliance between the Young Marshal, Yang Hucheng and the Communists disintegrated the moment the plane took off. Some of the younger officers blamed the Communists for having betrayed Zhang Xueliang and trapped their leader. They turned on Zhou Enlai, who only just managed to talk himself out of a sticky situation. But the Communists, at long last, had some respite, marking the occasion by moving their capital to Yan'an, a county seat within easy reach of Xi'an, equipped with adequate infrastructure to accommodate all the institutions of the Party.[14]

The Young Marshal was sentenced to ten years in prison on 31 December, although Chiang would keep him under house arrest for the rest of his life (he died in 2001, aged 100). Yang Hucheng was relieved of his post on 5 January 1937, and Xi'an taken over by Gu Zhutong, a trusted and distinguished general who had commanded the crack First Army.[15]

Extensive horse trading took place between Nanjing and Yan'an, closely overseen by Moscow. On 19 January the Comintern warned the Communist leadership that the 'peaceful resolution' of the so-called 'Xi'an Incident' could be undermined not only by the 'machinations of the Japanese imperialists and their agents', keen on igniting a civil war, but also by 'erroneous steps on your part'. Instructions were clear: 'No open Communist activities should be carried out in Xi'an; not a word should be said about the promises given by Chiang Kai-shek in Xi'an; no demands should be made for an immediate declaration of war on Japan.' Four days later, an even greater concession was made, as Moscow recommended an end to land distribution and the abrogation of the soviets as organs of power in order 'to facilitate the unification of all forces of the Chinese people in defence of their motherland'. The stick came with a carrot, as Stalin approved a transfer of US$800,000 to the Communists for the month of January alone. On 10 February, Mao undertook to end all attempts to overthrow the government, also recognising Nanjing as the legitimate government, renaming the soviet a Special Area Government and placing the Red Army under the nominal command of the Military Council in Nanjing. But Nanjing viewed the existence of two administrations as entirely unacceptable, and further demanded that the Marxist notion of class struggle be repudiated.[16]

On 11 February, Bogomolov, the Soviet ambassador in Nanjing, suggested that Chiang Kai-shek's son, Ching-kuo, be sent back from Russia to help with a pact between Nanjing and Moscow. Since Chiang Ching-kuo was a Communist, the hope was that he might sway his father. Another sweetener came in early March, when Stalin agreed to barter military equipment to the value of 50 million Mexican dollars, equivalent to more than US$13 million, in exchange for raw materials. On 17 March, the Generalissimo was informed that his son was on his way back home. Still Chiang stalled. The agreement paled in comparison to the deliveries from Nazi Germany. But, most of all, Chiang abhorred the Communists and harboured doubts about the truce. On 30 January, he had wondered whether it was wise to agree to terms 'now that they are exhausted and have nowhere to turn'. The Communists, he wrote in his diary a few weeks later, were 'stateless, inhumane, devoid of any morality'. They were also untrustworthy, as a report from the Bureau of Investigation on 24 February confirmed, explaining that they were planning to expand east of the Yellow River even as they paid lip service to the terms they had agreed upon.[17]

More haggling took place over the following months. Yet even as the precise terms of the agreement were being hammered out, the Communists benefited most. Since Nanjing wished to view the soviet districts as part of a national defence area, with the Red Army subsumed under a central command, in January it began paying 200,000 to 300,000 yuan a month for their maintenance. The exact monthly allowance was under debate, but it provided great relief to Yan'an, with money flowing in from both Moscow and Nanjing. During the Xi'an Incident their troops had occupied substantial new areas of Shaanxi, not least the strategically vital city of Tongguan, where mud-walled buildings now served as the local office of the Red Army.[18]

The economic blockade around the soviet was gradually lifted, and trade relations resumed. Flush with cash, the Communists bought a fleet of American lorries to operate a bus service between Xi'an and Yan'an. Hundreds of enthusiastic young radicals travelled to the red capital, to enrol in the Red University, renamed 'Anti-Japanese University', as well as in technical training institutes or the Communist Party school. Although the Communist Party remained nominally illegal in the rest of the country, conditions eased and arrests ceased, allowing underground agents to extend their reach and recruit more members. The Communists at last possessed a base where they could train new recruits without fear of interference.[19]

Nanjing did not advertise these changes, least of all the continued negotiations with Moscow. But they constituted a threat to Tokyo, where Japanese leaders feared an alliance between Nanjing, Moscow and Yan'an. Already during the

Xi'an Incident, as Communist troops had moved to occupy the heights around Tongguan, Tokyo had sensed the danger. In February Japan began to send reinforcements to the Kwantung Army in Manchuria, with warehouses and depots bulging with accumulated supplies designed for eventual use in a war against Nanjing. In June, increased military traffic along the railways was apparent everywhere in Manchuria, with troops converging towards Shanhaiguan, where the Great Wall met the Bohai Sea.[20]

***

On 7 July 1937 the Japanese engineered a clash on the Marco Polo Bridge, a granite structure spanning the Yongding River twelve kilometres southwest of Beiping. Within six hours of the incident, the railway line running south from Shanhaiguan to Tianjin had been seized, with 160,000 troops pouring through the Great Wall in heavy military trains. When negotiations stalled a few days later, relays of aircraft bombed parts of Tianjin into oblivion. Ferocious fighting followed. Beiping was spared, its commander having abandoned the former capital without a fight.[21]

Chiang Kai-shek, who for eight years had been building up his forces, now seized the initiative and deployed some of his top divisions around Shanghai. On 17 July he called for a war of resistance. Japan's plan was to occupy the five northern provinces of Hebei, Suiyuan, Shandong, Shanxi and Chahar, but the Generalissimo sought to draw their forces into a war of attrition in the Yangtze valley, where they were not prepared to fight. For weeks there were continuous movements of troops around the city, with 5 million gallons of petrol distributed to sixty-two points in central provinces north of the Yangtze.[22]

Mao, keen to obtain official recognition from Nanjing, cabled Chiang on 8 July to declare that 'the officers and men of the Red Army sincerely wish to give their all in the service of their country under your leadership.' In the ensuing weeks he mobilised his troops and sent 3,000 men to Jehol, Chahar and Hebei. But on 31 July, in the face of a Japanese onslaught, he instructed his troops to slow down and move at a pace of no more than twenty-five kilometres a day, with a pause every three days. 'There must be a difference between what we say we do and what we actually do,' read his cable. The next day he explained that 'we cannot allow ourselves to be restricted in campaigns and tactics,' and advocated 'dispersed guerrilla warfare', with the main forces kept safely behind the frontline.[23]

Japan had hoped to attain victory by occupying Beiping and Tianjin in the north. It was not prepared to fight in Shanghai, where it maintained a force so small that it was easily outmanoeuvred and put on the defensive on 13 August. After Japanese ships berthed along the Huangpu River had opened fire on enemy positions, Chiang Kai-shek sent Martin bombers to try to sink them. He also threw overwhelming numbers of soldiers at Japanese positions. Both attacks failed, but were renewed time and again over the following days, even as the enemy unleashed a continuous bombardment from the sea and from the air. Fragments of bodies were everywhere, splattered against buildings and fences, strewn on pavements, some difficult to remove. 'Heads, arms, legs lay far from mangled trunks,' observed one journalist. Even after sand and disinfectant had been sprinkled, the streets smelled like a charnel house in the summer heat. When Japan managed to land troops fifty kilometres north of the city, fighting moved from the centre towards the suburbs. For three long months the Chinese divisions managed to hold on to the city, even as Greater Shanghai was reduced to a mass of ruins, with endless blocks of gutted roofs and jagged walls protruding towards the sky. The soldiers fought ferociously, and 'in accordance with recognised tactical and technical principles', according to Evans Carlson, a military observer from the United States. But 'spirit, flesh and blood', he added, 'could not indefinitely prevail in the face of superior fire power in a pitched battle.' The tenacity of the resistance amazed foreign observers, used to seeing civil wars in which opponents often came to an understanding without a shot being fired. The formidable military machine deployed by Tokyo, on the other hand, appeared gruesome in its capacity to sow death, but below par in terms of tactics and strategy. The conflict caused an estimated 250,000 casualties. One-third of the central government's divisions were wiped out, with huge damage to its air force and naval power.[24]

Japan had counted on a quick victory in the north, hoping that the country would disintegrate with a dozen warlords fighting each other for power. Instead their invasion united the country. But the central government sorely lacked military equipment. In July Chiang Kai-shek repeatedly pleaded with Litvinov for help. On 21 August 1937 China and the Soviet Union signed a treaty of non-aggression. Since Moscow wished the war between China and Japan to be protracted, it began supplying its ally with planes, tanks and anti-aircraft artillery through Xinjiang province.[25]

Four days later, the Red Army was reorganised on the lines the central government had proposed and was renamed the Eighth Route Army, totalling 45,000 men led by Zhu De with Peng Dehuai as deputy. A New Fourth Army also appeared, formed from 10,000 troops who had been left behind in central China during the Long March. A United Front was formally recognised on 22 September. Thousands of political prisoners were released, among them Hilaire Noulens and his wife. Publications openly praising the Eighth Route Army appeared. 'Some 200 newspapers throughout China agitate on our behalf for free,' commented one Soviet adviser sarcastically, adding that 'there is almost no press censorship against us.' Communist headquarters opened in many cities. In Xi'an, Lin Zuhan, the man suspected of being the mastermind behind the Nanjing Incident in March 1927, became the representative of the Shaanxi base area. Large pen sketches of Karl Marx, Mao Zedong and Zhu De adorned his office walls, next to Sun Yat-sen and Chiang Kai-shek as an obligatory gesture towards the United Front. It seemed as if China now had two governments, one covering a country, the other in charge of eighteen counties strewn across the borders of Shaanxi, Gansu and Ningxia.[26]

Even before formal recognition was granted, Mao insisted on the absolute independence of the Eighth Route Army. A conference was convened in Luochuan, strategically located between Yan'an and Xi'an. Zhang Guotao, Zhou Enlai, Zhu De, Peng Dehuai and others were keen to fight and wanted to be part of the central government's overall strategy. But Mao prevailed, brushing aside the idea that their army could score a military success on the front. The aim, he pointed out, was to 'preserve and enlarge the Red Army' by holding back and exploiting losses among government troops. Mao proposed to expand the Communists' territory by sending small detachments behind enemy lines and seize control the moment the Nationalists were defeated.[27]

Class struggle, officially repudiated in the United Front, took centre stage. The domestic rival was more dangerous than the foreign enemy, according to Mao. 'Should the bourgeoisie follow the proletariat, or should the proletariat follow the bourgeoisie?' became the main question, meaning that during the war the Communist Party had to prevail over the Nationalist Party.[28]

In September, detachments of the Eighth Route Army began to pursue a course of action at which they had excelled for a decade before the Long March: to move into distressed terrain, 'incorporate stragglers and their rifles into our forces, and organise guerrilla units', and establish Party, government and army organs under the leadership of high-ranking cadres. Mao ordered his troops to 'confiscate the property of big landlords and mobilise the masses extensively' on entering new territory. By November, several divisions were moving behind enemy lines in Shanxi, Hebei, Henan and even Shandong.[29]

On one occasion Communist troops attacked the Imperial Japanese Army. On 25 September, as Japanese troops moved south into Shanxi towards Taiyuan, Lin Biao ambushed them at a narrow mountain pass called Pingxingguan. The ensuing clash resulted in the loss of several hundred soldiers on both sides, and was heralded as the Great Victory of Pingxingguan. It would be the only battle the Communists fought during the entire war that involved a full division. The military attaché Joseph Stilwell, who later became an admirer of the Communists, was unimpressed: 'Communist troops have at last had their wish fulfilled to get a chance to fight the Japanese, and the result was discouraging, their efforts being of no more effect than those of any other Chinese unit.' The ambush had no impact on the battle of Taiyuan, a two-month offensive involving huge clashes between six army groups, five divisions and close to half a million men, with Japan finally outflanking the central government troops and taking the provincial capital in early November.[30]

On 9 November, two days after the fall of Taiyuan, government troops evacuated Shanghai. The Japanese pressed their advantage, following the old warpath along the Yangtze valley, past Suzhou directly to the capital Nanjing. Their planes pulverised the countryside, as the area between Shanghai and Nanjing, one of the most populous on earth, became 'the graveyard of almost a million Chinese soldiers and civilians', to quote the Australian journalist Rhodes Farmer. Suzhou, an old imperial city known as the 'Venice of China', was systematically crushed under tonnes of explosives, as 'death rained upon the city from the circling, droning Japanese planes'. On 13 December, precisely four months after war began in Shanghai, the Japanese entered Nanjing. Here they committed one of the worst wartime atrocities in modern history, even though enemy soldiers had already left and resistance was at an end. During three weeks they slaughtered up to 200,000 unarmed civilians. Harold Timperley, correspondent of the *Manchester Guardian*, chronicled the massacre in his dispatches, describing soldiers on the rampage, shooting, machine-gunning, bayoneting or beheading civilians. Many thousands of women of all ages, including elderly women and even children, were raped, mutilated and killed. Letters arrived in Shanghai describing how civilians were sprayed with petrol and set afire. Bodies were dumped in ponds, trenches and mass graves or directly into the Yangtze River.[31]

The indiscriminate bombing of Canton began in November. Military supplies from the Soviet Union were not only flown to Xinjiang, but also delivered by freighter to the southern port. Tokyo's aim was to cut off these supplies, which were sent by railway to Wuchang, next to the arsenals of Hanyang. The third city making up Wuhan was Hankou, where Chiang Kai-shek set up his headquarters after his troops had retreated from Shanghai and Nanjing in November. The staff and records of the central government's civil ministries were dispersed among several cities with Hankou as the main haven. Chongqing, deep inland in

Sichuan, was selected as the venue for the executive, legislative, judicial and control councils. A flood of refugees joined the government in Hankou, packed in buses, lorries, junks and steamers. Entire schools and universities arrived from Beiping and Tianjin, banks, factories and mills from Shanghai.[32]

Before the fall of Nanjing, tens of thousands of tonnes of war supplies and modern machinery, mingled with the household effects of thousands of refugees, had been moved to Hankou and Chongqing. Huge mounds of goods, standing along the riverbank like a surreal dyke, were shipped either up the Yangtze River or by train, first up north towards Xuzhou, a major junction near the Shandong border, then inland to Zhengzhou before moving south to their final destination.

In March 1938, the Japanese occupied Jinan in Shandong province, tearing apart the defences built along the Yellow River. Their aim was to move south along the railway and link with Nanjing. But they encountered huge resistance in Tai'erzhuang, just fifty kilometres north of Xuzhou. After several days of ferocious combat, much of it at close quarters, troops under generals Bai Chongxi and Li Zongren inflicted a humiliating defeat on their enemy, the country's first major victory, and one that galvanised the nation. Hankou and other cities celebrated, but in May the victors found themselves besieged in Xuzhou and were forced to retreat.

Before the troops began their long trek to safety in Hankou, on 3 June Chiang Kai-shek ordered them to breach the dykes holding back the Yellow River near Zhengzhou. He and his advisers hoped that the waters would prevent a Japanese advance along the railway to Zhengzhou and further west to Tongguan in Shaanxi, opening the way towards Hankou and potentially all Sichuan. Initially, several attempts to blow up the dykes that confined the water to its elevated bed failed. On 10 June even the French ambassador in Shanghai realised that the level of the flood water was too low to flow southward. But a third set of explosives finally forced the river to leave its bed, and a vast sheet of water began to move slowly across the great wheat-growing plains of Henan. This delaying strategy came at a huge cost to the local population. By some accounts half a million people perished, although these numbers are misleading since they are derived from all wartime casualties in the flooded areas between 1938 and 1947. One historian has suggested a much lower estimate of 30,000.[33]

The waters moved slowly but inexorably, advancing between five and twelve kilometres a day, a speed that a child could easily outpace. The villagers had time to flee, alerting each other to the oncoming flood, which took a month to cross the border into Anhui. Journalists, local or foreign, reported enormous numbers of refugees but rarely commented on the death toll, even when such diseases as cholera became rampant in the wake of the disaster. A team of observers flying over the flooded sections in July noted that 'few towns have been completely submerged and none seem to have been washed away,' while small hillocks abounded in parts of the countryside, criss-crossed by elevated roadways. Even the Japanese spokesman, keen to blame Chiang Kai-shek, conceded that most losses were confined to property and crop damage, with refugees marooned for a few days. Father F. Clougherty, chairman of the International Relief Committee, reported that there had been eight cases of illness requiring isolation among the 9,000 refugees in his care. When, in September 1938, several districts in Henan released data on the extent of the damage, they mentioned widespread agricultural losses and hundreds of thousands of victims awaiting relief from distress.[34]

The entire area, stretching from Zhengzhou to Xuzhou, remained waterlogged for several months, hampering the movement of the heavily mechanised forces of the enemy. The breach, however pitiless, had worked. The Japanese did not take Zhengzhou until 1944 while Shaanxi remained free, preventing in turn the invasion of Sichuan province.

Hankou was bombed in February 1938, with fighting confined to the skies over the following months. Unable to advance along the railways after the fall of Xuzhou, the Japanese began to follow the banks of the Yangtze River instead, first assaulting the river fortress of Madang on 24 June before moving towards the heavily fortified port of Jiujiang, 250 kilometres downstream from

Hankou. The population of Jiujiang, like the inhabitants of so many other cities captured by the Imperial Japanese Army, was subjected to a reign of terror, with mass executions and systematic rape. One bloody battle followed another along the westward advance of the Japanese, who managed to approach Hankou only towards the end of October. Throughout, Japan made heavy use of chemical weapons, employing poison gas to compensate for its dwindling troops. In September, a second Japanese force tried to move across the Dabie Mountains north of Hankou, occupying Macheng, the erstwhile capital of Zhang Guotao's soviet, on 24 October.[35]

A stalemate followed, prompting the Japanese to open a third front in the south, as they planned to move along the railway from Canton towards Hankou via Changsha, much as the Northern Expedition had done over a decade earlier. Canton fell on 27 October after the longest and bloodiest battle of the Sino-Japanese War, with China sustaining over a million military and civilian casualties. Japan, too, paid in blood and treasure, suffering its heaviest losses of the war. At home, its economy was bankrupt. Although on four occasions the Imperial Army would attempt to take Changsha, it ceased to expand further inland. The battle gave the central government enough time to retreat safely towards Chongqing, which would remain the capital of Free China until the end of the war. Chiang's strategy now became one of 'using space to gain time'.[36]

**

Even as Soviet pilots joined their Chinese counterparts in dog fights with Japanese fighter planes in the skies high above the temporary capital, Chiang was again elected Party leader on 29 March 1938. This time, the slogan was 'One Doctrine, One Leader, One Organisation'. The aim was to transform the Generalissimo into a genuine dictator, on the basis that total power was apparently required in times of war. But it was obvious to all that, unlike his counterparts in Berlin and Rome, he was locked in a United Front with another doctrine, another leader and another organisation. Furthermore, an organic law provided for a People's Political

Council, designed 'to unify national strength; to utilise the best minds of the nation, and to facilitate the formulation and execution of national policies'. When it met in Hankou on 7 July 1938, some 120 out of a total of 200 seats were allocated to independent candidates, smaller groups as well as the Chinese Communist Party and the National Salvation Association. The meeting lasted nine days and was marked by lively debates as well as a few 'clashes between the Communists and Right Wing leaders'.[37]

Chen Duxiu, released from prison in the interests of the United Front after serving three years of an eight-year sentence, was also in Hankou. He had changed his views on communism, reverting to the humanist values he had embraced in his earlier career. In Hankou he advocated a union of all political forces that were independent of both the Nationalist Party and the Communist Party on the basis of a programme of freedom and democracy. He would be relentlessly denounced as a Trotskyist by the Communist Party in the following years, dying in 1942 at the age of sixty-two in a small town outside Chongqing.[38]

Mao did not attend the People's Political Council but sent his warmest regards. At home and abroad, he had become a household name. Edgar Snow, who had introduced the leader to a wider public in November 1936, published *Red Star over China* in September 1937, even as the Japanese were tearing Shanghai apart. The book was an instant success, selling 12,000 copies in the United States within the first month of publication. It was immediately translated into Chinese, turning Mao into a national figure. The photograph on the cover of the book, showing Mao wearing a military cap with a single red star, would be an iconic image for decades to come.[39]

Snow had been carefully vetted and had spent several months in Bao'an, with every detail of his visit closely supervised: 'Security, secrecy, warmth and red carpet'. Mao offered the American journalist a mythical version of his own life, describing his childhood, youth and career as a revolutionary. He checked and corrected every word Snow wrote.[40]

Red Star over China presented the mysterious leader of the Chinese Communist Party as an 'accomplished scholar of classical

Chinese, an omnivorous reader, a deep student of philosophy and history, a good speaker, a man with an unusual memory and extraordinary powers of concentration, an able writer, careless in his personal habits and appearance but astonishingly meticulous about details of duty, a man of tireless energy and a military and political strategist of considerable genius'. Mao was the poor child of the soil who had pulled himself up through sheer willpower and pride, determined to fight for his humiliated compatriots. He was a man of simple habits, living in a loess cave, growing his own tobacco leaves. He was down to earth, a rebel with a lively, rustic sense of humour. He worked tirelessly. He was a poet. He was a philosopher. He was a great strategist. But most of all he was a man of destiny, called upon by deep historical forces to regenerate his country. 'He might very well become a very great man,' Snow concluded.[41]

Even as Mao's star was rising, a challenger arrived from Moscow. Stalin, who was now shipping large amounts of war supplies to Chiang Kai-shek, sent Wang Ming back to China in November 1937 to ensure that the Communists did their share of fighting against Japan within the United Front. In Yan'an, Wang acted like an imperial envoy, passing on orders to his underlings: the Nationalist Party and the Communist Party, he asserted, both represented the people and should make mutual concessions. Wang criticised the decisions taken by Mao at the Luochuan conference, pointing out that Chiang was the head of the military headquarters with the power to command the Eighth Route Army. Wang Ming's words seemed like a 'direct blow on the head' for Mao, not least because Zhou Enlai and several others agreed with Wang. Sidelined, Mao sulked, later complaining that his authority 'did not extend beyond my cave'.[42]

Wang Ming, Stalin's most faithful student, was also instructed to take all necessary measures to eradicate Trotskyism from the ranks of the Party. 'Trotskyists must be hunted down, shot, destroyed. These are international provocateurs, fascism's most vicious agents,' Stalin explained in a private meeting. On his way back to China, Wang Ming stopped in Xinjiang, where he reportedly ordered that half a dozen Chinese Communist Party members, compromised during the purges in Moscow, be summarily shot.[43]

Chief among the suspects in Yan'an was Zhang Guotao. Zhang, who two years earlier had set up an alternative Central Committee, had already been taken to task by his rival Mao a few months earlier. In meetings lasting up to a week, he was attacked by Zhang Wentian, one of the erstwhile 'Bolshevists' who was acting on Mao Zedong's behalf. Forty of Zhang Guotao's underlings were arrested. In a public denunciation meeting, one young man jumped up and took him to task. Not all that glitters is gold, the speaker charged, since flies also glitter: 'Zhang Guotao is a fly in the Chinese Communist Party.' Wang Ming now grilled Zhang, telling him that 'you yourself are not a Trotskyist, but you have been used by them.' Zhang scrambled to prove his innocence. A few months after Wang Ming and Zhou Enlai had set off for Hankou, Zhang managed to abscond, abandoning Yan'an and the Communist Party to defect to the central government.[44]

Mao, although sidelined, maintained a firm grip on the Eighth Route Army. Red troops continued to advance behind enemy lines, filling a power vacuum, occasionally ambushing the enemy, more often than not consolidating their power in the countryside. On 20 January 1938 they destroyed the railway line outside Baoding, the capital of Hebei, only 120 kilometres from both Beiping and Tianjin. The countryside in north China was rapidly reverting to the lawless years that had followed the collapse of the empire in 1911, with remnant government soldiers, irregular troops, bandit gangs, partisans and self-defence units all fighting each other for turf, occasionally forming an alliance against the Japanese. The Communists prevailed, sometimes with the cooperation of the Nationalist Party, often without. They were far more experienced and also more determined, besides benefiting from a better organisation. In February 1938 the Communists and independent partisans could be spotted a mere twenty kilometres to the south of Tianjin, trying to cut the communication lines on which the Japanese depended. On 24 February, units from the Eighth Route Army took Bazhou, seventy kilometres to the west of Tianjin. Between the two railways in Hebei running parallel to each other, the one from Beiping to Hankou, the other from Tianjin to Nanjing, the Communists by March controlled eighteen counties – as well as every phase of local life.[45]

In county towns and larger villages, they held elections, ensuring that the only acceptable candidates were their own. Independent delegates who persisted in presenting themselves were quickly arrested and denounced as traitors or spies. The duly elected committees in turn appointed reliable cadres to all key positions, asked for voluntary payments and took over the public treasure in the name of nationalism and resistance. The bandits who roamed the countryside were eliminated, some shot, while partisans and other armed units were integrated within Communist ranks. As more recruits joined the guerrilla units, they were equipped with swords, spears and hand grenades. Twelve small arsenals were operating in the territory, making grenades from scrap iron and home-made gunpowder. A sprawling spy system alerted the base area to garrison changes in enemy-controlled cities. Five other such areas existed in the three provinces of Hebei, Chahar and Shanxi.[46]

In defying the directives of the Central Committee, Mao was supported by Liu Shaoqi, a quiet and earnest leader in the labour movement who had joined the Chinese Communist Party in 1921 and had spent time in Moscow. Liu made his mark by organising an underground network in Beiping and Tianjin, becoming Party secretary of north China in 1936. In April 1938, Mao and Liu urged the Eighth Route Army to move even deeper into north China. In July, Xu Xiangqian established a base area along the Hebei, Henan and Shandong borders. Its government, like that of the other base areas, was supposedly under the nominal control of Hankou, with Chiang Kai-shek overseeing an undercover army of guerrillas who farmed by day and fought by night, staying in touch through a network of sixty military radio stations. In reality it was autonomous. Constrained by Stalin and the necessities of the United Front, the grip the Communists exerted was firm but relatively benign: there was no class struggle and no major land distribution. The soldiers were also very polite, addressing elderly women as 'aunty' or 'grandmother'. Some even offered to sweep the floor. Foreign missionaries could work without fear of molestation, while merchants could travel in relative safety. But the propaganda was relentless, with books and pamphlets for the literate, lectures for the others, all pounding home a simple message: the Communists would protect the villagers from the common enemy, Japan. Surveillance was tight, as a complete register of the population was compiled so that safe-conduct passes could be issued. Even a stroll to a neighbouring village required passing through several checkpoints. Soon more detailed information about each person was added to the records, including notes about their political background. This was easily accomplished, since in any village everybody knew everything about everyone. The system was based on what one observer called a 'method of doubt': the Communists were suspicious of all, including themselves, viewing any interest in anything beyond their own ideology as a potential threat. 'They are so trained in duplicity that duplicity becomes second nature, and after a while they no longer trust anyone at all.'[47]

Soon the screws were applied. Temples, monasteries and churches were taken over, Confucianism denounced in compulsory village meetings for the feudal bonds that held the fabric of social life together. Emancipation was the key word, as people were set against each other in so-called 'struggle meetings', denouncing all authority, whether village elders, clan leaders or simply parents and siblings. That change was overdue had been widely accepted since the May Fourth Movement two decades earlier. The Communists, however, wanted to destroy the old order overnight, replacing all authority with their own.[48]

It helped that as early as March 1938 the Japanese began to retaliate against raids along the railway lines with the complete destruction of villages suspected of harbouring guerrilla fighters. More than 200 villages were incinerated in Hebei, with extensive loss of life. After a brief battle with the Communists who had occupied the county seat for months, a column of 500 Japanese soldiers entered the walled city of Anguo. They looted the place before burning it to the ground. Hundreds of bodies were piled high in the streets, bayoneted rather than shot. The greater the exactions, the firmer the subsequent grip of the Communist Party.[49]

A few months later, the Communists recaptured Anguo and invited Haldore Hanson, an American freelance journalist, to visit the city and witness how they were fighting the Japanese. A great show of activity was prepared for his benefit, with anti-American and anti-British posters erased from the walls, replaced with more complimentary ones featuring the Great Powers. Everywhere he went, several minders accompanied Hanson. The people he interviewed seemed to be perfectly free, insisted that they were perfectly free, and knew exactly what to say and when to say it. Like so many others, Hanson was deceived by the outward docility of the people and the discipline of the army. In Anguo the troops were reviewed for his benefit, as some 20,000 uniformed guerrillas shouted anti-Japanese slogans in English under an American flag. 'The only evidence of Communist leadership was the display of the hammer-and-sickle flag at all mass meetings,' Hanson opined, portraying the guerrilla fighters as 'Communists' in name only, true partisans close to the people who might very well, one day, defeat the Japanese, if given proper weapons. Other foreign journalists joined the fray, visiting different areas under Communist control. Zhu De went out of his way to present himself and his Party as true democrats. Although responsible for the abduction and occasional murder of dozens of foreign missionaries, he went so far as to attend a Catholic mass in the presence of foreign journalists. Christianity and Communism, he told three Americans who visited him in Shanxi province on his personal invitation, had 'similar motives', striving for peace and justice.[50]

By September 1938, the ranks of the Eighth Route Army had trebled from 30,000 to at least 100,000 troops. That same month, after a stalemate of almost ten months in a leadership divided into two factions, word arrived from Georgi Dimitrov, confirming Mao Zedong rather than Wang Ming as the undisputed head of the Party. There was no directive from the Comintern, not even a written recommendation, just an oral account of a conversation brought back from Moscow by Wang Jiaxiang, the Soviet-trained ideologist sent to the Kremlin by Mao to secure his grip over the Party.[51]

Mao treated this oral message from Moscow as holy writ, using it to summon the entire leadership back to Yan'an. Wang Jiaxiang opened the plenum, quoting Dimitrov's remark. Wang Ming offered little resistance, and was promptly replaced by Liu Shaoqi. Now that Wang was no longer a threat, Mao proceeded to use almost exactly the same language as his rival to recommend 'unprecedented unity against Japan' under the 'unified leadership of the national leader and supreme commander', namely Chiang Kai-shek. He even sent Chiang a letter, delivered personally by Zhou Enlai, expressing his 'boundless admiration' for him. This was Mao's way of disarming his enemy while submitting to Stalin. Chiang Kai-shek saw straight through the ploy, suspecting that yet more demands would follow the letter. These came in the guise of a request, among others, to permit Chinese Communist Party members to join the Nationalist Party. Chiang concluded that the Communists, like the proverbial Trojan horse, were once again trying to infiltrate the ranks, and rejected the proposal out of hand. One month later, behind closed doors, Mao refused to accept the principle of a unified command under the United Front or to take orders from the central government, insisting instead on complete autonomy for the Eighth Route Army to expand its territory and establish a foundation for a future victory. Every Communist had to grasp a simple principle, namely that 'political power grows from the barrel of a gun.'[52]

***

Chiang was not duped, but his dependence on aid from Moscow meant he had to play along. After Canton had been cut off and Hankou abandoned in favour of Chongqing, supplies were sent overland from Chita, first across the vast steppes of Mongolia to Lanzhou and then further south to Chengdu. Petrol depots and repair shops were built along the 2,500-kilometre route, with more than 200 lorries arriving daily by the end of 1939, bringing 30,000 tonnes of supplies. Camel caravans and convoys of donkey carts also arrived every day, uninterrupted by the rain, which made crossing the tundra difficult for heavy vehicles. Oil, pig bristles, tea, hemp and gold were carried back. Moscow sought to lengthen the war and spared no effort in pursuit of that goal, dispatching military instructors, planes, war material and credit to the tune of US$250 million. In Chengdu alone, the Russian mission boasted 1,000 members, half of them pilots, the other half handling propaganda.⁵³

When the lorries arrived in Lanzhou, some turned eastward and drove to Yan'an instead. Supplies to Yan'an increased after September 1938, when it became apparent to Moscow that the central government troops would be unable to hold on to Hankou. That same month a Yan'an delegation flew from Lanzhou to Spassk, 220 kilometres north-east of Vladivostok, successfully negotiating for artillery supplies and howitzers as well as motor oil.⁵⁴

Still, Stalin took no chances, bulking up his troops along the border with Manchuria until they outnumbered the Kwantung Army. For good measure, Stalin also ordered a purge of Siberia after a high-ranking general defected to Tokyo. One victim was Vasily Blyukher, later beaten to death, as well as 4,000 officers and military commissars. Between August 1937 and May 1938, some 11,000 Chinese living inside Siberia within a hundred kilometres of the frontier were arrested and deported, while 160,000 Koreans were relocated with great brutality, with hundreds shot or dying in transit.⁵⁵

Believing that Stalin's purges had weakened his fighting machine, the Kwantung Army saw an opportunity. They aimed for a weak spot, namely the deserted sand plains slashed by deep ravines along a small river near Nomonhan on the border with Outer Mongolia. In May 1939 the Japanese sent a cavalry unit, which was crushed. They persisted, building up a large armoured force and attacking again a month later. Stalin, who feared that the Japanese might smash their way across Mongolia and cut the Trans-Siberian Railway, sent Georgy Zhukov to the rescue. Over the following weeks Zhukov, not one for half measures, amassed a huge force combining mobile artillery, mechanised brigades, aircraft and 500 tanks. On 20 August he counter-attacked, tearing through the enemy and comprehensively pulverising their forces. Tokyo was shocked, its dismay compounded by the fact that on 23 August the Soviet Union signed a pact with Japan's ally Germany. Tokyo accepted a ceasefire on 16 September, its generals determined never to face Soviet tanks again. The Nomonhan Battle is little remembered and rarely mentioned, but it had a decisive effect on the evolution of the Second World War. Masanobu Tsuji, a leader in the Kwantung Army, would become a vocal proponent of attacking Pearl Harbor instead, as Tokyo began to covet the oil in the Dutch Indies rather than the deposits in Eastern Siberia. On 17 September, one day after the truce, the Soviet Union invaded Poland, dividing up the country with Germany.[56]

The Molotov–Ribbentrop non-aggression pact prompted outrage in Chongqing. Two months later, when Moscow and Tokyo signed a commercial treaty, Chiang Kai-shek's hope that the Soviet Union might enter the war with Japan was dashed. Yan'an, on the other hand, welcomed the pact, cheering it as a great victory. For years, the Comintern had promoted a United Front against fascism, but now Moscow had signed a pact with the Nazis. Every Communist Party was required to reverse course and toe the new line, namely opposition to the 'international reactionary capitalist class' which had tried to provoke a war between the Soviet Union and Germany. In Yan'an, Mao condemned the war in Europe as an 'imperialist war': 'whether it be Germany, Italy, or Japan, or whether it be Britain, the United States, or France, all the imperialist states participating directly or indirectly in the war have only a counter-revolutionary goal, a goal of plundering the people, an imperialist goal.' Mao concluded: 'oppose the imperialist war and organise a revolutionary war.'[57]

From the beginning there had been clashes between government units and the guerrilla fighters. As the Eighth Route Army poured onto the plains of north China, everywhere its soldiers attacked and absorbed partisan units or local armed forces under the government's command. As Jacques Guillermaz, a French military attaché in China and later eminent sinologist, pointed out, the Communists always followed the same scheme, namely provoke or exploit disorder, liquidate or incorporate all autonomous troops and set up a new administration. In Hebei, rather than fighting the Japanese, they repeatedly confronted government troops, managing to dislodge the head of the Baoding Field Headquarters. In Shanxi, from December 1939 onwards, ceaseless battles took place between the Eighth Route Army and the provincial troops of Yan Xishan. In Shandong, more than half of all casualties among the Communists were due to clashes with government forces. Bound by Moscow, Chiang Kai-shek was reluctant to react. But among the generals and their troops discontent mounted over the ceaseless depredations of guerrilla fighters. In June 1939 the Generalissimo put his foot down, formally warning Zhou Enlai, the Communist representative in Chongqing. When the Soviet Union invaded Finland on 30 November that year, a torn Chiang Kai-shek refused to veto Moscow's expulsion from the League of Nations. Deliveries of weapons were suspended overnight, even as central government troops began to knock out half a dozen red garrisons in Gansu and Ningxia, ensuring that both provinces – and the route from Chita to Yan'an via Lanzhou – remained in government hands.[58]

As the fighting resumed, the gloves came off and violence was ratcheted up. There were frequent reports of people being buried alive. Guillermaz noted that this was one of the most common forms of capital punishment the Communists inflicted, an observation largely confirmed by contemporary reports to Chongqing, although the practice apparently vanished in 1941. In April 1940, Yan Xishan reported that 200 soldiers had been buried alive after a division tried to cross a river guarded by the Communists. That same month, Xu Ming, the Communist head of Tunliu county, imposed the same penalty on fourteen people. In May 1940, after the New Fourth Army captured Sixian county in Anhui, the magistrate Zhu Tianxiu was buried alive. In Anguo, the Belgian missionary Raymond de Jaegher witnessed the wholesale massacre of known anti-Communists in early 1940. An underling of He Long explained that burying a man in a hole up to the waist with his hands tied behind his back, a sentinel making sure that no one could help him, was the best method. In Weixian, to the south of Hebei, forty-five village leaders were buried alive. General Shi Yousan, the central government's commander in south Hebei, issued a proclamation designating the Eighth Route Army a 'public enemy'.[59]

A state of terror was imposed on the local population, even those living far behind enemy lines. In Hebei, after Communist control had systematically supplanted the central administration, with some local officials summarily executed, enrolment in Party organisations became compulsory. All contact with the outside world was cut off. Legal tender was outlawed, replaced with paper notes issued by each base area. The wealthy were dispossessed or taxed out of existence. People lived in dreadful poverty, not least those caught between the reprisals of the Japanese and those of the Communists. The situation deteriorated after torrential rains caused widespread flooding in the autumn of 1939. The guerrilla fighters took the opportunity to attack the Japanese with renewed vigour, prompting even greater reprisals from the enemy. When the harvest failed in parts of the province, still inundated in March 1940, there were no food reserves left, these having been commandeered either by the guerrillas or by the Japanese forces. Millions were reduced to starvation, some eating the bark of trees or even earth. In Gaoyang, according to local missionaries, not a day went by without an encounter with guerrilla fighters, who incinerated entire villages and exacted contributions in grain, pushing a great many people to take to the roads to beg, many dying in regions which were even more deprived. The Japanese, on the other hand, retaliated without any discrimination, randomly burning and murdering. Whether trapped by the Communists or the Japanese, it was inevitably the wretched villagers who paid the price.[60]

The violence was not confined to Hebei. In Shanxi in March 1940, as they occupied new territory far behind enemy lines, the Communists executed hundreds of individuals considered politically unreliable, the majority of them local notables who had sided with Yan Xishan. At every level they replaced government officials with so-called 'poor peasants and workers' under their thumb. Well-to-do landowners who failed to toe the Party line were denounced as 'traitors' and 'capitulators', their assets seized and redistributed. Throughout the province, a radical revolutionary agenda led to the deaths of many villagers considered to be 'rich'.[61]

Missionaries were not exempt. Their land, too, was collectivised, their churches closed if the Japanese had not burned them down. In Yanjiaping, south of Chahar, the Trappists were required to perform public work or join the army. They were lucky: in Baoding, once again, the missionaries were ransomed.[62]

Violent reprisals by the Communists also took place in Manchuria. Once the Kwantung Army had conquered the region in September 1931, they brutally suppressed all opposition, including Russians suspected of promoting communism. So fierce was the clampdown that in 1935 Moscow abandoned its stretch of the Chinese Eastern Railway, selling the rights to Tokyo for a quarter of its value. A variety of partisans, volunteers, Korean nationalists and guerrilla fighters, not to mention local bandits, appeared during these years, including Zhao Shangzhi, one of the first Chinese Communist Party members in Manchuria and a graduate of the Whampoa Academy. In 1934, he emerged as leader of the North-east Anti-Japanese United Army, a Communist umbrella organisation welcoming all those fighting the Japanese. During the Long March, the guerrilla fighters lost touch with the Central Committee and drifted apart. By 1935, several base areas had appeared, mostly in the mountain range stretching along the Korean border from Dandong up north to Siberia, with guerrilla fighters living in caves deep inside the forests. They were equipped with first-rate Russian weapons, and even had sewing machines made in the Soviet Union. The Kwantung Army, much like Chiang Kai-shek south of the Great Wall, struggled to dislodge them, despite repeated military campaigns known as 'liquidate on the spot'. The Japanese began to ruthlessly enforce a 'protected village' programme, concentrating the villagers in enclosed settlements where everyone could be closely monitored. Their previous homes were burned, their crops destroyed and entire districts set ablaze.[63]

Still, the villagers fared little better under the Communists, who not only raided, pillaged and ransomed, but also burned, hanged and killed villagers suspected of working for the Japanese. At first, individuals were targeted. A propaganda team would arrive in the middle of the night with a blacklist, assemble the villagers, deliver a speech, read out a death sentence and drive a large nail in the back of the head of alleged collaborators. Later entire villages were razed to the ground. The Third Army under Zhao Shangzhi began 'burning and beating the local population, causing them to hate them', according to a report to the Central Committee dated May 1938. 'The Anti-Japanese United Army is worse than the bandits!' local people exclaimed. In the name of 'ethnic extirpation', minority people known as the Suoli were machine-gunned in one hamlet, including thirty women and children: 'they acted like fascists trying to exterminate a race,' according to the Communists' own report. When, on one occasion, foresters refused to comply with Zhao Shangzhi's orders, sixty of them were massacred, their bodies piled high in a demonstration of brute force. His approach was not uncommon, and was based on a simple principle, namely that one had to inflict a level of violence greater than that used by the enemy. As Zhao phrased it, 'the people are afraid of the Japanese, so they follow them. If the people are more afraid of us than of the Japanese, they will follow us!' Ultimately, due to mass desertions, fighting between different armed factions, defections to the enemy, widespread fear among the population and ruthless suppression by the Japanese, the Communists had to flee, crossing the border into Siberia in 1942. Zhao Shangzhi stayed behind and died at the hands of the Japanese. The city of Zhuhe was renamed Shangzhi in his honour in 1946.[64]

***

On 8 December 1940, Chief of Staff He Yingqin and his deputy Bai Chongxi sent a warning letter to the Red Army. The two generals explained that their Communist counterpart in the United Front had been included in the order of battle and allocated an operational area but had failed to follow orders from the supreme commander, instead carrying out subversive activities, marching into Hebei and Chahar and attacking central government units. 'The objective of your troops is that in all territories in the rear of the enemy, political structures and public organisations which are not in line with those of your own must be done away with. You are virtually lending a helping hand to the enemy and in fact you are acting as vanguards for the aggressors.' The generals may have been biased, but the Soviets agreed. Marshal Semyon Timoshenko, the people's commissar for defence, pointed out that the Chinese Communists were eager to direct their military forces against the central government and 'ignore the danger from Japan'.[65]

The letter was addressed to Zhu De, commander of the Eighth Route Army, but also specifically to Ye Ting, who headed the New Fourth Army. The main force of the New Fourth Army, established in December 1937 with the consent of Chiang Kai-shek, had moved in January 1938 towards Nanchang, the very city Ye Ting had besieged more than ten years earlier after defecting to the Communists. Remnants of the New Fourth Army were also scattered across the Yangtze valley, from Jiangxi all the way to the north of Hankou where Zhang Guotao had once reigned. The New Fourth Army was theoretically commanded by Gu Zhutong, the Nationalist general in charge of Jiangsu and south Anhui. But, like the Eighth Route Army, Ye Ting and his guerrilla fighters ignored orders and used the opportunity to establish base areas and enlist more recruits instead. Over the summer of 1940, they tried to cross the river and expand into the north of Jiangsu, clashing with guerrillas who had pledged allegiance to the central government. In early October, they besieged and destroyed a local garrison of over 20,000 soldiers under the command of Han Deqin at Huangqiao, a small hamlet in Jiangsu just across the Yangtze. Vast quantities of ammunition, rifles, pistols, machine guns and several mortars were captured by the New Fourth Army, which they used to push further into north Jiangsu and south Shandong, attacking government troops when and where they could. Caodian, a government stronghold where Han Deqin was waiting for reinforcements from Shandong, was besieged in November, although the Communists suffered huge casualties.[66]

Throughout the Sino-Japanese War, France, Britain and the United States had been careful not to antagonise Japan, refraining from overtly helping China. Even as the Nazi flag was raised over

Versailles in June 1940, Japan pressured French Indo-China to close the railway linking the port of Haiphong in Vietnam to Kunming, which had developed into a major transit centre to Chongqing. Shortly afterwards, when Britain temporarily closed the Burma Road linking Lashio to Kunming, China was more isolated than ever. Japan intensified its carpet-bombing of Chongqing, a city which would become the most bombed in history with around 3,000 tonnes of explosives dropped on it between 1939 and 1942. Mao seized his chance and intensified his attacks on government troops, hoping to take over parts of central China. On 12 July 1940, he ordered the New Fourth Army to concentrate all their forces on northern Jiangsu, the main thrust of the troops being the garrison in Huangqiao: 'all our forces', he wrote, 'should deal with Han Deqin and the other diehard troops in northern Jiangsu.' But on 27 September Japan signed a Tripartite Pact with Germany and Italy. This freed both Britain and the United States from all constraints in their dealings with China, with Roosevelt rapidly agreeing to help the Generalissimo. The Burma Road was reopened. In December, medical and military supplies from the United States were shipped to Vladivostok, then by rail to Chita, where they followed the familiar trail south to Lanzhou and Chengdu. Moscow, in November, had also resumed its military help, with a new contract for barter trade worth US$170 million concluded the following month. Chiang calculated that war between Russia and Germany was imminent, and that Moscow counted on him to keep Japan from attacking Siberia. Retaliation, at long last, became possible.[67]

On 9 December the Generalissimo ordered all Communist forces, including the New Fourth Army, to move north of the Yangtze River by the end of the year. Yan'an agreed, instructing Ye Ting first to delay, then to march north through the town of Maolin in Anhui province. The troops walked into a trap, paying for what they had done in Huangqiao. On 6 January 1941, some 80,000 government troops surrounded and attacked the 9,000 guerrilla fighters, capturing or eliminating them over the next ten days. Only 2,000 men were able to escape. Ye Ting was detained and later sent to a military tribunal. On 17 January, the

Generalissimo ordered the New Fourth Army disbanded. Yan'an never complied, reorganising it under the command of Chen Yi.[68]

Both sides were keen to keep the Maolin battle, later referred to as the New Fourth Army Incident, under wraps. But the conclusion was foregone: while the pretence of a United Front would prevail for another four to five years, a full-fledged clash between the two adversaries was inevitable.

7
Biding Time
(1941–1945)

On 13 April 1941, to the dismay of Chongqing, Moscow signed a neutrality pact with Tokyo. The pact precluded the Soviet Union from assisting China militarily. To make matters worse, the same day a declaration was signed whereby Moscow recognised Manchukuo's territorial integrity, while Japan reciprocated for Mongolia. It violated every agreement signed between China and the Soviet Union, not least the non-aggression pact of 1937. In Chongqing, the tone turned resolutely anti-Soviet, with articles in the press lambasting Moscow. Simmering resentment of the Comintern's material and moral support for the Communists surfaced in what one diplomat called an 'explosion of anti-Communist passion'. When less than two months later 3 million German troops crossed the Russian border in a three-pronged attack, taking Stalin completely by surprise, few in Chongqing expressed sympathy. Chiang Kai-shek himself had repeatedly predicted the offensive, even giving 21 June 1941 as a date. His fear now was that Russia would go down too fast, his hope that Moscow's assistance to the Communists would dwindle.[1]

Japan, instead of using the opportunity to march into Siberia and claim the oilfields, was still shaken by its crushing encounter with Soviet armour two years earlier. Tokyo preferred to wait for the Germans to take Moscow first. But as it became apparent that the Nazis were barely advancing across the vast Russian plains, Tokyo opted instead for a desperate gamble, namely a lunge towards the rich deposits of oil, rubber and tin to be found in South-east Asia. A trade embargo against Japan made the colonial possessions of Britain and the Netherlands even more compelling, although it entailed control of the Pacific, which, in turn, implied a pre-emptive strike against the naval power of the United States. On 7 December 1941, the Japanese launched a surprise attack on Pearl Harbor, forcing the United States to enter the war. By February 1942, all of South-east Asia was under Japan's direct or indirect control, including the American Philippines, British Hong Kong, Dutch Indonesia, Siam, the Malay States, Singapore and Burma. All supply roads to Chongqing, with the exception of the laborious caravan trail across Mongolia, were now closed.

In Chongqing the Americans had been replacing the Russians as early as March 1941, when Congress passed the Lend-Lease Act, including China in its policy of supplying Allied nations with food, oil and war materiel. Pilots began arriving, recruited and trained by Claire Chennault, a retired US Army captain who had served as an adviser to the Chinese Air Force since the Marco Polo Bridge Incident in July 1937. In a great reversal, even as the Americans arrived, the Russian military specialists began leaving Chongqing, recalled to defend their own country. But the Americans did not match the Russians in their financial and military aid. Roosevelt was willing to lend a hand, but stuck to a 'Europe First' policy, meaning that China had to play second fiddle, never receiving parity with either Britain or the Soviet Union. With limited outside support, Chiang began to curtail his military operations and prepare instead for the inevitable confrontation with the Communists.[2]

The moment Germany invaded the Soviet Union, Mao, like all Communists, had to change his tone once more, switching from a denunciation of the 'imperialist war', allegedly waged by France, Britain and the United States, back to a condemnation of 'international fascism', to be fought hand in hand with France, Britain, the United States and other allies. This he did effortlessly, calling for an 'International United Front against

Fascism' on 23 June 1941. Moscow was pleased, agreeing on 9 July to send US$1 million in instalments to Yan'an, even as all aid to Chongqing ceased. The money, as always, came with strings attached, namely the creation of a national United Front and a commitment to bog down the Japanese troops if they were to attack the Soviet Union. Yan'an promised to 'improve relations' with the central government, but protested that its troops were too weak, its ammunition running too low and its territory too small to enable it to coordinate significant military operations. It asked for more weapons and more ammunition. After their pleas had been turned down and the German troops moved closer to Moscow, the Communists began to doubt their protector, becoming openly hostile. The same pattern would repeat itself over the following years, namely admonitions from Moscow to unite with Chongqing and fight the Japanese, invariably followed by pledges made and then broken by Yan'an.[3]

Mao, like Chiang, counted on the United States and the Soviet Union to defeat Japan. He, too, dug in, determined to preserve his forces instead of fighting the enemy. He began to turn his attention towards the Party, keen to whip its ranks into shape and prepare it for the civil war looming on the horizon.

***

For several years, Mao had laboured to establish himself as a Marxist theoretician, considered an indispensable attribute for any Communist leader worth his salt. In this task he was helped by Chen Boda, a bookish but ambitious young man trained in Moscow who would become his ghost-writer. Together they penned *On New Democracy*, a pamphlet published in January 1940 that portrayed the Communist Party as a broad front striving to unite all 'revolutionary classes', including the 'national bourgeoisie', in the fight against imperialism and capitalism. China, Mao opined, was a semi-colonial and semi-feudal society demanding a revolution in two stages: first a democratic revolution, then a socialist revolution. The new democracy, he explained, was not the old bankrupt democracy dominated by a bourgeois minority so commonly found in capitalist countries, but a 'joint dictatorship of all revolutionary classes', a true majority protected by the leadership of the Communist Party. Mao welcomed all the 'revolutionary people', including 'intellectuals' and even elements of the 'bourgeoisie'. He promised a multi-party system, universal and equal suffrage, democratic freedoms and protection of private property. It was an entirely fictitious programme, but one that held broad popular appeal.[4]

Several years earlier, the central government had organised an election of deputies to a National Assembly, tasked with adopting a constitution for the Republic of China. After war broke out in 1937 the delegates had been unable to convene. In November 1940, after the Nationalist Party had retreated to the safety of Chongqing, the National Assembly was summoned once again. But when central government troops clashed with Communist forces the following month, the convocation was postponed yet again, this time until the end of the war. Mao, in November 1937, had opposed popular representation, partly because in his view a 'large number of Party members are of petty bourgeois origin'. But when Chongqing postponed the National Assembly he seized the opportunity to launch a campaign in favour of 'constitutional government', ordering that Associations for the Promotion of Constitutional Government be established throughout the territories under Communist control. In March 1940, as part of the New Democracy, Mao introduced elections for People's Political Councils, to be based on a so-called 'One Third' system (also called 'Three-Thirds'). It worked as follows: Communist Party members should account for a third, representing the 'proletariat' and the 'poor'; 'progressive elements' who did not belong to the Communist Party, representing the 'petty bourgeoisie', should also be allocated a third; and 'intermediate elements', standing for the 'enlightened gentry', should be given the final third. Determining who was 'progressive' and who 'enlightened' was entirely up to the Chinese Communist Party, as was the decision to ban those defined as 'traitors' or 'counter-revolutionaries' from the electoral process.[5]

The One Third system, much like the New Democracy, was based on a Leninist principle called 'democratic centralism', which meant that all major political decisions were reached by a voting process which was binding upon all Communist Party members. In this system, Party members voted for a National Congress every few years, members of the congress in turn approving the membership of the Central Committee. The Central Committee, once elected, nominally selected a Politburo, or Central Political Bureau, composed of a few dozen members. Day-to-day decisions were made by a much smaller Standing Committee, often composed of seven or eight elderly members. The most powerful person was the Chairman. In practice, the power structure was inverted, as supreme power flowed from the hands of the man at the top of the pyramid. Those eligible to vote were presented with a list of candidates, merely ratifying decisions taken at the highest level. As Mao explained, from the National Congress down to the provincial, county, district and township congresses, at all levels the respective government bodies were to be elected in a 'joint dictatorship of all the revolutionary classes'. 'Only a government based on democratic centralism can fully express the will of all revolutionary people and fight the enemies of the revolution most effectively.'[6]

The One Third system was implemented from February 1941 onwards and completed towards the end of 1942. The world on paper was far removed from the reality on the ground, and much arm-twisting was required to persuade non-Party members to present themselves at the elections. Individuals stigmatised by the Party as 'rich peasants' and 'landlords' not surprisingly objected that they had been targets during land reform and would be used again for political purposes. 'They used you in the past, they will use you again,' as one of them put it succinctly. Party cadres, on the other hand, were just as suspicious, fearing that their grip on power would be diluted. In some places, including the recently conquered sub-district of Longdong, no more than the facade of a One Third system was offered, while in reality all non-Party candidates were deemed to be 'rotten' and summarily excluded. In other cases, contrariwise, local cadres were accused of being too lax, admitting local thugs or opium smokers. Yet always the Party had to have an absolute majority, regardless of the idea of three separate tranches. One example of a problematic situation to be avoided was Ansai county, where just twenty-four out of thirty-four elected people were Party members. By 1944 the overwhelming majority of elected candidates across fourteen counties in Shaanxi were 'poor peasants', ensuring that 'Communist Party members and progressive forces, from the point of view of their class background, combine to represent an enormous majority.'[7]

Candidates deemed suitable were elected to a People's Political Council. The council was supposed to elect and supervise the government. But it was made clear from the beginning that the system reflected 'neither a separation of powers' between the supervisory and the executive nor the existence of 'two equal powers' between the supervisory and the executive. At every level, the government remained the organ of executive power, and elected council members could not use their supervisory role 'to restrain the government's executive power'. Their role was further whittled down when elected council members were discouraged from devoting themselves to committee work by taking leave of absence from their daytime job. 'One full-time member per council for each county is enough,' since the emergence of a countervailing power to the clout of the Party was to be avoided.[8]

To call the elections a sham would miss the point. Although the Communists had never represented more than a fraction of the entire population, they were convinced that they stood for a majority of villagers and workers, repressed by a capitalist minority bent on using every trick in the book to maintain power. In the Communist view, the democracy of their opponents was a sham, a thinly disguised dictatorship of the bourgeoisie, whereas their own dictatorship of the proletariat was the only true democracy. It was a quintessential Orwellian attempt to twist the meaning of words and turn the world upside down ('war is peace, freedom is slavery, ignorance is strength'). In the name of the proletarian majority, eternal vigilance was required, based on the widespread fear that 'landlords', 'traitors', 'counter-revolutionaries' and other nefarious elements could use the elections to worm their way into the Party and subvert it from within. This was made abundantly clear in February 1943, when it was explained at the highest level that enemies had infiltrated the ranks as a result of a 'misunderstanding' of the electoral system, with some cadres erroneously believing that 'anyone can come' and present themselves for election. 'Without thorough elimination of spies and traitors we cannot build a stable New Democracy,' the Party thundered.[9]

The Communist Party lost no opportunity to trumpet its New Democracy, either through unrelenting press propaganda in Free China, where Communist publications were allowed, or through interviews granted with foreigners in Yan'an, where Nationalist publications were banned. In Chongqing, Zhou Enlai was tireless in propagating the Communist Party's many achievements. On 20 November 1941, he spent a full hour with members of the British Parliamentary Mission, complaining that the central government paid only lip service to the cause of democracy. Zhou requested that the mission exert its influence on foreign opinion to bring about an early assembling of a 'constitutional parliament in China', and help towards the granting of 'individual liberty in the exercise of free speech'. Most foreigners were duped, but not the Russians. As Dimitrov wrote in his diary, Zhou Enlai was 'organising secret conferences with Chiang Kai-shek's enemies and foreign correspondents that are directed against Chiang Kai-shek'.[10]

Mao also received the occasional foreign visitor to promote his message of freedom and democracy. One such was Carel Brondgeest, a Dutch engineer who escaped from Japanese-occupied Beiping to Chongqing via Yan'an in January 1942. Mao told him that the Communists always 'strictly kept' their promises, and had even taken measures to limit the representation of the Communist Party in any government department to no more than one-third. 'We do not have the slightest intention of promoting a proletarian revolution with dictatorship,' Mao explained. His aim, on the contrary, was to 'build a new democratic republic where all classes enjoy equal rights'. A few months later, René d'Anjou and Georges Uhlmann, two Frenchmen, also visited Yan'an, reporting back to the world that the Communists, thanks to the

One Third system, were 'more democratic' than the Nationalists. William Band, an English professor of physics who left Yenching University in Beiping the moment the Japanese took over the institution in December 1941, reported that the Communists had established the 'first full democratic government the country had ever known in its long history'. This 'democratic system', Band and his wife helpfully added, was 'patterned after that used in Soviet Russia'. Not one of these foreign visitors ever encountered a single member of the Nationalist Party in Yan'an.[11]

Party membership grew, reaching 800,000 by the end of 1941, a far cry from the situation before the outbreak of the war in 1937. But recruitment was hasty, with many local members having joined for practical rather than ideological reasons. A great many were illiterate. As a detailed survey of village branches across thirteen counties showed, three out of four members could not read. The majority were roped in by acquaintances keen to reach a quota set by the Party. In some cases villagers merely attending a public meeting were signed on without even a cursory background check. Half of the recruits had no inkling of what the Communist Party was, and one in five could not explain why they had joined. Many hoped to obtain some kind of material benefit. Only a third expressed commitment to the organisation and a willingness to work for it. 'Peasants', the report concluded, had a 'backward and narrow mentality', and spurned the United Front. Most of all, a majority of local district and county leaders simply had no idea what was happening in the villages and were unable to say whether regular Party meetings were being held.[12]

A second group of recruits were at the other end of the social spectrum. Attracted by the promise of a more democratic future, many thousands of students, teachers, artists, writers and journalists poured into Yan'an. The vast majority were idealists, young volunteers keen to fight for equality, justice and freedom, the proclaimed values of the Communist Party. They were disenchanted with their government, which they viewed as incompetent, corrupt and repressive, dominated by a clique unconcerned by widespread poverty and injustice and insincere in their commitment to democracy. Yan'an was the new

Mecca, the name of a mysterious valley somewhere in the north where a different world existed, one where government officials lived cheek by jowl with the peasants, devoted entirely to their wellbeing. Many undertook an arduous journey to the promised land, trekking through difficult terrain on foot, avoiding enemy forces, slipping through the blockade to reach the hallowed destination. On seeing the heights of Yan'an, with its octagonal pagoda towering on a hill to the south of the city, some volunteers were reduced to tears, hugging each other, a few belting out the Internationale.

With help from Moscow, Mao initially used the young idealists to undermine his rivals, not least Wang Ming. Pavel Mif, Wang Ming's erstwhile mentor, was among the many victims of Stalin's Great Purge, executed as a counter-revolutionary in September 1939. A few months later, the Personnel Department of the Comintern specifically recommended that Wang Ming be discarded from the Chinese Communist Party's leadership. A list of other leaders to be excluded from key positions followed, most of them belonging to the group of 'Bolsheviks' who had dominated the Politburo under Wang Ming in the early 1930s. These included Bo Gu, the bookish young man who had become Party secretary and taken Mao to task at the Ningdu Conference in October 1932. All had been fervent followers of their master in Moscow, who now threw them to the wolves. The Comintern recommended instead some of Mao's most trusted followers, including Lin Biao, Deng Xiaoping, He Long and Xu Xiangqian. Mao's position was cemented. 'Mao Zedong is certainly the most important political figure in the Chinese Communist Party. He knows China better than the other leaders, knows the people, understands politics and generally frames issues correctly,' the report concluded.[13]

Mao waited until September 1941 to fire a warning shot across the bows of his rivals. In an opening statement to a plenum of the Politburo, he systematically reviewed the history of the Chinese Communist Party, condemning everyone who had crossed him in the past for their 'left opportunism', 'subjectivism', 'dogmatism' or 'sectarianism'. Mao offered a canonical version of the Party's history, one in which a long series of errors against the correct Party line had been committed until he had finally triumphed, leading the Red Army to Yan'an on the Long March. Wang Ming was not identified by name, but few had any doubts as to the identity of the 'left opportunist' who had been even worse than Li Lisan. All of them had something in common: 'they took on the outward appearance of Marxists, but they were sham Marxists.'

In a thinly veiled attack on the 'Bolsheviks' who had for so long used their training in Moscow to dominate the Party, Mao scoffed at these 'sham Marxists' who invoked *Das Kapital*, the *Anti-Dühring* and other works by Marx and Engels, but failed to offer a solution to any of the country's practical problems. He called instead for the sinification of Marxism, urging all leading cadres to establish small study groups to bring theory and practice together in solving concrete issues within China. In mass meetings, everyone was required to 'get up on the platform and speak'.[14]

Careful listeners realised that what was to come was a test of loyalty to Mao. On 16 March 1942, Li Weihan, one of the 'Bolsheviks' who had been blacklisted by the Comintern, viciously denounced Zhang Wentian, also on the Moscow list. Zhang was the director of a Central Research Institute, an organisation Mao singled out for harbouring so-called 'Red Professors' who needed to be brought down a peg or two. In an editorial in the *Liberation Daily*, the Party's mouthpiece in Yan'an, Hu Qiaomu, a loyal follower, denounced these 'theoreticians' as 'garbage'. Assailed from all sides, the 'Red Professors' soon declared that the Marxist and Leninist works they had been studying were 'less useful than shit'.[15]

Mao also encouraged the young volunteers to attack 'dogmatism' and its alleged practitioners. They needed little prodding. Soon after arriving in Yan'an, they had been quickly disabused. Instead of equality, they found a rigid hierarchy. Every organisation had three different kitchens, the best food being reserved for the senior leaders. From the amount of grain, sugar, cooking oil, meat and fruit to the quality of health care and access to information, an individual's position in the Party hierarchy determined everything. Even the quality of tobacco and writing paper varied according to rank. Medicine was scarce for those on the lower rungs of the ladder, although leading cadres had personal doctors and sent their children to Moscow. At the apex of the Party stood Mao, driven around in the only car in Yan'an and living in a large mansion with heating especially installed for his comfort.[16]

Encouraged to express themselves, the young volunteers joined the fray. In one essay after another, they took to task the 'dogmatism' of the Communist Party. Mao personally polished and revised several of their essays. Ding Ling, a young writer who had set the literary world on fire with her iconoclastic stories in the late 1920s, exposed the leadership's cavalier treatment of women in an editorial published to mark International Working Women's Day. Others expressed discontent with the way the red capital was run. But none went as far as a young man named Wang Shiwei. In an essay entitled 'Wild Lilies' he took the 'big shots' to task for their arrogance, their unjustified privileges and their inhumanity towards ordinary people, whom they 'looked upon as a race apart'. They binged on food even when the amount of soup to nourish the sick was restricted. Above all, they suppressed freedom of speech and alienated the young volunteers.[17]

Mao's response came in May 1942. In a speech delivered at the launch of the Yan'an Forum on Literature and Art, he invoked the work of Stalin and his propagandist-in-chief, Andrei Zhdanov. Zhdanov, in the opening address to the first Soviet Writers' Congress in 1934, had paid tribute to the 'guiding genius' of Stalin, invoking the famous line of his master in which writers were characterised as 'engineers of the human soul'. In an age of class struggle, Zhdanov pointed out, all good writing was political. Mao, likewise, declared that art was a tool of political struggle. Humanism, he contended, was the very embodiment of the kind of bourgeois literature from which revolutionary writers must break free. Creative freedom, he further explained, was a sham of the bourgeoisie, while writers and artists, compared to the proletariat, were the most 'ignorant', 'carrying around a lot of exploiters' filth in their heads'. 'Or,' as Mao said, 'to put it more elegantly, their innermost souls are still in the kingdom of the petty bourgeoisie.' In short, art must serve the revolution.[18]

Two close followers now stepped to the fore. One was Zhou Yang, a literary theorist with a sharp tongue who headed the Cultural Committee under the Central Committee. He was China's Zhdanov, tightening up every publication throughout all areas controlled by the Communist Party to ensure that his master's vision prevailed. To impose ideological control over every writer and artist, Zhou Yang began a close collaboration with Kang Sheng. A sinister figure with a pencil moustache and thick spectacles, always dressed in black, Kang had been trained in Moscow, where he had helped the secret police persecute hundreds of students from China during the Great Terror. But Kang had arrived in Yan'an together with Wang Ming, so his name had appeared on the Comintern's blacklist. Kang worked hard to redeem himself, launching a pitiless campaign to eradicate any lingering influence of free thinking among the young volunteers. One by one, they were interrogated in front of large crowds, made to confess in endless indoctrination meetings and forced to denounce each other in a bid to prove themselves. A contrite Ding Ling saved herself by pointing the finger at Wang Shiwei, whom she described as 'despicable, petty, capricious, complex, and shady'. She would soon join the ranks of the cultural warriors working for Mao, although she, too, would eventually meet her fate in a similar campaign a decade later.[19]

Some suspects were locked up in caves, others taken to mock executions. For months on end, life in Yan'an was a relentless succession of interrogations and rallies conducted in an atmosphere of fear, suspicion and betrayal. Any attempt to contact the outside world was interpreted as evidence of espionage. The pressure was too much for some, who broke down, lost their minds or committed suicide. Mao demanded absolute loyalty from intellectuals, who were forced to reform themselves ideologically by studying and discussing essays by himself, Stalin and others.

Kang Sheng, his keen henchman, also investigated the rank and file to find spies and undercover agents. This campaign, known as the 'Rectification Movement', peaked in the summer of 1943, when a virtual state of siege was introduced in Yan'an, with suspects ordered to stay at their place of work and guards stationed at the gates of offices and schools. A mournful silence enveloped the city, as private conversations became dangerous. Even married men were not allowed to see their families. 'Fear, fear, and again fear sums up the general atmosphere in Yenan,' noted one Russian living in the red capital. By now, people were being made to confess their crimes, imaginary or otherwise, in batches of several hundred at a time. The majority pleaded guilty to espionage. In some organisations the number of exposed agents allegedly serving on behalf of either the Nationalists or the Japanese reached a perfect 100 per cent. All principles, whether moral or ideological, were cast aside to make way for a tried-and-tested survival mechanism, namely self-humiliation. The Communist Party now had a hold on every individual, keeping records of their every confession.[20]

Writers and artists, by most accounts, were hit the hardest, with a great many forced to perform manual work, more often than not useless and insulting tasks, including the obligatory knitting of socks. Uneducated people crammed with dogma came to the fore, ensuring that art served the revolution. Not a single good novel was produced.[21]

But well beyond Yan'an, outside the relatively privileged circles of culture and education, the Rectification Movement was actually much harsher, even though far less is known about it. Mao needed educated people. He sought to break them and transform them into his obedient servants, not dispose of them. Village cadres, on the other hand, were dispensable, just like ordinary people, who were also subjected to the campaign. In Shenfu county (later renamed Shenmu), 150 kilometres north of Yan'an, the Rectification Movement identified 400 suspects. One in four was killed or driven to suicide, with victims jumping from cliffs or into rivers. In Longdong county, acclaimed as the home of the One Third system, 500 people were arrested, many meeting a similar fate. Longdong was in the eastern part of Gansu province. Not far away, on the other side of the government blockade, was Zhenyuan, where special facilities were set up to welcome young people who had managed to escape the campaign, many of them arriving exhausted and badly famished. How many died will never be known, but in 1944 Zhu Shaoliang, deputy chief of staff of the Military Commission in Chongqing, suggested that 3,000 young people suspected of being spies or traitors had been physically liquidated. Wang Ming – admittedly somewhat biased – later testified from Moscow that 'it became common practice in all sub-divisions to arrest people, hang them up by their arms, beat them, even kill.' Cadres in charge of the campaign would summon the villagers, line them up and order them to confess to being 'counter-revolutionaries', 'enemy spies' or 'traitors'. Those who 'confessed' were allowed to go home. Those who were stubborn were tortured and placed under surveillance. The result was that not only the young volunteers but the vast majority of the population, at one point or another, became suspects. By December 1944, even Moscow expressed its dismay at the 'repulsive manner' in which Kang Sheng had purged the grassroots.[22]

Mao also needed experienced leaders, but not before they submitted to his will and kissed the ring. For this purpose he set up a Central General Study Committee, which he packed with trusted underlings. Chief among these was Liu Shaoqi, who would emerge as his Number Two. The Study Committee ran everything in Yan'an, in effect converting the Communist Party into Mao's personal dictatorship. Leading members who had crossed Mao in the past were humiliated, forced to write confessions and apologise publicly for their mistakes. Zhou Enlai, who was one of them, tried hard to redeem himself by proclaiming his undying support for Mao. This was deemed insufficient, so he was tested in a series of denunciation meetings where he was forced to describe himself as a 'political swindler' who lacked principles. It was a gruelling exercise in self-abasement, but Zhou managed to emerge from the ordeal as Mao's faithful assistant, determined never to oppose him again. Unlike Stalin, Mao rarely had his rivals shot, transforming them instead into accomplices who were on permanent probation, forced to work tirelessly to prove themselves. The one exception was Wang Ming, who by one account was slowly poisoned and kept a virtual prisoner in Yan'an. By the end of 1944 Georgi Dimitrov stepped in to plead on his behalf. He survived, travelling to Moscow in 1956 for medical treatment and never returned, dying in 1974 under Soviet protection.[23]

When the Rectification Campaign ended in 1944, around 15,000 alleged enemy agents and spies had been unmasked. Mao had allowed the terror to run amok, assuming the role of a self-effacing, distant yet benevolent leader. He then stepped in to curb the violence, letting Kang Sheng take the blame. Some 90 per cent of those who had confessed, it had come to light, were not in fact real spies or traitors and were to be rehabilitated immediately. Those who had managed to survive the horror turned to Mao as a saviour.[24]

Mao, on launching the Rectification Campaign in 1942, had called for the 'sinification of Marxism'. It soon became clear what this meant: instead of poring over Marx and Lenin, all and sundry should immerse themselves in the writings of Mao Zedong. Foreign admirers, including venerable sinologists of every hue, have applauded the audacity with which Mao allegedly adapted the tenets of Marxism–Leninism to the specific conditions of China, but they have missed a simple point: Mao was just following directives from Moscow. On 15 May 1943, Stalin dissolved the Comintern. This came three months after the battle of Stalingrad, a brutal clash of steel, flesh and fire which stopped the Germans and turned the tide of war. Two months later, German and Italian troops surrendered to the Allies in Tunisia. Stalin could see victory beckoning ahead, and began to plan the endgame. Instead of 'socialism in one country', he now insisted that Communists in different countries adapt their organisation 'to the peculiarities of the concrete historical situation and to problems immediately resulting from this situation'. In short, each Communist Party was enjoined to adapt in a flexible, independent way to the specific conditions they faced. The resolution to dissolve the Comintern insisted on the 'deep differences of the historic paths of development of various countries, the differences in their character and even contradictions in their social orders, the differences in the level and tempo of their political, social and economic development, the differences in the degree of consciousness and organization of workers'. 'Any sort of international centre would encounter insuperable obstacles in solving the problems facing the movement in each country,' the resolution further determined. Stalin was not cutting loose the Communist parties outside the Soviet Union, of course. He was trying to present himself as a true democrat, keen on more American supplies and lend-lease war materiel. But he was also thinking strategically. The Communist parties in the countries he would conquer on his march east and west had to appear genuinely popular and indigenous, not mere puppets manipulated by Moscow.[25]

Only six weeks after the Comintern's dissolution, on 1 July 1943, the twenty-second anniversary of the founding of the Chinese Communist Party, Mao announced that the Rectification Campaign had 'guaranteed ideological and political unanimity in the Party'. His verdict signalled the beginning of an unlimited cult of personality. A few months earlier, at a Politburo meeting from which the bedridden Wang Ming was absent, Mao had emerged as Chairman of the Communist Party. All now had to acclaim the Chairman and study 'Mao Zedong Thought', a term coined four days later by Wang Jiaxiang, the Soviet-trained ideologist who had helped Mao sideline Wang Ming in 1938: 'Mao Zedong Thought is China's Marxism–Leninism, China's Bolshevism, and China's communism.' By far the most enthusiastic sycophant, however, was Liu Shaoqi, who unhesitatingly acclaimed the Chairman as a 'great revolutionary leader' and 'master of Marxism–Leninism'.[26]

Liu's praise prompted others to rally around their leader in a great show of fealty, acclaiming him as the 'great revolutionary helmsman', a 'saving star', a 'genius strategist' and a 'genius politician'. Some penned poems, others wrote essays. One of the greatest admirers was Zhou Enlai:

> There is nothing clearer from the developments over these three years than that all who opposed or doubted Comrade Mao Zedong's leadership or views in the past have now been proven utterly wrong. The twenty-two-year history of our

Party proves that throughout this entire historical period, only Comrade Mao Zedong's views have consistently developed into a Sinicised Marxist-Leninist line, which is the line of Chinese communism. Comrade Mao Zedong's orientation is the orientation of the Chinese Communist Party. Comrade Mao Zedong's line is the line of Chinese Bolshevism.[27]

The panegyrics were 'nauseatingly slavish', commented Theodore White and Annalee Jacoby, two American journalists. When Mao stood up and spoke, hardened men tempered by years of guerrilla warfare would studiously take notes 'as if drinking from the fountain of knowledge'.[28]

The Party's mouthpiece *Liberation Daily*, overseen by Mao himself, used giant headlines to proclaim that 'Comrade Mao Zedong is the Saviour of the Chinese People!' By the end of 1943, portraits of Mao could be seen everywhere, prominently displayed next to those of Marx, Engels, Lenin and Stalin. Badges featuring his likeness circulated among the Party elite, while his profile appeared in gold relief on the facade of a huge auditorium in Yan'an. People sang to his glory: 'The East is Red, the Sun is Rising; China has Brought Forth a Mao Zedong; He Seeks the People's Happiness.'[29]

In April 1945, after a seventeen-year interval, a Party Congress was finally convened. Hundreds of the delegates had been persecuted during the Rectification Campaign, some of them replaced by men loyal to Mao. All hailed their leader, who was elected to all the top organs of the Party. Mao Zedong Thought was enshrined in the Party constitution. In his opening report, Liu Shaoqi mentioned the Chairman's name more than a hundred times, referring to him as 'the greatest revolutionary and statesman in all of Chinese history' as well as 'the greatest theoretician and scientist in all of Chinese history'.[30]

The Rectification Campaign had unfolded over two years, leaving few people untouched. The economy was neglected, just as the financial contributions of the central government came to an end after the New Fourth Army Incident in early 1941. From 1937 to 1941, the government in Yan'an had relied heavily on outside aid to finance its operations. The Chongqing appropriation accounted for 75 to 90 per cent of its total budget. Stalin, too, quietly contributed, sending some US$350,000 in 1940, followed by US$1 million in 1941. But after the Nazis had invaded the Soviet Union, financial assistance vanished. Without Chiang Kai-shek's help, deprived of financial assistance from Moscow, the Communists were forced to become self-sufficient. But the region they controlled was sparsely populated and mired in poverty. Yan'an was surrounded by brittle loess plateaus covered with meagre shrubs and an occasional stunted tree, although the valleys and the foothills were studded with green fields. The villagers, who for generations had scraped a meagre living from the soil, had to produce more in order to feed the leaders, cadres and soldiers of the Communist Party. They also had to take time out from work to praise the many benefits of communism in compulsory village meetings, besides attending struggle sessions designed to uncover counter-revolutionary spies.

Since the red capital was in no position to subsidise the regions it controlled, each commander imposed his own heavy taxes on the local population. In Yan'an county, the average amounted to 35 per cent of the annual yield, or roughly five times the burden imposed by the central government. Some farmers, crushed by taxation, decided to move on to greener pastures. From Yan'an around 800 families managed to abscond in the spring of 1942, while 500 households left the adjoining region of Ansai. Few counties were spared. The people who remained behind lacked enthusiasm, aware that any surplus they produced would be procured. 'The general mood among the peasants when it comes to production is low,' one report stated. They feared that 'after procurement of grain there will be procurement of money.' Xie Juezai, the commissar in charge of the economy, observed in his private diary that in some cases the amount of grain the state levied was equivalent to the entire year's harvest: 'there is nothing left to eat once grain taxes have been paid.'[31]

The Communist Party, which issued its own currency, decided to print more of it, which led to rampant inflation. Inflation was also widespread in Free China, but the price differentials that developed on either side of the blockade were disadvantageous to the Communists. More had to be exported for less, causing severe shortages and the general impoverishment of the entire population. So much unbacked currency was pumped into the economy that it was driven out of circulation on the black market. Already in 1942, Mao himself noted that '[In the worst times, we] have neither clothes to wear, nor oil for cooking, nor paper to write on, nor vegetables to eat. Soldiers have no stockings and shoes and cadres have no quilts in the [harsh] winter.'[32]

The Communist Party attempted to remedy the situation by launching a frugality campaign, cutting the number of government employees and reducing their food rations. They also ordered the soldiers to take part in production. In 1944, as the situation became critical, local cadres tried to boost the number of people working in the fields. 'No One is Idle' became the slogan, as women, students, even children were press-ganged into special production teams.[33]

This made a difference, but the key to economic survival was found elsewhere, in a robust plant with grey-green leaves, bearing a pod that burst open into a beautiful, frilly flower with red, white or lilac petals. The poppy was an ideal crop for the arid provinces of the north-west, not least Shaanxi, where opium had been produced since the mid-nineteenth century. The Communists had long dealt in opium, reintroducing the crop in Yongxin county near their base in Jinggangshan in 1928. The milky latex harvested from the seed pods, once processed into a brown paste, kept the economy afloat. Even this, however, the Communists initially managed to botch, as inexperienced cadres ignored advice from local farmers, ruining hundreds of hectares by planting the seeds too early. Still, cultivation flourished, with the Communist Party producing 150 tonnes of opium in 1943, contributing 40 per cent of total revenue. Opium in effect saved the Communists from economic ruin.[34]

By April 1944, Mao had turned the Party into an instrument of his own will. Throughout, foreigners had been banned from Yan'an, except for a handful of visitors. Having cleaned the house, Mao was ready to invite guests. Posters attacking the central government were removed, loud slogans painted over. There were so many of them that a small army had to be deployed for the purpose. Model villages, set up specifically to demonstrate the advantages of communism, were spruced up, talks rehearsed with their inhabitants, all expected to act the part. Opium was an issue, with poppies gently swaying in fields near the red capital. Once special teams had destroyed all the plants along the main road, Yan'an was ready to display itself to the world.[35]

***

Two days after Japan had struck Pearl Harbor, the Republic of China declared war on the Axis Powers, the military coalition uniting Berlin, Rome and Tokyo (the war with Japan had so far been undeclared). Chongqing faced a mammoth task. It was cut off from most of the world and received limited outside support, yet had to administer a country the size of a continent, much of it laid waste by years of warfare, and continue to fight a savage, pitiless enemy. Air bombardments of the capital and other cities were continuous, with hundreds of planes on occasion participating in a single raid. Carpet bombing of Chongqing claimed over 10,000 civilian lives during the entire war, although the population, by all accounts, endured the hardship with great calm, even if they sometimes had to spend up to twenty hours in shelters without water or electricity. Thanks to a sophisticated network of underground bunkers, as well as ferocious fighting in the skies by the Chinese Air Force, the average number of people killed or injured for every bomb dropped by the Japanese decreased from 5.5 in 1939 to less than one for every 3.5 bombs by May 1940. Most damage was caused by fire, with the city constantly rebuilding itself, replacing frail timber structures with new, more resistant buildings.[36]

Worst of all, the central government was trapped in a vicious cycle of inflation. It had to finance the war even as its enemy increasingly controlled or severely impaired the key to recovery, namely transportation, preventing the efficient distribution of fuel and food supplies throughout Free China. Chiang Kai-shek had obtained full tariff autonomy in 1929, but taxes on imports and exports, a major source of income before 1937, hardly existed. The government's tax base was drastically reduced, its grip on the country precarious, not least north of the Yangtze River. Whatever revenue was raised could only cover a small portion of the cost of the war, with a budget deficit that could not be bridged by selling war bonds. Without substantial foreign help, the only solution was to issue paper currency, which inevitably led to inflation. A hundred yuan in 1940 would have bought a pig, but no more than a chicken in 1943. By 1945 it was barely enough for a fish.[37]

Historians never fail to highlight how inflation undermined living standards in Free China. Yet few seem to realise that rising prices, in no small measure, were due to a 'currency war' deliberately engineered by Japan. Tokyo, keen to generate funds for the war, attacked the country's legal tender by printing vast amounts of counterfeit notes and establishing 'puppet' banks that issued unbacked currencies in the hope of undermining Chongqing. These counterfeit notes and puppet currencies circulated widely and wreaked havoc on the economy. Also overlooked in standard accounts is one very simple fact: inflation was just as devastating in regions occupied by the Japanese and a great deal higher still in Yan'an. In occupied Canton, inflation was so crippling that it brought about a frozen economy and so high a crime rate that the Japanese could no longer ensure safety in the city. In the surrounding countryside, once prosperous farmers lived on the brink of starvation. In Shanghai, inflation led to constant strikes, including by the police and the post office. Up north in Beiping, food was increasingly difficult to obtain, since the farmers produced less and the merchants refused to sell.[38]

In Yan'an, the greatest victims of inflation were the villagers. But in Free China it was precisely the rural population who were least affected by galloping prices. Like all producers, their income was linked to the prices of the goods they sold. As late as 1944, even as inflation was causing a rapid decline in industrial production, it did not greatly affect the agricultural population. In the early years of inflation even ordinary workers were better off, since most employers, whether in industry or commerce, either supplied rice at a greatly reduced price or gave one free meal a day. As a foreign observer remarked in 1941, 'especially the poorer classes of labourers and manual workers are earning more real money than ever before in their lives, and for them this inflationary boom is a period of real prosperity which they hope will continue indefinitely.'[39]

Hardest hit were schoolteachers, college professors and government employees, people on fixed incomes who saw their standards of living steadily decline. Students, too, suffered, including in Kunming, where a great many universities had relocated during the war. 'There is no city in the world with a higher rate of inflation than Kunming,' wrote one visitor in 1943, noting that prices there changed more in a day than they did in a year in the United States. These circles also happened to be the central government's most vocal critics. The Nationalist Party, like the Communist Party, was a Leninist organisation based on the principle of democratic centralism. But whereas Mao Zedong had widely advertised his New Democracy, with promises of a multi-party system, equal suffrage and democratic freedoms, Chiang Kai-shek seemed to have little to offer when he responded in 1943 with *China's Destiny*, a book setting forth his own vision of the future. He repeated the very themes that had preoccupied his erstwhile mentor Sun Yat-sen, explaining that China was not yet ready for any kind of democracy; that its government had historically promoted a planned economy; that the idea of a market economy was incompatible with the specific characteristics of China's economy; that the government would prevent the emergence of large monopolies by placing private property under strict state control; and that land property rights would be abolished in favour of collective farms. On the relation between the individual and the state, Chiang pointed out, no 'individual freedom' in which people could just drift apart like 'loose grains of sand' would be tolerated. To critical readers, Chiang seemed the dictator, Mao the democrat.[40]

In Chongqing and elsewhere, a steadily growing number of disenchanted students and scholars began pointing to the gross incompetence, corruption, nepotism and bribery of the central government, not to mention its use of the secret police. Abroad, too, Chiang was increasingly portrayed as a feudal leader out of touch with his own people, if not a fascist dictator reducing his country to serfdom. Reinforcing the hugely influential work of Edgar Snow, a number of American journalists based in Chongqing, notably Theodore White, Jack Belden and Graham Peck, published searing indictments of the central government. They contrasted the feudal, deceitful ways of Chongqing, where they were granted every freedom, to the democratic ways of Yan'an, where they had never set foot.[41]

In the White House too, opinion was tilting away from Chongqing towards Yan'an. As early as 1938, Captain Evans Carlson, who had visited Yan'an, reported to President Franklin D. Roosevelt that Mao was a dreamer and a genius. Carlson had Roosevelt's ear, having served in 1933 as an executive officer of the Marine Corps Detachment at the president's retreat at Warm Springs, Georgia. 'The Chinese Communist group (so-called) is not Communistic in the sense that we are accustomed to use the term,' he argued. 'They are selfless men who use their power to improve the welfare of those they lead. They are incorruptible.'[42]

One of Chiang Kai-shek's greatest critics was General Joseph Stilwell, sent to China in 1942 as chief of staff to the Generalissimo and commander of all US forces and lend-lease material in China. Stilwell knew China, having served as military attaché there from 1935 to 1939. He disdained all things Chinese, not least Chiang Kai-shek, whom he described as 'obstinate, pig-headed, ignorant, intolerant, arbitrary, unreasonable, illogical, ungrateful, grasping', condemning him as a 'conceited despot', 'the world's greatest ignoramus' and an 'insect', although he hesitated to call Chiang a dictator, since no one obeyed his orders. Stilwell, another American who had never set foot in Yan'an, went on to compare the 'corruption, neglect, chaos' of the central government with the Communist programme: 'Reduce taxes, rents, interest. Raise production, and standard of living. Participate in government. Practice what they preach.'[43]

Roosevelt finally met Chiang Kai-shek in person at the Cairo conference where the leaders of the Allied Powers convened in November 1943 to agree on a strategy to defeat Japan. The president had already made the acquaintance of Soong Mei-ling, who had toured the United States and stayed as a guest at the White House several months earlier. He had not liked her, and nor did he take to the Generalissimo. By then, Roosevelt had come to view a united government merging Chongqing and Yan'an as indispensable in fighting the Japanese, making this a condition for any further financial and military support.[44]

In April 1944, after several years of positional warfare, Japan launched Operation Ichigo, a major campaign intended to open a route to French Indo-China by creating a railway link all the way from Beiping to Canton via Hankou. The Japanese also sought to destroy several airbases in south-east China that American bombers used against their forces in Asia. Ferocious battles took place in several provinces, resulting in devastating losses among the government troops. In June 1944, an apprehensive Roosevelt sent his vice-president to China. The Allies had just landed in Normandy. With their forces fully committed to Europe, they increasingly viewed Yan'an as a promising wartime ally in China. Stilwell, who was scathing of the feebleness of the war effort mounted by Chongqing, encouraged Roosevelt in his views. As one Nationalist general commented at the time, there were 940,000 Japanese in China as opposed to 750,000 Germans on the western front in Europe. It took an enormous effort, requiring no less than several million tonnes of munitions as well as 13,000 aircraft, to effect a landing in Normandy. Yet the Americans expected Chiang Kai-shek to continue to fight the Japanese more or less single-handedly while the United States contributed a mere 20,000 tonnes monthly, with 60 per cent of these supplies earmarked for the United States Army Air Forces in Kunming and two-thirds of the remaining 40 per cent reserved for the Burma Expeditionary Force.[45]

In Chongqing, Vice-President Henry A. Wallace insisted on unity with the Communists. When Chiang pointed out that the Communists were subject to orders from Moscow, Wallace countered that the Comintern had been abolished in 1943. He also mentioned remarks made by Martel Hall, a bank manager who had travelled through Communist territory in 1943 and spoke highly of the Communist Party. The American bank manager, he implied, was better informed than anyone in Chongqing. Wallace also urged friendly relations between China and the Soviet Union, insisting that Stalin had personally conveyed the need for 'a united China eager to carry on the war against Japan'. Roosevelt's envoy, furthermore, expressed a desire to see an increase in agricultural production in China, praising developments he had observed in the Soviet Union. On Stalin's invitation, Wallace had travelled to Chongqing via Alaska and Siberia, where the labour camps had been carefully disguised and model villages prepared for the vice-president and his party. On the tour was Magadan, a mining centre in the Kolyma valley where thousands of prisoners extracted precious metals. Wallace had been deeply impressed by Soviet accomplishments in the region, holding them up as an example for the Generalissimo to emulate. Wallace also asked that an American observation group should be sent directly to Yan'an to gather intelligence and establish relations with the Chinese Communist Party. Chiang, dependent on American aid, reluctantly agreed. Had Wallace been an envoy sent by Moscow, he could scarcely have done a better job.[46]

The mission, composed of eight soldiers and a diplomat, landed in Yan'an on 22 July 1944. The red capital was on full alert, Mao ready to perform his act, flanked by all the leaders at the airport with a band playing military music. The diplomat was John Stewart Service, second secretary at the American Embassy in Chongqing. Colonel David Barrett was the head of the mission. Mao made a simple calculation: Japanese troops were crushing Chiang Kai-shek, boosting the Communist Party's chances of a deal.[47]

John Service was the most inquisitive, formulating clear questions on the nature of the Communist Party's economic programme and its vision for the future. David Barrett was initially more guarded, but he too was soon won over, joining Service in vociferously criticising Chiang Kai-shek, his regime and their troops, all condemned as inept and unreliable. John Service wrote back to Washington, listing the many achievements of the Communist Party. He recommended full support, becoming one of the most influential and enthusiastic proponents of the cause within the State Department. After the civil war resumed a year later, Service gave Philip Jaffe, a devoted Stalinist businessman who provided Soviet intelligence agents with information, a top-secret document revealing the central government's order of battle, with the exact disposition of their troops. Before he passed away in 1999, Service admitted that he had deliberately ignored Mao's persecution of his enemies during the Rectification Campaign. 'I wanted them to win.'[48]

Foreign journalists, likewise, arrived. They encountered model workers and model peasants, all of them carefully selected and groomed by the regime. With minders accompanying their every step, they were taken on guided tours to visit model schools and model hospitals. Every answer given to the journalists was written down and later subjected to evaluation, with individuals whose performance was deemed unsatisfactory listed by name. Even villagers pretending to work along the road used to ferry the correspondents from one showcase site to another were taken to task for appearing too contrived. Farmers equipped with hoes did not look up as the foreigners passed by, producing an unnatural effect. In one village, dogs had been locked away, which created an artificial quiet. The foreign journalists, only too happy to be herded around and fully prepared to help dispel the hostile stereotypes of the nature of communism that prevailed in Chongqing, remained oblivious of any such minor incongruities.[49]

One of the first to report back to the world was Harrison Forman of the *New York Herald Tribune*. 'The Chinese people need democracy,' Mao told him, since 'only when there is democracy can China's unity continue after the war.' The Chairman, like other leaders, was dressed no differently from his orderlies, in a faded blue cotton tunic and baggy pants, with rope sandals on his feet, a far cry from the pomp and extravagance of Chongqing. The soldiers, instead of taking from the peasants, cultivated the land themselves, transforming a wasteland of barren hills and valleys into lush agricultural fields, troopers chanting as they wielded picks, hoes and shovels. Forman himself spent an evening sitting under the stars, watching the soldiers and their wives perform a native dance. They cheered the success of the United Nations, established in the summer of 1945.[50]

Countless similar reports appeared. Brooks Atkinson wrote that Yan'an was an 'agrarian or peasant democracy', Communist in name only. The *New York Times* enthusiastically titled his article 'Yenan, A Chinese Wonderland City'. Like others, he viewed the Chinese Communist Party as a red turnip, scarlet on the outside only. Theodore White, one of the most influential reporters of that time, admitted decades later that Mao always spoke 'in the most rigid Marxist terms', expressing ideas that 'seemed so unrealistic and orthodox that I found them not worth the reporting'. In the United States, as a congressman who had worked as a medical missionary in China pointed out, 'a year ago [one] could hardly find words good enough with which to describe our Chinese allies [in Chongqing], now [one] can hardly find words bad enough.'[51]

Some of these reporters were agents recruited by Moscow. One example was Günther Stein, at that time a key member of the Soviet Military Intelligence (GRU) ring operated by Richard Sorge, a German journalist active as an agent in East Asia whom the Japanese hanged as a spy in 1944. Stein, a tireless defender of the Chinese Communist Party, wrote that behind the blockade 'Communists Set Up New Democracy'. Sir Humphrey Prideaux-Brune, a British career diplomat in China since 1911, drily observed that Stein was disappointed with Chongqing and concentrated his sympathies on the Communists, 'as has happened to various other people with strong pro-Chinese sympathies but a relatively limited China background'.[52]

Towards the end of 1944, the British Embassy commented that ever more visitors were coming to Yan'an, noting that they had 'much to say that was positive, and practically nothing that is contrary to the regime'. Chinese journalists were less impressed. The Communists, they alleged, 'suppress facts for their own ends', 'fabricate stories' and 'alter the truth in order to attack and undermine the central government'. They observed widespread censorship and lack of religious freedom, finding all the temples on the road to Yan'an destroyed. They complained that the tours were 'conducted' and they were not allowed 'free contact' with the population. They highlighted an atmosphere of distrust, with one correspondent being warned that his 'personal safety' could not be guaranteed after he had managed to slip away from his minders. All of them noted that prices were much higher than in Free China. Bookshops, they said, sold nothing but political literature. The newspapers carried daily diatribes against the central government. The One Third system was eyewash. One journalist was impertinent enough to ask why he could not find a single Nationalist Party member in all of Yan'an.[53]

Günther Stein, operating on behalf of Moscow, also assured the world that no link whatsoever existed between Mao and Stalin. A similar message came from the Soviet Union. One week before Wallace was sent to Chongqing, Stalin met the American ambassador Averell Harriman to tell him that Chiang Kai-shek was wrong to be suspicious of the Chinese Communists, who were nothing but patriots keen to join the fight against Japan. With a flick of the hand, he laughingly dismissed the 'so-called Communists' in the north as no more than 'Margarine Communists'. In September, Molotov reinforced the message, explaining to Harriman that in China 'some of these people call themselves "Communists" but they have no relation whatever to communism.' They were just expressing their 'dissatisfaction at their economic condition' by 'calling themselves Communists'. Once economic conditions had improved, Molotov continued, they would 'forget this political inclination'. The Soviet government, he concluded, could not be blamed in any way for this situation nor should it be associated with these 'Communist elements'.[54]

Moscow, in short, successfully manoeuvred Washington into continuing its own long-standing policy of forcing the central government into a coalition with the Chinese Communist Party.

***

Throughout the war Roosevelt had insisted that Joseph Stilwell be made commander of all armies in China. But Stilwell had a lacklustre record. Soon after arriving in China to serve as the

Generalissimo's chief of staff, he had been assigned command of two Nationalist armies in Burma that the Japanese swept aside. Stilwell ordered a counter-offensive, directly countermanding Chiang Kai-shek's orders, resulting in a disaster which cost the central government some of its best troops. The American general abandoned his soldiers the moment the Japanese gained the upper hand.[55]

Chiang Kai-shek ignored Roosevelt's requests, until an ultimatum arrived from the White House on 16 September 1944, ordering him to place Stilwell in 'unrestricted command' of all his forces 'at once', and making it a condition for the 'continued efforts the United States proposes to take to maintain and increase our aid to you'. Chiang called the president's bluff, viewing the ultimatum as tantamount to the complete subordination of his country. Always stubborn, he insisted instead that Stilwell be replaced. Patrick Hurley, a special envoy Roosevelt had sent to China in August to help smooth relations between Chiang and Stilwell, backed the Generalissimo. In November 1944, the tall and imposing General Albert Wedemeyer was sent to replace Stilwell. When he took over from his predecessor, he found that no American war plans for China proper existed. Still, the general restored morale within a few months, established good relations with Chiang Kai-shek and helped shape powerful armies under his guidance.[56]

Hurley, an impeccably groomed businessman from Oklahoma with a brushy moustache and a full head of white hair, was keen to create a united front, visiting Yan'an with an offer from Chiang Kai-shek to legalise all political parties and give the Chinese Communist Party a number of government posts. He arrived on 7 November, to be greeted at the airport by Zhou Enlai and Colonel David Barrett. Mao, not one to waste a good opportunity, pushed hard, calling for a coalition government, in effect aiming to place Yan'an on an equal footing with the internationally recognised Republic of China. Among several prerequisites, the Chairman demanded a joint military council with equal numbers of Nationalist and Communist generals. Hurley agreed to everything. For good measure, the American envoy himself added demands for democracy and liberty to the draft declaration before signing a copy. The moment Hurley left Yan'an, a delighted Mao dispatched several cables to Moscow.[57]

The Americans failed to discern what the British found obvious, namely that no coalition could be formed when both sides possessed their own armed forces and distrusted each other. London pointed to Greece as an inauspicious precedent, where a government-in-exile led by the prominent liberal Georgios Papandreou had entered a coalition with Communist forces in May 1944. The Communist ministers threw sand in the machine of the 'National Unity' government, resigning like clockwork when it was time for a coup. The moment the British entered Athens after the withdrawal of German forces on 13 October, Communist guerrilla fighters spread out to take control of the countryside and a string of cities. The coalition collapsed in December, to be followed from 1946 to 1949 by a civil war that would leave Greece in ruins.[58]

In Chongqing, the reaction to the Communist proposal was sheer dismay. T. V. Soong immediately pointed out to Hurley, who had only just been made ambassador, that 'you have been sold a bill of goods by the Communists.' 'The National Government will never grant what the Communists have requested,' he added. Chiang Kai-shek rejected out of hand the idea of a coalition government, demanding instead control over Communist troops. The Chairman, in turn, dismissed this as a complete surrender, and threatened to publish the document which Hurley had co-written with the Communists and signed without having first consulted the United States' ally in Chongqing. Mao, who knew full well that his conditions were unacceptable, had in effect cornered Hurley and was now in a good position to argue that an alliance with Chiang Kai-shek was impossible.[59]

Hurley realised he had been tricked. One month later, Chiang introduced him to his secret police chief, who produced evidence of an undercover plan initiated by the Office of Strategic Services, the American intelligence agency. One of their agents, Colonel William Bird, who was in Yan'an on David Barrett's team, had developed an ambitious blueprint for cooperation between Washington and the Communists, proposing to bring over enough American experts to train and equip up to 25,000 guerrilla fighters. Hurley, who had been kept in the dark about the operation, exploded. He concluded that Barrett and Bird had surreptitiously offered the Communists recognition as an armed belligerent behind his back and had undermined his efforts at building a coalition. He complained to Roosevelt, who terminated the Bird initiative.[60]

A few weeks later, while Hurley was visiting Washington, he reversed course, denouncing any kind of collaboration with Yan'an and urging Washington to fully endorse Chongqing. 'All the arguments and all the documents submitted should indicate to you', he wrote to Roosevelt on 18 February 1945, 'that the Chinese Communist Party is not democratic; that its purpose is to destroy the control of the government by the Kuomintang before there has been an opportunity to adopt a constitution or to return the control of the Government to the people on a democratic basis.' By now, negotiations between the two sides had been dragging on fruitlessly in one form or another for more than nine months. As Wang Shijie, the negotiator representing the central government, pointed out, the Communists were continually changing or increasing their demands, making new ones every time the central government suffered a military reverse at Japanese hands.[61]

Hurley's volte-face cut short Mao's attempt to obtain substantial financial and military aid from the United States. He turned to Moscow instead, with talk rife among leaders about the 'common spirit of the fraternal parties' and how the Soviet Union would fight for the Chinese Communist Party.[62]

Further evidence of the Soviet Union's potential entry into the war against Japan came in February 1945. In November 1943, Chiang Kai-shek had been invited to meet his British and American counterparts in Cairo, who had among other matters declared that Manchuria and Taiwan would be restored to the Republic of China once Japan was defeated. But in February 1945, when Roosevelt, Churchill and Stalin met in Yalta, a Soviet holiday resort on the Black Sea, Chiang was not invited as one of the four Great Powers. Months earlier, in October 1944, General

Douglas MacArthur had landed his troops on Leyte in the Philippines. Fierce fighting followed, with the battle for Manila alone claiming 100,000 civilian deaths, leaving the city in ruins. An amphibious assault on Japan looked daunting and was expected to prove extremely costly in terms of American lives. The secret atomic bomb had not yet been tested, and a frail Roosevelt sought to gain Soviet support in the war against Japan. Stalin agreed to break his non-aggression pact with Japan and enter the Pacific War three months after Germany's surrender, but not without major concessions. These included an occupation zone in Korea, possession of Sakhalin Island just to the north of Hokkaido and control of Port Arthur and Dairen (Dalian) in Manchuria. Stalin also demanded joint control over the Chinese Eastern Railway, the rights to which Moscow had sold to Tokyo ten years earlier. Chiang Kai-shek was never consulted, as Roosevelt in effect bartered exclusive Soviet access to Manchuria in exchange for help from Stalin. The president also accepted Moscow's request for two months' supply of food and fuel for 1.5 million troops, sending hundreds of shiploads of lend-lease materiel to Siberia in the following months, including 500 Sherman tanks.[63]

In Yan'an, Mao had an inkling of what was happening when on 18 February 1945 *Izvestia*, a Soviet mouthpiece, published an editorial highlighting Moscow's desire to 'solve the Far Eastern problem taking due account of the interests of the Chinese Communists'. On 25 February, Mao sent a cable to Moscow, congratulating Stalin on the spectacular victories of the Red Army, which was advancing deep into Germany. The Chairman was all flattery, expressing his awe for Stalin's genius. When, on 5 April, Moscow broke its pact with Tokyo, Mao began to eye Manchuria. 'What would be the significance for the Chinese Revolution if the North-east were to come under our leadership?' he enquired rhetorically on 31 May at the end of the Seventh Party Congress. 'At present, these few base areas of ours are separated from one another by the enemy. None of our strongholds and base areas are stable. Without any industry, they are in danger of being eliminated. For this reason, we must contend for the cities, contend for any solid piece of land. If we had a large piece of a genuine base area, including the North-east, then speaking from the point of view of the entire nation, the victory of the Chinese Revolution would have a basis, a strong and solid basis.' The question, increasingly, was when, rather than if, the Red Army would enter Manchuria.[64]

8
Civil War
(1945–1949)

On 6 August 1945, Hiroshima was erased in a blinding flash of light. Three days later, after a second atomic bomb had wiped out Nagasaki, close to a million Soviet troops stormed into Manchuria with tactical aircraft in support. The operation had been carefully prepared over several months, with armoured trains carrying elite troops along the Chinese Eastern Railway towards Harbin, making daily gains of up to seventy kilometres. A separate drive from Vladivostok was launched southward into Korea, where the port of Rashin was soon captured. The Japanese offered little opposition. Within days the Russians were in control of all strategic points in Manchuria. Stalin had fulfilled the promise he had made at Yalta, namely to declare war on Japan three months after Germany's surrender.[1]

The unconditional surrender of Japan was met with jubilation across China, but took both Chiang Kai-shek and Mao Zedong by surprise. In Chongqing, shouts of joy as well as firecrackers were heard all over the city, 'sporadic at first but growing to a volcanic eruption of sound and happiness within an hour'. A flood of cheering, laughing and weeping people poured through the streets, with searchlights dancing festively across the sky. Dressed in a simple khaki uniform without any decorations, the Generalissimo read a victory message over the radio, then walked out of the broadcasting studio to meet an ecstatic crowd. One of the bloodiest chapters in its history was over, as liberation had finally come to China.[2]

The formal surrender ceremony between China and Japan took place on 21 August 1945 at the Zhijiang Airfield in Hunan, as Major General Takeo Imai handed over a map showing the positions of his 1,000,000 troops in the country. They were allowed to retain their arms and maintain public order until the arrival of government troops, who were being rushed to all the key cities south of the Great Wall in a spectacular sea operation, the largest aerial troop movement of the Second World War, conducted under the command of General Albert Wedemeyer. Some 80,000 soldiers of the Sixth Army were flown to Nanjing to reclaim their erstwhile capital. In Shanghai, shabbily clothed soldiers stepped out of giant transport aircraft, blinking at the sight of a large crowd who welcomed them as liberators.[3]

In Yan'an, the rapid advance of the Soviet troops left Mao so stunned that he was uncertain how to react. The Communists had hoped that the Red Army would deliver a blow to the Japanese troops in Inner Mongolia and Kalgan, adjacent to the territories they controlled, rather than remaining in Manchuria. Stalin, moreover, had been awed by the atomic bombs, and was anxious to avoid a direct conflict with the United States. Moscow had signed a treaty with Chongqing in July in which the concessions wrangled from the Allies at the Yalta Conference, not least control over Port Arthur and the Chinese Eastern Railway, had been endorsed. As a dejected Mao noted at a Politburo meeting on 23 August, 'The Soviet Union, for the sake of international peace and under the restraints of the Sino-Soviet Treaty, is not able to help us and cannot properly do so.'[4]

Stalin advised Mao to reach an agreement with Chiang. The Chairman, on two occasions, had declined an invitation to travel to Chongqing, and public opinion was turning against him. Now he reluctantly agreed. On 27 August, Patrick Hurley flew to Yan'an to meet him and ensure his safety on the trip to Chongqing. Hurley, looking dapper in an elegant suit with a bow tie, and Mao, dressed in a bulky field jacket and wearing a pith helmet, stepped out of the plane the following day, welcomed by a party that included Chiang Ching-kuo, representing his father. Chiang and Mao, who had not seen each other for twenty years, assumed contrived smiles at a formal reception held on the first evening, toasting each other with millet wine. Mao stayed a full six weeks, biding his time, hoping for a reversal in fortune.[5]

Chance beckoned a few weeks later. When the Soviets had crossed the Amur River into Manchuria, accompanying them dressed in Soviet uniforms were members of the North-east Anti-Japanese United Army, the Communist guerrilla fighters who had fled into Siberia in 1942. Thoroughly trained soldiers of the Red Army's 88th Brigade, they knew the region intimately, and were posted in no fewer than fifty-seven strategic locations throughout Manchuria, commanding city garrisons and local governments.[6]

Even as the Soviets fanned out across Manchuria, on 30 August a regiment of the Eighth Route Army under Zeng Kelin moved towards Shanhaiguan, the coastal gateway to Manchuria. Here Soviet troops helped Zeng take over the city and move on to Shenyang (previously known as Mukden), where they arrived by train on 5 September. The Soviet commander welcomed them, but asked Zeng and his 2,000 soldiers to remain on the train until orders were received from Moscow. Two days later a cable arrived from Stalin: the Communists were welcome, provided they avoided any mention of the Eighth Route Army. Zeng opted to rename his unit the 'People's Autonomous Army of the North-east'. As local partisans, they were allowed to take over the garrison, establish a provisional municipal government, disarm 15,000 partisans and formally run the city. On 10 September, members of the North-east Anti-Japanese United Army joined Zeng. In a mere three days, they were handed 1,000 automatic weapons, 20,000 rifles and 156 cannons from the Shenyang arsenal. Port Arthur, under Soviet control by virtue of the Yalta Treaty, also began to welcome Communist troops. The port faced Yantai across the Bohai Sea, and in mid-September Communist troops in Shandong began to be ferried across the 170-kilometre divide.[7]

The man in charge of Manchuria was Rodion Malinovsky, a marshal who had fought at Stalingrad and contributed to Soviet military supremacy in Central Europe. On 14 September, he sent a colonel to Yan'an by plane, accompanied by Zeng Kelin. The message to the leadership was the same: no Communist troops should enter Manchuria until the Soviets had departed, and soldiers of the Eighth Route Army should withdraw from Shenyang and other cities, although local armed forces were welcome. The colonel recommended that the Communist Party send a group of high-ranking officials to Manchuria to ensure more efficient cooperation. Mao Zedong and Zhou Enlai were both in Chongqing, dragging out the negotiations with Chiang Kai-shek. Liu Shaoqi therefore took the initiative, making sure Peng Zhen, Chen Yun and several other ranking members were on board when the colonel flew to Shanhaiguan a few days later.[8]

Mao and Zhou cabled their approval from Chongqing. Mao was now ready to conclude an agreement with Chiang, declaring on 18 September: 'We must stop [the] civil war and all parties must unite under the leadership of Chairman Chiang to build a modern China.' He stalled for another three weeks, finally making a formal statement on 10 October, the anniversary of the 1911 revolution that had brought about the overthrow of the Qing empire. Back in Yan'an a few days later, Mao explained to his comrades-in-arms that the agreed statement in Chongqing was 'a mere scrap of paper'.[9]

Liu had worked around the clock, frantically ordering units dispersed throughout the north to make their way to Manchuria from Communist-controlled areas. 'Make sure you are not discovered by the Soviets, the British, the Americans or the Nationalists when entering Manchuria [...] Once you are inside Manchuria you must change the designation of your military unit,' he ordered.[10]

Peng Zhen, a tall, strapping man close to Liu Shaoqi who had distinguished himself for his eagerness in persecuting alleged traitors during the Rectification Campaign, took his team by train from Shanhaiguan to Shenyang. Here, the Communists were allowed to reinvent themselves as 'local partisans'. They switched names several times, settling for the 'North-east Democratic

League Army'. Peng Zhen was its political commissar, Lin Biao, who had arrived from Shandong, its commander. With Soviet acquiescence, they recruited demobilised soldiers, puppet troops and bandit fighters. By the end of September they numbered 13,000 men, swelling to 60,000 one month later. By November, in Shenyang alone over 100,000 Communist soldiers controlled the city and the surrounding countryside, while 195,000 troops were deployed in strategic locations throughout Soviet-occupied territory, not including some 20,000 detachments at the county level. They were well armed: the Soviets handed over weapons confiscated from the Kwantung Army, including 3,700 rifles, army mortars and grenade launchers, 600 tanks, 861 planes, approximately 12,000 machine guns and over 2,000 automatic weapons. There were also a staggering 679 arsenals, designed to churn out yet more weapons.[11]

Not all divisions of the Eighth Route Army moved into Manchuria. Even as Mao was in Chongqing, negotiating the terms for a coalition government, Zhu De acted in complete defiance of Chiang Kai-shek's order that his troops remain at their posts, instead serving ultimatums on Japanese garrisons in Shandong, Shanxi, Chahar and Hebei, and closing in on several big cities north of the Yellow River. Even before Mao had landed in Chongqing, Communist troops clashed with government forces near Qingdao and Tianjin. They occupied Nanyuan, where Beiping's principal airport was located, and took control of Wanping, the site of the Marco Polo Bridge Incident in 1937.[12]

The strategy the Communists were pursuing soon became clear: surround the cities, cut off food and fuel supplies and starve them into submission. The central government, once its troops reached all the main cities south of the Great Wall, faced the mammoth task of administering a country the size of a continent that had been laid waste by eight years of warfare, an undertaking that the Communists were determined to undermine. They did what they were best trained to do, namely destroy, sabotage and cripple. In pitiless partisan warfare, everything that tore society apart operated to the Communists' advantage. 'Between Beiping and Tianjin one sees a succession of derailed trains, destroyed telephone poles and road blocks, while everywhere north and south and west of the area rail communications are torn and impassable,' wrote William Langdon, the American consul-general in Kunming who travelled through all of liberated China, on 13 October 1945. 'In the absence of Japanese to harass, they harass their own people,' he continued. One example was the Kailan mines north of Tianjin, where 'they prey on and terrorise' the workers, who had to be protected by sizeable military detachments.[13]

Besides being cost-effective, the Communist strategy had many other advantages. It imposed a huge burden on the central government and greater misery on the population, since every economic asset under its jurisdiction, whether a factory or a stretch of railway, required round-the-clock protection, tying down large numbers of troops. From a propaganda point of view, it was also helpful that the government seemed inept, unable to make something as simple as a telegraph line function properly. Outside Kaifeng, the Communists blew up the dykes holding back the Yellow River, making 1.7 million people homeless. Inside Beiping itself, an estimated 4,000 underground agents were active, doing their utmost to influence local malcontents, including Korean and Japanese civilians. By November resentment at the government's failure to remedy the economic chaos which had replaced the relatively stable conditions under the Japanese was widespread. In December, the American consul in Beiping reported Communist activity in 'wrecking railways, requisitioning food stuffs and enforcing compulsory conscription' in central Hebei.[14]

In north China the Communists came armed with Japanese rifles, machine guns and mortars. Many soldiers were as young as sixteen, with rudimentary military training. The villages were organised into collectives, which, according to a French consular expert, were 'not popular'. Families kept no food reserves for fear of requisitioning, and would grind their grain on a day-by-day basis. Conscription was so heavy that in numerous fields sorghum and corn were left to rot, since few villagers were left behind to reap the harvest. In Yantai, a port city of 180,000 in Shandong that the Communists seized on 23 August to facilitate the dispatch of troops to Manchuria, every man between the ages of twenty and forty-five was enlisted, and young girls and women compelled to join a 'support corps'. All boats were grounded, and 300 of them commandeered to transport troops to Dalian.[15]

With Soviet help, the Communists also tried to prevent the government troops from entering Manchuria. The Soviets assisted Zeng Kelin in taking over Shanhaiguan, through which all trains to Manchuria had to pass. Stalin allowed the Communists to occupy Kalgan (Zhangjiakou), the strategic city where Yan Xishan had once established his headquarters. Before the fall of the empire, camel caravans had regularly assembled in this key gateway through the Great Wall to carry tea chests to Russia. Nestled in the midst of a great sweep of valley rising towards snow-capped promontories, the city was known as 'Beijing's Northern Door', on account of its strategic position for any army contemplating an attack on the ancient capital. The Japanese had turned Kalgan into an economic and industrial centre, leaving behind an enormous cache of ammunition and weapons, including sixty tanks.[16]

Chiang Kai-shek knew full well that the Soviets were cooperating with the Communists in Manchuria, but he was in no position to quarrel with Stalin. Control of Manchuria, with its steel mills, huge reserves of iron ore and coal, dense forests and rich farmland, was vital from an economic point of view, and strategically a key to control of the country as a whole. Chiang placed General Du Yuming in charge of reclaiming the region. His troops were denied permission to land in Port Arthur and Dalian, under Soviet control following the Sino-Soviet Treaty. In October 1945, when ships from the US Seventh Fleet sailed instead to Yingkou, a minor harbour with rail connections to the interior, red sentries met them on the dock with orders not to permit anyone to disembark. Even as the deputy mayor, flanked by two gunmen, explained that Communist troops would oppose any attempt to land troops ashore, Du Yuming and his soldiers could see how trenches and barricades were being built on both sides of the river. Instead, General Du went ashore further south at Qinhuangdao, captured Shanhaiguan from the Communists on 16 November, breached the Great Wall and lunged forward along the railway, meeting little opposition. In less than three weeks he covered the 300 kilometres from the Great Wall to the industrial base of Shenyang, where the Communists had evacuated the city. Under pressure to fulfil their commitments to the central government, the Soviets relented and allowed Du Yuming's troops to be airlifted into Changchun, further north along the railway from Shenyang.[17]

Just three days after Du Yuming had reclaimed Shanhaiguan, Mao instructed Peng Zhen to ask 'our friends to delay the arrival of central government troops in Manchuria as much as possible'. Stalin opted for a compromise, betting on both sides, and allowed Chiang Kai-shek to take over a number of cities while the Communists became entrenched in the countryside. But no American representative was allowed north of the Great Wall.[18]

The reason for the ban on Allied Powers soon became clear: the Red Army had looted cities in Manchuria. James McHugh, one of the first businessmen allowed into Shenyang, reported that the troops had been let loose 'for three days of rape and pillage'. They 'stole everything in sight, broke up bathtubs and toilets with hammers, pulled electric light wiring out of the plaster, built fires on the floor and either burned down the house or at least left a big hole in the floor'. Women cut their hair and dressed like men to avoid being raped. In the city, 'factories lay like raddled skeletons, picked clean of their machinery.' Shenyang, one reporter wrote, 'has been reduced from a great industrial city to a tragic, crowded way station on the Russian-controlled railway to Dairen [Dalian]'. The systematic plunder of Manchuria's industrial infrastructure would later be valued at US$2 billion.[19]

For several months an uneasy stalemate prevailed, with Du Yuming's troops garrisoned in Shenyang and Changchun, and the Communists in the surrounding countryside. The Americans, still keen on ending all military conflict, intervened. In December 1945, President Truman sent General George C. Marshall, a tall, slender man with grey hair and intense blue eyes who had organised the war effort under Roosevelt as chief of staff. It was he who had insisted a few years earlier that Stilwell be given charge of all the armies in China. Despite all evidence to the contrary,

Marshall still believed that the Communists were not doctrinaire ideologists, but merely rural reformers who could help shape a democratic China. In the words of one historian, he was 'just about the least fitting man to send to China'.[20]

Before setting out for Nanjing, Marshall met with Stilwell. Shortly after the meeting, Marshall halted all negotiations for the sale of US surplus property in China, using this as a bargaining chip in his negotiations with Chiang Kai-shek. At a welcoming banquet, he spoke 'like a colonial governor', lecturing every civil and military official attending the occasion. His message was straightforward, namely, that financial and military aid was dependent on a truce with the Communists. The *New York Times*, on 16 December, conveyed a loud and clear message: 'Truman Says Aid to China Hinges on Ending of Strife and Unification of Nation'. Even as the Americans were insisting that Communists be excluded from the governments of Italy and France, Marshall was demanding a coalition government in China. American aid, at this point, was already pitifully limited. Like Europe, China came out of the war with a collapsed economy, tens of millions of displaced people, severe shortages of foodstuffs, its factories and transportation destroyed and entire cities reduced to rubble. The government could barely function on its own, let alone fight a civil war against an opponent armed and backed by Moscow.[21]

Nanjing had little choice but to acquiesce, even though the prospect of a lasting agreement between the two camps seemed more remote than ever. The Communists, on the other hand, had nothing to lose: they used the truce to regroup and expand even further in Manchuria, entrenching themselves in the countryside away from major cities and the railways. The suave and unassuming Zhou Enlai, Mao's envoy to the peace talks, was a master of deception, cultivating a close relationship with Marshall to present the Communists as true democrats. Zhou even persuaded Mao solemnly to declare that 'Chinese democracy must follow the American path'. A ceasefire agreement was hammered out and announced on 10 January 1946. That same day, as Chiang announced the truce at the People's Consultative Conference, he further lifted all wartime restrictions on speech, publication, religion and assembly. All political parties were now equal before the law.²²

On the very day that the ceasefire agreement was reached, the Communists used five regiments to attack government troops in Yingkou. A few weeks later, Du Yuming continued his march into Manchuria, occasionally encountering scattered resistance from Lin Biao's troops. In March, the Soviets finally began to withdraw their troops. After the last Soviet tank had rumbled across the border in April, Chiang ordered Du to fight the Communists. Crowds cheered large groups of veteran soldiers, wearing parkas and high-laced Arctic boots, as they passed through the stone gates of Shenyang on their way to fight for Siping, a strategic railway centre between Shenyang and Changchun seized by the Communists several weeks earlier. Lin Biao did not believe that his troops, outnumbered and outgunned, were ready to resist the full onslaught of the government forces and defend a fifty-kilometre front without secure flanks. But Mao adamantly insisted that the city must be held at all costs. He was prepared to sacrifice tens of thousands of lives, betting on a decisive showdown that would allow the Communists to take all Manchuria in one fell swoop.²³

After weeks of bitter house-to-house fighting, Lin Biao's severely battered forces were finally forced to retreat northward, with the government soldiers in close pursuit, harrying the Communists across the Sungari River. Du Yuming's troops were now within striking distance of Harbin, the only city still in Communist hands. Lin Biao's men were in a state of virtual collapse, with soldiers deserting in large numbers. When interviewed years later by an army officer from the People's Liberation Army, one of the soldiers remembered that during the rout even military officers and political commissars absconded: 'some went home, some became bandits, and some surrendered.'²⁴

Once again George Marshall lent a hand. His own man in the field, Lieutenant General Alean Gillem, had informed him that 'the Communists are definitely the aggressors,' but Marshall was not swayed. He had just visited Yan'an, where the Chairman had presented himself as a liberal reformer and true democrat. Marshall even wrote to the president to assure him that the

300,000 Communists in Manchuria were large in number 'but little more than loosely organised bands'. On 31 May he wrote to Chiang, complaining that 'under the circumstances of the continued advance of the Government troops in Manchuria [...] a point is being reached where the integrity of my position is open to serious question.' Marshall, therefore, demanded that Chiang 'immediately issue an order terminating advances, attacks or pursuits by Government troops'.[25]

The new ceasefire, designed to last two weeks, became a four-month truce that changed the course of the civil war. After two prominent members of the Democratic League, established in 1941 as an umbrella group in favour of democracy, were gunned down in Kunming in July 1946, leaving the city's academic community cowed into silence, President Truman himself wrote to Chiang to warn that the 'generous attitude' of the United States could not be expected to continue if 'genuine progress' was not made towards a 'peaceful settlement of China's internal problems'. And yet, from the moment the marines had arrived in north China in October 1945 to help oversee the repatriation of Japanese troops, the Eighth Route Army had targeted the Americans with ambushes, skirmishes, firefights and acts of sabotage. Weeks before Truman's admonition, seven marines guarding a bridge outside Beidaihe were ambushed, captured and held to ransom for over a week. Days later, three marines were killed and a dozen injured in a Communist attack fifty kilometres south-east of Beiping.[26]

The truce gave the retreating Communists time to recondition their troops, recruit soldiers from the countryside and receive more training, advice and aid from Moscow. Hundreds of Soviet technical advisers and military experts lent a hand. In Dalian the arsenals were put to work, churning out bullets and shells by the million, as well as automatic rifles and tommy guns. Trainloads of materiel also arrived across the border from Siberia and North Korea, carrying not just weapons but also fuel, medicine, even clothing and shoes. Ships were also used, with regular communications established along the Amur and the Sungari River between Blagoveshchensk, Khabarovsk, Komsomolsk-on-Amur and the Chinese city of Jiamusi, which served as the

Communists' rear base. In the first six months of 1947 alone, up to 210,000 tonnes of war supplies were transferred from North Korea. In return, the Communists sent foodstuffs and other local products, shipping a million tonnes of grain to Russia in 1947. The Soviets also opened sixteen military institutions, including air force, artillery and engineering schools. Five were located in Dalian and two in Harbin. Some Chinese officers went to the Soviet Union for advanced training, while others took refuge in the Russian enclaves of Port Arthur and Dalian.[27]

Hostilities resumed in October 1946, although Chiang Kai-shek maintained a fragile ceasefire in Manchuria, focusing instead on Kalgan, the main stronghold south of the Great Wall still in Communist hands. On 1 October government troops entered the city almost without firing a shot. As in the past, the Communists had employed scorched-earth tactics before leaving, burning to the ground airport hangars, the municipal building and the bank. The railway station was a sooty mass of wreckage. Some fifty factories had been either dynamited or entirely stripped of electric-light installations, furniture, rugs and even window frames, to be used as fuel in the harsh winter. Besides Kalgan, Du Yuming took without a fight one city in south Manchuria, Andong, where the Communists likewise destroyed all municipal buildings, the railway station and the airport before withdrawing.[28]

Villages outside Kalgan were starving, but nothing prepared government troops for what they found in Xiwanzi, a hamlet in Chongli county. Fu Zuoyi, the general in charge, cabled back to Nanjing that on 9 December, during their retreat from Kalgan, the Communists had massacred over a thousand villagers. Many were machine-gunned, although some victims had their skulls crushed by rocks. Entire families were killed, including children and even infants, with all twelve members of one family surnamed Zheng annihilated. The majority of the victims were Catholic, and all had apparently refused to convert to Marxism. Some 300 locals had been locked inside the local church and a three-storey seminary, which were both burned to the ground, leaving unrecognisable the charred remains of the victims. One foreign journalist who travelled to the site saw 200 frozen bodies stacked in a courtyard, their clothes stripped off for use by the Communists. Contemporaries termed it the 'Little Lidice', after the small Czech town outside Prague that the Germans annihilated in 1942 in reprisal for the assassination of Reinhard Heydrich. But there was nothing small about Xiwanzi. In Lidice the Nazis executed 173 men over the age of 15 and deported 184 women and 88 children to concentration camps, where most were gassed to death. Xiwanzi was 'little' only in the manner in which history, or rather historians, consigned it to oblivion. In other villages too, scores of civilians were killed, missions sacked and foreign priests abducted.[29]

***

The grain sent to the Soviet Union, as well as the cannon fodder recruited by the Communists, came directly from the countryside. In May 1946, even as Marshall imposed a new truce, the Communists abandoned the moderate policy of rent reduction that had prevailed under the United Front. Mao issued a new directive ordering that all the land should be confiscated from 'traitors', 'tyrants', 'bandits' and 'landlords', to be distributed to the poor peasants. This would fully unleash the revolutionary potential of the countryside, overthrowing the old order and flushing out every last government reactionary. Accompanying the campaign was a great deal of propaganda, not least *The Hurricane*, a novel by Zhou Libo, an editor of the literary supplement of the *Liberation Daily* in Yan'an. He had been transferred in 1946 to Manchuria to join a work team charged with galvanising the countryside. The team was assigned to Yuanbao, a town 130 kilometres east of Harbin. The novel purported to describe how, under the leadership of the Chinese Communist Party, the peasants of Yuanbao had seized power from local tyrants and abolished thousands of years of feudal land ownership. In public trials, depraved landlords were forced to confess their sins, the irate masses raising their sticks and beating the villains to death. Like the proverbial spark that could set the prairie alight, their revolutionary zeal took them to other towns and villages, sweeping away all remnants of feudalism like a hurricane. The novel, an instant hit, became a textbook for other work teams in charge of land reform, and would win the highly coveted Stalin Prize for Literature in 1951.[30]

The reality, however, was somewhat different. Most villagers in Manchuria viewed Nanjing as their legitimate government and knew very little about communism. 'When we went there, at the time the villagers didn't know what we Communists were like or what the Eighth Army was. They had no idea,' recalled Han Hui, a twenty-two-year-old cadre at the time. In Yuanbao only a few local riff-raff and vagrants were interested in the cause, and they were the ones who became Party activists. One of the first tasks of the work team was to divide the villagers into 'landlords', 'rich peasants', 'middle peasants', 'poor peasants' and 'labourers'. This took place in long meetings in the evening, as the work team pored over the backgrounds of every villager, using information gathered from newly recruited activists.[31]

Few of these artificial class distinctions corresponded to the reality in the village, where most people lived in roughly similar conditions. In Yuanbao there were no landlords. Han Laoliu, who would be portrayed as the archetypical villain in Zhou Libo's novel, had been elected head of the local peasant association by the villagers. He had no land of his own, but collected rent on behalf of an absentee owner. Like many others, he ate coarse grain and had only a few clothes to keep him warm in the winter. His greatest claim to wealth was two small windowpanes built into his earth-walled house covered with a layer of straw. 'In reality Han Laoliu had nothing worthwhile,' remembered one villager. 'It's not quite like what's written in that book,' he added.

The next task was to persuade those identified as 'poor peasants' and 'labourers' to turn hardship into hatred. This, too, required weeks of persistent persuasion, as the work team had to convince them that the 'rich' were behind their every misfortune, having exploited their labour since time immemorial. In so-called 'speak bitterness' meetings, participants were encouraged to tap into a reservoir of grievances. Some vented genuine frustrations that had long been bottled up; others were coerced into inventing accusations against their richer neighbours. But weeks of indoctrination also produced true believers who no longer needed prodding by the work team. A number of these saw an opportunity, ready to become revolutionary zealots, eager to break the bonds of friendship for the cause. Drawn to an ideology that promised liberation, they relished becoming champions of the exploited, forging a better world full of hope and light. As one missionary caught up in land reform noted, 'They knew their parts well and spoke sharply the proper Party phrase at the proper time with the proper emphasis.'

After months of patient work in Yuanbao, the Communists turned a majority against a few carefully targeted victims. Armed militia sealed off the village. Everyone wore a strip of cloth identifying their class background: landlords white, rich peasants pink, middle peasants yellow. The poor sported red. One by one the victims were dragged out on to a stage where the crowd, screaming for blood, denounced them as 'landlords', 'tyrants' and 'traitors', demanding that accounts be settled. Victims were mercilessly mocked, humiliated, beaten, sometimes killed as an orgy of violence engulfed the village. In some cases the targets of revolutionary ire were first tortured to make them reveal the location of their assets, real or imagined. Liu Fude remembered: 'There were people who only needed to be told to hit somebody and they would do so. For instance Madame Ding, she was that kind of person.' Madame Ding, who worked for Zhou Libo, claimed: 'I did exactly as he told me to do. This is what Zhou Libo would say: "That Sun Liangba can be taken to task," that's what he would say. So I would beat him.'

A few of those labelled 'rich peasants' tried to hide in the fields, only to freeze to death. In one village alone, out of a population of roughly 700, seventy-three people were killed. The pact between the Party and the poor was sealed in blood as all the land and assets of the victims were distributed to the crowd. The land was paced, measured and distributed to the poor, the name of the beneficiary carved on a wooden board marking the boundary of each plot. Grain was loaded into baskets, furniture packed off, pigs herded away. Even pots and jars were placed in rattan hampers, making it look like moving day. 'So what did I get?' Liu Yongqing pondered when interviewed more than fifty years after the looting, his skin leathery and tanned, his hair sparse and grey. 'I got a jar. A water jar.' Lü Kesheng, a man with an open face topped by a dense crop of white hair, was less fortunate: 'I got a horse. A horse leg, not a whole horse. We [slaughtered and] divided a horse between four families.'

Once everything in the village had been mopped up, down to the last handful of grain, the poor climbed into their carts in the middle of the night and visited other villages, hoping to find new struggle targets. Soon hundreds of carts converged on the county seat, each one crammed with villagers armed with banners, pitchforks and red-tasselled spears. 'The rats in the city are even fatter than the pigs in the village.' In the county as a whole, 21,000 from a population of 118,000 were targeted, meaning that, since every villager had been implicated in a crime, all feared the return of the central government. As the civilians of a town outside Siping were told after their leaders had been executed, 'You executed the Nationalist landlords and gentry. When the Nationalists come back in future, you too will be dead.' Many young men joined the army, whether voluntarily or recruited under duress.[32]

Yuanbao was one of the first places where land was traded for blood, but in 1947 every village that came under Communist control underwent a similar ritual: people were divided into classes, the poor worked up into a fever pitch of hatred, victims humiliated, beaten and sometimes killed, and the victors handed the spoils. One of the most violent regions was Shanxi province, where Kang Sheng oversaw land reform in 1947, fomenting all-out class warfare in the countryside by forcing every villager to take a stance. In a hamlet called Haojiapo, he watched approvingly as the farmers forced landlords to kneel on broken bricks. The victims were then beaten and spat upon and had excrement poured over them. In parts of the region under his control, even farmers classified as 'middle peasants' were arrested, beaten, tortured and then stripped of their property. In some places one out of five people was branded as a 'landlord'. It was sufficient for one of the poor to point at a villager and call him a 'landlord' for his fate to be sealed. In Xing county alone, over 2,000 people were killed, including 250 elderly and 25 children – the latter called 'little landlords'.[33]

Violence was at the heart of the campaign, with anyone in a position of authority overthrown, but Kang Sheng and others went too far. Liu Shaoqi reported disapprovingly that in Hebei some people had been buried alive, dismembered, shot or throttled to death. Sometimes the bodies of the victims were chopped up and hung from trees. In Chifeng, Inner Mongolia, hanging was common, 'coupled with freezing, burning, dragging, and so on'. Orders came from above to reduce the level of violence and limit errors made in identifying enemies of the revolution, but many activists ignored these directives. As Gao Wangling, the foremost historian of land reform, stated, 'local cadres believed that resorting to force was the only way to carry out land reform and effectively deprive landlords of their possessions in order to redistribute them.'[34]

***

Land reform was implemented behind closed doors, with very little reliable information filtering out of the territories controlled by the Communists. Public opinion was, by contrast, increasingly taking the government to task. Inflation was one reason. After the surrender of Japan it had continued to soar, with the cost of living reaching approximately 30,000 times the level of 1936. What would have bought a pig in 1940 was no longer enough to purchase a box of matches in 1947. Inflation embittered a great many people, not least teachers, students and professional workers. When they demonstrated or otherwise manifested their discontent, all too often they faced repressive measures that only heightened popular resentment. Chiang tried to bring inflation under control by banning the export of foreign currency and gold bullion, imposing a ceiling on interest rates and freezing all wages, but these measures had no lasting effect. When his government began to encroach on matters of industry and private commerce, it alienated bankers, merchants and industrialists. T. V. Soong angered a range of investors first by refusing to fully redeem gold certificates sold during the war, then by repurchasing at far less than their maturity value US dollar certificates bought by patriotic overseas Chinese.[35]

Soldiers were barely paid, and even officers could not support their families on their regular income. Some of them inflated their bills or sold military equipment on the black market. Graft, embezzlement and corruption became rampant. Tax collectors accepted bribes. The police extorted money by threatening the poor with arrest and imprisonment. No easy solution to the problem existed, in part because so much of the countryside was effectively cut off from the cities and every stretch of road or railway needed round-the-clock protection against sabotage.

In Taiwan, where administrative control was handed over to the central government after fifty years of Japanese colonial rule, the high-handed, corrupt behaviour of the mainland authorities, including arbitrary seizure of private property, provoked public protests in February 1947. When soldiers fired on the demonstrators, slaying at least three, outrage spread across the island, prompting the local governor to use troops to quell widespread unrest. The violent suppression of all dissent, known as the 'White Terror', continued for many decades, with estimates of the immediate death toll varying from 4,000 to 10,000. The massacre, following on widespread accusations of ineptitude and corruption, did not sit well in Washington.[36]

The government needed help. Financial assistance was required to curb inflation, rebuild the country and buy arms and munitions. Beginning in April 1948, the Marshall Plan, designed by the very man who had tried against all odds to engineer a coalition between Chiang Kai-shek and the Communists, provided US$13 billion in economic and technical assistance to help the recovery of Europe. This sum did not include the US$12 billion in American aid that Europe had already received between the end of the war and the start of the Plan. But support from Allied Powers for China was minimal. Even after a Republican majority finally pushed Congress to provide an aid package, which was only passed in April 1948, the total military aid China received from August 1945 onwards amounted to somewhere between US$225 million and $360 million. Even Japan received more.[37]

As Zhang Junmai, a veteran diplomat, campaigner for parliamentary democracy and unsparing critic of the central government noted later, even if an efficient government had existed it would have been no match for the combined forces of Moscow and Yan'an. Yet even as trainloads of equipment moved back and forth across the border between Manchuria and Siberia, the United States began refusing to license military equipment for China. In September 1946, Truman imposed an arms embargo which lasted until July 1947, when the government was allowed to purchase a three-week supply of infantry ammunition. In March 1947, the president proclaimed the Truman Doctrine, committing the United States to support democratic nations against authoritarian threats, and extended immediate economic and military aid to Greece and Turkey to counteract Soviet influence. During a cabinet discussion on China, he rejected more aid for Nanjing. 'It would be pouring sand in a rat hole,' he opined.[38]

War resumed in January 1947, as Chiang tried to consolidate the north of China before resuming his campaign in Manchuria. Yan'an was bombed and occupied in March, its caves found abandoned since a spy in the ranks of Hu Zongnan's forces had given the Communists advance notice of the attack. But Chiang focused his military efforts primarily on Shandong province, facing south Manchuria across the Bohai Sea. Lin Biao seized the opportunity to attack and annihilate isolated units in Manchuria. By then, the Communist military strength north of the Great Wall was over 400,000, roughly equal to the total under Du Yuming's command. In June, Lin marched his combat units on to Siping, which had been in government hands for over a year. His soldiers were no longer simple peasants armed with swords and a few rifles. The Communists had gained recruits and organised a modern army equipped with huge firepower, not least several battalions that began to shatter the city's fortifications with large-calibre and anti-aircraft artillery. By one account, up to 10,000 shells a day were lobbed into Siping, an offensive previously unmatched in intensity and ferocity in the civil war. But once the defences had been breached the Communists encountered stubborn resistance, as government troops ensconced themselves, turning buildings, bunkers and pillboxes into redoubts. After two weeks of fierce fighting at close quarters, with battles for streets, factories and houses, nearly half the city had been levelled.[39]

Far away, in the countryside around Beiping and Tianjin, artillery fire was audible as the Communists sought to cut railways and isolate all major cities in the hope of disrupting supply lines to Siping. In Tanggu, the main port outside Tianjin, Communist forces threatened to attack after the last of 1,900 US marines had sailed home. Towards the end of June, two mechanised armies from Shenyang and Changchun came to Siping's defence, converging in a pincer movement that forced the Communists to abandon the city's flaming ruins. Casualties for all involved were huge, with estimates on each side varying from 15,000 to 20,000. Even as Lin Biao withdrew, the government's failure to obtain a US$500 million loan from the United States pushed the currency to dizzying heights in Beiping, Shanghai, Nanjing and other cities.[40]

For months on end, the Communists relentlessly hammered the cities under government control. As winter approached, Lin Biao again began cutting off railway connections and the supply of coal to Jilin, Changchun, Siping, Shenyang, Yingkou and Manchuria's gateway at Shanhaiguan. But Chiang Kai-shek surmised that the loss of Manchuria would open all of north China to the Communists and was determined to hold on whatever the cost, pouring more troops into the region.[41]

By December 1947, the Communists had managed to increase their troops to 730,000. Protected by thick mist and glacial weather that severely limited the government's use of aircraft, they bypassed the heavily defended cities and attacked several smaller and more vulnerable positions near Shenyang. Pressing their military advantage, they isolated and wiped out several government divisions. In the following months, Lin Biao picked off peripheral cities that served as Shenyang's outer defences. In March 1948, he returned to Siping, this time with a vengeance, taking the severely undermanned garrison in a single day.[42]

In every town and village liberated by the Communists, standard procedures were followed. All able-bodied men were recruited into the army, the women enlisted in support units. Children were used as informants, sometimes organised into teams to keep an eye on all the roads out of town and search travellers. Numerous denunciation meetings followed, as inhabitants were offered an opportunity to prove themselves by pointing the finger at others. Grain procurements increased vastly, with stacks of rice and queues of horsecarts and sledges seen in some villages. Prices were officially fixed, forcing shops to downgrade to mere stalls or close altogether, replaced by state-operated stores and cooperatives. Since many people found their incomes inadequate, one sector of the economy that did thriving business was trade in second-hand goods. No civil or criminal courts existed, as the Public Security Bureau, the Labour Union or occasionally the duly elected Communist mayor handled most legal cases.[43]

By summer 1948, the government was holding on to just three cities, namely Changchun, Shenyang and Jinzhou, representing 1 per cent of Manchuria. A tug of war began between Wei Lihuang, who assumed overall command of the troops in Manchuria in October 1947, and the Generalissimo. Wei, a veteran of the Burma campaign who was considered one of the country's most talented battlefield tacticians, openly defied orders to withdraw from Changchun and Shenyang. Instead of retreating towards Jinzhou, which Chiang Kai-shek believed would be easier to supply, Wei Lihuang insisted on making a stand and defending Shenyang and Changchun to the last.[44]

In April 1948, Lin Biao approached Changchun, which had become an isolated outpost some 300 kilometres removed from Shenyang. Shenyang, in turn, was 250 kilometres north of Jinzhou. Changchun had served as the capital of Manchukuo, the puppet state of the Japanese, who had transformed the place into a modern, wheel-shaped city with broad avenues, shade trees and public works. The Japanese built spacious, cream-coloured buildings for the imperial bureaucracy, dotting the city with elegant villas for themselves and their local collaborators. The Soviets had dismantled much of the infrastructure, demolishing industrial installations and leaving many of its houses stripped bare. When Lin Biao and his troops arrived outside the gates,

Zheng Dongguo, the defending commander, refused to surrender. On 30 May, Lin Biao ordered that the city be starved into submission: 'Turn Changchun into a city of death.'[45]

Inside were an estimated 500,000 civilians, many of them refugees who had fled the advancing Communists and were trapped on their journey south to Beiping after the railway lines had been cut. A garrison of 100,000 troops defended the city. They imposed a curfew, confining people to their homes overnight. No one was allowed to leave, and people who refused to submit to searches by sentries were liable to be shot on the spot. Yet an air of goodwill prevailed in the first weeks of the siege, as emergency supplies were dropped by air.[46]

Soon the situation deteriorated. Changchun was surrounded by 200,000 troops who dug trenches and cut off the underground water supply. On more than fifty occasions the attackers hurled themselves on to the city's defences in what Zheng Dongguo called 'human waves'. This was one of the first uses of the term, which would appear regularly over the coming fifteen months, in different contexts. Two dozen anti-aircraft guns and heavy artillery bombarded the city all day long, concentrating their fire on government buildings. The beleaguered troops built three defensive lines of pillboxes around Changchun. A vast no man's land, quickly taken over by outlaws, soon separated the besieged and the assailants.[47]

On 12 June, to prevent a famine, Chiang Kai-shek cabled an order reversing the ban on people leaving Changchun. Even without enemy fire, his planes, forced to fly at an altitude of 3,000 metres to evade Lin Biao's anti-aircraft artillery, often missed their target and could not possibly parachute in enough supplies to meet the needs of more than half a million people. Every departing person was subjected to rigorous inspection and, to avoid further burdening the city, was prohibited from returning. They were forbidden to take metallic objects such as pots or pans, as well as gold, silver and even salt. Once outside the city gates, the refugees had to cross the no man's land, a dark and dangerous terrain dominated by gangs, usually army deserters, who preyed on the defenceless crowds. The most skilful escapees managed to hide a piece of jewellery, a watch or a fountain pen, even though they risked being shot. A few saved their treasures by bundling them deep inside a burlap bag filled with dirty rags, including urine-soaked baby clothes, hoping that the smell would repel the robbers.[48]

Few ever made it past the Communist lines. Lin Biao had placed a sentry every fifty metres along barbed wire and trenches four metres deep. Every exit was blocked. He reported to Mao: 'We don't allow the refugees to leave and exhort them to turn back. This method was very effective in the beginning, but later the famine got worse, and starving civilians would leave the city in droves at all times of day and night, and after we turned them down they started gathering in the area between our troops and the enemy.' Lin Biao described the desperation of the refugees trying to get through the perimeter he had imposed, depicting how they:

> knelt in front of our troops in large groups and begged us to let them through. Some left their babies and small children with us and absconded, others hanged themselves in front of sentry posts. The soldiers who saw this misery lost their resolve, some even falling on their knees to weep with the starving people, saying, 'We are only following orders.' Others covertly allowed some of them through. After we corrected this, another tendency was discovered, namely the beating, tying up and shooting of refugees by soldiers, some to death (we do not yet have any numbers for those injured or beaten to death).[49]

Half a century later, Wang Junru, who was fifteen when the Communists forced him to enrol in the army, recalled that he had been ordered to drive back hungry civilians during the siege: 'We were told they were the enemy and they had to die.'[50]

By the end of June, 30,000 people were trapped in the area between the Communists, who would not allow them to pass, and the Nationalists, who refused to let them re-enter the city. Hundreds died every day. Two months later, more than 150,000 civilians were pressed inside the death zone, reduced to eating grass and leaves, doomed to slow starvation. Dead bodies were strewn everywhere, their bellies bloated in the scorching sun. 'The pungent stench of decomposition was everywhere,' remembered one survivor.[51]

The situation inside the city was little better. Some 330 tonnes of grain were required daily to feed the population, although at best 84 tonnes were delivered by plane. Everything was requisitioned in the defence of Changchun. Soon soldiers began turning on civilians, taking their food at gunpoint. They slaughtered the army horses, then dogs, cats, even birds. Ordinary people ate rotten sorghum, corncobs, bark stripped from trees, insects and leather belts. A few turned to human flesh, which apparently sold at $1.20 a pound on the black market.[52]

Autumn saw temperatures plunge, with survivors struggling to stay warm. They stripped floorboards, rooftops, sometimes entire buildings in the search for fuel. Trees were chopped down, and even signboards were pilfered for wood. Asphalt was ripped from the streets. An estimated 40 per cent of the housing stock went up in smoke. Heavy bombardment by artillery at point-blank range added to the misery, as ordinary people sheltered in shanties strewn with debris and decomposing bodies, while the garrison's top brass took refuge behind the massive concrete walls of the Central Bank of China.[53]

The siege lasted 150 days, with at least 160,000 civilians dying of hunger and disease during the blockade. On 16 October, the Generalissimo ordered Zheng Dongguo to evacuate the city and cut southward towards Shenyang. 'If Changchun falls, do you really think Beiping will be safe?' Zheng was asked. He gave a sigh: 'No place in China will be safe.'[54]

The soldiers, too weak to march to Shenyang, turned their guns instead on their superiors, handing the city over to Lin Biao. The fall of Changchun was the single most important event of the entire civil war. It demonstrated steely resolve as well as the grim effectiveness of the Communists' attrition warfare, conducted without regard for loss of civilian life. Few garrison commanders were willing to subject their city to a similar fate.

Shenyang, too, was under siege. Inside this island of dwindling resistance, there were 1.2 million civilians, swollen to about 4 million by refugees fleeing the Communists, as well as 200,000 troops. Unlike Changchun, people could leave. Planes of General Claire Chennault's commercial airline shuttled in and out, evacuating about 1,500 passengers to safety each day, but few could afford to bribe their way on board. The majority left by train, rattling west towards the edge of the city's defence perimeter where the line ended. By the summer of 1948, every month some 140,000 pressed their way through the military lines around Shenyang to join the exodus. They continued their perilous journey on foot, joining a flood of misery pouring out of Manchuria – refugees escaping from beleaguered cities, farmers fleeing a bloodied countryside, most of them stumbling forward on foot, a few hobbling on crutches or sticks. From Jinzhou they were packed on to special trains to Shanhaiguan, where they found a makeshift refugee centre serviced by a single tap with running water. Many people quickly moved on to Beiping and Tianjin, even though few could be housed or adequately fed. Wherever they were in China, refugees always moved away from the Communists. Despite all the widely advertised merits of the Chinese Communist Party, nowhere during the civil war did anyone ever witness people fleeing a region controlled by the government towards the Communists.[55]

Many civilians were too poor or too sick to leave Shenyang, and as early as February they began to starve or die of disease. As a foreign reporter noted in July 1948: 'I walked down the desolate streets past the emaciated bodies of the dead in the gutters, pursued by unbearably pitiful child beggars and women crying out for help.'[56]

The coup de grâce came in September 1948, as Lin Biao deployed 300,000 men to encircle Jinzhou. Military engineers blew holes in the city walls. After sustaining 34,000 casualties, the city fell on 15 October, leaving Shenyang entirely isolated. A rescue force of 90,000 men, hacking its way through enemy lines outside Shenyang, walked straight into a trap, to be crushed a week later by Lin Biao. Fighting continued for about a week, often in bloody hand-to-hand combat after artillery fire had demolished the walls. When the most senior officer still alive in Shenyang surrendered on 1 November, the battle for Manchuria was over.[57]

***

Prices in Shanghai rose fivefold overnight. On the international market the gold yuan sank to one-tenth of its original value. A wave of defeatism swept across China. The United States advised its citizens as far south as Nanjing and Shanghai to evacuate the area. In the north, panic set in as an army of 750,000 fighters, reinforced with tanks, heavy artillery and other weapons captured from government troops, marched across the frozen plains of Manchuria through the Great Wall in a southward thrust towards Beiping. General Fu Zuoyi, a rough-and-ready commander who had begun his career as an officer in Yan Xishan's army, was in command of the entire area along a corridor stretching south of the Great Wall from Kalgan to the Taku Forts outside Tianjin, built during the Ming dynasty to protect the city from sea raiders. He stood little chance, as the Communists moved swiftly to surround Tianjin in November 1948, forcing him to pull his troops back inside the walls of Beiping. Here, too, Lin Biao drew a perimeter around the ancient capital, cutting off electricity and water supplies.[58]

Soon a strange silence set in, occasionally disturbed by shell explosions or bursts of machine-gun fire. At first Fu seemed determined to defend Beiping, ordering the digging of trenches and erection of street barricades, with soldiers going from house to house to commandeer billets. Since both airports outside the city were in Communist hands, an airstrip was constructed on the polo ground of the old Legation Quarter, where decades earlier Li Dazhao and others had been arrested in the Russian Embassy. In the dead of winter, forced-labour gangs dressed in padded gowns pulled down telephone poles, trees and even buildings on the approach to the runway to allow cargo planes to deliver vital supplies. Martial rule was imposed. Lorries with soldiers carrying sub-machine guns careened through the streets, reminding the population of their presence. Outside the city walls, thousands of homes were needlessly levelled, ostensibly to provide a good field of fire for the defending troops.[59]

Everyone in Beiping knew of the fate of Changchun, transformed into a 'city of death' by the very general who was now camping outside the gated walls. The prospect of watching Beiping, China's centre of traditional culture and learning since the Ming, destroyed for no good reason tormented Fu Zuoyi. He had seen what the Communists had done in Xiwanzi, the 'Little Lidice'. At first he asked Chiang for permission to resign, but when the Generalissimo refused, he resumed secret negotiations through his daughter, who was a Communist Party member. Fu surrendered on 22 January 1949. All his 240,000 troops were absorbed into the People's Liberation Army, as the Communists had renamed the Red Army in October 1947.[60]

For eight days Beiping seemed to float in a twilight zone, as government soldiers, some of them still armed, wandered about the city freely. Chiang Kai-shek's portrait on Tiananmen Square was removed before a People's Liberation Army vanguard entered the west gates on 31 January 1949. A lorry led the procession, its loudspeakers blaring the continuous refrain, 'Welcome to the Liberation Army on its Arrival in Beiping! Welcome to the People's Army on its Arrival in Beiping! Congratulations to the People of Beiping on their Liberation!' Soldiers followed, marching six abreast in full battle regalia, red-cheeked and seemingly in high spirits. Behind the soldiers came students, carrying large portraits of Mao Zedong and Zhu De. A military band closed the parade. There were no jubilant crowds, only curious onlookers relieved to have survived the siege. On Tiananmen Square, a hastily sketched portrait of Mao Zedong went up. The Chairman himself only entered the city several months later, driving to the Summer Palace on the outskirts in a bullet-proof Dodge limousine, made in Detroit for Chiang Kai-shek's personal use.[61]

Liberation in the countryside brought increased requisitions and compulsory recruitment into the army. In Hengshui, people were left on a starvation diet once they had paid their taxes in kind.

In villages clustered around Beiping, some farmers even came to the imperial capital to buy grain in order to meet their dues in kind. In Gengcun, where most of the 300 villagers shared the same surname Geng, people worked from dawn to dusk to pay taxes and surtaxes, usually in cash and grain but also submitting stalks of coarse native grass as well as timber. One hundred soldiers were billeted in the village. Denunciation meetings and mass trials accompanied land distribution, with a few people identified as 'tyrants' or 'landlords' inevitably ending up being killed. One man who once owned twelve acres of land was the designated victim and his mud hut, land and draught animals were distributed to villagers identified as 'poor peasants', all called Geng. In some places the family members of class enemies were driven away and prohibited from begging for food within a radius of twelve kilometres from their native villages. At every level, people were ruled by fear and mutual surveillance, encouraged to watch each other and denounce the merest whiff of deviant behaviour.[62]

Cangzhou, once a thriving industrial centre of 120,000 inhabitants just south of Tianjin, had no more than 50,000 people left by April 1949. The city was divided into wards, with an elder responsible for each street of each ward. Here, as everywhere else, mutual surveillance backed up by robust militia ensured public order. Many factories and shops were boarded up, with luxury items such as cigarettes and cosmetics banned outright. On market day, stallholders offered homespun cloth, vegetables, meat, bicycle accessories, shoes and some clothing items; but, with prices beyond the average wage earner, there were few buyers. Mass trials and denunciation meetings took place on the public square. Attendance was compulsory, with beatings liberally administered to exact the right kind of confession from the victims, some of whom were repeatedly attacked by a mob and later paraded through the streets. 'One small landholder said his entire family was condemned because his earthen home was roofed with tile,' a local journalist who had managed to disguise himself as a trader observed.[63]

The conquest of north China opened the door to massive recruitment. Japan had never managed to extract more than 400,000 tonnes of grain from the region, an amount the Communists were able to match by displaying the same disregard for the welfare of the local population. It was sufficient to feed an army of 1.2 million men. But procurements from Manchuria could support 5 million troops. An agricultural surplus in Manchuria, in other words, complemented a human surplus in north China, with the railways between both regions used to achieve a balance between supplies and boots on the ground.[64]

With a vast countryside pressed into service, the number of troops in the People's Liberation Army soared. So did the use of human-wave tactics, which from October 1948 onwards was widely reported in cables to Nanjing. Lin Biao had deployed the tactic during the siege of Changchun, and used it again in his assault on Tianjin. In Taiyuan, the capital of Shanxi which boasted extensive industrial plants including steel mills and arsenals, Xu Xiangqian sent his troops in one wave after another against the city. Yan Xishan, the model governor who had managed to hold on to his province for more than three decades, was determined to fend off the Communists. His men were forced to shoot the assailants by the hundreds, the human-wave technique exhausting not only the bullets but also the morale of the garrison. By April 1949, when the city was finally taken, both sides had suffered huge casualties, measured in multiple tens of thousands. A few years later, when General Maxwell Taylor, who had overseen the withdrawal of American troops from Korea in 1953, remarked to Chiang Kai-shek on how outdated some of the weapons of the Chinese Communists had been during the Korean War, the Generalissimo pointed out that they employed human waves, with 200 troops overwhelming every ten enemy soldiers, regardless of the death rate. Chiang's point was simple: the combined forces of the United Nations had been unable to prevail in Korea in 1951, much as his own men had been swept aside in China in 1949.[65]

Even as fierce fighting still raged in the north, in November 1948 over a million troops moved towards Xuzhou. As in 1938, control of the country's arterial railways was vital, not least the junction where the trunk line running from Beiping southward to Nanjing intersected with the railway meandering from Tianshui in the west to Haizhou on the Yellow Sea in the east. Xuzhou was the key to Nanjing and the gateway to the prosperous Yangtze valley. The Communists mustered a force of almost 400,000 troops who marched straight out of Manchuria, past Beiping, bearing down on Xuzhou. They were joined by another 200,000 who swept in from the neighbouring province of Shandong, where the Communists controlled large parts of the countryside as well as the port of Yantai. The government deployed 400,000 troops in the flat, water-laced plains around the railway junction. General Chen Yi, the bald and stocky commander of the Communist troops, moved swiftly to cut all railway lines, subjecting the main airfield to heavy artillery bombardment. Du Yuming, the general who had pursued Lin Biao in Manchuria, moved his men over rutted roads and torn-up rail tracks to establish a new line of defence to the east of the city, using the autumn floods to defend the swampy ground to the north.[66]

Both sides clashed in the greatest battle in Chinese history, known as the 'Huaihai Campaign'. In the fight for the heartland of the country, tanks and heavy artillery were deployed, with government planes controlling the skies, using cloudless days and nights to wreak havoc on the enemy. Both armies pounded ancient towns with moats and crenellated walls, reducing them to smouldering ruins set amid fields sown with winter wheat. Women could be seen poking forlornly through roofless huts and blackened walls, hoping to retrieve some of their possessions. As one Communist general later recalled, the People's Liberation Army wiped out village after village with blanket shelling: 'In fighting Du Yuming, we practically flattened the villages, using thousands of shells and countless bombs.' One returning pilot working for the government reported that every village in sight was burning, the fields 'covered with bodies'.[67]

Supporting Chen Yi and his troops were more than 5 million men and women, sometimes even children, conscripted by Deng Xiaoping. Deng imposed strict recruitment quotas for each village and threatened severe punishment if they were not met. These pick-and-shovel crews not only provided logistical support, carrying food and materiel on their backs to the front, but were also used as human shields, sometimes forced to march before the troops. Dense waves of unarmed villagers overwhelmed the government troops. Lin Jingwu, an ordinary soldier fighting from the trenches, remembered years later that his hands went numb from firing bullets into a sea of civilians. He felt sick at the idea of slaying them and tried to close his eyes, but kept on shooting. In the Huaihai Campaign, they kept coming and coming, with no regard for casualties.[68]

Du Yuming held nothing back, mauling his opponents badly and surprising those who believed that the Communists would take Chiang Kai-shek's capital within days. But it was not enough, as relentless pressure forced him to retreat inside Xuzhou, where his troops quickly ran out of food. Horses were slaughtered, and civilians reduced to scouring the streets for bark and roots. Xuzhou became a repeat of Shenyang, with women and children in small villages caught between enemy lines outside the city walls freezing to death in the absence of fuel. Du Yuming, disguised as an ordinary soldier, was captured as he tried to slip away, with his troops surrendering after the enemy boomed offers of food and shelter incessantly over loudspeakers. By 10 January 1949 the battle was over. Chen Yi had dealt a fatal blow to Chiang Kai-shek.[69]

A few weeks later, the defeated Generalissimo stepped down, reading a formal statement from a small drawing room in the Ministry of National Defence in Nanjing. His vice-president continued peace talks with the Communists, but it was too little, too late. Everywhere people were apathetic, beaten down by inflation and heavy taxes, sometimes even openly hostile to the government. Despite a muzzled press, the abuses of an increasingly repressive regime were widely reported. The brutal methods the police employed in the hunt for underground agents particularly alienated large sections of the urban population. A powerful Communist propaganda machine presided over by Zhou Enlai mercilessly exploited every shortcoming of the government, unfailingly contrasting these with the vision of democracy and social reform promised by the Communists. After more than a decade of war, people craved peace at any cost.

Once the Communists had poured across the Yangtze, the country's last great defensive barrier, they moved with great speed. Nanjing was taken on 23 April 1949, followed by Wuhan on 17 May. 'Shanghai will be China's Stalingrad,' the general appointed to defend the country's financial powerhouse vowed. But after a wary wait of several weeks, with Chen Yi controlling the countryside, the 'Paris of the East' fell on 25 May with barely a shot fired, much to the relief of the local population. Many, including business leaders and gangster triads, had quietly switched sides, prepared for the takeover by years of patient underground work. In Shanghai as elsewhere, no foreign concessions existed, since they had been relinquished on 1 January 1943, in the middle of the war. A banner went up near the American Club, proclaiming 'Welcome to the People's Liberation Army'. Within a few days a huge portrait of Mao Zedong was also hoisted over the Great World Amusement Centre, Shanghai's seething six-floor recreational building. Red flags fluttered over shop doorways, while lorries bedecked with red banners carried students and workers jubilantly waving pennants. Even as machine guns still rattled in the distance, Communist songs blared from loudspeakers in the city centre. In June, a string of authoritative newspapers, including several that had been critical of the central government, closed down. The Communist Control Committee explained that freedom of the press was allowed, but only for 'those who serve the interests of the people'.[70]

With the entire Yangtze valley under Communist control, government troops that had not yet surrendered continued their retreat further south. Canton, the city where Sun Yat-sen had first set up a Nationalist government, once again became a temporary capital. On Shameen, the former enclave for foreign diplomats, government officials bought up plush stone mansions shaded by banyan trees. For a few brief weeks, the city became a boom town, creaking under the extra load of refugees, with new arrivals from all over the country vying to obtain a remaining house or apartment. This lasted until 14 October 1949, when Canton fell 'with scarcely more than a quiet sigh'. Chiang Kai-shek and his followers hastily withdrew all the way back to their wartime capital of Chongqing.[71]

Even as the Communists were driving south towards Canton, another army was following the railway west of Xuzhou. Ahead lay a vast borderland with frontiers that adjoined the People's Republic of Mongolia, the Soviet Union, Tibet, India and Afghanistan. The railway went as far as Tianshui, in the southern corner of Gansu province. Peng Dehuai was in charge, taking his 150,000 men to the provincial capital of Lanzhou, the gateway to the north-west, including the Yumen oilfields. Further west along the ancient silk road lay Qinghai, home of one of the most efficient provincial regimes in the country. Ma Bufang, a trim, burly Muslim general, had used a firm hand to transform the province under his purview, lining the smooth, metalled highways with willow and poplar saplings, cleaning up the cities, irrigating the countryside and building hospitals and medical facilities. In Xining, the capital, one-third of the population went to school; food, clothing and tuition were provided free to all students. Qinghai thrived when most of the country was heaving under the weight of civil war. But Ma Bufang's cavalry of 40,000 armed Muslim horsemen was no match for Peng Dehuai.[72]

Next came Xinjiang, a vast region where deserts, mountains, steppes and lakes formed a harsh but beautiful landscape, hiding valuable resources in oil, coal, gold, tungsten, uranium and rare-earth metals. The province was home to a heterogeneous population, as waves of migration had left behind Uighurs, Kazaks, Chinese, Taranchis, Kirghiz, Mongols, White Russians, Uzbeks, Tajiks, Tatars and Manchus, among others. Relations between these different peoples were sometimes strained, on occasion violent, in particular in the nineteenth century when revolts against the Qing had flared up. Not until 1884 had the region been fully colonised by the empire. After 1917, the Soviets had repeatedly helped Sheng Shicai, governor of the province, to repress local rebellions, in exchange for trading privileges as well as concessions for oilwells, tin and wolfram mines. In November 1940, Moscow, seeking a buffer state against Japan, had taken virtual control of the region, only to leave in 1944. Peng Dehuai approached the outskirts of Urumqi in October 1949, forcing the local garrison to surrender. By then, his supply lines were stretched to the limit. Unable to feed his troops, Peng turned to Moscow for help. Within weeks, Soviet traders, engineers and advisers were once again swarming through the region. Convoys of lorries with Russian troops in full winter clothing could be seen rumbling along the streets of Urumqi at night.[73]

Encircled on all sides, Chiang Kai-shek moved the seat of his government from Chongqing to Chengdu. 'We are concentrating our troops so that the battle for the southwest can be sustained,' he announced, even as the Communists were only ten kilometres from the refugee capital. All of the air force's planes began evacuating government officials in an exodus to Taipei, capital of Taiwan. Chiang himself was one of the last to board a plane, leaving with his son Ching-kuo on 10 December, never to return.[74]

One year later a mere 40,000 troops of the People's Liberation Army conquered Tibet, scaling the 4,000-metre passes to enter a bleak plateau and approach Lhasa on 7 October 1950. They wiped out all armed opposition at Chamdo, establishing a weak theocratic government under their thumb. By then, only Hong Kong, Macau and Taiwan still eluded the reach of the Chinese Communist Party. For most people across the length and breadth of the People's Republic of China, the cost of their liberation was yet to be realised.

Notes

PREFACE

1 CA, *Zhejiang geming lishi wenjian huiji (shengwei wenjian): 1926–1927*, Report from Provincial Party Committee, 27 Sept. 1927, p. 118; CA, *Jiangsu geming lishi wenjian huiji (shengwei wenjian): 1929.6–1929.8*, Report from Provincial Party Committee, 18 June 1929, p. 49.
2 Carlos A. Cunha, *The Portuguese Communist Party's Strategy for Power: 1921–1986*, New York and London: Garland, 1992, p. 199; Royal Institute of International Affairs, 'World Communism in Figures', *World Today*, 14, no. 5 (May 1958), p. 215; John H. Hodgson, 'The Finnish Communist Party', *Slavic Review*, 29, no. 1 (March 1970), p. 76; Gansu sheng dang'anguan (eds), *Gansu sheng dang'anguan zhinan* (Guide to the Gansu provincial archives), Lanzhou: Gansu renmin chubanshe, 1997, pp. 164–5.
3 NARA, RG 165, MID 2657-1-276/420, 'Situation Report', Report No. 8778, 28 Feb. 1934.
4 He Xiya, *Zhongguo daofei wenti zhi yanjiu* (A Study of the Bandit Problem in China), Shanghai: Taidong tushuju, 1925; see also Patrick Fuliang Shan, 'Insecurity, Outlawry and Social Order: Banditry in China's Heilongjiang Frontier Region, 1900–1931', *Journal of Social History*, 40, no. 1 (Autumn 2006), pp. 25–54; virtually any newspaper on any day in republican China will carry information about bandits in one part or another of the country, although, as Xu Youwei and Philip Billingsley have argued, historians in the People's Republic, their world revolving around the Communists, only began to 'discover' bandits at the turn of the twentieth century, closely followed by their Western counterparts; see Xu Youwei and Philip Billingsley, 'Out of the Closet: China's Historians "Discover"

Republican-Period Bandits', *Modern China*, 28, no. 4 (Oct. 2002), pp. 467–99.
5 PRO, FO 371/8040, 'Bolshevism in China', 4 July 1922, p. 3.
6 Joseph Esherick, *Accidental Holy Land: The Communist Revolution in Northwest China*, Berkeley, CA: University of California Press, 2022, p. 128.
7 Jung Chang and Jon Halliday, *Mao: The Unknown Story*, London: Jonathan Cape, 2005, p. 192.
8 Edgar Snow, 'Interviews with Mao Tse-tung, Communist Leader', *China Weekly Review*, 14 and 21 Nov. 1936.
9 The foremost historian of these alternative traditions is Gregor Benton; see, among others, Gregor Benton and Alan Hunter, *Wild Lily, Prairie Fire: China's Road to Democracy, Yan'an to Tian'anmen, 1942–1989*, Princeton: Princeton University Press, 1995.
10 Michael Walker, *The 1929 Sino-Soviet War: The War Nobody Knew*, Lawrence, KS: University Press of Kansas, 2017.
11 Robert Marquand, 'Modern China's Founding Legend: Heavy on Myth?', *Christian Science Monitor*, 22 May 2006.
12 Mikhail L. Titarenko (ed.), *VKP (b), Komintern i Kitai: Dokumenty* (The CPSU, the Comintern and China: Documents), Moscow: AO 'Buklet', 1994–2007.
13 Harold H. Fisher, *The Communist Revolution: An Outline of Strategy and Tactics*, Stanford, CA: Stanford University Press, 1955, p. 13.
14 Arthur Waldron, two decades ago, highlighted the shortcomings of this approach, pointing instead at the importance of traditional military strategy in his pioneering review essay entitled 'The Life of Mao Zedong', *Orbis*, 44, no. 4 (Autumn 2000), pp. 637–47.

1 INCUBATION (1921–1926)

1 David Andress, *The Terror: The Merciless War for Freedom in Revolutionary France*, New York: Farrar, Straus & Giroux, 2005, p. 147; Simon Schama, *Citizens: A Chronicle of the French Revolution*, New York: Alfred A. Knopf, 1989, pp. 668–9.
2 Karl Marx, 'Provisional Rules of the Working Men's International Association', Karl Marx and Friedrich Engels, *Collected Works*, vol. XX, New York: International Publishers, 1985, pp. 14–16.
3 Rosa Luxemburg, *The Essential Rosa Luxemburg*, Chicago, IL: Haymarket Books, 2007, p. 90.

4 Victor Serge and Natalia Sedova Trotsky, *The Life and Death of Leon Trotsky*, Chicago, IL: Haymarket Books, 2015, p. 15; James Ryan, '"Revolution is War": The Development of the Thought of V. I. Lenin on Violence, 1899–1907', *Slavonic and East European Review*, 89, no. 2 (April 2011), pp. 248–73.
5 PRO, FO 371/13239, Shanghai Publicity Bureau, 'New Bulletin', Aug. 1928, p. 19.
6 Jennifer Siegel, *For Peace and Money: French and British Finance in the Service of Tsars and Commissars*, Oxford: Oxford University Press, 2014, pp. 169–71.
7 Peter Neville, *Mussolini*, Abingdon: Routledge, 2015, p. 46.
8 Joseph Fletcher, 'The Heyday of the Ch'ing Order in Mongolia, Sinkiang and Tibet', in Dennis Twitchett and John K. Fairbank (eds), *The Cambridge History of China*, Cambridge: Cambridge University Press, 1978, vol. 10, part 1, pp. 375–85; Pär Cassel, *Grounds of Judgment*, New York: Oxford University Press, 2012, p. 8.
9 A. L. P. Dennis, 'The Origin of the "Open Door"', *Current History*, 27, no. 5 (Feb. 1928), pp. 651–3.
10 On the dealings at Versailles, see Bruce A. Elleman, *Wilson and China: A Revised History of the Shandong Question*, London: Routledge, 2002.
11 PRO, FO 371/8040, 'Bolshevism in China', 4 July 1922, p. 3.
12 Liu Jianyi, 'The Origins of the Chinese Communist Party and the Role Played by Soviet Russia and the Comintern', doctoral dissertation, York University, 2000, pp. 123–6; Liu's work is pioneering in understanding the importance of the Foreign Office archives and using them to highlight the crucial role played by agents from Moscow in the development of communism in China.
13 Li Dazhao, 'The Victory of Bolshevism', in Jonathan Spence et al. (eds), *The Search for Modern China: A Documentary Collection*, New York: W. W. Norton & Company, 1999, pp. 236–8, with stylistic changes.
14 Liu, 'The Origins of the Chinese Communist Party', pp. 132–3.
15 PRO, FO 371/5341, A. D. Blackburn, 'Summary of Intelligence of the Shanghai Intelligence Bureau', Aug. 1920, p. 208.
16 Liu, 'The Origins of the Chinese Communist Party', pp. 101–3.
17 PRO, FO 371/6612, 'Weekly Report of the Special Bureau of Information', 27 Nov. 1920, p. 106; PRO, FO 371/6602, G. C. Denham, 'Bolshevism and Chinese Communism', 9 Aug. 1921, p. 120; on the Centrosoyuz, see also Liu, 'The Origins of the Chinese Communist Party', p. 104.
18 PRO, FO 371/5341, G. C. Denham, 'Memorandum respecting Bolshevism in the Far East', 7 April 1920, pp. 83–4.

19 Abel Bonnard, *In China*, New York: E. P. Dutton, 1927, p. 126.
20 MAE, 513PO/A/428bis, Chengdu Consulate, 'Télégramme Circulaire du Ministère de l'Intérieur', 24 Feb. 1921.
21 MAE, 513PO/A/428, 'L'action bolchévique en Chine', 30 April 1925, pp. 15–17; also NARA, RG 263, SMP, box 1, document 5, D. S. McKeown, 'History of the Communist Movement in Shanghai', 8 May 1933.
22 Marie-Claire Bergère, *Sun Yat-sen*, Stanford, CA: Stanford University Press, 1998, pp. 257–8.
23 Ibid., p. 274.
24 Tony Saich, *Finding Allies and Making Revolution: The Early Years of the Chinese Communist Party*, Leiden: E. J. Brill, 2020, pp. 19–20.
25 PRO, FO 228/3211, 2 Nov. 1919, quoted in Liu, 'The Origins of the Chinese Communist Party', p. 143; PRO, FO 371/6602, G. C. Denham, 'Bolshevism and Chinese Communism', 9 Aug. 1921, p. 121.
26 PRO, FO 371/5340, Shanghai Intelligence Bureau Report for June 1920, 14 July 1920, p. 39; Ishikawa Yoshihiro, *The Formation of the Chinese Communist Party*, New York: Columbia University Press, 2013, p. 90.
27 PRO, FO 371/6602, G. C. Denham, 'Bolshevism and Chinese Communism', 9 Aug. 1921, p. 120.
28 Ishikawa, *The Formation of the Chinese Communist Party*, p. 90.
29 Hollington K. Tong, 'Russian Soviet Would Befriend China', *Millard's Review of the Far East*, 5 June 1920, p. 24; the key sentence is 'the Government of the Soviets returns to the Chinese people without demanding any kind of compensation the Chinese Eastern Railway.' Historians routinely write about the '25 July 1919 Karakhan Declaration' and its enthusiastic reception in China during the May Fourth Movement, but the text did not reach Irkutsk until February 1920, the French version only being transmitted to Beijing by the chairman of its Provincial Revolutionary Committee, Iakov Davidovich Ianson, on 26 March; see M. V. Kryukov, 'Vokrug "Pervoi Deklaratsii Karakhana" po Kitaiskomu voprosu, 1919', *Novaia i noveishaia istoriia*, no. 5 (2000), pp. 30–43; the late arrival of the declaration is clearly noted in Chow Tse-tsung, *The May 4th Movement: Intellectual Revolution in Modern China*, Cambridge, MA: Harvard University Press, 1960, p. 211.
30 MAE, 513PO/A/428bis, Military Attaché, 'Bolshevisme en Extrême-Orient', 25 April 1921; 'Résumé des Renseignements', 23 June 1921.

31 MAE, 513PO/A/428bis, M. Beauvais, French Consul in Canton, 'Le mouvement socialiste à Canton', 19 May 1921; the title of the newspaper was *Huzhu ribao*.
32 Claude Cadart, *Mémoires de Peng Shuzhi: L'envol du communisme en Chine*, Paris: Gallimard, 1983, pp. 205–7; Shanghai: *Laodong jie*, Beijing: *Laodong sheng*; more generally, see Yoshihiro, *The Formation of the Chinese Communist Party*, pp. 168 ff., and Saich, *Finding Allies and Making Revolution*, pp. 61–2.
33 Saich, *Finding Allies and Making Revolution*, pp. 70–7.
34 Ibid., p. 69; PRO, FO 371/6602, G. C. Denham, 'Bolshevism and Chinese Communism', 9 Aug. 1921, p. 119.
35 PRO, FO 371/8040, G. C. Denham, 'Anarchism and Communism in Canton', 25 July 1922, p. 27.
36 NARA, RG 59, file 893.000/3817, quoted in C. Martin Wilbur, *Sun Yat-sen: Frustrated Patriot*, New York: Columbia University Press, 1976, p. 324, f. 74; John Foord, 'New Hope for China', *New York Times*, 26 Sept. 1920.
37 Saich, *Finding Allies and Making Revolution*, pp. 89–92.
38 Ibid., pp. 92–6, 109, 112 and 122.
39 'Minutes of the Second Congress of the Communist International', Seventh Session, 30 July 1920; see also Hu Shi, 'China in Stalin's Grand Strategy', *Foreign Affairs*, 1950.
40 MAE, 513PO/A/428, 'L'action bolchévique en Chine', 30 April 1929.
41 J. B. Powell, 'Red Envoy to Peking Opposes Chinese Soviet', *Chicago Daily Tribune*, 27 Jan. 1923; the aid and assistance from the Soviet Union were kept secret.
42 'Canton is Army's Aim', *Los Angeles Times*, 4 Feb. 1923.
43 MAE, 513PO/A/542, 'La question sociale au Kouang-Tong en 1923', 20 Feb. 1924; Harry A. Franck, *Roving through Southern China*, New York: The Century Co., 1925, pp. 266–71.
44 Brian T. George, 'The State Department and Sun Yat-Sen: American Policy and the Revolutionary Disintegration of China, 1920–1924', *Pacific Historical Review*, 46, no. 3 (Aug. 1977), pp. 400–2; Bergère, *Sun Yat-sen*, p. 313.
45 'Telegram from A. Joffe to H. Sneevliet', 1 May 1923, reproduced in Tony Saich, *The Origins of the First United Front in China: The Role of Sneevliet [Alias Maring]*, Leiden: E. J. Brill, 1991, vol. 2, p. 527.
46 Alexander V. Pantsov, *Victorious in Defeat: The Life and Times of Chiang Kai-shek, China, 1887–1975*, New Haven, CT: Yale University Press, 2023, pp. 88–9.

47 Robert Service, *Trotsky: A Biography*, Cambridge, MA: Harvard University Press, 2009, p. 310; the orators are mentioned in Cadart, *Mémoires de Peng Shuzhi*, pp. 331–2.
48 Note by Baranovsky on the Meeting between the Nationalist Party's Delegation and Trotsky, 27 Nov. 1923, in Mikhail L. Titarenko et al. (eds), *VKP(b), Komintern i Kitai: Dokumenty* (The All-Union Communist Party of Bolsheviks, the Comintern and China: Documents), Moscow: AO 'Buklet', 1994, vol. 1, p. 307; Chiang, 'Diary', 27 Nov. 1923, quoted in Guoshiguan (eds), *Jiang Zhongzheng nianpu changbian*, Taipei: Guoshiguan, 2014, vol. 1, p. 226; Chiang's talk is mentioned in Edna Lee Booker, *News is my Job: A Correspondent in War-torn China*, New York: Macmillan, 1940, p. 181.
49 Resolution on the Issue of the National Liberation Movement in China, 28 Nov. 1923, in Titarenko, *VKP(b), Komintern i Kitai*, vol. 1, pp. 308–11; Chiang, 'Diary', 28 Nov. 1923, quoted in *Jiang Zhongzheng nianpu changbian*, vol. 1, p. 228; Chiang's conclusion: Letter to Liao Zhongkai, 14 March 1924, in Chiang Kai-shek, *Soviet Russia in China: A Summing Up at Seventy*, New York: Farrar, Straus & Cudahy, 1958, p. 26.
50 N. Mitarevsky, *World Wide Soviet Plots*, Tianjin: Tientsin Press, 1927, p. 131.
51 Ibid., p. 134.
52 Booker, *News is my Job*, pp. 182–3; Dan Jacobs, *Borodin: Stalin's Man in China from Moscow*, Cambridge, MA: Harvard University Press, 1981, pp. 124–5 and 135.
53 The diary is quoted at length in A. I. Cherepanov, *Zapiski voennovo sovetnika v Kitae* (Notes of a Soviet adviser in China), Moscow: Nauka, 1964, p. 71; Sun Yat-sen, *Zhongguo Guomindang diyici quanguo daibiaohui xuanyan* (Manifesto of the first national congress of the Nationalist Party), Guangzhou: Xinmin yinshuguan, 1924.
54 Jacobs, *Borodin*, p. 134.
55 MAE, 513PO/A/542, G. Dufaure de la Prade, Consul in Canton, 'Ecole de bolchévisme à Canton', 22 Nov. 1924; PRO, FO 371/11621, G. R. V. Steward, Military Attaché, 'Enclosure', 21 March 1925; for the curriculum, see HIA, Huston (Jay C.) Papers, box 2, 2 April 1924.
56 Mitarevksy, *World Wide Soviet Plots*, p. 34.
57 Jacobs, *Borodin*, pp. 149–50.
58 Ibid., p. 152.
59 Cherepanov, *Zapiski voennovo sovetnika v Kitae*, pp. 112–14; Pantsov, *Victorious in Defeat*, p. 103; '30 Chinese Reds Die in Battle

in Canton', *New York Times*, 13 Oct. 1924; also HIA, Huston (Jay C.) Papers, box 2, Douglas Jenkins, American Consul General, Report on Canton, 13 Oct. 1924.
60 'Further Fighting Expected as Canton Ruins Smoulder', *Atlanta Constitution*, 17 Oct. 1924; 'War in Canton', *South China Morning Post*, 16 Oct. 1924; 'Fires Set by Reds Burning Fiercely in Canton', *Atlanta Constitution*, 16 Oct. 1924.
61 Booker, *News is my Job*, p. 180.
62 MAE, 513PO/A/428, 'L'action bolchévique en Chine', 30 April 1929, pp. 12–13.
63 NARA, RG 263, SMP, box 1, document 5, D. S. McKeown, 'History of the Communist Movement in Shanghai', 8 May 1933, p. 8.
64 Booker, *News is my Job*, pp. 185–7.
65 MAE, 513PO/A/428, 'Message d'adieu de Sun Yat-sen', March 1925; Wilbur, *Frustrated Patriot*, pp. 278–9; Sun Yat-sen, *Sun Zhongshan congshu* (Collected writings of Sun Yat-sen), Shanghai: Guangyi shuju, 1928, pp. 53–4.
66 PRO, FO 371/10944, Secret Intelligence Services Report, 24 Feb. 1925, pp. 32–3; NARA, RG 263, SMP, box 1, document 5, D. S. McKeown, 'History of the Communist Movement in Shanghai', 8 May 1933, pp. 11–12.
67 McKeown, 'History of the Communist Movement in Shanghai', pp. 11–12; PRO, FO 371/10944, H. P. King, 'Developments', 15 June 1925, p. 237.
68 MAE, 513PO/A/435bis, Report on the May 30 Incident, 14 June 1925, including, in English, annex 7, 'Resume of the Incident of May 30, June 1 and June 2' dated 22 June 1925.
69 MAE, 513PO/A/435bis, Letter by Student Association of Tsing Hua College, 6 June 1925; also E. Finley Johnson, 'Report of the International Commission of Judges Appointed to Inquire into the Causes of the Disturbances at Shanghai May 30th, 1925', 9 Nov. 1925, p. 33.
70 PRO, FO 371/10944, H. P. King, 'Developments', 15 June 1925, pp. 234–5.
71 Edna Booker astutely pointed at the pivotal role students played in the spread of the Communist movement; see Booker, *News is my Job*, p. 189; MAE, 513PO/A/434bis, Fernand Roy, Consul in Chongqing, 'Agitation anti-Anglaise', 11 July 1925.
72 Earl A. Seele, *Donald of China*, New York: Harper, 1948, pp. 239–40; Wang Fanxi, *Memoirs of a Chinese Revolutionary, 1919–1949*, New York: Columbia University Press, 1991, p. 8; Cheng Woo-fee, letter to the editor, *China Press*, 5 Jan. 1926, quoted in Zack Woerner, 'A Reluctant Imperialist: Justice Elias Finley Johnson and

China's May 30th Movement', Senior Thesis, Bryn Mawr College, 2012, pp. 62–3.
73 HIA, Huston (Jay C.) Papers, box 2, Douglas Jenkins, Consul General in Canton, Despatch 298 to Secretary of State, 7 May 1925, as well as Douglas Jenkins, 'Military and Political Situation', 17 June 1925.
74 PRO, FO 371/11621, p. 79.
75 The key documents are in PRO, FO 371/11630 and 11631; some historians appear hesitant as to which side opened fire first, despite a slew of witnesses, including the Danish consul, the Swedish consul and a lieutenant of the US Marine Corps; a year later, in negotiations with acting consul J. F. Brenan, Eugene Chen could not explain why he had not called for an inquiry into the shooting a year earlier; he quietly dropped claims for compensation, asking instead for financial assistance to relieve the burden of unemployment caused by the strike against Britain, which was unsurprisingly declined (FO 371/11630).
76 PRO, FO 371/12501, Extract from Report on Canton after the Shameen Incident by General Galen (Vasily Blyukher), 20 Sept. 1925, p. 204; Kit-ching Chan Lau, *China, Britain and Hong Kong, 1895–1945*, Hong Kong: Chinese University Press, 1990, p. 180.
77 PRO, FO 371/12501, Extract from Report on Canton after the Shameen Incident by General Galen, 20 Sept. 1925, p. 204.
78 Mitarevsky, *World Wide Soviet Plots*, pp. 145–7.
79 'Soviet Intrigue in Canton', *Hongkong Telegraph*, 27 May 1925.
80 Yueh Sheng, *Sun Yat-sen University in Moscow and the Chinese Revolution: A Personal Account*, New York: Paragon Book Gallery, 1971, pp. 69–70; Gregor Benton (ed.), *Prophets Unarmed: Trotskyists in Revolution, War, Jail, and the Return from Limbo*, Leiden: E. J. Brill, 2015, pp. 47–51.
81 Mitarevksy, *World Wide Soviet Plots*, pp. 51 and 56.
82 MAE, 513PO/A/428, 'La propagande bolchevique en Chine', 23 June 1925; also Report from Harbin dated 16 June 1925, mentioning the arrest of a group of sixty-two agitators paid by Moscow.
83 MAE, 513PO/A/428, French Consulate, Harbin, 'L'action bolchévique en Mandchourie', including a report dated 28 June 1925 by Consul General Grandt to the People's Commissariat for Foreign Affairs in Moscow, 24 July 1925.
84 Julie Lien-ying How, 'Soviet Advisors with the Kuominchun, 1925–1926: A Documentary Study', *Chinese Studies in History*, 19, nos 1–2 (Winter 1985), pp. 13–15; Mitarevksy, *World Wide Soviet Plots*, pp. 30–5 and 41–9.

85 Mitarevksy, *World Wide Soviet Plots*, pp. 51 and 114–17; Yueh, *Sun Yat-sen University in Moscow*, p. 133.

2 FOMENTING REVOLUTION (1926–1927)

1 Mitarevksy, *World Wide Soviet Plots*, pp. 34–7; 'Kissanka' was a pseudonym for Kuibyshev.
2 Letter from Kuibyshev, 13 Jan. 1926, in Titarenko, *VKP(b), Komintern i Kitai: Dokumenty*, vol. 2, p. 21.
3 C. Martin Wilbur and Julie Lien-ying How, *Missionaries of Revolution: Soviet Advisers and Nationalist China, 1920–1927*, Cambridge, MA: Harvard University Press, 1989, pp. 188–92.
4 Jacobs, *Borodin*, pp. 188–90.
5 Jacobs, *Borodin*, pp. 198–9; Ch'en Li-fu, *The Storm Clouds Clear over China: The Memoir of Ch'en Li-fu, 1900–1993*, Stanford, CA: Stanford University Press, 1994, p. 26; Chiang, 'Diary', 12 Feb. 1926.
6 Chiang, *Soviet Russia in China*, pp. 42–3.
7 Michael Tsin, *Nation, Governance, and Modernity in China: Canton, 1900–1927*, Stanford, CA: Stanford University Press, 2000, pp. 165–6; Jacobs, *Borodin*, p. 202.
8 Tsin, *Nation, Governance, and Modernity in China*, p. 166.
9 Chiang, *Soviet Russia in China*, pp. 43–4.
10 Donald A. Jordan, *The Northern Expedition: China's National Revolution of 1926–1928*, Honolulu, HI: University Press of Hawaii, 1976, pp. 14–15; Jacobs, *Borodin*, p. 212.
11 Ruth Altman Greene, *Hsiang-Ya Journal*, Hamden, CT: Archon Books, 1977, pp. 42–4; 'Changsha under the Reds', *North-China Herald*, 6 Nov. 1926.
12 '12,000 are Rescued from Wuchang City', *New York Times*, 7 Oct. 1926; Ch'en, *The Storm Clouds Clear over China*, p. 43.
13 'The General Desire for Peace', *North-China Herald*, 6 Nov. 1926; Vera Vladimirovna Vishnyakova-Akimova, *Two Years in Revolutionary China, 1925–1927*, Cambridge, MA: Harvard University Press, 1971, p. 251.
14 Jacobs, *Borodin*, p. 216; Vishnyakova-Akimova, *Two Years in Revolutionary China*, p. 253.
15 Vishnyakova-Akimova, *Two Years in Revolutionary China*, p. 254.
16 Mitarevksy, *World Wide Soviet Plots*, pp. 145–7.
17 Ibid., pp. 147–9.

18 'Hankow Acclaims Bolshevist Agent', *New York Times*, 13 Dec. 1926.
19 'Violent Speeches at Hankow Meeting', *South China Morning Post*, 24 Dec. 1926.
20 John B. Powell, *My Twenty-Five Years in China*, New York: The Macmillan Company, 1945, p. 135; also NARA, RG 165, MID 2657-1-342, John Magruder, 'Russia in Chinese Nationalist Movement (From Observations in Hankow)', G-2 Report No. 7017, 15 April 1927.
21 Vishnyakova-Akimova, *Two Years in Revolutionary China*, pp. 286–8.
22 'Hankow Rioters Battle in Concession Streets', *New York Times*, 6 Jan. 1927; 'American Women Stoned', *Atlanta Constitution*, 10 Jan. 1927.
23 Mitarevksy, *World Wide Soviet Plots*, pp. 140–1.
24 Vishnyakova-Akimova, *Two Years in Revolutionary China*, p. 219.
25 Greene, *Hsiang-Ya Journal*, pp. 50–1.
26 Mitarevksy, *World Wide Soviet Plots*, p. 139.
27 S. T. Tung, 'Land Reform, Red Style', *Freeman*, 25 Aug. 1952, quoted in Richard J. Walker, *China under Communism: The First Five Years*, New Haven, CT: Yale University Press, 1955, p. 131.
28 Extract from Protocol 65 of the Politburo Meeting, 29 Oct. 1926, in Titarenko, *VKP(b), Komintern i Kitai*, vol. 2, p. 498.
29 Stuart R. Schram and Nancy J. Hodes (eds), *Mao's Road to Power: Revolutionary Writings, 1912–1949*, Armonk, NY: M. E. Sharpe, 1994, vol. 2, pp. 420–2.
30 'Report on the Peasant Movement in Hunan', Feb. 1927, in ibid., pp. 435–7 and 447.
31 Ibid., p. 430.
32 Mitarevksy, *World Wide Soviet Plots*, pp. 148–9.
33 L. W. Han, 'Sino-British Relations', *North-China Herald*, 14 July 1937.
34 Brian Farrell provides excellent background on the Washington Conference and its implications in Brian P. Farrell, S. R. Joey Long and David J. Ulbrich (eds), *From Far East to Asia Pacific: Great Powers and Grand Strategy, 1900–1954*, Berlin: Walter De Gruyter, 2022; Joseph Gordon, 'China Wins Tariff Independence', *Current History*, 34, no. 4 (July 1931), p. 549.
35 PRO, FO 371/17064, Miles Lampson, Farewell Report, 24 Aug. 1933, pp. 168–9.
36 *Jiang Zhongzheng xiansheng nianpu changbian*, vol. 2, 10 and 17 Feb. 1927, pp. 21 and 23.

37 MAE, 513PO/A/434, Telegram from Consul General in Shanghai and Statement from Mrs Giles, 29 March 1927.
38 Report by John Davis, Consul in Nanjing, 'Anti-Foreign Outrages at Nanking on March 24, 1927', reproduced in full in H. R. Misselwitz, *The Dragon Stirs*, New York: Harbinger House, 1941, pp. 38–40.
39 Roy C. Smith, 'Nanking, March 24, 1927', *United States Naval Institute Proceedings*, 58 (Jan. 1928), pp. 1–21.
40 MAE, 513PO/A/434, 'Rapport de mission', including the testimony of Madame Roger Caplain, 29 March 1927; Roy Smith, who was in charge of the rescue operation and the USS *Noa*, wrote that the looting stopped 'as if by magic': Smith, 'Nanking'; see also William R. Braisted, *Diplomats in Blue: New Perspectives on Maritime History and Nautical Archaeology*, Gainesville, FL: University Press of Florida, 2009, pp. 131–9.
41 GSG, 002-060100-00001-079, Draft Summary of Daily Events, 25 March 1927.
42 Hu Shih, 'China in Stalin's Grand Strategy', *Foreign Affairs*, 1950, pp. 18–19.
43 PRO, FO 371/12501, 'Document No. 22', dated early 1927, pp. 175–8; also PRO, FO 371/12407, 'Report on the Situation in Shanghai', 15 April 1927, p. 123.
44 'Police Stations Raided in Chapei', *North-China Herald*, 26 March 1927; Misselwitz, *The Dragon Stirs*, pp. 24–5.
45 'Fall of Shanghai and Nanking', *North-China Herald*, 26 March 1927; 'Labour's Campaign of Murder', *North-China Herald*, 26 March 1927; 'After the Flames', *North-China Herald*, 26 March 1927; see also Jordan, *The Northern Expedition*, p. 116.
46 GSG, 002-060100-00001-076, Draft Summary of Daily Events, 22 March 1927; GSG, 002-020100-00012-068, Telegram from Chiang Kai-shek to Bai Chongxi, 24 March 1927.
47 Extract from Protocol 87 of the Politburo Meeting, 17 Feb. 1927, in Titarenko, *VKP(b), Komintern i Kitai*, vol. 2, pp. 619–20.
48 'Nanking, Hankow and Hangchow All Show Evidences of Unrest', *China Press*, 5 April 1927; 'Nationalists Assume All Responsibility for Nanking Riots', *China Press*, 5 April 1927.
49 Extract from Protocol 78 of the Politburo Meeting, 13 Jan. 1927, and Letter from Gregori Voitinksy, 21 Jan. 1927, both in Titarenko, *VKP(b), Komintern i Kitai*, vol. 2, pp. 579–80 and 602; telegrams to Wang: S. I. Hsiung, *The Life of Chiang Kai-shek*, London: Peter Davies, 1948, pp. 263–4.
50 GSG, 002-060100-00002-002, Draft Summary of Daily Events, 1 April 1927.

51 GSG, 002-020100-00025-052, Message from the Central Supervisory Commission to the Central Executive Committee, 2 April 1927; GSG, 002-060100-00002-002 and 003, Draft Summary of Daily Events, 3 April 1927; Chiang, 'Diary', 3 April 1927, in *Jiang Zhongzheng nianpu changbian*, vol. 2, p. 48.

52 Wang Jingwei and Chen Duxiu, 'Wang Jingwei, Chen Duxiu lianhe xuanyan', 5 April 1927, in Zhongyang dang'anguan (eds), *Zhonggong zhongyang wenjian wenji* (Selected documents from the Central Committee), Beijing: Zhonggong zhongyang dangxiao chubanshe, 1989, vol. 3, pp. 593–4; GSG, 002-060100-00002-004, Draft Summary of Daily Events, 5 April 1927.

53 'Peking Orders Execution of Russian Agents', *Chicago Daily Tribune*, 9 March 1927; 'Chang for Expulsion of Bolsheviks', *Manchester Guardian*, 4 April 1927.

54 PRO, FO 371/12501; Hallett Abend, *My Life in China*, New York: Harcourt, Brace, 1943, pp. 51–2; see also Wu Aitchen, *China and the Soviet Union*, London: Methuen, 1950, pp. 188–95.

55 See, among others, Harriette Flory, 'The Arcos Raid and the Rupture of Anglo-Soviet Relations', *Journal of Contemporary History*, 12, no. 4 (Oct. 1977), pp. 707–23; the Beijing raid, by contrast, is rarely mentioned, one notable exception being Bruce A. Elleman, *Modern Chinese Warfare, 1798–1989*, London: Routledge, 2001, p. 173.

56 GSG, 002-060100-00002-005 and 006, Draft Summary of Daily Events, 7 and 8 April 1927.

57 'G.L.U. Agitation in Shanghai', *North-China Herald*, 2 April 1927; PRO, FO 371/12407, 'Report on the Situation in Shanghai', 15 April 1927, p. 123; 'Soldiers and Pickets Clash in Shanghai', *South China Morning Post*, 8 April 1927; 'two regiments' mentioned in *Jiang Zhongzheng nianpu changbian*, 12 April 1927, vol. 2, p. 54.

58 PRO, FO 371/12407, 'Report on the Situation in Shanghai', 15 April 1927, p. 123; 'Nationalists Raid Labor Centers', *China Press*, 13 April 1927; a great deal has been published about 'gangsters' hired to slaughter the Communists on 12 April. But an editorial published on 13 April by the General Labour Union to protest against the raid does not mention any 'gangsters', nor were 'gangsters' reported by any journalist, either foreign or local ('Radical Faction of Kuomintang Aims to Paralyse all Activities in Shanghai', *China Press*, 13 April 1927); a letter of protest published by Zheng Zhenduo, Hu Yuzhi and others on 15 April on the events of the preceding days mentioned outrage at the killings, but not any 'gangsters'; see 'Zhabei jumin shi yifeng shu' (Letter by ordinary people from Zhabei), *Shishi xinbao*, 15 April 1927; most of the evidence for these 'gangsters' goes back to a single line by a journalist who merely

heard a rumour that a meeting had taken place between a gangster leader and the mayor of the International Settlement (Powell, *My Twenty-Five Years in China*, pp. 158–9).

59 Brian P. Farrell, 'Twilight in China: Great Powers and the Defence of Shanghai, 1925–1937', in Farrell, Long and Ulbrich, *From Far East to Asia Pacific*, pp. 113–50, especially p. 138; also Arthur Ransome, *The Chinese Puzzle*, London: George Allen & Unwin, 1927, p. 146.

60 'Another General Strike is Called for Today', *China Press*, 13 April 1927.

61 The key witness accounts are in 'Zuori jiesan Zhabei gongren youxing qingxing' (The circumstances of the dispersal of the workers' parade in Zhabei yesterday), *Shenbao*, 14 April 1927.

62 'Jiuchadui jiaoxie shi zhi sishangzhe lian shisan ri Baoshanlu chongtu shijian' (Casualties during the disarming of the pickets and during the clashes on Baoshan Road the following day), *Shishi xinbao*, 18 April 1927, p. 3.

63 Ibid.; GSG, 002-020100-00025-048, Telegram from Yang Hu and Chen Qun to Chiang Kai-shek, 14 April 1927; historians like Frederic Wakeman (*Policing Shanghai, 1927–1937*, Berkeley, CA: University of California Press, 1995, p. 123) who write about 'four thousand' Communists being slaughtered in the streets of Shanghai in April generally refer to Harold Isaacs, an author who in 1932 provided a lurid description of alleged massacres in China in a piece entitled *Five Years of Kuomintang Reaction*. Isaacs was an American journalist who arrived in Shanghai in 1930 and quickly became embroiled in Communist politics. But even Isaacs made no such claim, and merely writes that 'a number' of labour leaders were killed while 5,000 workers were arrested (see Harold R. Isaacs, *Five Years of Kuomintang Reaction*, Shanghai: China Forum Publishing Co., 1932, p. 5). A subsequent book published in 1938, entitled *The Tragedy of the Chinese Revolution*, prefaced by Trotsky himself, placed responsibility for the failure of the 'revolution' in China squarely on Stalin, Trotsky's nemesis. Yet this book did not mention a massacre of 'thousands' in Shanghai either. To this day the 'Shanghai massacre' represents, for true believers, the key moment when, after the defeat of the German October in 1923, Stalin's short-sighted insistence on a United Front in China brought the world revolution to a bloody conclusion.

64 Wang's arrest was reported in the *Shishi xinbao*, 7 May 1927, p. 9; in 1996 an article confirmed, on the basis of archival evidence, that Wang had been arrested, then delivered to Yang Hu, who had him interrogated and executed by firing squad on 12 April; see Ye Lei, 'Wang Shouhua lieshi shi bei Du Yuesheng huomai de ma?' (Was

martyr Wang Shouhua really buried alive by Du Yuesheng?), *Shanghai dangshi yanjiu*, no. 2 (1996), pp. 33–4.
65 'Another General Strike is Called for Today', *China Press*, 13 April 1927.
66 'Cantonese Factions Fight in Big Cities', *Boston Daily Globe*, 13 April 1927.
67 The figures are from MAE, 513PO/A/433, 'A.s. des incidents du 15 Avril', 16 April 1927; PRO, FO 371/12404, Telegram No. 38, p. 183; Communists quoted in Tsin, *Nation, Governance, and Modernity in China*, pp. 169–70.
68 'How the Reds were Executed', *New York Times*, 30 April 1927.
69 MAE, 513PO/A/433, 'A.s. de Mr. Doriot', 7 March 1927.
70 'Changsha Situation: All Communist Leaders Have Disappeared', *South China Morning Post*, 9 June 1927; more than a dozen armed pickets were shot, while the labour unions and peasant associations were dissolved in the following weeks. No doubt a great many people in the countryside were killed in the years to come, although some historians have written about a tide of terror without providing any substantial evidence; Philip Short claims that in 1927 some 300,000 people were killed in four neighbouring counties in Hunan, an allegation repeated in Wikipedia; his endnote refers to a book published in 1975 by Angus McDonald; McDonald, however, asserts that some 300,000 people were killed not in 1927, but 'in the decade that followed', although he, too, offers no evidence to substantiate his claim. I have been unable to find any articles in the foreign or Chinese press or any reference in Taiwanese, French or British archives referring to mass killings in Leiyang, Chaling or Liyang counties in 1927, although a commercial slump is mentioned for Liuyang; Philip Short, *Mao: The Man who Made China*, London: I. B. Tauris, 2017, p. 188; Angus McDonald, *The Urban Origins of Rural Revolution, Elites and the Masses in Hunan Province, China, 1911–1927*, p. 316. A great many fantastic figures, often reaching in the hundreds of thousands, have been offered without much evidence by a range of historians on killings of Communists in Hunan and Hubei in the two years after April 1927, although careful reading of dozens of volumes of reports compiled by the provincial Party committees and other local branches of the Chinese Communist Party between April 1927 and January 1930 yields, depending on how one computes often overlapping and very rough figures, at most 25,000 in each province; see CA, *Hunan geming lishi wenjian huiji* and *Hubei geming lishi wenjian huiji*, volumes from 1927 to 1930.

71 Vincent Sheean, *Personal History*, New York: Garden City Publishing, 1937, pp. 238–40; 'Hankow and Nanking', *South China Morning Post*, 28 June 1927.
72 'Radical Faction in Hankow Placed under Ban', *China Press*, 28 and 29 June 1927; Misselwitz, *The Dragon Stirs*, pp. 119–28.
73 Vishnyakova-Akimova, *Two Years in Revolutionary China*, p. 219.
74 Louis Fisher, 'China – Seen from Moscow', *Nation*, 30 Nov. 1927, p. 613.
75 Jacobs, *Borodin*, pp. 290 and 310; Schram and Hodes, *Mao's Road to Power*, vol. 3, 7 Aug. 1927, p. 36; Extract from Protocol 119 of the Politburo Meeting, 11 Aug. 1927, in Titarenko, *VKP(b), Komintern i Kitai*, vol. 3, pp. 71–2.
76 'From the Chinese Press', *China Weekly Review*, 20 August 1927.
77 CA, *Jiangxi geming lishi wenjian huiji: 1927–1928*, Report on the Question of Bandits in Fuzhou, Sept. 1927, pp. 35–9, and Circular by the Jiangxi Provincial Committee, 8 Sept. 1927, pp. 38–41; Chang Kuo-t'ao, *The Rise of the Communist Party, 1928–1938*, Lawrence, KS: University of Kansas Press, 1972, vol. 2, p. 46.
78 The five Russians presented themselves later that month to the British consul, asking for transit visas to Canton via Hong Kong: see PRO, FO 371/12411, Consul Kirke to Sir M. Lampson, 6 Oct. 1927, p. 35; on the looting, see PRO, FO 371/12410, Consul Kirke to Sir M. Lampson, 26 Sept. 1927, p. 216; see also 'Lawless Mob of Communist Soldiers Now Rules Swatow', *China Press*, 27 Sept. 1927.
79 PRO, FO 371/12410, Consul Kirke to Sir M. Lampson, 26 Sept. 1927, p. 216; PRO, FO 371/12411, Consul Kirke to Sir M. Lampson, 6 Oct. 1927, p. 35; on executions, see also 'Renyi jingsha muwu renquan' (Random plunder and murder without regard to human rights), *Chenbao*, 12 Oct. 1927, p. 6; see also Laura M. Calkins, 'Recapturing an Urban Identity: Chinese Communists and the Commune at Shantou, 1927', *Studies on Asia*, series IV, vol. 1, no. 2 (Summer 2011), pp. 35–73.
80 Margarete Buber-Neumann, *Von Potsdam nach Moskau*, Munich: Ullstein-Taschenbuchverlag, 2002.
81 'Attack on Club', *South China Morning Post*, 23 Nov. 1927; CA, *Guangdong geming lishi wenjian huiji (shengwei wenjian): 1927*, 'Report to the Central Committee', November 1927, p. 149; 'Boycotters Draw Final Dividend', *North-China Herald*, 26 Nov. 1927; 'Canton's Fire Epidemic', *South China Morning Post*, 29 Nov. 1927.
82 CA, *Guangdong geming lishi wenjian huiji (shengwei wenjian): 1927*, various letters and reports dated 26 Nov. and 1 and

8 Dec. 1927, pp. 153, 165 and 185; Letter from the Centre to the Guangdong Provincial Committee, 23 Sept. 1927, in Zhongyang dang'anguan (eds), *zhongyang zhangyang wenjian xuanji (1927)*, Beijing: Zhonggong zhongyang dangxiao chubanshe, 1991, vol. 3, p. 374; discovery of two bombs: 'The Failure of the Labour Peasant Uprising in Canton', *China Weekly Review*, 31 Dec. 1927.

83 HIA, Huston (Jay C.) Papers, box 2, Frederick W. Hinke, Vice Consul in Canton, 'The Communist Coup d'Etat at Canton'; HIA, Huston (Jay C.) Papers, box 14, 'Peasants, Workers and Soldiers Revolt of December 11–13, 1927 at Canton, China', Despatch No. 699, 30 Dec. 1927; on Fu Sinian, see Wang Fan-sen, *Fu Ssu-nien: A Life in Chinese History and Politics*, Cambridge: Cambridge University Press, 2000, p. 71.

84 The estimates are in Hinke, 'The Communist Coup d'Etat at Canton', p. 18; 'Peasants, Workers and Soldiers Revolt', p. 27; PRO, FO 371/12411, 17 Dec. 1927, p. 227; MAE, 513PO/A/433, 'La situation à Canton', 23 Dec. 1927.

85 'Much Activity against Local Soviet', *North-China Herald*, 24 Dec. 1927; 'Nationalist China "Breaks" with Soviet Union', *China Weekly Review*, 24 Dec. 1927; 'Presence Undesirable', *South China Morning Post*, 20 Dec. 1927.

3 RED TERROR (1927–1931)

1 Ye Ting is quoted in M. N. Roy, *Revolution and Counterrevolution in China*, Delhi: Ajanta Books International, 1946, reprint 1986, p. 459; the Canton Soviet decrees are in MAE, 513PO/A/433, Translation of Handbills, Canton, 31 Dec. 1927.

2 Pang Yong-Pil, 'Peng Pai from Landlord to Revolutionary', *Modern China*, 1, no. 3 (July 1975), pp. 297–322.

3 'Outrages by Red Troops', *South China Morning Post*, 8 Nov. 1927.

4 Report on the Revolutionary Violence in Hailufeng, 9 Nov. 1927, in Zhonggong Haifeng xianwei dangshi bangongshe (eds), *Hailufeng geming shiliao: 1927–1933* (Historical sources on the revolutionary history of Hailufeng: 1927–1933), Guangzhou: Guangdong renmin chubanshe, 1986, vol. 2, p. 19; CA, *Guangdong geming lishi wenjian huiji (shengwei): 1927*, Report from the Guangdong Provincial Committee to the Central Committee, Nov. 1927, p. 155; Chen Xiaobai, *Hailufeng chihuo ji* (Account of the red terror in Hailufeng), Hailufeng: Hailufeng tongxianghui, 1932, p. 26.

5 Fernando Galbiati, *P'eng P'ai and the Hai–Lu–Feng Soviet*, Stanford, CA: Stanford University Press, 1985, p. 294; Chen, *Hailufeng chihuo ji*, p. 27.
6 Chen, *Hailufeng chihuo ji*, p. 27; HIA, Huston (Jay C.) Papers, box 14, Jay Huston, 'Communism in South China: The Hai–Lu–Feng Soviet', 7 Feb. 1928, pp. 3–7.
7 Huston, 'Communism in South China', pp. 5–7; 'Communist Reign of Terror at Swatow', *North-China Herald*, 14 Jan. 1928.
8 'The Fiends of Swabue', *North-China Herald*, 18 Feb. 1928.
9 Chen, *Hailufeng chihuo ji*, p. 27; Huston, 'Communism in South China', 7 Feb. 1928, pp. 3–7.
10 'Outrages by Red Troops', *South China Morning Post*, 8 Nov. 1927; Zhang Fakui is quoted in MAE, 513PO/A/433, 'La situation à Canton', 31 Dec. 1927.
11 'Communist Reign of Terror at Swatow', *North-China Herald*, 14 Jan. 1928.
12 'The Fiends of Swabue', *North-China Herald*, 18 Feb. 1928; 'Swatow Fears Coming of Communists', *South China Morning Post*, 29 March 1928.
13 MAE, 513PO/A/433, 'La situation à Canton', 7 April 1928; 'Xi Zhongxun zhuzheng Guangdong ersan shi' (Xi Zhongxun resolves a number of issues in Guangdong), *Nanfang ribao*, 9 Aug. 2013; also John Gittings, 'How a Maoist Mob Hunted Down Family', *Guardian*, 23 Jan. 1985.
14 'Nine Months of Communist Misrule in Hunan', *North-China Herald*, 14 May 1927; 'Letters from the Yangtze Valley', *Times of India*, 30 May 1927; 'Changsha Situation', *South China Morning Post*, 9 June 1927.
15 'Letter from the Hunan Provincial Committee', 30 Aug. 1927, in Schram and Hodes, *Mao's Road to Power*, vol. 3, p. 42.
16 Peng Gongda, 'Guanyu Hunan qiushou baodong jingguo baogao' (Report on the Autumn Harvest Uprising) in Zhongyang dang'an-guan (eds), *Jiandang yilai zhongyao wenxuan xuanbian* (Selection of important texts on Party history), Beijing: Zhongyang wenxian chubanshe, 1992, vol. 4, pp. 545–6.
17 'Excitement in Various Places', *China Press*, 12 Oct. 1927.
18 'The Communism of Hunan', *North-China Herald*, 12 Nov. 1927; 'A People in Fear', *South China Morning Post*, 28 Dec. 1927.
19 'The Communism of Hunan', *North-China Herald*, 12 Nov. 1927.
20 The admirer was Agnes Smedley, a fellow traveller who spent time with Zhu De in the 1930s; Agnes Smedley, *China Fights Back*, London: Victor Gallancz, 1938, p. 90; see also Zhonggong

zhongyang wenxian yanjiushi (eds), *Zhu De nianpu* (A chronology of Zhu De's life), Beijing: Renmin chubanshe, 1986, pp. 34–5.
21 'Two Cities Looted and Burned', *South China Morning Post*, 19 Jan 1928.
22 Huang Kecheng, 'Huiyi Xiangnan baodong' (Recalling the insurrection in south Hunan), *Jindai lishi*, 1980, no. 4, pp. 3 and 6; 'Orgy of Massacre', *South China Morning Post*, 5 March 1928; 'Refugees from Leiyang Describe Reds' Work', *South China Morning Post*, 13 March 1928; monks also mentioned in 'Gongchan zhanling Leiyang' (Communists occupy Leiyang), *Chenbao*, 4 March 1928; on the burning of main buildings in the region, see also 'Xiangsheng changong qingxiang jihua' (Plan for the elimination of Communists in Hunan), *Yishibao*, 8 March 1928, p. 6.
23 Huang, 'Huiyi Xiangnan baodong', pp. 6–7; executions and maiming in 'Refugees from Leiyang Describe Reds' Work'; 'Xiangnan gonghuo zhi canku' (Communist cruelty in south Hunan), *Minguo ribao*, 17 April 1928; 'Leiyang tusha' (Massacre in Leiyang), *Yishibao*, 9 March 1928; 'Chaling gongjun chaihui Zhuping lu' (Road to Zhuping destroyed by Chaling Communists), *Chenbao*, 13 March 1928, p. 6; the gouging of eyes, as well as other methods of torture, was also confirmed in the witness statement of a German engineer employed by a local mining company; he and his wife were seized by the Communists and forced to witness their depredations; see 'Red Atrocities', *South China Morning Post*, 15 March 1928.
24 Huang, 'Huiyi Xiangnan baodong', pp. 6–7; *Zhu De nianpu*, p. 63.
25 'Spring Offensive', *South China Morning Post*, 14 March 1928.
26 Schram and Hodes, *Mao's Road to Power*, vol. 3, pp. 55–6.
27 'The Communists in Kiangsi', *North-China Herald*, 21 July 1928; opium mentioned in 'Optimistic Spirit in Kiangsi', *North-China Herald*, 25 May 1929.
28 'Troops Sent from Canton', *China Press*, 29 Aug. 1928; 'Communist Forces in Retreat from Three Cities', *China Press*, 27 Aug. 1928.
29 'New Massacre by China Reds', *Los Angeles Times*, 8 April 1928; '"Red" Scare in Kuangtung', *North-China Herald*, 1 Sept. 1928.
30 Misselwitz, *The Dragon Stirs*, p. 73; Chiang, 'Diary', 12 and 14 May 1928, quoted in *Jiang Zhongzheng nianpu changbian*, vol. 2, pp. 240–1 and 246.
31 The French consul investigated the affair, arriving on the premises at seven in the morning, ninety minutes after the explosion occurred; see MAE, 513PO/A/435, R. Blondeau, 'A.s. attentat du 4 juin', 14 June 1928.
32 'Forces Take Field to Suppress Insurgent Troops', *China Press*, 24 Aug. 1928.

33 The poem is entitled 'Jinggangshan' and can be found in Schram and Hodes, *Mao's Road to Power*, vol. 3, p. 61; the manner in which land reform should be carried out was codified in the 'Jinggangshan Land Law', in the same volume, pp. 128–30; the quotations by Mao are in his Report to the Central Committee, 25 Nov. 1928, same volume, pp. 81–121, especially pp. 96–7, 104–5 and 111; the report on the economy: Yang Kaiming, 'Report on the Hunan-Jiangxi Border Soviet', in Jinggangshan geming bowuguan (eds), *Jinggangshan geming genjudi* (The Jinggangshan base area), Beijing: Zhonggong dangshi ziliao chubanshe, 1987, p. 249, quoted in Chang and Halliday, *Mao*, p. 62, with changes in the translation of the original.

34 Peng Dehuai, *Memoirs of a Chinese Marshal*, Beijing: Foreign Languages Press, 1984, p. 231.

35 Letter from the Fourth Red Army to the Central Committee, 20 March 1929, in Schram and Hodes, *Mao's Road to Power*, vol. 3, pp. 147–52.

36 'Border Town Sacked', *North-China Herald*, 23 Feb. 1929; 'Brigands' Trail in Kiangsi', *North-China Herald*, 9 March 1929.

37 'The Minister in China (MacMurray) to the Secretary of State', 25 Jan. 1929, *Foreign Relations of the United States: Diplomatic Papers, 1929*, Washington: Government Printing Office, 1943, vol. 2, doc. 414; Edouard Young, 'La mission de Nananfu du 18 au 27 janvier 1929', *Annales de la Congrégation de la Mission*, 1929, vol. 94, pp. 890–8; 'Held by Communists', *South China Morning Post*, 2 March 1929.

38 Rudolf Bosshardt was the first to be released as the result of a change in Communist policy towards a 'United Front' in April 1936: NARA, 893.00B/1089, C. E. Gauss, 'Release of the Reverend R. A. Bosshardt', 17 April 1936; Eleanor Harrison and Edith Nettleton were clumsily beheaded in October 1930 and buried in a forest, only given a proper burial in 1936; see 'Missionaries beheaded by Communists', *North-China Herald*, 14 Oct. 1930; 'Missionary Murders, British Policy and the Communist Situation', *China Weekly Review*, 18 Oct. 1930. They were not the only ones: in December 1934 . a unit commanded by Nie Rongzhen took John and Betty Stam, graduates of the Moody Bible Institute of Chicago, up a hill in Anhui province and beheaded them, although the couple managed to save their baby daughter: Powell, *My Twenty-Five Years in China*, p. 262; 'China Reds Take Warpath', *Los Angeles Times*, 23 March 1929.

39 Letter to the Central Committee, 5 April 1929, in Schram and Hodes, *Mao's Road to Power*, vol. 3, pp. 155–6; Walter Laqueur

pointed this out eloquently in his *Guerrilla Warfare: A Historical and Critical Study*, London: Routledge, 1997.
40 'Communist Scare in Nanchang', *North-China Herald*, 3 Aug. 1929.
41 Extract from Protocol 8 of the Meeting of the Comintern's Far Eastern Section, 29 Jan. 1929, in Titarenko, *VKP(b), Komintern i Kitai*, vol. 3, p. 518.
42 Robert Service, *Stalin: A Biography*, Basingstoke: Macmillan, 2004, pp. 293 and 340; Letter from Pavel Mif, 7 June 1929, in Titarenko, *VKP(b), Komintern i Kitai*, vol. 3, pp. 559–61; see also the 7 June 1929 letter on the 'peasant issue' to which these documents refer, in Mikhail L. Titarenko (ed.), *Kommunisticheskii Internatsional i kitaiskaia revoliutsiia. Dokumenty i materialy*, Moscow: Nauka, 1986, pp. 179–89, specifically p. 184 in defence of Mao.
43 MAE, 513PO/A/428bis, Louis Reynaud, Consul in Harbin, 'Perquisitions au Consulat Général de l'U.R.S.S.', 29 May 1929.
44 'Chinese Arrest Red Rail Chiefs', *Los Angeles Times*, 11 July 1929; 'China in a Coup to Seize Rail Holdings', *New York Herald Tribune*, 11 July 1929.
45 Powell, *My Twenty-Five Years in China*, p. 173.
46 The key historian of the conflict is Michael Walker, *The 1929 Sino-Soviet War: The War Nobody Knew*, Lawrence, KS: University Press of Kansas, 2017.
47 Powell, *My Twenty-Five Years in China*, p. 174.
48 Lars T. Lih et al. (eds), *Stalin's Letters to Molotov*, New Haven, CT: Yale University Press, 1995, p. 182; Extract from Protocol 102 of the Politburo Meeting, 15 Oct. 1929, in Titarenko, *VKP(b), Komintern i Kitai*, vol. 3, p. 616.
49 Membership in *Communism in China*, document A, 1932, p. 5, quoted in James P. Harrison, 'The Li Li-San Line and the CCP in 1930 (Part 1)', *China Quarterly*, no. 14 (June 1963), p. 183; 'Circular No. 60', 8 Dec. 1929, Zhongyang dang'anguan (eds), *Zhonggong zhongyang wenjian xuanji (1929)*, p. 564.
50 'Circular No. 30', 26 Feb. 1930, Zhongyang dang'anguan (eds), *Zhonggong zhongyang wenjian xuanji (1930)*, p. 28.
51 Letter from the Politburo, 12 Oct. 1930, in Titarenko, *VKP(b), Komintern i Kitai*, vol. 3, p. 1,048.
52 Chang and Halliday, *Mao*, p. 73.
53 Mao Zedong, 'A Single Spark Can Start a Prairie Fire', 5 Jan. 1930, *Selected Works of Mao Tse-tung*, Beijing: Foreign Languages Press, 1965, vol. 1, pp. 117–28.
54 'Telegram of the Chinese Revolutionary Military Commission on Attacking Nanchang and Regrouping at Wuhan', 25 June 1930, in Schram and Hodes, *Mao's Road to Power*, vol. 3, pp. 457–9.

55 NARA, RG 165, MID 2657-1-276/306, Morris B. De Pass, 'Situation Report', G-2 Report 7792, 11 Aug. 1930, p. 17; MAE, 513PO/A/433, Telegram from the Hankou Consul, 30 July 1930; see also NARA, RG 165, MID 2657-1-276/332, C. J. Kanaga, 'Report on Trip to South of Yangtze, Report No. 7978, 31 March 1931; Kanaga collected witness accounts about the events of July 1930; 'Communists' Occupation of Changsha', *China Weekly Review*, 2 Aug. 1930; the use of villagers as barrier troops is mentioned in 'Foreigners in Flight before Chinese Reds', *New York Times*, 4 Aug. 1930; the practice was reported and denounced by He Yingqin in a report to the Nationalist Party's People's Convention in May 1931, although he was referring not to the siege of Changsha but to more general attacks: He Yingqin, 'Communist Movement in Kiangse', HIA, Huston (Jay C.) Papers, box 1; estimate of casualties is in 'Proof is Found Soviet Directed Changsha Affair', *Christian Science Monitor*, 13 Aug. 1930, and 'Reds Executed 2,000 in Changsha Seizure', *North-China Herald*, 6 Aug. 1930.

56 MAE, 513PO/A/433, Marcel Baudez, Hankou Consul, 'Situation politique', 12 Aug. 1930; Mao Zedong, Letter to the Southwest Jiangxi Special Committee, 19 Aug. 1930, in Schram and Hodes, *Mao's Road to Power*, vol. 3, p. 483; 'How Changsha Was Relieved', *North-China Herald*, 19 Aug. 1930.

57 Mao Zedong, Letter to the Central Committee on the General Situation, 19 Aug. 1930, in Schram and Hodes, *Mao's Road to Power*, vol. 3, p. 483, and 'Reds Executed 2,000 in Changsha Seizure', *North-China Herald*, 6 Aug. 1930.

58 Chang, *The Rise of the Communist Party, 1928–1938*, vol. 2, pp. 19–20.

59 Chen Yaohuang, 'Zhonggong Xiang'exi suqu de fazhan ji qi neibu zhengsu' (The development and purge of the Hunan and West Hubei Soviet), *Guoshiguan xueshu jikan*, no. 15 (2008), pp. 48–9; 'Terrible Massacres', *South China Morning Post*, 24 Aug. 1929; 'From the Chinese Press', *China Weekly Review*, 12 Oct. 1929.

60 'Communists Active near Hankou', *North-China Herald*, 29 July 1930; C. T. Liang, '"Red Scare" Overshadows Central China', *China Weekly Review*, 9 Aug. 1930; 'Hankow's Cost of Living', *North-China Herald*, 29 July 1930.

61 Mao Zedong, Telegram on Attacking Nanchang and Regrouping at Wuhan, 25 June 1930, in Schram and Hodes, *Mao's Road to Power*, vol. 3, p. 459.

62 'Lessening Shanghai Strikes', *China Press*, 9 April 1928; Jack Gray, *Rebellions and Revolutions: China from the 1800s to*

2000, Oxford: Oxford University Press, 1990, p. 226; Pantsov, *Victorious in Defeat*, p. 189.
63 The key historian of the Central Plains War is Peter Worthing, 'A Tale of Two Fronts: China's War of the Central Plains, 1930', *War in History*, 25, no. 4 (Nov. 2018), pp. 511–33.
64 'Peking Police Outlined', *South China Morning Post*, 2 Aug. 1930; on the appointment of He Yingqin, see 5 Aug. 1930, *Jiang Zhongzheng nianpu changbian*, vol. 3, p. 202, and 'No Traces of Communists in Nanchang', *China Press*, 10 Aug. 1930.
65 'Use of Buffaloes', *South China Morning Post*, 6 Sept. 1930; 'Heavy Defeat of Communists', *South China Morning Post*, 8 Sept. 1930.
66 The best witness accounts are in MAE, 513PO/A/63bis, Fernand Thieffry, 'La Prise de Ki-an', 23 Feb. 1931, as well as the diary by Édouard Barbato, *Annales de la Congrégation de la Mission*, vol. 96, 1931, pp. 539–79.
67 'Red Defeat at Kianfu', *South China Morning Post*, 21 Nov. 1930; MAE, 513PO/A/63bis, 'La Prise de Ki-an', 23 Feb. 1931; 1 Jan. and 8 Feb. 1931 in *Jiang Zhongzheng nianpu changbian*, vol. 3, pp. 332 and 356; MAE, 513PO/A/63bis, Report from Consul, 23 Feb. 1931.
68 Schram and Hodes, *Mao's Road to Power*, vol. 3, pp. 718–19.
69 'Letter to Lin Biao', 14 June 1929, in ibid., pp. 176–89; Titarenko, *VKP(b), Komintern i Kitai*, vol. 3, p. 1,274.
70 CA, *Jiangxi geming lishi wenjian huiji: 1930 (1)*, Report by the West Jiangxi Special Committee, 18 May 1930, p. 132 and Liu Zuofu, Report by the West Jiangxi Special Committee, 22 July 1930, pp. 222–3 and 254; later investigation: CA, *Jiangxi geming lishi wenjian huiji: 1930 (2)*, Work Report on West Jiangxi, 5 Sept. 1930, pp. 57–8; 1,000 deaths is the estimate given in Minutes of West Jiangxi Meeting, 13 Oct. 1930, in Jiangxi sheng dang'anguan (eds), *Zhongyang geming genjudi shiliao xuanbian* (Selection of historical materials on the central revolutionary base areas), Nanchang: Jiangxi renmin chubanshe, 1982, vol. 1, p. 631.
71 Letter to the Central Committee, 14 Oct. 1930, in Schram and Hodes, *Mao's Road to Power*, vol. 3, p. 554; Letter from the Far Eastern Bureau of the Comintern's Executive Bureau, 10 Nov. 1930, in Titarenko, *VKP(b), Komintern i Kitai*, vol. 3, p. 1,109.
72 Report from the Jiangxi Provincial Committee, May 1932, *Zhongyang geming genjudi shiliao xuanbian*, vol. 1, pp. 478–80.
73 Ibid., also p. 436 for 'the thousands and tens of thousands'; the best article on the purge, which includes the estimate of 2,000 killed, is Ch'en Yung-fa, 'The Futian Incident and the Anti-Bolshevik League: The "Terror" in the CCP Revolution', *Republican China*, 19, no. 2 (April 1994), pp. 1–51.

74 Gordon Y. M. Chan, 'The Communists in Rural Guangdong, 1928–1936', *Journal of the Royal Asiatic Society*, 13, no. 1 (April 2003), pp. 83–4.
75 Record of a Conversation between Gailis, Mif and Malyshev with Ren Bishi, 19 Feb 1931, in Titarenko, *VKP(b), Komintern i Kitai*, vol. 3, pp. 1,276–8.
76 Wang, *Memoirs of a Chinese Revolutionary, 1919–1949*, pp. 63–4, 128 and 151–2.
77 NARA, RG 59, 893.00B, Despatch 8072, Edwin Cunningham, Consul General in Shanghai, 'Communist Activities in Shanghai during 1931', 11 Jan. 1932.
78 Ibid.; MAE, 513PO/A/428, Report by Jacques Meyrier, Consul in Shanghai, 25 June 1932.
79 Frederick S. Litten, 'The Noulens Affair', *China Quarterly*, no. 138 (June 1994), pp. 492–512; also Christopher Baxter, 'The Secret Intelligence Service and China: The Case of Hilaire Noulens, 1923–1932', in Christopher Baxter et al. (eds), *Britain in Global Politics: From Gladstone to Churchill*, London: Palgrave, 2013, pp. 132–52.
80 Litten, 'The Noulens Affair', pp. 496–7; Edgar Snow, as well as Harold Isaacs, are mentioned in MAE, 513PO/A/428, Report by Jacques Meyrier, Consul in Shanghai, 25 June 1932.
81 'Government Air Squad Blows Ningtu City to Bits', *China Press*, 21 July 1931; the quotation comes from Chang and Halliday, *Mao*, p. 97; villagers rallying to the government side in Philip C. C. Huang, Lynda Schaefer Bell and Kathy Le Mons Walker, *Chinese Communists and Rural Society, 1927–1934*, Berkeley, CA: Center for Chinese Studies, University of California, 1978, p. 20; 'Reds' Retreat Described', *North-China Herald*, 11 Aug. 1931.

4 THE SOVIETS (1931–1934)

1 Abend, *My Life in China*, pp. 150–1.
2 Ibid., p. 167; Powell, *My Twenty-Five Years in China*, p. 233.
3 'Death and Desolation in China', *Times of India*, 24 Aug. 1931; Abend, *My Life in China*, p. 155; Booker, *News is my Job*, p. 246.
4 'Martial Law Laid All around Harbin', *Washington Post*, 6 Feb. 1932; Misselwitz, *The Dragon Stirs*, p. 284.
5 Booker, *News is my Job*, pp. 248–51; Abend, *My Life in China*, pp. 174–94; 'Chapei and the Future', *China Press*, 24 March 1932.

6 'Fall of Juichin Looms in Drive on Communists', *China Press*, 7 Aug. 1931.
7 NARA, RG 165, MID 2657-1-276/420, 'Situation Report', Report No. 8778, 28 Feb. 1934.
8 Agnes Smedley, *China's Red Army Marches*, London: Lawrence & Wishart, 1936, pp. 297–303.
9 Edgar Snow, *Red Star over China*, New York: Grove Press, 1971, p. 428.
10 Pavel Mif, 'A New Rise of the Chinese Revolution', 14 May 1930, translated in NARA, RG 59, 893.00B/719; 'Introduction' and 'Investigation of Caixi Townships', in Schram and Hodes, *Mao's Road to Power*, vol. 4, pp. lxvi and 635–6; CA, *Jiangxi geming lishi wenjian huiji: 1932 (1)*, General Report on the Jiangxi Soviet, May 1932, p. 148.
11 CA, *Jiangxi geming lishi wenjian huiji: 1931*, pp. 259–60; CA, *Jiangxi geming lishi wenjian huiji: 1932 (1)*, General Report on the Jiangxi Soviet, May 1932, p. 152.
12 CA, *Jiangxi geming lishi wenjian huiji: 1932 (1)*, General Report on the Jiangxi Soviet, May 1932, pp. 156–7; CA, *Jiangxi geming lishi wenjian huiji: 1933–1934*, Reports on Taxation, 26 March and 7 April 1933, pp. 74 and 90–1.
13 'The Economic Policy of the Chinese Soviet Republic', 1 Dec. 1931, and 'Unfold a Mass Movement to Support a National Currency', 28 Aug. 1933, both in Schram and Hodes, *Mao's Road to Power*, vol. 4, pp. 160–2 and 502–3; CA, *Jiangxi geming lishi wenjian huiji: 1933–1934*, Government Orders, 1 and 5 April 1933, pp. 81 and 84–5.
14 'The Economic Policy of the Chinese Soviet Republic', 1 Dec. 1931, in Schram and Hodes, *Mao's Road to Power*, vol. 4, pp. 160–2; CA, *Jiangxi geming lishi wenjian huiji: 1933–1934*, Government Orders, 1 and 5 April 1933, pp. 81 and 84–5; on tungsten in Jiangxi, see 'Recaptured Red Areas Begin Rehabilitation', *China Press*, 10 Oct. 1934; Mao's brother Mao Zemin was in charge of the mines; see Long Huanqi, 'Mao Zemin ban Zhonghua wukuang gongsi', in Shu Long (ed.), *Mao Zemin*, Beijing: Junshi kexue chubanshe, 1996, p. 77 (this article came to my attention thanks to a reference in Chang and Halliday, *Mao*).
15 CA, *Jiangxi geming lishi wenjian huiji: 1931*, Report from Southwest Jiangxi, 1931, p. 260.
16 'Faxing jingji jianshe gongzhai tiaoli' (Regulations for the Issuance of Economic Constructions Bonds), *Hongse Zhonghua*, no. 96, 26 July 1933; HIA, Chen Cheng Collection, 'Wei faxing sanbaiwan jingji jianshe gongzhai' (Issuance of Three Million Dollar Economic Constructions Bonds), proclamation no. 26, 28 Aug.

1933; 'Investigation of Changnang Township', 18 Nov. 1933, in Schram and Hodes, *Mao's Road to Power*, vol. 4, pp. 607–8; CA, *Jiangxi geming lishi wenjian huiji: 1933–1934*, Report from the Jiangxi Provincial Committee, 17 June 1933, p. 153; a detailed history of the three bond issues appears in King-yi Hsü, 'Agrarian Policies of the Chinese Soviet Republic, 1931–1934', doctoral dissertation, Indiana University, 1971, pp. 446–54.

17 'Investigation of Ganggang Township', 18 Nov. 1933, in Schram and Hodes, *Mao's Road to Power*, vol. 4, p. 609.

18 CA, *Jiangxi geming lishi wenjian huiji: 1931*, p. 107; 'Investigation of Changnang Township', 18 Nov. 1933, and 'Investigation of Caixi Township', 26 Nov. 1933, both in Schram and Hodes, *Mao's Road to Power*, vol. 4, pp. 586, 599 and 630.

19 On the army see PRO, FO 371/18091, Gerald Yorke, 'An Account of the Chinese Soviet Republic in Kiangsi', Nov. 1933, p. 103; 'Resolution of the CCP on Winning Initial Revolutionary Successes in One or More Provinces', 9 Jan. 1932, in Tony Saich and Benjamin Yang (eds), *The Rise to Power of the Chinese Communist Party: Documents and Analysis*, London: Routledge, 2005, p. 563; 'The Fight for Kanchow', *North-China Herald*, 29 March 1932.

20 'China is Preparing Huge Drive on Reds', *New York Times*, 28 Sept. 1933; Hallett Abend, 'Nanking Red Drive Ending in Draw', *New York Times*, 11 Sept. 1932.

21 PRO, FO 676/58, Letter from China Inland Mission, Ganzhou, 19 May 1930, pp. 22–4 (page numbers missing, given here in sequential order); PRO, FO 371/18091, Gerald Yorke, 'An Account of the Chinese Soviet Republic in Kiangsi', Nov. 1933, pp. 104–6.

22 A key document on the many achievements of the soviet can be found in 'Report of the Central Executive Committee', 24–25 Jan. 1934, in Schram and Hodes, *Mao's Road to Power*, vol. 4, particularly pp. 695–6; the hospital is mentioned in *Mao Zedong nianpu*, vol. 1, p. 394, quoted in Chang and Halliday, *Mao*, p. 106.

23 Chan, 'The Communists in Rural Guangdong, 1928–1936', pp. 84–6.

24 CA, *Shaanxi geming lishi wenjian huiji (shengwei wenjian): 1927–1929*, Report from the Provincial Party Committee, 26 Sept. 1927, pp. 88–92; CA, *Shaanxi geming lishi wenjian huiji (shengwei wenjian): 1930–1931*, Report to the Central Committee, 30 April 1930, p. 75, also Report from the Provincial Committee, 13 Sept. 1930, p. 211; CA, *Shaanxi geming lishi wenjian huiji (shengwei wenjian): 1932 (2)*, Letter to the Central Committee, 23 Sept. 1932, p. 98.

25 CA, *Henan geming lishi wenjian huiji (yizhongben): 1927–1934*, Statistics of the Party Organisation, April 1930, p. 105; CA, *Henan geming lishi wenjian huiji (shengwei wenjian): 1931–1932*, Report to

the Central Committee, 25 March 1931, p. 37, and Report from the Henan Military Committee, 30 May 1931, p. 76; CA, *Hebei geming lishi wenjian huiji (jia di jiu ce): 1932.7–1932.9*, Agenda from the Four Prefectural Centres in South Hebei, 13 Aug. 1932, p. 305; CA, *Hebei geming lishi wenjian huiji (jia di shijiu ce): 1928.3–1936.3*, Report from the Tianjin Municipal Party Committee, 13 Dec. 1932, p. 352.

26 CA, *Zhejiang geming lishi wenjian huiji (shengwei wenjian): 1926–1927*, Report from Provincial Party Committee, 27 Sept. 1927, p. 118; release of prisoners: GSG, 001-014500-00011-001, Report by He Yingqin, 10 Feb. 1928; CA, *Zhejiang geming lishi wenjian huiji (dixian wenjian): 1931–1936*, Report on Organising the Railway Workers, 23 Aug. 1932, p. 25, and Report from the Wenzhou County Committee, 6 July 1931, pp. 90–4; CA, *Shandong geming lishi wenjian huiji (jiazhongben di jiu ji): 1931.3–1932.12*, Report from the Provincial Party Committee, 5 June 1932, p. 337, and Report from the Provincial Party Committee, 13 Sept. 1932, p. 379.

27 'More Executions at Hankou', *New York Times*, 21 Dec. 1927; 'More Executions in Hankow', *North-China Herald*, 31 March 1928; CA, *Hubei geming lishi wenjian huiji (shengwei wenjian): 1928*, Report to the Central Committee, May 1928, p. 377.

28 CA, *Hubei geming lishi wenjian huiji (quntuan, Suwei'ai wenjian): 1927–1933*, Report from Provincial Conference, 6 March 1927, p. 40 and Conference Report, 7 March 1927, p. 63; CA, *Hubei geming lishi wenjian huiji (shengwei wenjian): 1929*, Report by Cao Dajun, 16 May 1929, p. 66; William T. Rowe, *Crimson Rain: Seven Centuries of Violence in a Chinese County*, Stanford, CA: Stanford University Press, 2007, pp. 272–6 provides a long list of atrocities committed by General Xia Douyin in fighting the Communists in Hubei in 1927; while there is little doubt that he burned and killed suspected Communists without pity, the alleged atrocities, and indeed Xia Douyin himself, are barely mentioned in the many reports compiled by the various Communist organisations themselves in Hubei; see CA, *Hubei geming lishi wenjian huiji (shengwei wenjian): 1926–1927*, as well as CA, *Hubei geming lishi wenjian huiji (quntuan, Suwei'ai wenjian): 1927–1933*; Xia Douyin appears in half a sentence in 'Report on Work in Huang'an', 14 Dec. 1927, CA, *Eyuwan suqu geming lishi wenjian huiji (Edongbei tewei, Edongnan tewei wenjian): 1927–1934*, p. 1; Rowe bases most of his evidence on the Hankou edition of the *Minguo ribao* (Republican Daily), which was published by Dong Biwu, the very person who established the Communist cell in Macheng; see *Zhongguo jindai*

lishi cidian, 1840–1949, Nanchang: Jiangxi renmin chubanshe, 1986, p. 297.

29 CA, *Xiang'exi suqu geming lishi wenjian huiji (Suwei'ai, quntuan wenjian): 1930–1932*, Report to the Central Committee, 29 March 1931, pp. 48 and 58–9.

30 CA, *Xiang'exi suqu geming lishi wenjian huiji (shengwei wenjian): 1927–1932*, Deng Zhongxia, Report, 15 Oct. 1930, p. 29; CA, *Xiang'exi suqu geming lishi wenjian huiji (zhongyang fenju wenjian): 1931–1934*, Report about the Situation in Xiang'exi, 19 Dec. 1932, p. 314; 'Rehabilitating Central China Districts Recovered from the "Reds"', *China Weekly Review*, 24 Dec. 1932; the classification of 'rich', 'middle' and 'poor' is to be found in literature seized in Jianli and translated in PRO, FO 676/130, Report from the Consul, Hankou, 18 April 1932.

31 CA, *Xiang'exi suqu geming lishi wenjian huiji (shengwei wenjian): 1927–1932*, Deng Zhongxia, Report, 15 Oct. 1930, pp. 29–30; CA, *Xiang'exi suqu geming lishi wenjian huiji (zhongyang fenju wenjian): 1931–1934*, Report about the Situation in Xiang'exi, 19 Dec. 1932, pp. 286–94; MAE, 513PO/A/428, Report from Marcel Baudez, Consul in Hankou, 10 May 1932.

32 CA, *Xiang'exi suqu geming lishi wenjian huiji (zhongyang fenju wenjian): 1931–1934*, Report about the Situation in Xiang'exi, 19 Dec. 1932, pp. 285–6.

33 Ibid., pp. 283–4, also Report on the Current Situation and the Xiang'exi Party, 21 Feb. 1932, p. 141; CA, *Xiang'exi suqu geming lishi wenjian huiji (shengwei wenjian): 1927–1932*, Deng Zhongxia, Report on the Red 26th Army, 19 Oct. 1930, p. 36.

34 CA, *Xiang'exi suqu geming lishi wenjian huiji (zhongyang fenju wenjian): 1931–1934*, Song Panming, General Report to the Central Committee about the Situation in Xiang'exi, 22 Nov. 1931, p. 114, also Report to the Central Committee from the Xiang'exi Central Committee, 25 Feb. 1932, p. 145; 'Rehabilitating Central China Districts Recovered from the "Reds"', *China Weekly Review*, 24 Dec. 1932.

35 Yueh, *Sun Yat-sen University in Moscow*, pp. 114–17 and 241; Xiao Ke, 'Hong'er, liu juntuan huishi qianhou' (Reminiscences about the Second and Sixth Red Armies), *Jindaishi yanjiu*, 1981, no. 1, p. 16; CA, *Xiang'exi suqu geming lishi wenjian huiji (zhongyang fenju wenjian): 1931–1934*, Report on the Struggle against Counter-Revolutionary Groups in Xiang'exi, 16 April 1932, pp. 195–6, as well as Report on the General Situation in Xiang'exi, 24 Oct. 1932, p. 256; retreat to Sangzhi: Chang, *The Rise of the Communist Party, 1928–1938*, vol. 2, p. 293.

36 CA, *Hubei geming lishi wenjian huiji (shengwei wenjian): 1926–1927*, 'Report on Work in Huang'an', 14 Dec. 1927, p. 438 mentions 500; CA, *Eyuwan suqu geming lishi wenjian huiji (Edongbei tewei, Edongnan tewei wenjian): 1927–1934*, Report on Work in Huang'an, 14 Dec. 1927, p. 6 mentions a thousand.

37 CA, *Eyuwan suqu geming lishi wenjian huiji (yizongben): 1929–1934*, Report to the Central Committee, 8 Sept. 1929, p. 18; CA, *Eyuwan suqu geming lishi wenjian huiji (shengwei wenjian): 1929–1934*, Agenda about Military Issues for the Congress of Party Representatives, 2 Dec. 1929, pp. 40–1.

38 Gregor Benton, *Mountain Fires: The Red Army's Three-Year War in South China, 1934–1938*, Berkeley, CA: University of California Press, 1992, pp. 310–13; 'wiping out entire villages' is mentioned in 'Communist Raids in Hupeh', *North-China Herald*, 20 July 1929.

39 CA, *Eyuwan suqu geming lishi wenjian huiji (shengwei wenjian): 1929–1934*, Zeng Zhongsheng, Report to the Central Committee, 10 Feb. 1931, pp. 221–3.

40 The reports are in CA, *Eyuwan suqu geming lishi wenjian huiji (zhongyang fenju wenjian): 1931–1934*, Report to the Central Committee, Notice Number Seven, 10 June 1931, p. 60; Resolutions of an Enlarged Meeting, June 1931, p. 90; see also Chang, *The Rise of the Communist Party, 1928–1938*, vol. 2, pp. 245–6 and 277.

41 CA, *Eyuwan suqu geming lishi wenjian huiji (yizongben): 1929–1934*, Report on the Purge, 22 Nov. 1931, p. 129; Chang, *The Rise of the Communist Party, 1928–1938*, vol. 2, pp. 197, 245–6 and 277; William Rowe, using a chronology of Zhang Guotao's life published in the People's Republic, writes that on 28 June 1931 Zhang vowed to eradicate every landlord and rich peasant; but the facts do not support this chronology; on 30 June 1931 Zhang explicitly pointed out that 'opposing rich peasants is not the same as exterminating rich peasants'; see CA, *Eyuwan suqu geming lishi wenjian huiji (zhongyang fenju wenjian): 1931–1934*, Zhang Guotao, Report to an Enlarged Meeting, 30 June 1931, p. 136 (Rowe, *Crimson Rain*, p. 314, quoting Sheng Renxue, *Zhang Guotao nianpu ji yanlun*, Beijing: Jiefangjun chubanshe, 1985, p. 32); 600 were arrested: Chang, *The Rise of the Communist Party, 1928–1938*, vol. 2, p. 276; Xu Xiangqian, *Lishi de huigu* (A look back at history), Beijing: Jiefangjun chubanshe, 1987, pp. 159 and 161–3; Xu Xiangqian, *Xu Xiangqian huiyi lu* (Memoirs of Xu Xiangqian), Beijing: Jiefangjun chubanshe, 2007, pp. 108–16.

42 CA, *Eyuwan suqu geming lishi wenjian huiji (shengwei wenjian): 1929-1934*, Report to the Central Committee, 2 Aug. 1933, p. 363; GSG, 002-090300-00062-393, Cable by Liu Zhenhua to Chiang Kai-shek, 5 Nov. 1933; 'Grim Result of Red Occupation

in Hupeh', *China Weekly Review*, 23 Dec. 1933; slaughter: Benton, *Mountain Fires*.

43 George B. Cressey, *The Land of the 500 Million*, New York: McGraw-Hill, 1955, p. 178.

44 CA, *Sichuan suqu geming lishi wenjian huiji (shengwei wenjian): 1926–1927*, Plan for an Uprising in Dazhu County, Oct. 1927, p. 264; CA, *Sichuan suqu geming lishi wenjian huiji (shengwei wenjian): 1928–1929.2*, Report to the Central Committee, 29 Jan. 1928, p. 15; CA, *Sichuan suqu geming lishi wenjian huiji (shengwei wenjian): 1930–1931*, Report to the Central Committee, June 1931, p. 481.

45 Liu Xiang: 'Ruin Wrought by War Lords', *Los Angeles Times*, 13 Aug. 1933; 'Reds in Szechuen', *North-China Herald*, 8 Feb. 1933; 'The Communists in Szechuen', *North-China Herald*, 22 March 1933, Chang, *The Rise of the Communist Party, 1928–1938*, vol. 2, p. 331; MAE, 513PO/A/435, Report from the Consul, Chengdu, 25 Feb. 1933, and a similar observation in PRO, FO 371/17061, Report, 23 Jan. 1933, pp. 74–6.

46 Chang, *The Rise of the Communist Party, 1928–1938*, vol. 2, pp. 332 and 349; on Bazhou, see GSG, 002-090300-00056-375, Tongnanba Bandit Disaster Temporary Emergency Relief Department, telegram, 12 April 1933, as well as 'Szechuen-Shensi Red Terror', *North-China Herald*, 12 July 1933; vermin: MAE, 513PO/A/435, Report from the Consul, Chengdu, 25 Feb. 1933; Liu Xiang's cable is in GSG, 002-090300-00071-316, 19 March 1934.

47 Chang, *The Rise of the Communist Party, 1928–1938*, vol. 2, p. 350; Norman D. Hanwell, 'Within Chinese Red Areas', *Asia*, 37, no. 1 (Jan. 1937), pp. 58–61; money to Shanghai: PRO, FO 371/18091, Report by the Consul General, Chongqing, 13 Nov. 1933, pp. 127–30.

48 Chang, *The Rise of the Communist Party, 1928–1938*, vol. 2, pp. 350–61; roads torn up: PRO, FO 371/18091, Report by the Consul General, Chongqing, 13 Nov. 1933, pp. 127–30; Norman D. Hanwell, 'When Chinese Reds Move In' *Asia*, 36, no. 10 (Oct. 1936), pp. 631–6; on the concealment of land, see the pioneering work of Gao Wangling, *Zudian guanxi xinlun: Dizhu, nongmin he dizu* (A new perspective on tenure relationships: Landlords, peasants and rent), Shanghai: Shanghai shudian chubanshe, 2005.

49 Chang, *The Rise of the Communist Party, 1928–1938*, vol. 2, p. 361.

50 'Introduction', in Schram and Hodes, *Mao's Road to Power*, vol. 4, pp. lvii–lx; Letter to the Central Committee, 30 Sept. 1932, in Titarenko, *VKP(b), Komintern i Kitai*, vol. 4, part 1, pp. 187–8.

51 'Introduction', in Schram and Hodes, *Mao's Road to Power*, vol. 4, pp. lxiv–lxvii.
52 'Defeated Reds Retreat to Kiangsi Border', *South China Morning Post*, 24 Feb. 1933; Tyler Dennett, 'Japan Overruns Jehol', *Current History*, 38, no. 1 (April 1933), pp. 124–8; 'Japan Stuns World, Withdraws from League', UPI Archives, 24 Feb. 1933; Abend, *My Life in China*, p. 204; Peter Worthing, *General He Yingqin: The Rise and Fall of Nationalist China*, Cambridge: Cambridge University Press, 2016, pp. 147–8.
53 Appeal to Save Grain for the Red Army, June 1933; On the Solution to the Grain Problem, 16 June 1933; Report of the Central Executive Committee, 24–25 Jan. 1934, all in Schram and Hodes, *Mao's Road to Power*, vol. 4, pp. 402–3, 408 and 686.
54 Mao Zedong, Preliminary Summing Up of the Land Investigation Movement, Aug. 1933, in Schram and Hodes, *Mao's Road to Power*, vol. 4, pp. 510–11.
55 PRO, FO 371/18091, Gerald Yorke, 'An Account of the Chinese Soviet Republic in Kiangsi', Nov. 1933, pp. 104–5; also NARA, RG 165, MID 2657-1-281/139, W. S. Drysdale, Military Attaché, 'Anti-Communist Operations in Kiangsi', G-2 Report No. 8960, 6 Nov. 1934; Peter Fleming, *One's Company: A Journey to China*, New York: Charles Scribner's Sons, 1934, p. 234.
56 PRO, FO 371/18091, Gerald Yorke, 'An Account of the Chinese Soviet Republic in Kiangsi', Nov. 1933, p. 106; PRO, WO 106/5312 (also in FO 676/130), Lt. Dewar Durie, Report on the Blockade, 25 Nov. 1933, p. 20.
57 PRO, FO 371/18091, Gerald Yorke, 'An Account of the Chinese Soviet Republic in Kiangsi', Nov. 1933, pp. 106–11.
58 Ibid., p. 112; PRO, FO 106/5312, Lt Dewar Durie, Report on the Blockade, 25 Nov. 1933, p. 31; Frank Dikötter, *Crime, Punishment and the Prison in Modern China*, New York: Columbia University Press, 2002, pp. 280–6.
59 Fleming, *One's Company*, p. 184; Yorke, *China Changes*, pp. 207–8; Fuzhou Consul quoted in PRO, FO 676/156, Miles Lampson to Foreign Office, 18 Sept. 1933, pp. 109–19; the Special Movement Corps is mentioned in NARA, RG 165, MID 2657-1-276/445, W. S. Drysdale, 'Situation Report', Report No. 9035, 31 Jan. 1935, p. 5; see also footnote 42 in Xu Youwei and Philip Billingsley, 'Behind the Scenes of the Xi'an Incident: The Case of the Lixingshe', *China Quarterly*, no. 154 (June 1998), p. 297.
60 Telegram from the Comintern to Arthur Ewert and the Central Committee, 25 March 1934; Arthur Ewert, Report, 2 June 1934, both in Titarenko, *VKP(b), Komintern i Kitai*, vol. 4, part 1, pp. 584

and 602; loss of a fifth, meaning 5,000 were lost out of 25,000 troops: Ch'en Yung-fa, *Zhongguo gongchan geming qishinian* (Seventy years of the Chinese revolution), Taipei: Lianjing chuban shiye gongsi, 2nd edn, 2001, p. 270.

61 On soldiers and red terror, see 'Wei jianjue jingong diren huifu Menling' (On taking back Menling), *Hongse Zhonghua*, 14 May 1934; the key text is Zhang Wentian, 'Shi jianjue de zhenya fangeming hai shi zai fangeming qianmian de kuangluan?' (Should we resolutely suppress the counter-revolution or should we become utterly confused because of the counter-revolution?), *Hongse Zhonghua*, 28 June 1934; this text has been translated by a pioneer of documentary research on the Chinese Communist Party, namely Hsiao Tso-liang, *The Land Revolution in China, 1930–1934: A Study of Documents*, Seattle: University of Washington Press, 1969, pp. 285–90; at the time Hsiao Tso-liang did not have access to the order of 23 May 1934, which can be found in 'Zhonghua suwei'ai gongheguo renmin weiyuanhui xunling' (Order from the People's Committee of the Chinese Soviet Republic), *Hongse Zhonghua*, 23 May 1934; Zhang Wentian's text was part of the so-called Ch'en Ch'eng Collection, named after a general who participated in the blockade of the soviet and seized large amounts of material from the Communists which later found their way to both the Bureau of Investigation in Taipei and the Hoover Institution at Stanford University. For decades little more was available on the soviet in terms of primary material.

62 'On the Problem of Deserters from the Red Army', 15 Dec. 1933, in Schram and Hodes, *Mao's Road to Power*, vol. 4, pp. 641–2; the appeal to the pioneers is in 'Bosheng mofanying "wuwu" jie quanti jiaru hongjun' (The entire model battalion in Bosheng county joins the Red Army on the anniversary of Karl Marx's birthday), *Hongse Zhonghua*, 14 May 1934; 'Luo Man tongzhi zai Ruijin fayan' (Li Weihan gives a speech in Ruijin), *Hongse Zhonghua*, 18 Sept. 1934; 'Communist Strength Broken in Kiangsi', *China Press*, 29 April 1934.

63 'Refugees in Kiangsi Form Own Defense', *China Press*, 2 Dec. 1933; see Luo Man (Li Weihan), 'Gannan bu yinggai luohou' (South Jiangxi should not be backward), *Hongse Zhonghua*, 21 Sept. 1934; 'Ganzhou Chutan qu xianxiang yanzhong' (Grave issues in the Ganzhou Chutan region), *Hongse Zhonghua*, 24 July 1934, quoted in Cao Boyi [Tsao Po-i], *Jiangxi suwei'ai zhi jianli jiqi bengkui (1931–1934)* (Rise and fall of the Chinese soviet in Jiangxi, 1931–1934), Taipei: Guoli zhengzhi daxue dongya yanjiusuo, 1969, pp. 642–3; the conclusion of Cao Boyi referred to here is on p. 645.

64 'Red Capital Filled with Dead When Taken Over', *China Press*, 14 Nov. 1934; 'Former Red Area in China is Gaunt', *New York Times*, 28 Jan. 1935; 'Tingzhou', *Dagongbao*, 3 Nov. 1934, p. 3; 'Ruijin shoufu jingguo xiangqing' (A detailed account of the recovery of Ruijin), *Dagongbao*, 13 Nov. 1934, p. 3; Li Yushu, 'Jiehou zhi Ruijin' (Ruijin after the sack), *Dagongbao*, 18 Dec. 1934; 'Thrilling Defence against Reds', *North-China Herald*, 6 Feb. 1935; the peak is called Cuiweifeng, and has been turned into a 'scenic spot'.

65 'Kuloudui cheng shan' (Heaps of corpses), *Dagongbao*, 10 April 1935, p. 3; around Ji'an: GSG, 002-090300-00089-038, Cable by Lu Xingrong to Chiang Kai-shek, 29 Dec. 1934; Wang Hao, *Shoufu feiqu zhi tudi wenti* (Land problems in the territories recovered from the bandits), Nanjing: Zhengzhong shuju, 1935, p. 49.

5 SURVIVAL (1934–1936)

1 'The Chinese Soviet Mystery Man', *North-China Herald*, 30 Jan. 1935; 'Otto Braun is Dead', *New York Times*, 23 Aug. 1974.

2 Otto Braun, *A Comintern Agent in China, 1932–1939*, London: Hurst, 1982, pp. 81–3; Nym Wales (Helen Foster Snow), *The Chinese Communists: Sketches and Autobiographies of the Old Guard*, Westport, CT: Greenwood Publishing, 1972, pp. 245–6; Chang and Halliday, *Mao*, pp. 158–9; on Otto Braun, one should read Freddy Litten, 'Otto Brauns frühes Wirken in China (1932–1935)', *Working Papers*, no. 124, Munich: Osteuropa-Institut, 1988.

3 Braun, *A Comintern Agent in China, 1932–1939*, pp. 89–90; Chen Jitang's deal is mentioned in Sun Shuyun, *The Long March*, London: HarperPress, 2006, p. 70.

4 Braun, *A Comintern Agent in China, 1932–1939*, pp. 89–90; the diary and desertion strategy appear in Sun, *The Long March*, pp. 74–6.

5 Shi Zhongquan, *Changzheng xing* (The Long March), Beijing: Zhonggong dangshi chubanshe, 2006, p. 43; Braun, *A Comintern Agent in China, 1932–1939*, pp. 89–90; 'Defence of Kwangsi', *South China Morning Post*, 15 Nov. 1934.

6 Braun, *A Comintern Agent in China, 1932–1939*, pp. 89–90; 'Kwangsi Quiet', *South China Morning Post*, 5 Dec. 1934; *Central China Post*, Guilin, 12 Dec. 1934, quoted in HIA, Hanwell (Norman David) Papers 1928–1944, box 3, 'Communists let [sic] by Chu Teh and Mao Tse-tung'.

7 Yan Daogang, 'Jiang Jieshi zhuidu changzheng hongjun de neimu' (The inside story of Chiang Kai-shek's pursuit of the Red Army during the Long March), *Wenshi jinghua*, no. 10 (1996), p. 24.
8 'Liping Plundered', *South China Morning Post*, 29 Dec. 1934; 'Red Advance into Kweichow', *North-China Herald*, 9 Jan. 1935; Braun, *A Comintern Agent in China, 1932–1939*, pp. 91–2.
9 Braun, *A Comintern Agent in China, 1932–1939*, pp. 93–4; 'Kweichow War', *South China Morning Post*, 24 Jan. 1935.
10 Braun, *A Comintern Agent in China, 1932–1939*, pp. 95–107; see also the meticulous research of Frederick S. Litten, 'The Myth of the "Turning-Point": Towards a New Understanding of the Long March', *Bochumer Jahrbuch zur Ostasienforschung*, no. 25 (2001), pp. 2–44.
11 The series of defeats inflicted at Tucheng and elsewhere is mentioned in PRO, FO 371/19264, J. W. O. Davidson, Report, British Consulate General, Chongqing, 11 Feb. 1935, pp. 74–5; S. W. Lovat Fraser, Military Attaché, Minute on Communism, 28 Feb. 1935, pp. 102–3; the quotations from a survivor are in Sun, *The Long March*, pp. 125; Braun, *A Comintern Agent in China, 1932–1939*, pp. 108–111.
12 'Nothing but his own interests' is quoted in PRO, FO 371/17061, H. F. Handley Derry, Consul General in Kunming, 'Political Situation in Kweichow', 16 Feb. 1933, p. 199; *Reuters*, Guiyang, 10 April 1935, and *Reuters*, Guiyang, 11 April 1935, both in Hanwell, 'Communists let [sic] by Chu Teh and Mao Tse-tung', box 3.
13 'Reds in Szechuen', *North-China Herald*, 8 Feb. 1933; 'Missionaries in Szechwan Flee Red Approach', *China Press*, 16 Feb. 1933; 'Marshal Chang and Gen. Chiang Confer at Kweiyang', *China Weekly Review*, 20 April 1935; see also NARA, RG 165, MID 2657-1-276/443, G-2 Report No. 9016, 3 Jan. 1935.
14 Braun, *A Comintern Agent in China, 1932–1939*, p. 113; GSG, 002-060100-00095-010, 10 April 1935.
15 Sun, *The Long March*, p. 128; Sun also provides the quotation from Lin Biao on page 129, which departs so much from the original that I have retranslated it entirely; the original can be found in Nie Rongzhen, *Nie Rongzhen huiyilu* (Memoirs of Nie Rongzhen), Beijing: Jiefangjun chubanshe, 2007, p. 206.
16 *North China Daily News*, Guiyang, 3 April 1935; *Reuters*, Guiyang, 14 April 1935, both in Hanwell, 'Communists let [sic] by Chu Teh and Mao Tse-tung', box 3.
17 *Reuters*, Guiyang, 21 April 1935, in Hanwell, 'Communists let [sic] by Chu Teh and Mao Tse-tung', box 3; Braun, *A Comintern Agent in China, 1932–1939*, p. 116; PRO, FO 371/19266, H. I. Harding,

Consul General, Kunming, 'Communist Invasion of Yunnan', 8 and 15 May 1935, pp. 140–5 and 168–70.

18 *Reuters*, Guiyang, 21 April 1935, in Hanwell, 'Communists let [sic] by Chu Teh and Mao Tse-tung', box 3; 'Huili Relieved', *South China Morning Post*, 29 May 1935; Braun, *A Comintern Agent in China, 1932–1939*, p. 116; PRO, FO 371/19266, H. I. Harding, Consul General, Kunming, 'Communist Invasion of Yunnan', 8 and 15 May 1935, pp. 140–5 and 168–70; Peng, *Memoirs of a Chinese Marshal*, pp. 369–70.

19 'Red Advance', *South China Morning Post*, 9 May 1935, p. 117; 'Zhongyangjun yi zengfang Huili' (Central troops reinforce Huili), *Yunyang ribao*, 26 May 1935; 'Red China Away', *North-China Herald*, 20 March 1935.

20 The propaganda is expertly recounted in Sun, *The Long March*, p. 156.

21 Chang and Halliday, *Mao*, pp. 153–4.

22 Sun, *The Long March*, pp. 157–61.

23 The evangelisation of the region is invoked in 'Letters from High Altitudes', *North-China Herald*, 2 June 1928; MAE, 513PO/A/63, S. P. Valentin, Report on Luding, 16 June 1935; also Georges Bechamp, Chengdu Consulate, 'A.s. de la lettre de Mgr Valentin', 29 June 1935; aircraft mentioned in 'Reds Beaten Back in Szechuen', *North-China Herald*, 12 June 1935; destruction of bridge in 'Luting Taken', *China Press*, 12 June 1935, and Sun, *The Long March*, p. 162; the quotation admiring the bridge is in 'The Red Attack on Tachienlu', *North-China Herald*, 31 July 1935; repair mentioned in 'Reds Reduced in Numbers', *North-China Herald*, 4 Sept. 1935.

24 Sun, *The Long March*, pp. 22–4.

25 Braun, *A Comintern Agent in China, 1932–1939*, p. 120.

26 Ibid., pp. 122–3.

27 Chang, *The Rise of the Communist Party, 1928–1938*, vol. 2, pp. 361–5.

28 '40,000 Chinese Reds Preparing Chengtu Attack', *New York Times*, 21 April 1935; 'Troops' Plight', *South China Morning Post*, 24 April 1935; Chang, *The Rise of the Communist Party, 1928–1938*, vol. 2, pp. 366–70.

29 Chang, *The Rise of the Communist Party, 1928–1938*, vol. 2, pp. 361–5; 'Heavy Fighting Reported on Chengtu Front', *China Press*, 6 June 1935.

30 Braun, *A Comintern Agent in China, 1932–1939*, pp. 135–41; Chang, *The Rise of the Communist Party, 1928–1938*, vol. 2, pp. 379 and 434.

31 Braun, *A Comintern Agent in China, 1932–1939*, pp. 136–42; quotation about plunderers in J. C. Keyte, *The Passing of the Dragon: The Story of the Shensi Revolution and Relief Expedition*, London: Hodder & Stoughton, 1913, p. 227, quoted in Mark Selden, 'The Guerrilla Movement in Northwest China: The Origins of the Shensi–Kansu–Ninghsia Border Region (Part I)', *China Quarterly*, no. 28 (Dec. 1966), p. 63; 'Szechwan Reds Said to Have Entered Kansu', *China Press*, 27 Sept. 1935.

32 NARA, RG 165, MID 2055-622/174, W. S. Drysdale, 'Comments on Current Events', Report No. 8409, 12 Oct. 1932, p. 5; PRO, FO 371/20233, Military Attaché, Nanjing, 'Communist Situation: China', 2 June 1936, p. 98; views of the Japanese Assistant Naval Attaché quoted in PRO, FO 371/20952, T. J. N. Hilken, Report, 20 July 1937, p. 173.

33 MAE, 513PO/A/322, Auguste Wilden, Ambassador in Nanjing, Report to Minister of Foreign Affairs, 17 Dec. 1932; H. Bonnafous, Manager of the Consulate in Harbin, 'Les préparatifs militaires à Vladivostok', 24 Oct. 1934; Louis Reynaud, Consul in Harbin, 'Les incidents de frontière soviéto-mandchous', 18 Dec. 1935; Wilden was one of the first foreign ambassadors, besides his Russian colleague, to move his residence from Beijing to Nanjing.

34 'Nanking Denies Understanding with Reds', *China Weekly Review*, 5 Oct. 1935.

35 Rudolf A. Bosshardt, *The Restraining Hand: Captivity for Christ in China*, London: Hodder & Stoughton, 1936, pp. 31–2, 39, 48 and 56.

36 PRO, FO 371/19266, K. E. F. Millar, 'Journey to and from Szechuan and Subsequent Travel in Hunan', 24 April 1935, pp. 40–1; Bosshardt, *The Restraining Hand*, pp. 65–8; volunteers: PRO, FO 371/19264, Report of Trip Made by Three Volunteers, 4 March 1935, pp. 159–61.

37 PRO, FO 371/20233, Military Attaché, Beijing Embassy, 'Communist Situation in China', 3 Feb. 1936, pp. 11–23; PRO, FO 371/20232, S. L. Burdett, Consul in Changsha, 2 Dec. 1935, pp. 182–7; 'Reds' Main Body Estimated at Fifteen Thousand', *South China Morning Post*, 24 Dec. 1935; clothing and shoes: Bosshardt, *The Restraining Hand*, p. 145.

38 PRO, FO 371/20233, H. I. Harding, Consul in Kunming, 'Communists', 14 April 1936, pp. 56–63; 'Communists Flee from Yunnan', *North-China Herald*, 2 Sept. 1936.

39 Chang, *The Rise of the Communist Party, 1928–1938*, vol. 2, pp. 426–8.

40 Liu Tong, *Beishang: Dang zhongyang yu Zhang Guotao douzheng jishi* (A record of the struggle between the Central Committee and Zhang Guotao), Nanning: Guangxi renmin chubanshe, 2004, pp. 201–11.
41 '15,000 Reds Lay Siege to Minhsien', *New York Times*, 2 Sept. 1936; 'Communist Defeat', *South China Morning Post*, 7 Nov. 1936; Sun, *The Long March*, p. 227.
42 Mao Zedong, 'On Tactics against Japanese Imperialism', 27 Dec. 1935, in Schram and Hodes, *Mao's Road to Power*, vol. 5, p. 92.
43 Zhongyang dang'anguan (eds), *Zhonggong zhongyang kangri minzu tongyi zhanxian wenjian xuanbian* (Central Committee selected documents of the national United Front in the war against Japan), Beijing: Dang'an chubanshe, 1985, vol. 3, p. 674; membership numbers in Benjamin Yang, *From Revolution to Politics: Chinese Communists on the Long March*, London: Routledge, 1990, p. 233.
44 John L. Buck, *Land Utilization in China*, Nanjing: University of Nanking, 1937, extensively analysed in the peerless Gray, *Rebellions and Revolutions*, pp. 156–61.
45 PRO, FO 371/17064, Miles Lampson, Ambassador, Farewell Report, 24 Aug. 1933, pp. 199 and 216.
46 James C. Thomson, *While China Faced West: American Reformers in Nationalist China, 1928–1937*, Cambridge, MA: Harvard University Press, 1969, pp. 35–8; roads: Department of Overseas Trade, *Economic Conditions in China to September 1st, 1929*, London: His Majesty's Stationery Office, 1930, p. 26; railways: Chang Jui-te, 'Technology Transfer in Modern China: The Case of Railway Enterprise (1876–1937)', *Modern Asian Studies*, 27, no. 2 (1993), p. 291; Department of Overseas Trade, *Trade and Economic Conditions in China, 1931–33*, London: His Majesty's Stationery Office, 1933, p. 120.
47 Braun, *A Comintern Agent in China, 1932–1939*, p. 130.
48 Alvin D. Coox, *Nomonhan: Japan against Russia 1939*, Stanford, CA: Stanford University Press, 1988, p. 93.
49 Georgi Dimitrov, 'Unity of the Working Class against Fascism', 13 Aug. 1935, in Georgi Dimitrov, *Selected Works*, Sofia: Sofia Press, 1972, vol. 2, pp. 86–119.
50 Wang Ming, 'Message to Compatriots on Resistance to Japan', 1 Aug. 1935, in Saich and Yang, *The Rise to Power of the Chinese Communist Party*, pp. 692–7; 'Students Strike to Stir Chinese over Autonomy', *New York Herald Tribune*, 11 Dec. 1935.
51 Mao Zedong, cable to Zhu De, 1 Jan. 1936, *Mao Zedong quanji*, vol. 8, p. 157.
52 Powell, *My Twenty-Five Years in China*, pp. 322–3.

53 Report from Bogomolov on Conversation with Zhang Xueliang, 28 Nov. 1935, doc. 309, in Andrei M. Ledovskii et al. (eds), *Russko-kitaiskie otnosheniia v XX veke: Materialy i dokumenty*, Moscow: Nauka, 2010, vol. 3, pp. 473–4; Mao Zedong, cables on 20 and 25 Jan. 1936, *Mao Zedong quanji*, vol. 8, pp. 173 and 175–8.

54 Mao Zedong, cables on 9 and 11 April 1936, *Mao Zedong quanji*, vol. 8, pp. 336–7 and 340.

55 MAE, 513PO/A/229, Henri Hoppenot, 'Campagne contre les Communistes au Chansi', 19 March 1936; the proclamation issued on 21 Feb. 1936 is enclosed in NARA, 893.00/13696, Nelson Johnson, 'Communist Situation in Northwest China', 7 Aug. 1936.

56 NARA, RG 165, MID 2657-1-276/475, Joseph Stilwell, 'Situation Report', Report No. 9330, 27 March 1936; NARA, RG 165, MID 2657-1-276/479, Joseph Stilwell, 'Situation Report', Report No. 9369, 22 May 1936.

57 'Spravka o peregovorov', 19 Oct. 1936, doc. 352, and 'O dal'nevostočnyh problemah', 1 Dec. 1936, doc. 311, both in Ledovskii, *Russko-kitaiskie otnosheniia v XX veke*, vol. 3, pp. 478–80 and 576–7; Reports on Discussions between Deng Wenyi and Wang Ming, 17, 22 and 23 Jan. 1936, in Titarenko, *VKP(b), Komintern i Kitai*, vol. 4, part 2, pp. 941–58.

58 NARA, 893.00/13696, Nelson Johnson, 'Communist Situation in Northwest China', 7 Aug. 1936; NARA, RG 165, MID 2657-1-276/484, Joseph Stilwell, 'Situation Report', Report No. 9446, 31 July 1936.

59 Mao Zedong, 'Guangyu liangguang shibian de huatan' (About the Southwest Incident), in *Mao Zedong quanji*, vol. 8, pp. 413–5.

60 Notes of Conversation between Bogomolov and Zhang Xueliang, 24 July 1936, doc. 347, in Ledovskii, *Russko-kitaiskie otnosheniia v XX veke*, vol. 3, pp. 569–70.

61 F. F. Liu, *A Military History of Modern China*, Princeton: Princeton University Press, 1956, p. 101; Chiang's request for Blyukher's advice is in Notes of Conversation between Blyukher and Deng Wenyi, 20 Jan. 1936, doc. 320, in Ledovskii, *Russko-kitaiskie otnosheniia v XX veke*, vol. 3, p. 499.

62 Letter from Dimitrov to Stalin, 27 July 1936, and Telegram from the Comintern Secretariat to the Central Committee, 15 Aug. 1936, in Titarenko, *VKP(b), Komintern i Kitai*, vol. 4, part 2, pp. 1,067–71; the cable is translated in Alexander Dallin and F. I. Firsov, *Dimitrov and Stalin, 1934–1943: Letters from the Soviet Archives*, New Haven, CT: Yale University Press, 2000, pp. 102–6.

63 'A Letter from the Chinese Communist Party to the Chinese Guomindang', 25 Aug. 1936, and 'The Heart of our Policy is to

Unite with Chiang to Resist Japan', 30 Aug. 1936, in Schram and Hodes, *Mao's Road to Power*, vol. 5, pp. 323–32 and 334; Ch'en, *The Storm Clouds Clear over China*, p. 120.

64 'Government Troops Take Communist Stronghold', *China Press*, 26 June 1936; Mao Zedong, Letter to Wang Ming, 25 Aug 1936, in *Mao Zedong quanji*, vol. 9, p. 65; on the failure to obtain aircraft and heavy artillery, see Yang Kuisong, 'Sulian daguimo yuanzhu Zhongguo hongjun de yici changshi' (The Soviet Union's attempt to deliver massive aid to the Chinese Red Army), *Jindaishi yanjiu*, 1995, no. 1, p. 266.

65 'Mohammedans Resist Red Invasion', *China Press*, 30 Oct. 1936; 'Reds Cornered in North-West', *North-China Herald*, 25 Nov. 1936; Mao Zedong, 'Wei Xu Xiangqian qicao de zhi Hu Zongnan xin' (Xu Xiangqian's draft letter to Hu Zongnan), 18 Oct. 1936, in *Mao Zedong quanji*, vol. 9, pp. 202–3; Chiang's diary is dated 25 Oct. 1936 and quoted in *Jiang Zhongzheng nianpu changbian*, vol. 5, p. 169.

66 Edgar Snow, 'Interviews with Mao Tze-tung, Communist Leader', *China Weekly Review*, 14 and 21 Nov. 1936.

67 PRO, FO 371/20991, Sir Hughe Knatchbull-Hugessen to Anthony Eden, 12 Feb. 1937, pp. 9–15.

68 Abend, *My Life in China*, pp. 223–4; John H. Jouett, 'War Planes over Asia', *Asia*, vol. 37 (1937), pp. 827–30.

69 Seele, *Donald of China*, pp. 318–19; Chiang Kai-shek's diary, 28 Nov. 1936, quoted in *Jiang Zhongzheng nianpu changbian*, vol. 5, p. 190; one observer: PRO, FO 371/20970, Hughe Knatchbull-Hugessen, Ambassador, 'Political Situation in China', 2 March 1937, p. 44; Yang Hucheng quoted in Wu Tien-wei, *The Sian Incident: A Pivotal Point in Modern History*, Ann Arbor: Center for Chinese Studies, University of Michigan, 1976, p. 71, with slight stylistic changes to the quotation.

6 UNITED AGAIN (1936–1941)

1 'Sian the Progressive City', *North-China Herald*, 15 July 1936; Entry for 4 Dec. 1936, *Jiang Zhongzheng nianpu changbian*, vol. 5, p. 194; 'Tsingtao Tension', *South China Morning Post*, 4 Dec. 1936.

2 PRO, FO 371/20970, Hughe Knatchbull-Hugessen, Ambassador, 'Political Situation in China', 2 March 1937, pp. 40–4; Entry for 9–12 Dec. 1936, *Jiang Zhongzheng nianpu changbian*, vol. 5, pp. 195–8.

3 Itoh Mayumi, *The Making of China's War with Japan: Zhou Enlai and Zhang Xueliang*, London: Palgrave Macmillan, 2016, pp. 134–7; cable from Mao in Zhongyang dang'anguan (eds), *Zhongguo gongchandang guanyu Xi'an shibian dang'an shiliao xuanbian* (Selected archival documents on the Xi'an Incident), Beijing: Zhongguo dang'an chubanshe, 1997, p. 174; cable to Mao: Ye Zilong, *Ye Zilong huiyilu* (Memoirs of Ye Zilong), Beijing: Zhongyang wenxian chubanshe, 2000, p. 39, quoted in Chang and Halliday, *Mao*, p. 183.
4 Entry dated 12 Dec. 1936, *Jiang Zhongzheng nianpu changbian*, vol. 5, p. 198.
5 Chang, *The Rise of the Communist Party, 1928–1938*, vol. 2, pp. 480–1; cables and speech by Mao, as well as cable to Zhang Xueliang, 13 and 14 Dec. 1936, in *Zhongguo gongchandang guanyu Xi'an shibian dang'an shiliao xuanbian*, pp. 178–81; execution of Chiang: Zhang Youkun et al. (eds), *Zhang Xueliang nianpu* (A chronology of Zhang Xueliang's life), Beijing: Shehui kexue wenxian chubanshe, 1996, vol. 2, p. 1,124; cable to Moscow, mentioned in comments on Comintern Telegram dated 16 Dec. 1936, in Titarenko, *VKP(b), Komintern i Kitai*, vol. 4, part 2, p. 1,086, note 2.
6 Chiang knew: GSG, 002-060100-00120-016, 16 Dec. 1936; Extract from Dimitrov's Diary, 14 Dec. 1936, doc. 364, in Ledovskii, *Russko-kitaiskie otnosheniia v XX veke*, vol. 3, p. 610.
7 Itoh, *The Making of China's War with Japan*, p. 154.
8 Comintern Telegram dated 16 Dec. 1936, in Titarenko, *VKP(b), Komintern i Kitai*, vol. 4, part 2, pp. 1,085–6; Chang, *The Rise of the Communist Party, 1928–1938*, vol 2, p. 484; cables to Zhang Xueliang, 14 and 15 Dec. 1936, in Schram and Hodes, *Mao's Road to Power*, vol. 5, pp. 544–6, 550 and 561.
9 Cable to Zhou Enlai, 21 Dec. 1936, in Schram and Hodes, *Mao's Road to Power*, vol. 5, p. 561; Worthing, *General He Yingqin*, pp. 169–70.
10 Mao's telegram informing Zhou Enlai of the cable from Moscow is dated 20 Dec. 1936, in *Mao Zedong quanji*, vol. 9, p. 460; Seele, *Donald of China*, p. 316; Hu Shi's piece was reproduced many times, for instance in the *Dongnan ribao*, 21 Dec. 1936; I used the version copied on 18 Dec. 1936 in GSG, 002-060100-00120-018; many calls for Chiang's release appeared in the newspapers on 15 December 1936 and can be found in GSG, 002-060100-00120-015.
11 Seele, *Donald of China*, p. 327; HIA, Soong, T. V. (Tzu-wen) Papers 1920-1999, box 59, 'TVS Diary of Xian Incident – 1936', pp. 1–15.
12 GSG, 002-060100-00120-024 and 002-060100-00120-025, Diary of Events, 24 and 25 Dec. 1936, and 'TVS Diary of Xian

Incident – 1936', pp. 14–15; the fictive dialogue on the evening of 24 December, reproduced word for word in a recent biography of Chiang Kai-shek, is based on Zhou Enlai's official biography, namely Jin Chongji et al. (eds), *Zhou Enlai zhuan (1898–1976)* (A biography of Zhou Enlai, 1898–1976), Beijing: Zhongyang wenxian chubanshe, 2009, vol. 1, p. 375, which relies on Shen Bochun, *Xi'an shibian jishi* (A true record of the Xi'an Incident), Beijing: Renmin chubanshe, 1979, p. 157, which, in turn, offers not a shred of evidence; there is nothing about such a dialogue either in Chiang Kai-shek's diary or in his secretary's draft record of events, which devotes over a hundred pages to covering the twelve days in Xi'an; it is a curious fact of historiography that biographers of Chiang Kai-shek who claim to have read his diary would instead rely on the alleged words of his adversary, Zhou Enlai, a person described by Laszlo Ladany as 'one of those men who never tell the truth and never tell a lie', since for them there is no distinction between the two; see Laszlo Ladany, *The Communist Party of China and Marxism, 1921–1985: A Self-Portrait*, Stanford, CA: Hoover Institution Press, 1988, p. 209; a further myth is that during the negotiations, Stalin, or Zhou, or both, agreed to releasing Chiang Kai-shek's son, hostage in Moscow, but this was only undertaken several months later (see p. 180).

13 'Gen. Chiang Freed', *New York Times*, 26 Dec. 1936; 'Chiang Freed after Ransom', *Washington Post*, 26 Dec. 1936; the journalist is Abend, *My Life in China*, p. 231; Chiang: GSG, 002-060100-00120-029, Diary of Events, 29 Dec. 1936; Liu, *A Military History of Modern China*, p. 102.

14 Chang, *The Rise of the Communist Party, 1928–1938*, vol. 2, pp. 489–90.

15 *Jiang Zhongzheng nianpu changbian*, vol. 5, pp. 216–18.

16 Telegram from the Comintern, 19 Jan. 1937, in Titarenko, *VKP(b), Komintern i Kitai*, vol. 4, part 2, pp. 1,089 and 1,092; transfer of funds mentioned in Yang Kuisong, *Mao Zedong yu Mosike de enen yuanyuan* (Mao and Moscow), Nanchang: Jiangxi renmin chubanshe, 1999, p. 163; cable of 10 February in *Mao Zedong nianpu*, vol. 1, p. 652; Chiang, *Soviet Russia in China*, pp. 79–81.

17 Note from Bogomolov to Litvinov, 11 Feb. 1937, doc. 377, in Ledovskii, *Russko-kitaiskie otnosheniia v XX veke*, vol. 3, pp. 626–7; Extract of Politburo Resolution, 8 March 1937, doc. 3, in ibid., vol. 4, part 1, p. 40; Chiang's diary, 30 Jan. and 18 Feb. 1937, mentioned in GSG, 002-060100-00121-030 and 002-060100-00121-045; GSG, 002-080200-00276-081, Bureau of Investigation, Report,

24 Feb. 1937; meeting of 8 and 9 June: *Jiang Zhongzheng nianpu changbian*, vol. 5, pp. 312–13.
18 Instructions to Gu Zhutong, 31 Jan. 1937, in *Jiang Zhongzheng nianpu changbian*, vol. 5, p. 235.
19 Snow, *Red Star over China*, pp. 396–9.
20 FO 371/20991, Military Attaché, Tokyo, 'Japanese Troops in Manchuria', 14 April 1937, p. 147; Abend, *My Life in China*, p. 232.
21 Abend, *My Life in China*, pp. 246–8.
22 FO 371/20952, Knatchbull-Hugessen, Report, 3 Aug. 1937, pp. 150–1.
23 Cable dated 16 July 1937, in Schram and Hodes, *Mao's Road to Power*, vol. 5, p. 699; cable dated 1 Aug. 1937, in ibid., vol. 6, p. 7; the cable dated 28 July 1937 is quoted in Yang Kuisong, 'Kangri zhanzheng baofa hou Zhongguo gongchandang duiri junshi zhanlüe fangzhen de yanbian' (The evolution of the Chinese Communist Party's military strategy after the outbreak of the war against Japan), *Jindaishi yanjiu*, no. 2 (1988), p. 108, although the author does not provide any location data.
24 PRO, FO 371/20970, Berkeley Gage, Report to Anthony Eden, 8 Sept. 1937, pp. 296–319; Booker, *News is my Job*, p. 293; Rhodes Farmer, *Shanghai Harvest: A Diary of Three Years in the China War*, London: Museum Press, 1945, p. 46; Abend, *My Life in China*, pp. 253–5; Evans F. Carlson, *Twin Stars of China*, New York: Dodd, Mead, 1940, p. 27; estimates have been ventured by the pre-eminent historian of the battle, Peter Harmsen, *Shanghai 1937: Stalingrad on the Yangtze*, Oxford: Casemate, 2013, p. 247.
25 PRO, FO 371/20952, Lord Chilston, Embassy in Moscow, 7 Aug. 1937, p. 269; Ch'en, *The Storm Clouds Clear over China*, p. 124.
26 'China Frees Communists under Pact with Russia', *New York Herald Tribune*, 5 Sept. 1937; Soviet adviser: Short Note on Conversation with Andrianov, 2 Feb. 1938, in Titarenko, *VKP(b), Komintern i Kitai*, vol. 5, p. 81.
27 Braun, *A Comintern Agent in China, 1932–1939*, pp. 213–14; Chang, *The Rise of the Communist Party, 1928–1938*, vol. 2, pp. 530–40.
28 Mao Zedong, 'The Situation and our Tasks', 1 Sept. 1937, in Schram and Hodes, *Mao's Road to Power*, vol. 6, p. 36.
29 Cables dated 25 Sept. 1937, in ibid., pp. 57 and 60; Chang, *The Rise of the Communist Party, 1928–1938*, vol. 2, p. 558.
30 NARA, RG 165, MID 2657-1-276/516, Joseph Stilwell, G-2 Report No. 9599, 18 Oct. 1937, p. 3.
31 Booker, *News is my Job*, p. 354; Harold J. Timperley, *What War Means: Japanese Terror in China*, London: Victor Gollancz, 1938.

32 'China's Leaders Flee Nanking', *Chicago Daily Tribune*, 17 Nov. 1937; Booker, *News is my Job*, p. 338.

33 The oft-quoted but rarely discussed estimate of half a million is a loose extrapolation of another figure, namely 890,000, compiled in 1947 by two researchers who counted every death in every disaster, including drought, disease and famine in the region throughout the war from June 1938 to March 1947, implying that the population fared much better during seven years under Japanese rule than in 1938 (Han Qitong and Nan Zhongwan, *Huangfanqu de sunhai yu shanhou jiuji* [Damage, rehabilitation and relief in the Yellow River's flooded areas], Shanghai: Xingzhengyuan shanhou jiuji zongshu, 1948); most historians who invoke these numbers give less than a paragraph to the actual flood and the tragedy that unfolded; MAE, 513PO/A/78, Frédéric Knobel, Cable from French Embassy to Hong Kong Consulate, 10 June 1938; recent estimate of 30,000: Jia Zhongwei, 'Kangzhan shiqi: Huayuankou juedi zhanlüe zhi yunyong, xiaoguo yu lishi fansi', *Fengchuanmei*, 20 Aug. 2021.

34 'Yellow River Flood Still Spreading', *North-China Herald*, 13 July 1938; 'Flood Havoc', *South China Morning Post*, 5 July 1938; 'Yellow River Flood Flows into Anhwei', *South China Morning Post*, 2 Aug. 1938; 'Ravages by Floods', *South China Morning Post*, 2 Sept. 1938; elevated roadway mentioned in 'Japanese Weaken North China Army', *New York Times*, 6 Aug. 1938.

35 Peter Harmsen, *Storm Clouds over the Pacific, 1931–1941*, Oxford: Casemate, 2018, pp. 146–8.

36 Estimate of a million in Stephen R. MacKinnon, *Wuhan, 1938: War, Refugees, and the Making of Modern China*, Berkeley, CA: University of California Press, 2008.

37 Ch'en, *The Storm Clouds Clear over China*, p. 136; 'New Political Council Ends Nine-Day Hankow Session', *New York Times*, 17 July 1938.

38 Wang, *Memoirs of a Chinese Revolutionary, 1919–1949*, p. 205.

39 Lee Feigon, *Mao: A Reinterpretation*, Chicago, IL: Ivan R. Dee, 2002, p. 67; Robert M. Farnsworth, *From Vagabond to Journalist: Edgar Snow in Asia, 1928–1941*, Columbia, MO: University of Missouri Press, 1996, p. 222.

40 Chang and Halliday, *Mao*, p. 192.

41 Snow, *Red Star over China*, p. 92; Feigon, *Mao*, pp. 67–9.

42 Gao Hua, *How the Red Sun Rose: The Origins and Development of the Rectification Movement*, Hong Kong: Chinese University Press, 2000, pp. 150–1; Chang, *The Rise of the Communist Party, 1928–1938*, vol. 2, pp. 565–72; comment by Mao: Schram and Hodes, *Mao's Road to Power*, vol. 6, p. xl.

43 Short Note on Conversation between Wang Ming, Kang Sheng and Stalin, 11 Nov. 1937, in Titarenko, *VKP(b), Komintern i Kitai*, vol. 5, pp. 74–5, translated in Ivo Banac (ed.), *The Diary of Georgi Dimitrov, 1933–1949*, New Haven, CT: Yale University Press, 2003, p. 67; Chang, *The Rise of the Communist Party, 1928–1938*, vol. 2, pp. 574–5.
44 Chang, *The Rise of the Communist Party, 1928–1938*, vol. 2, pp. 573–9.
45 MAE, 513PO/A/78, Henry Jacomy, 'Le banditisme et les guérillas chinoises', 20 May 1938; 'New China State', *New York Times*, 23 March 1938.
46 Ibid.
47 'Chinese Still Rule Big Area in the North', *New York Times*, 3 July 1938; 'Radio Stations behind Lines of Foe Aid China', *Washington Post*, 29 Aug. 1938; Raymond J. de Jaegher, *The Enemy Within: An Eyewitness Account of the Communist Conquest of China*, Garden City, NY: Doubleday, 1952, pp. 46–8 and 200–1.
48 de Jaegher, *The Enemy Within*, pp. 50–79.
49 'Chinese Increase Thrusts at Enemy', *New York Times*, 27 March 1938; 'Japanese Troops Loot and Destroy Walled City of Ankwo', *Daily Boston Globe*, 29 June 1938; de Jaegher, *The Enemy Within*, p. 88.
50 de Jaegher, *The Enemy Within*, pp. 197–9; Haldore Hanson, 'Inside the Japanese Lines', *China Press*, 22 Aug. 1938; 'Reds Attend Mass in Northern China', *New York Times*, 20 Feb. 1938.
51 Estimate in Braun, *A Comintern Agent in China, 1932–1939*, p. 231; 'Chinese Still Rule Big Area in the North', *New York Times*, 3 July 1938; 'Radio Stations Behind Lines of Foe Aid China', *Washington Post*, 29 Aug. 1938.
52 Gao, *How the Red Sun Rose*, pp. 179–89; Chiang, *Soviet Russia in China*, pp. 87–8; Mao Zedong, 'The Question of Independence and Autonomy under the United Front' and 'Problems of War and Strategy', 5 and 6 Nov. 1938, in Schram and Hodes, *Mao's Road to Power*, vol. 6, pp. 546 and 552.
53 MAE, 513PO/A/322, Chongqing, 16 Oct. 1939, 11 Nov. 1939 and 25 Nov. 1940.
54 MAE, 513PO/A/322, 'Soviet Assistance to the 8th Army and Others' (in English), 30 Sept. 1938.
55 Alvin D. Coox, 'L'Affaire Lyushkov: Anatomy of a Defector', *Soviet Studies*, 19, no. 3 (Jan. 1968), pp. 405–20; John J. Stephan, '"Cleansing" the Soviet Far East, 1937–1938', *Acta Slavica Iaponica*, 10 (1992), pp. 47–8.
56 The key historian on the Nomonhan Battle is Coox, *Nomonhan*.

57 Mao Zedong, 'Outline of a Speech', 14 Sept. 1939, in Schram and Hodes, *Mao's Road to Power*, vol. 7, pp. 190–200.
58 Jacques Guillermaz, *Histoire du Parti Communiste Chinois*, Paris: Payot, 1975, pp. 353–4; deliveries suspended: John W. Garver, *Chinese-Soviet Relations, 1937–1945: The Diplomacy of Chinese Nationalism*, Oxford: Oxford University Press, 1988, pp. 100–5.
59 Guillermaz, *Histoire du Parti Communiste Chinois*, p. 353; Yan Xishan: GSG, 002-090300-00212-212, 23 April 1940, Cable by Yan Xishan; Xu Ming: GSG, 002-090300-00212-173, 25 April 1940, Cable by Yan Xishan; Sixian: GSG, 002-090300-00212-189, 6 May 1940, Cable to Chiang Kai-shek; Anguo: de Jaegher, *The Enemy Within*, pp. 191–2; Weixian: GSG, 002-090300-00218-119, 16 Jan. 1940, Cable to Chiang Kai-shek; Shi Yousan: 'Communist Troops', *South China Morning Post*, 24 Jan.1940.
60 MAE, 513PO/A/78, 'Développement du communisme au Hopei', 15 July 1940; 'Communisme en Chine du Nord', 23 July 1940; flood and famine: 'Flood in Hopei', *South China Morning Post*, 29 July 1939; 'Famine in China: Four Million Face Starvation', *South China Morning Post*, 14 March 1940; 'Famine in Hopei', *South China Morning Post*, 3 June 1940; MAE, 513PO/A/63, 'Lettre du R. P. Pégourié', 28 Dec. 1939.
61 See Liu Qingjun, 'Reinterpreting the Chinese Revolution: The Balance between Radical and Moderate Approaches, 1937–1945', *Modern China*, 48, no. 2 (March 2022), pp. 1–35.
62 MAE, 513PO/A/78, Reports dated 5 Aug. and 2 Sept. 1940.
63 Powell, *My Twenty-Five Years in China*, p. 176 mentions a quarter of the value; caves as well as 'liquidate-on-the-spot' campaigns mentioned in PRO, FO 371/18091, Report by the Consulate General of Mukden, 11 Aug. 1934, p. 231; Russian weapons and 'protected village' programme in NARA, 893.00 P.R. MUKDEN/109, William R. Langdon, American Consul General, Mukden, 'Political Review for November 1936', 9 Dec. 1936.
64 Twelve-centimetre nails in PRO, FO 371/18091, Report by the Consulate General of Mukden, 11 Aug. 1934, p. 232; May 1938 report, as well as 'fascists', in CA, *Dongbei diqu geming lishi wenjian huiji: 1938.1–1938.5*, Zhang Lansheng, Report, 1 May 1938, p. 306; burning and raiding of villages, foresters as well as the killing of three dozen Suoli women and children mentioned in CA, *Dongbei diqu geming lishi wenjian huiji: 1939.5–1939.12*, Ma Zhongyun, Report to the Central Committee, 12 June 1939, pp. 107–8; quotation by Zhao in CA, *Dongbei diqu geming lishi wenjian huiji: 1929–1944*, Zhou Baozhong, Letter to the Comintern, 20 Feb. 1938, p. 232.

65 NARA, RG 59, CA, 'Chinese Communists, Jan.–July 1944' and 'Text of the Joint Telegram Sent on December 8, 1940'; Vasili Chuikov, *Mission to China: Memoirs of a Soviet Military Adviser to Chiang Kaishek*, Norwalk, CT: EastBridge Books, 2003, p. 14.
66 Gregor Benton, *New Fourth Army: Communist Resistance along the Yangtze and the Huai, 1938–1941*, Berkeley, CA: California University Press, 1999, p. 480; also Gregor Benton, 'The South Anhui Incident', *Journal of Asian Studies*, 45, no. 4 (Aug. 1986), pp. 681–720; on Caodian, see Sherman Xiaogang Lai, 'A War within a War: The Road to the New Fourth Army Incident in January 1941', *Journal of Chinese Military History*, 2, no. 1 (Jan. 2013), pp. 20–1.
67 3,000 tonnes mentioned in Don Moser, *China, Burma, India*, Alexandria, VA: Time-Life Books, 1978, p. 8; Mao Zedong, Cable on Central China, 12 July 1940, in Schram and Hodes, *Mao's Road to Power*, vol. 7, pp. 496–7; Douglas Robertson, 'Vladivostok Road Sends Aid to China', *New York Times*, 22 Dec. 1940; Soviet contract mentioned in MAE, 513PO/A/322, 'Accord de Troc', 8 Feb. 1941; for the resumption of Soviet aid, and the overall context, see Lai, 'A War within a War', pp. 1–27.
68 Lai, 'A War within a War'.

7 BIDING TIME (1941–1945)

1 MAE, 513PO/A/322, 'Réaction de Tchongking', 27 June 1941, and 'Les répercussions à Tchongking', 30 April 1941; Chiang Kai-shek's prediction: Dimitrov, *Diary*, p. 166.
2 Taylor, *The Generalissimo*, pp. 178–9.
3 Mao Zedong, Decision on the International United Front, 23 June 1941, in Schram and Hodes, *Mao's Road to Power*, vol. 7, p. 764; Notes from the Politburo's Meeting, 3 July 1941, in Titarenko, *VKP(b), Komintern i Kitai*, vol. 5, p. 540; Dallin and Firsov, *Dimitrov and Stalin, 1934–1943*, pp. 142–3; hostile: Peter Vladimirov, *The Vladimirov Diaries: Yenan, China, 1942–1945*, New York: Doubleday, 1975, p. 20; see also Dimitrov, *Diary*, p. 193.
4 Mao Zedong, 'On New Democracy', 15 Jan. 1940, in Schram and Hodes, *Mao's Road to Power*, vol. 7, pp. 330–69.
5 See Frank Dikötter, *The Age of Openness: China before Mao*, London: Hurst, and Berkeley, CA: University of California Press, 2008, pp. 21–2; Mao Zedong, 'The Situation and Tasks in the Anti-Japanese War', 12 Nov. 1937, in Schram and Hodes, *Mao's Road*

to Power, vol. 6, pp. 153–5; Mao Zedong, 'On the Promotion of Constitutional Government', 20 Feb. 1940, and 'On the Question of Political Power', 6 March 1940, both in Schram and Hodes, *Mao's Road to Power*, vol. 7, pp. 432–3 and 424–8; see also Arthur A. Cohen, *The Communism of Mao Tse-tung*, Chicago, IL: University of Chicago Press, 1964, pp. 93–5.

6 Mao Zedong, 'On New Democracy', 15 Jan. 1940, in Schram and Hodes, *Mao's Road to Power*, vol. 7, p. 342.

7 CA, *Shaanxi geming lishi wenjian huiji: 1942*, Summary of Work on the One Third System in the Northwest Region, 12 June 1942, pp. 139–144; the success of the system in Longdong, by contrast, was applauded as nothing short of 'astounding' by an early historian who relied on propaganda material; see Tetsuya Kataoka, *Resistance and Revolution in China: The Communists and the Second United Front*, Berkeley, CA: University of California Press, 1974, p. 240; class background: CA, *Xibeiju geming lishi wenjian huiji: 1944*, Research on the One Third System by the Northwestern Bureau, 23 March 1944, pp. 219–20.

8 CA, *Shaanxi geming lishi wenjian huiji: 1942*, The Experience of the Consultative Committees in the Shaanxi–Gansu–Ningxia Area, 19 Nov. 1942, pp. 286–7.

9 CA, *Xibeiju geming lishi wenjian huiji: 1943 (1)*, Draft Directive on Eliminating Traitors, March 1943, pp. 33–4.

10 PRO, FO 371/35777, Sir Horace J. Seymour to Anthony Eden, 29 Dec. 1942, p. 20; Banac, *The Diary of Georgi Dimitrov*, p. 227.

11 PRO, FO 371/35777, 'Extracts from a Report by C. A. M. Brondgeest', 1 Feb. 1943, p. 21; report by René d'Anjou and Georges Uhlmann: PRO, FO 371/35801, Sir Horace J. Seymour to Anthony Eden, 29 July 1943, pp. 3–4; Claire and William Band, *Dragon Fangs: Two Years with Chinese Guerrillas*, London: George Allen & Unwin, 1947, pp. 144–5.

12 CA, *Shaanxi geming lishi wenjian huiji: 1942*, The Issues of the Baojia System and the Work of Party Branches, 1942, pp. 315–45.

13 RGASPI, 495-225-71 and 495-74-314, quoted in Alexander V. Pantsov, *Mao: The Real Story*, New York: Simon & Schuster, 2012, p. 334.

14 Mao Zedong, 'Oppose Subjectivism and Sectarianism', 10 Sept. 1941, in Schram and Hodes, *Mao's Road to Power*, vol. 7, pp. 808–11; see also 'Reform our Study', 19 May 1941, in ibid., pp. 747–54.

15 Gao, *How the Red Sun Rose*, pp. 336–8.

16 Chang and Halliday, *Mao*, pp. 193–4 and 238–40.

17 On Ding Ling during the Rectification Movement one should read ch. 14 in Charles Alber, *Enduring the Revolution: Ding Ling and*

the *Politics of Literature in Guomindang China*, London: Praeger, 2002; much of great interest has been written about Wang Shiwei, not least by Gregor Benton, who also translated 'Wild Lilies', in his 'Introduction to "The Yenan Literary Opposition"', *New Left Review*, no. 92 (July–Aug. 1975), pp. 93–6, and Dai Qing, *Wang Shiwei and 'Wild Lilies': Rectification and Purges in the Chinese Communist Party, 1942–1944*, Armonk, NY: M. E. Sharpe, 1994.

18 Mao Zedong, 'Talks at the Yan'an Forum on Literature and Art', May 1942, in Schram and Hodes, *Mao's Road to Power*, vol. 8, pp. 102–32.

19 Gao, *How the Red Sun Rose*, pp. 410–1.

20 Vladimirov, *The Vladimirov Diaries*, pp. 137–44 and 161.

21 Ibid., p. 211.

22 Shenfu and Longdong: GSG, 002-090105-00009-158, Deng Baoshan to He Yingqin, 15 Jan. 1944; GSG, 002-090300-00212-110, Zhu Shaoliang, Report, 15 Jan. 1944; Wang Ming, *Mao's Betrayal*, Moscow: Progress Publishers, 1979, pp. 59 and 149; Moscow: Letter from Georgi Dimitrov to Mao Zedong, 22 Dec. 1944, in Titarenko, *Kommunisticheskii Internatsional i kitaiskaia revoliutsiia*, pp. 295–6.

23 Gao Wenqian, *Zhou Enlai: The Last Perfect Revolutionary*, New York: PublicAffairs, 2007, p. 88; Vladimirov, *The Vladimirov Diaries*, p. 106; Georgi Dimitrov to Mao Zedong, 22 Dec. 1944, in Titarenko, *Kommunisticheskii Internatsional i kitaiskaia revoliutsiia*, pp. 295–6.

24 Gao, *How the Red Sun Rose*, p. 648; Peter J. Seybolt, 'Terror and Conformity: Counterespionage Campaigns, Rectification, and Mass Movements, 1942–1943', *Modern China*, 12, no. 1 (Jan. 1986), p. 40.

25 Executive Committee of the Communist International, 'Resolution of the Executive Committee Presidium of the Communist International', 15 May 1943, various versions to be found online, including at the National Security Archive, from which this translation is drawn.

26 Raymond F. Wylie, *The Emergence of Maoism: Mao Tse-tung, Ch'en Po-ta, and the Search for Chinese Theory, 1935–1945*, Stanford, CA: Stanford University Press, 1980, pp. 205–6; Gao, *How the Red Sun Rose*, pp. 668–70; Li Jihua, 'Dui Mao Zedong geren chongbai de zisheng' (The propagation of Mao's cult of personality), *Yanhuang chunqiu*, no. 3 (March 2010), pp. 40–5.

27 Gao, *How the Red Sun Rose*, pp. 668–70.

28 Theodore H. White and Annalee Jacoby, *Thunder out of China*, London: Victor Gollancz, 1947, p. 217.

29 Chang and Halliday, *Mao*, p. 268; PRO, FO 371/35777, 'Extracts from a Report by C. A. M. Brondgeest', 1 Feb. 1943, p. 21.

30 Stuart R. Schram, 'Party Leader or True Ruler? Foundations and Significance of Mao Zedong's Personal Power', in Stuart R. Schram (ed.), *Foundations and Limits of State Power in China*, London: School of Oriental and African Studies, 1987, p. 213.
31 The contribution from the central government, as well as the taxes imposed in Yan'an, are discussed in Ch'en Yung-fa, 'The Blooming Poppy under the Red Sun: The Yan'an Way and the Opium Trade', in Tony Saich and Hans van de Ven (eds), *New Perspectives on the Chinese Communist Revolution*, Armonk, NY: M. E. Sharpe, 1995, pp. 263–98; the contribution from the Soviet Union is detailed in a series of telegrams dated 23 Feb. 1940 (USD350,000) and 3 July 1941 (USD1 million), in Titarenko, *VKP(b), Komintern i Kitai*, vol. 5, pp. 404–6 and 540; villagers fleeing and general mood: CA, *Shaanxi geming lishi wenjian huiji: 1942*, The Northwest Bureau on Problems during Spring Ploughing, 7 April 1942, pp. 113–15; Xie Juezai, *Xie Juezai riji* (Diary), Beijing: Renmin chubanshe, 1984, vol. 1, p. 579.
32 Inflation: CA, *Xibeiju geming lishi wenjian huiji: 1944*, Research by the Northwest Bureau on Trade, 15 March 1944, pp. 213–15; Mao quoted in Ch'en, 'The Blooming Poppy under the Red Sun', pp. 263–98.
33 CA, *Xibeiju geming lishi wenjian huiji: 1943 (1)*, Feb. 1943, On the Policy of Streamlining Government, pp. 40 and 45; CA, *Xibeiju geming lishi wenjian huiji: 1944*, Orders by the Northwest Bureau on Spring Ploughing, 30 Jan. 1944, pp. 10–11; see also Ch'en, 'The Blooming Poppy under the Red Sun'.
34 On the botched attempt at growing opium in Nanniwan, see CA, *Xibeiju geming lishi wenjian huiji: 1943 (1)*, Investigation of Nanniwan, Feb. 1943, p. 272; for opium production, see the exhaustive research by Ch'en, 'The Blooming Poppy under the Red Sun'.
35 Vladimirov, *The Vladimirov Diaries*, pp. 214–18.
36 MAE, 513PO/A/80, Reports on Chongqing, French Embassy, 30 Oct. 1940, 1 June 1941, 2 Aug. 1941, 1 and 2 Sept. 1941.
37 Associated Press Report, 24 July 1947, quoted in Michael Lynch, *Mao*, London: Routledge, 2004, p. 141.
38 Michell Li, 'Inflation in Eastern China during the Second Sino-Japanese War', *Journal of Economics Library*, 6, no. 4 (Dec. 2019), pp. 338–53; MAE, 513PO/A/77, 30 Sept. 1943, 'Situation politique en Chine', also 'Note sur la situation politique', Feb. 1944.
39 PRO, FO 371/41579, 'From Chungking to Foreign Office', 7 May 1944, p. 171; PRO, FO 371/27715, Ian Morrison, 'The Future of Free China', May or June 1941, p. 65.

40 Robert Payne, *Chinese Diaries: 1941–1946*, New York: Weybright & Talley, 1970, p. 262; Chiang Kai-shek, *China's Destiny*, New York: Roy Publishers, 1947, pp. 127, 137, 173, 210, 271–4, 277.

41 See Kenneth E. Shewmaker, *Americans and Chinese Communists, 1927–1945: A Persuading Encounter*, Ithaca, NY: Cornell University Press, 1971.

42 Evans F. Carlson, *Evans F. Carlson on China at War, 1937–1941*, Beijing: Foreign Languages Press, 2004, pp. 10, 32–3 and 61; see also Kenneth E. Shewmaker, 'The American Liberal Dream: Evans F. Carlson and the Chinese Communists, 1937–1947', *Pacific Historical Review*, 38, no. 2 (May 1969), pp. 207–16.

43 Joseph W. Stilwell, *The Stilwell Papers*, New York: William Sloane Associates, 1948, pp. 193, 206, 214–15 and 316.

44 Pantsov, *Mao*, pp. 530–6.

45 HIA, Soong, T. V. (Tzu-wen) Papers 1920–1999, box 36, Memorandum from Ho Feng-shan to T. V. Soong, 25 Sept. 1944.

46 *United States Relations with China, with Special Reference to the Period 1944–1949*, Washington, DC: Department of State, 1949, Summary Notes of Conversations between Henry Wallace and Chiang Kai-shek, 21–24 June 1944, pp. 549–59; also Robert P. Newman, *Owen Lattimore and the 'Loss' of China*, Berkeley, CA: University of California Press, 1992, chap. 8.

47 Vladimirov, *The Vladimirov Diaries*, pp. 233–4.

48 Ibid., pp. 252–8; NARA, RG 59, 893.00/9-2844, John Service, Report Approved for Transmission by David Barrett, 'The Need of American Policy Toward the Problem Created by the Rise of the Chinese Communist Party', 3 Sept. 1944; in a telephone conversation with Jonathan Mirsky in 1999, Service admitted that his actions could be considered treasonous; Jonathan Mirsky, 'In Whose Service? The Reckless Actions of a Pro-Mao "China Hand" in the State Department', *Wall Street Journal*, 20 Dec. 2009; on the United States' failure to understand China, one should read Tang Tsou, *America's Failure in China, 1941–1950*, Chicago, IL: University of Chicago Press, 1963.

49 CA, *Xibeiju geming lishi wenjian huiji: 1944*, Material on Visits by Foreign Journalists, Aug. 1944, pp. 327–38.

50 Harrison Forman, 'A Visit to Communist China', *New York Herald Tribune*, 1 July 1944.

51 Brooks Atkinson, 'Yenan is Well Fed with Big Harvest', *New York Times*, 25 Sept. 1944, 'Yenan, a Chinese Wonderland City on 3 Kinds of Time', *New York Times*, 6 Oct. 1944, and 'Chinese Still Try to Unify Factions', *New York Times*, 26 Nov. 1944; White and Jacoby, *Thunder out of China*, new introduction to 1961 edition,

p. xiii; Shewmaker, *Americans and Chinese Communists, 1927–1945*, p. 17; the congressman: Walter Judd, *What is the Truth about China?*, Washington, DC: U.S. Government Printing Office, 1945.

52 Charles A. Willoughby, *Shanghai Conspiracy: The Sorge Spy Ring, Moscow, Shanghai, Tokyo, San Francisco*, New York: Dutton, 1952, pp. 76 ff., 249–50 and 276–7; PRO, FO 371/46164, Sir Humphrey Prideaux-Brune, 'Report by Günther Stein', 3 Jan. 1945, p. 30.

53 PRO, FO 371/41615, Sir H. Seymour to Mr Eden, 17 Oct. 1944, p. 187; PRO, FO 371/41582, 'Postal and Telegraph Censorship', 29 Nov. 1944, p. 252; PRO, FO 371/41614, Sir H. Seymour to Mr Eden, 31 Aug. 1944, p. 136.

54 PRO, FO 371/46164, Sir Humphrey Prideaux-Brune, 'Report by Günther Stein', 3 Jan. 1945, p. 30; 'The Ambassador in the Soviet Union (Harriman) to President Roosevelt', 11 June 1944, and 'The Ambassador in the Soviet Union (Harriman) to the Secretary of State', 5 Sept. 1944, in *Foreign Relations of the United States: Diplomatic Papers, 1944, China*, vol. 6, documents 90 and 238; I have changed the past into present tense.

55 Hans van de Ven, *China at War: Triumph and Tragedy in the Emergence of the New China*, Cambridge, MA: Harvard University Press, 2018, pp. 164–6.

56 'President Roosevelt to Generalissimo Chiang Kai-shek', 16 Nov. 1944, *Foreign Relations of the United States: Diplomatic Papers, 1944, China*, vol. 6, document 146; Joseph and Stewart Alsop, 'Before Marshall: Still Went', *Washington Post*, 14 Jan. 1946.

57 Vladimirov, *The Vladimirov Diaries*, p. 289.

58 PRO, FO 371/46164, 'Relations between the Kuomintang and the Communists', comment by G. F. Hudson dated 26 Jan. 1945, p. 75.

59 'The Ambassador in China (Hurley) to the Secretary of State', 31 Jan. 1945, in *Foreign Relations of the United States: Diplomatic Papers, 1945, China*, vol. 7, doc. 149; John N. Hart, *The Making of an Army 'Old China Hand'*, Berkeley, CA: Institute of East Asian Studies, University of California, 1985, pp. 59–60; Jonathan Fenby, *Generalissimo: Chiang Kai-shek and the China He Lost*, London: The Free Press, 2003, pp. 443–6; Vladimirov, *The Vladimirov Diaries*, p. 289.

60 'The Ambassador in China (Hurley) to the Secretary of State', 7 Feb. 1945, *Foreign Relations of the United States: Diplomatic Papers, 1945, China*, vol. 7, doc. 155; Hart, *The Making of an Army 'Old China Hand'*, p. 59.

61 'The Ambassador in China (Hurley) to the Secretary of State', 18 Feb. 1945, *Foreign Relations of the United States: Diplomatic Papers, 1945, China*, vol. 7, doc. 161; Wang Shijie: HIA, T. V. Soong

(Tzu-wen) Papers 1920–1999, box 23, Wang Shijie, Report on Negotiations with the Chinese Communists, 6 March 1945.
62 Vladimirov, *The Vladimirov Diaries*, pp. 311 and 347.
63 Stalin's requirements on seven typescript pages are mentioned in John R. Deane, *The Strange Alliance: The Story of our Efforts at Wartime Cooperation with Russia*, New York: Viking Press, 1947, p. 248; see also David M. Glantz, *The Soviet Strategic Offensive in Manchuria, 1945: 'August Storm'*, London: Frank Cass, 2003, p. 9, and Robert H. Jones, *The Roads to Russia: United States Lend-Lease to the Soviet Union*, Norman, OK: University of Oklahoma Press, 1969, pp. 184–5.
64 *Izvestia* editorial quoted in Chang and Halliday, *Mao*, p. 282; Vladimirov, *The Vladimirov Diaries*, p. 358; Mao Zedong, Conclusion at the Seventh Party Congress, 31 May 1945, in Schram and Hodes, *Mao's Road to Power*, vol. 8, p. 920.

8 CIVIL WAR (1945–1949)

1 'To the Bitter End', *Time*, 20 Aug. 1945.
2 White and Jacoby, *Thunder out of China*, p. 259; 'Victory', *Time*, 20 Aug. 1945; 'Wan Wan Sui!', *Time*, 27 Aug. 1945.
3 White and Jacoby, *Thunder out of China*, p. 263.
4 Vladimirov, *The Vladimirov Diaries*, pp. 498–501; Mao Zedong, 'The New Situation', 23 Aug. 1945, in Schram and Hodes, *Mao's Road to Power*, vol. 9, p. 51, with stylistic changes.
5 Vladimirov, *The Vladimirov Diaries*, pp. 505–12.
6 Michael M. Sheng, *Battling Western Imperialism: Mao, Stalin, and the United States*, Princeton, NJ: Princeton University Press, 1997, pp. 105–6.
7 Zeng Kelin, *Zeng Kelin jiangjun zishu* (Autobiography of Zeng Kelin), Shenyang: Liaoning renmin chubanshe, 1997, pp. 81–103 and 121; see also Sheng, *Battling Western Imperialism*, pp. 106–8.
8 Zeng, *Zeng Kelin jiangjun zishu*, pp. 105–13; Jin Chongji et al. (eds), *Liu Shaoqi zhuan* (A biography of Liu Shaoqi), Beijing: Zhongyang wenxian chubanshe, 2008, pp. 480–1.
9 Taylor, *The Generalissimo*, pp. 321–3.
10 Jin, *Liu Shaoqi zhuan*, pp. 480–1.
11 Zeng, *Zeng Kelin jiangjun zishu*, pp. 121–2; K. P. Ageenko, *Voennaia pomoshch SSSR v osvoboditelnoi borbe kitaiskogo naroda* (Military help from the Soviet Union during the war of liberation), Moscow: Voenizdat, 1975, p. 100.

12 'Chiang Invites Chief of Chinese Reds to Parlay', *New York Herald Tribune*, 16 Aug. 1945; 'Chungking and Yenan Troops in Clash', *Times of India*, 16 Aug. 1945; 'Chinese Reds Reported at Peiping Airport', *New York Herald Tribune*, 18 Aug. 1945.
13 NARA, 893.00/10-1345, William Langdon, 'Findings in Reoccupied China', 13 Oct. 1945.
14 NARA, 893.00/11-2945, Harry Stevens, Consul in Beiping, to Secretary of State, 29 Nov. 1945; 'The Consul at Peiping (Stevens) to the Secretary of State', 20 Dec. 1945, *Foreign Relations of the United States: Diplomatic Papers, 1945, China*, vol. 7, doc. 563; the breach of the dykes is mentioned in MAE, 513PO/A/77, Report by Colonel Yvon, 10 Nov. 1945; see also 'Events in Brief', *China Weekly Review*, 3 Nov. 1945.
15 MAE, 513PO/A/77, Report by Captain Asselot, 6 Oct. 1945; also on forced conscription in the same collection, Report by Colonel Yvon, 5 Oct. 1945; on Yantai, Report by Colonel Yvon, 5 Dec. 1945; GSG, 002-090300-00016-190, Cable from He Yingqin to Chiang Kai-shek on Yantai, 25 March 1946.
16 'The Short March', *Time*, 17 Dec. 1945.
17 NARA, 893.00/11-845, 'Situation at Yingkow', 8 Nov. 1945; also Taylor, *The Generalissimo*, pp. 323–4.
18 Ageenko, *Voennaia pomoshch SSSR v osvoboditelnoi borbe kitaiskogo naroda*, p. 99.
19 James M. McHugh, letter to his wife dated 30 June 1946, Cornell University Library, Division of Rare and Manuscript Collections, quoted in Hannah Pakula, *The Last Empress: Madame Chiang Kai-shek and the Birth of Modern China*, New York: Simon & Schuster, 2009, p. 530; 'Wounds', *Time*, 18 March 1946; William Gray, 'Looted City', *Time*, 11 March 1946; see also 'Soviet Removals of Machinery', 8 July 1947, US Central Intelligence Agency Report, CIA-RDP82-00457D000700010002-5.
20 Jonathan Fenby, *Modern China: The Fall and Rise of a Great Power, 1850 to the Present*, New York: Ecco, 2008, pp. 332–3.
21 'Truman Says Aid to China Hinges on Ending of Strife and Unification of Nation', *New York Times*, 16 Dec. 1945; Ch'en, *The Storm Clouds Clear over China*, p. 185.
22 Zhang Baijia, 'Zhou Enlai and the Marshall Mission', in Larry I. Bland (ed.), *George C. Marshall's Mediation Mission to China, December 1945 – January 1947*, Lexington, VA: George C. Marshall Foundation, 1998, pp. 213–14; Simei Qing, 'American Visions of Democracy and the Marshall Mission to China', in Hongshan Li and Zhaohui Hong (eds), *Image, Perception, and the Making of U.S.–China Relations*, Lanham, MA: University Press of America,

1998, p. 283; 'Chiang Says Liberty Will Follow Truce', *New York Herald*, 11 Jan. 1946.

23 Victor Shiu Chiang Cheng, 'Imagining China's Madrid in Manchuria: The Communist Military Strategy at the Onset of the Chinese Civil War, 1945–1946', *Modern China*, 31, no. 1 (Jan. 2005), pp. 72–114; Spencer Davis, 'Carts and Feet Carry Chinese into Manchuria', *Chicago Daily Tribune*, 25 March 1946; 'Clashes with Communists at Szepingkai', *South China Morning Post*, 25 March 1946.

24 Zhang Zhenglong, *Xuebai xuehong* (Snow is white but blood is red), Hong Kong: Dadi chubanshe, 1991, pp. 170–1.

25 'Lieutenant General Alean C. Gillem, Jr., to General Marshall', 30 March 1946; 'Memorandum by General Marshall to President Truman', 13 March 1946; 'General Marshall to Mr. Walter S. Robertson', 31 May 1946; all three in *Foreign Relations of the United States: Diplomatic Papers, 1945, China, 1946*, vol. 9, docs 236, 345 and 492.

26 'President Truman to President Chiang Kai-shek', 10 Aug. 1946, in *United States Relations with China* (also called the China White Paper), Washington, DC: Office of Public Affairs, 1949, p. 652; Henry I. Shaw, *The United States Marines in North China, 1945–1949*, Washington, DC: US Marine Corps, 1968.

27 Ageenko, *Voennaia pomoshch SSSR v osvoboditelnoi borbe kitaiskogo naroda*, pp. 108–9; NARA, 893.00B/12-1548, 'Report Prepared by Vice Consul Culver Gleysteen Regarding the Chinese Communists', 15 Dec. 1948; see also Chang and Halliday, *Mao*, p. 297; Sheng, *Battling Western Imperialism*, pp. 156–7; Steven I. Levine, *Anvil of Victory: The Communist Revolution in Manchuria, 1945–1948*, New York: Columbia University Press, 1987, p. 178.

28 Benjamin Welles, 'Chinese Reds Stripped Kalgan', *New York Times*, 19 Oct. 1946; Dick Wilson, 'Kalgan Bruised When Reoccupied by Government', *China Weekly Review*, 2 Nov. 1946; 'American-Trained Chinese Take Reds' Big City in South Manchuria', *Atlanta Constitution*, 27 Oct. 1946.

29 GSG, 002-090300-00147-092, Cable from Fu Zuoyi, 16 Dec. 1946; NARA, RG59, CA, 570.3001, Patrick O'Connor, 'Anti-Religious Actions by Reds', 20 Jan. 1947; Waldo Drake, '"Times" Reporter Views Church Ruined by Reds', *Los Angeles Times*, 2 Jan. 1947; 'Red Massacre Charged', *New York Times*, 26 Dec. 1946; no professional historian, to my knowledge, has mentioned the massacre.

30 Zhou Libo, *The Hurricane*, Beijing: Foreign Languages Press, 1955; see also David Der-wei Wang, *The Monster that is History: History,*

Violence, and Fictional Writing in Twentieth-Century China, Berkeley: University of California Press, 2004, pp. 166–7.

31 With the exception of the reference to the 'proper party phrase', which comes from Robert W. Greene, *Calvary in China*, New York: Putnam, 1953, pp. 77–9, all the quotations and details from Yuanbao in the following paragraphs are from interviews in the documentary directed by Chen Xiaoqing, *Baofeng zhouyu* (The hurricane), China Memo Films, 2006, which explores in excruciating detail the vast gap between the novel and what actually happened in Yuanbao; on the absence of revolutionary fervour in Manchuria, see Levine, *Anvil of Victory*, p. 199; on land reform as a political device to overthrow traditional elites one should also read the many essays by Qin Hui, for instance Bian Wu (Qin Hui), 'Gongshe zhi mi: Nongye jituanhua de zai renshi' (The myth of the commune: Revisiting the collectivisation of agriculture), *Ershiyi shiji*, no. 48 (Aug. 1998), pp. 22–36, and Qin Hui, *Nongmin Zhongguo: Lishi fansi yu xianshi xuanze* (Peasant China: Historical reflections and realistic choices), Zhengzhou: Henan renmin chubanshe, 2003.

32 The reference to Siping is in Liang Surong, *Da shi da fei: Liang Surong huiyilu* (Memoirs of Liang Su-yung), Taipei: Tianxia wenhua, 1995, p. 63.

33 Zhang Yongdong, *Yijiusijiu nianhou Zhongguo nongcun zhidu biange shi* (A history of changes in the Chinese countryside after 1949), Taipei: Ziyou wenhua chubanshe, 2008, pp. 23–4; Luo Pinghan, *Tudi gaige yundong shi* (A history of the campaign for land reform), Fuzhou: Fujian renmin chubanshe, 2005, pp. 182–4.

34 Report by Liu Shaoqi at the National Conference on Land Reform, Aug. 1947, Hebei Provincial Archives, 572-1-35, two versions of the same speech in documents 1 and 3, pp. 33–4; Gao Wangling and Liu Yang, 'On a Slippery Roof: Chinese Farmers and the Complex Agenda of Land Reform', *Études rurales*, no. 179 (June 2007), pp. 19–34.

35 'Report on China', *Time*, 13 Oct. 1947; NARA, RG59, CA 306.001, 'China: Background', 1947; Ch'en, *The Storm Clouds Clear over China*, p. xii.

36 One of the very first foreigners to report on the massacre was John W. Powell, 'Taiwan's Blood Bath', *China Weekly Review*, 29 March 1947, who put the death toll at 5,000; George H. Kerr, *Formosa Betrayed*, Boston, MA: Houghton Mifflin, 1965, provided an estimate of 10,000; Wedemeyer was sent on a fact-finding mission in the summer of 1947 and mentioned the massacre in his report; see Arnold A. Offner, *Another Such Victory: President Truman and*

the Cold War, 1945–1953, Stanford, CA: Stanford University Press, 2002, p. 327.

37 Freda Utley, *The China Story*, Chicago, IL: Henry Regnery, 1951, ch. 2; James Fitzgerald, *Abandoning an Ally: The Real Story behind 70 Million Killed in China and America's 'Forgotten War'*, self-published, 2016, p. 320.

38 Carsun Chang, *The Third Force in China*, New York: Bookman Associates, 1952, p. 172; Taylor, *The Generalissimo*, p. 358; Utley, *The China Story*, ch. 2; Truman quotation in Offner, *Another Such Victory*, p. 326.

39 Harold M. Tanner, *Where Chiang Kai-shek Lost China: The Liao-Shen Campaign*, Bloomington: Indiana University Press, 2015, pp. 89–96; John Roderick, 'Chiang Forces Badly Hit at Szepingkai', *Washington Post*, 3 July 1947.

40 'Reds in China Take Rail Town near Key Port', *New York Herald Tribune*, 19 June 1947; 'Chinese Reds are Forced out of Szepingkai', *New York Herald Tribune*, 28 June 1947.

41 Tanner, *Where Chiang Kai-shek Lost China*, pp. 89–96; Taylor, *The Generalissimo*, pp. 378–9.

42 'Worse & Worse', *Time*, 26 Jan. 1948.

43 NARA, 893.00B/4-1248, John M. Cabot, 'Communist Regime at Yingkow', 12 April 1948; NARA, 893.00B/4-2748, Edmund Clubb, Report on Conditions in Manchuria, 27 April 1948.

44 Tanner, *Where Chiang Kai-shek Lost China*, p. 115.

45 Zhang, *Xuebai xuehong*, p. 441.

46 'Northern Theater', *Time*, 2 June 1947.

47 GSG, 002-090300-00032-191, Cable on Changchun, 22 June 1948; GSG, 002-080200-00330-042, Cable by Li Keting to Chiang Kai-shek, 11 June 1948.

48 GSG, 002-060100-00240-012, Directive from Chiang Kai-shek, 12 June 1948; Fred Gruin, '30,000,000 Uprooted Ones', *Time*, 26 July 1948.

49 Zhang, *Xuebai xuehong*, p. 469.

50 Wang Junru interviewed by Andrew Jacobs, 'China is Wordless on Traumas of Communists' Rise', *New York Times*, 1 Oct. 2009.

51 GSG, 002-080200-00331-025, Cable from Li Keting, 24 June 1948; GSG, 002-090300-00188-346, Cable from Li Keting, 14 Aug. 1948; Duan Kewen, *Zhanfan zishu* (Autobiography of a war criminal), Taipei: Shijie ribaoshe, 1976, pp. 3–4.

52 GSG, 002-020400-00016-104, Cable to Chiang Kai-shek, 26 Aug. 1948; GSG, 002-080200-00426-044, Order from Chiang Kai-shek to Zheng Dongguo, 17 Aug. 1948; 'Time for a Visit?', *Time*, 1 Nov.

1948; Henry R. Lieberman, 'Changchun Left to Reds by Chinese', *New York Times*, 7 Oct. 1949.

53 Zheng Dongguo, *Wo de rongma shengya: Zheng Dongguo huiyilu* (Reminiscences of Zheng Dongguo), Beijing: Tuanjie chubanshe, 1992, ch. 7; Duan, *Zhanfan zishu*, p. 5; Wang Daheng, *Wo de bange shiji* (The first half-century of my life), online publication, Qingpingguo dianzi tushu xilie, pp. 7–8.

54 Zhang, *Xuebai xuehong*, p. 467; 'Time for a Visit?', *Time*, 1 Nov. 1948.

55 'Sick Cities', *Time*, 21 June 1948; Frederick Gruin, '30,000,000 Uprooted Ones', *Time*, 26 July 1948.

56 '300,000 Starving in Mukden's Siege', *New York Times*, 2 July 1948; Seymour Topping, *Journey between Two Chinas*, New York: Harper & Row, 1972, p. 312.

57 Taylor, *The Generalissimo*, pp. 385–9.

58 Doak Barnett, letter no. 25, 'Communist Siege at Peiping', 1 Feb. 1949, Institute of Current World Affairs; 'One-Way Street', *Time*, 27 Dec. 1948.

59 Doak Barnett, letter no. 25, 'Communist Siege at Peiping', 1 Feb. 1949, Institute of Current World Affairs.

60 Taylor, *The Generalissimo*, p. 396; Chang and Halliday, *Mao*, pp. 308–9.

61 Derk Bodde, *Peking Diary: A Year of Revolution*, New York: Henry Schuman, 1950, pp. 100–1; Doak Barnett, letter no. 25, 'Communist Siege at Peiping', 1 Feb. 1949, Institute of Current World Affairs; 'Defeat', *Time*, 7 Feb. 1949; Odd Arne Westad, *Decisive Encounters: The Chinese Civil War, 1946–1950*, Stanford, CA: Stanford University Press, 2003, p. 259; Bo Yibo, *Ruogan zhongda shijian yu juece de huigu* (Recollections of several important decisions and events), Beijing: Zhonggong zongyang dangxiao chubanshe, 1997, vol. 1, pp. 160–1.

62 NARA, 893.00B/4-2549, Edmund Clubb, Report on Conditions in the Countryside, 27 April 1949; Eugene Lai, 'Chinese Work Dawn to Dusk to Pay Red Tax', *Chicago Daily Tribune*, 13 Aug. 1948.

63 Eugene Lai managed to visit several areas under Communist control and published a series of articles in the *Chicago Daily Tribune*, dated 10, 11, 12 and 13 Aug. 1948.

64 NARA, RG 59, OIR Report 4387, 'Major Factors Controlling the Size of the Chinese Communist Armies', 25 June 1947.

65 GSG, 002-090300-00191-211, 002-090300-00191-283 and 002-090300-00193-122, Cables by Yan Xishan, 9 and 10 Oct., 13 Nov. 1948; GSG, 005-010205-00109-001, Conversation between Chiang Kai-shek and Maxwell Taylor, 27 Sept. 1954, p. 12.

66 'To Defend the Yangtze', *Time*, 20 Dec. 1948; Roy Rowan, *Chasing the Dragon: A Veteran Journalist's Firsthand Account of the 1946–9 Chinese Revolution*, Guilford, CT: Lyons Press, 2004, p. 146.
67 Frederick Gruin, 'Eighteen Levels Down', *Time*, 20 Dec. 1948; 'Crescendo', *Time*, 22 Nov. 1948; 'Or Cut Bait', *Time*, 29 Nov. 1948; Su Yu, *Su Yu junshi wenji* (Collected military writings by Su Yu), Beijing: Jiefangjun chubanshe, 1989, p. 455, quoted in Luo Pinghan, *Dangshi xijie* (Details in the history of the Communist Party), Beijing: Renmin chubanshe, 2011, p. 150.
68 Long Yingtai, *Da jiang da hai 1949* (Big river, big sea: Untold stories of 1949), Hong Kong: Tiandi tushu youxian gongsi, 2009, p. 221; see also Henry Lieberman, 'The "Human Sea" that Mao Commands', *New York Times*, 10 Dec. 1950; Lieberman spent twelve years in China, covered the civil war and was critical of both sides.
69 Topping, *Journey between Two Chinas*, p. 43.
70 'Swift Disaster', *Time*, 2 May 1949; Rowan, *Chasing the Dragon*, p. 201; 'The Weary Wait', *Time*, 23 May 1949; 'A Landmark Passes', *Time*, 25 June 1949.
71 Dwight Martin, 'Exile in Canton', *Time*, 17 April 1949; 'Next: Chungking', *Time*, 24 Oct. 1949.
72 Doak Barnett, letter no. 20, 'Kansu Province, Northwest China', 8 Oct. 1948, Institute of Current World Affairs.
73 On the history of Xinjiang, see Andrew D. W. Forbes, *Warlords and Muslims in Chinese Central Asia: A Political History of Republican Sinkiang, 1911–1949*, Cambridge: Cambridge University Press, 1986; the trade agreement concluded between Peng Dehuai and the Soviets, dated 5 Jan. 1950, is in RGASPI, 82-2-1242, pp. 20–39, quoted in Frank Dikötter, *The Tragedy of Liberation: A History of the Chinese Revolution, 1945–1957*, London and New York: Bloomsbury, 2013, p. 301; Russian troops mentioned in PRO, FO 371/92207, O. C. Ellis, Report from Tihwa, 15 Nov. 1950.
74 'Best Nationalist Troops Leaving China Mainland', *New York Herald Tribune*, 5 Dec. 1949.

Select Bibliography

ARCHIVES

GSG – Guoshiguan (Academia Historica), Taipei
    Chiang Kai-shek Archives (002)
        - Draft Summary of Daily Events (060100)
        - Special Telegrams (090105)
        - Special Documents (080200)
        - Intelligence on Communists (020400)
HIA – Hoover Institution Library and Archives, Palo Alto
    Allman (Norwood F.) Papers 1929–1987
    Chiang Kai-shek Diaries
    Hanwell (Norman David) Papers 1928–1944
    Huston (Jay C.) Papers 1917–1931
    Romerstein (Herbert) Collection 1864–2011
    Soong, T. V. (Tzu-wen) Papers 1920–1999
    Wedemeyer (Albert C.) Papers 1897–1988
MAE – Ministère des Affaires Etrangères, Nantes
    513/PO, Chine: Postes Diplomatiques et Consulaires
NARA – National Archives and Records Administration, Washington DC
    RG 59, Records of the Department of State
        - Internal Affairs of China (Decimal File 893)
        - Division of Chinese Affairs (CA)
        - Office of Intelligence Research (OIR)
        - Marshall Mission to China (Lot File 54 D 270)
    RG 165, Records of the War Department: Military Intelligence Division (MID)
    RG 263, Records of the Central Intelligence Agency: Shanghai Municipal Police (SMP)

RG 226, Records of the Office of Strategic Services: Research and Analysis Branch (R&A)
PRO – Public Records Office (The National Archives), London
    FO 371, Foreign Office: General Correspondence
    FO 676, Foreign Office: Various Embassies and Legations
    CO 129, Colonial Office: Hong Kong
    WO 208, War Office: Directorate of Military Operations and Intelligence

PUBLISHED ARCHIVES WITH RESTRICTED CIRCULATION

CA – Central Archives, Beijing
    Dongbei diqu geming lishi wenjian huiji, 70 vols (Dongbei)
    Eyuwan suqu geming lishi wenjian huiji, 6 vols (Eyuwan)
    Fujian geming lishi wenjian huiji, 21 vols (Fujian)
    Guangdong diqu geming lishi wenjian huiji, 68 vols (Guangdong)
    Hebei geming lishi wenjian huiji, 24 vols (Hebei)
    Henan geming lishi wenjian huiji, 11 vols (Henan)
    Hubei geming lishi wenjian huiji, 12 vols (Hubei)
    Hunan geming lishi wenjian huiji, 11 vols (Hunan)
    Jiangsu geming lishi wenjian huiji, 28 vols (Jiangsu)
    Jiangxi geming lishi wenjian huiji, 10 vols (Jiangxi)
    Nei Menggu geming lishi wenjian huiji, 1 vol. (Nei Menggu)
    Shaanxi geming lishi wenjian huiji, 22 vols (Shaanxi)
    Shandong geming lishi wenjian huiji, 8 vols (Shandong)
    Shanghai geming lishi wenjian huiji, 17 vols (Shanghai)
    Sichuan geming lishi wenjian huiji, 14 vols (Sichuan)
    Xiang'exi suqu geming lishi wenjian huiji, 4 vols (Xiang'exi)
    Zhejiang geming lishi wenjian huiji, 9 vols (Zhejiang)
    Zhongyang Xibeiju geming lishi wenjian huiji, 7 vols (Xibeiju)

PUBLISHED WORKS

Abend, Hallett, *My Life in China*, New York: Harcourt, Brace, 1943
Ageenko, K. P., *Voennaia pomoshch SSSR v osvoboditelnoi borbe kitaiskogo naroda* (Military help from the Soviet Union during the war of liberation), Moscow: Voenizdat, 1975
Alber, Charles, *Enduring the Revolution: Ding Ling and the Politics of Literature in Guomindang China*, London: Praeger, 2002

Andress, David, *The Terror: The Merciless War for Freedom in Revolutionary France*, New York: Farrar, Straus & Giroux, 2005
Banac, Ivo (ed.), *The Diary of Georgi Dimitrov, 1933–1949*, New Haven, CT: Yale University Press, 2003
Band, Claire and William Band, *Dragon Fangs: Two Years with Chinese Guerrillas*, London: George Allen & Unwin, 1947
Baxter, Christopher, 'The Secret Intelligence Service and China: The Case of Hilaire Noulens, 1923–1932', in Christopher Baxter et al. (eds), *Britain in Global Politics: From Gladstone to Churchill*, London: Palgrave, 2013, pp. 132–52
Benton, Gregor, 'Introduction to "The Yenan Literary Opposition"', *New Left Review*, no. 92 (July–Aug. 1975), pp. 93–6
— *Mountain Fires: The Red Army's Three-Year War in South China, 1934–1938*, Berkeley, CA: University of California Press, 1992
— *New Fourth Army: Communist Resistance along the Yangtze and the Huai, 1938–1941*, Berkeley, CA: California University Press, 1999
— (ed.), *Prophets Unarmed: Trotskyists in Revolution, War, Jail, and the Return from Limbo*, Leiden: E. J. Brill, 2015
— 'The South Anhui Incident', *Journal of Asian Studies*, 45, no. 4 (Aug. 1986), pp. 681–720
— and Alan Hunter, *Wild Lily, Prairie Fire: China's Road to Democracy, Yan'an to Tian'anmen, 1942–1989*, Princeton, NJ: Princeton University Press, 1995
Bergère, Marie-Claire, *Sun Yat-sen*, Stanford, CA: Stanford University Press, 1998
Bian Wu (Qin Hui), 'Gongshe zhi mi: Nongye jituanhua de zai renshi' (The myth of the commune: Revisiting the collectivisation of agriculture), *Ershiyi shiji*, no. 48 (Aug. 1998), pp. 22–36
Bo Yibo, *Ruogan zhongda shijian yu juece de huigu* (Recollections of several important decisions and events), Beijing: Zhonggong zongyang dangxiao chubanshe, 1997
Bodde, Derk, *Peking Diary: A Year of Revolution*, New York: Henry Schuman, 1950
Bonnard, Abel, *In China*, New York: E. P. Dutton, 1927
Booker, Edna Lee, *News is my Job: A Correspondent in War-torn China*, New York: Macmillan, 1940
Bosshardt, Rudolf A., *The Restraining Hand: Captivity for Christ in China*, London: Hodder & Stoughton, 1936
Braisted, William R., *Diplomats in Blue: New Perspectives on Maritime History and Nautical Archaeology*, Gainesville, FL: University Press of Florida, 2009

Braun, Otto, *A Comintern Agent in China, 1932–1939*, London: Hurst, 1982
Buber-Neumann, Margarete, *Von Potsdam nach Moskau*, Munich: Ullstein-Taschenbuchverlag, 2002
Buck, John L., *Land Utilization in China*, Nanjing: University of Nanking, 1937
Cadart, Claude, *Mémoires de Peng Shuzhi: L'envol du communisme en Chine*, Paris: Gallimard, 1983
Calkins, Laura M., 'Recapturing an Urban Identity: Chinese Communists and the Commune at Shantou, 1927', *Studies on Asia*, series IV, vol. 1, no. 2 (Summer 2011), pp. 35–73
Cao Boyi [Tsao Po-i], *Jiangxi suwei'ai zhi jianli jiqi bengkui (1931–1934)* (Rise and fall of the Chinese soviet in Jiangxi, 1931–1934), Taipei: Guoli zhengzhi daxue dongya yanjiusuo, 1969
Carlson, Evans F., *Evans F. Carlson on China at War, 1937–1941*, Beijing: Foreign Languages Press, 2004
—, *Twin Stars of China*, New York: Dodd, Mead, 1940
Cassel, Pär, *Grounds of Judgment*, New York: Oxford University Press, 2012
Chan, Gordon Y. M., 'The Communists in Rural Guangdong, 1928–1936', *Journal of the Royal Asiatic Society*, 13, no. 1 (April 2003), pp. 77–97
Chan Lau, Kit-ching, *China, Britain and Hong Kong, 1895–1945*, Hong Kong: Chinese University Press, 1990
Chang, Carsun, *The Third Force in China*, New York: Bookman Associates, 1952
Chang Jui-te, 'Technology Transfer in Modern China: The Case of Railway Enterprise (1876–1937)', *Modern Asian Studies*, 27, no. 2 (1993), pp. 281–96
Chang, Jung and Jon Halliday, *Mao: The Unknown Story*, London: Jonathan Cape, 2005
Chang Kuo-t'ao, *The Rise of the Communist Party, 1928–1938*, Lawrence, KS: University of Kansas Press, 1972
Chen Xiaobai, *Hailufeng chihuo ji* (Account of the red terror in Hailufeng), Hailufeng: Hailufeng tongxianghui, 1932
Chen Yaohuang, 'Zhonggong Xiang'exi suqu de fazhan ji qi neibu zhengsu' (The development and purge of the Hunan and West Hubei Soviet), *Guoshiguan xueshu jikan*, no. 15 (2008), pp. 35–75
Ch'en Li-fu, *The Storm Clouds Clear over China: The Memoir of Ch'en Li-fu, 1900–1993*, Stanford, CA: Stanford University Press, 1994
Ch'en Yung-fa, 'The Blooming Poppy under the Red Sun: The Yan'an Way and the Opium Trade', in Tony Saich and Hans van de Ven (eds),

New Perspectives on the Chinese Communist Revolution, Armonk, NY: M. E. Sharpe, 1995, pp. 263–98
—, 'The Futian Incident and the Anti-Bolshevik League: The "Terror" in the CCP Revolution', *Republican China*, 19, no. 2 (April 1994), pp. 1–51
—, *Zhongguo gongchan geming qishinian* (Seventy years of the Chinese revolution), Taipei: Lianjing chuban shiye gongsi, 2nd edn, 2001
Cheng, Victor Shiu Chiang, 'Imagining China's Madrid in Manchuria: The Communist Military Strategy at the Onset of the Chinese Civil War, 1945–1946', *Modern China*, 31, no. 1 (Jan. 2005), pp. 72–114
Cherepanov, A. I., *Zapiski voennovo sovetnika v Kitae* (Notes of a Soviet adviser in China), Moscow: Nauka, 1964
Chiang Kai-shek, *China's Destiny*, New York: Roy Publishers, 1947
—, *Soviet Russia in China: A Summing Up at Seventy*, New York: Farrar, Straus & Cudahy, 1958
Chow Tse-tsung, *The May 4th Movement: Intellectual Revolution in Modern China*, Cambridge, MA: Harvard University Press, 1960
Chuikov, Vasili, *Mission to China: Memoirs of a Soviet Military Adviser to Chiang Kaishek*, Norwalk, CT: EastBridge Books, 2003
Cohen, Arthur A., *The Communism of Mao Tse-tung*, Chicago, IL: University of Chicago Press, 1964
Coox, Alvin D., 'L'Affaire Lyushkov: Anatomy of a Defector', *Soviet Studies*, 19, no. 3 (Jan. 1968), pp. 405–20
—, *Nomonhan: Japan against Russia 1939*, Stanford, CA: Stanford University Press, 1988
Cunha, Carlos A., *The Portuguese Communist Party's Strategy for Power: 1921–1986*, New York and London: Garland, 1992
Dai Qing, *Wang Shiwei and 'Wild Lilies': Rectification and Purges in the Chinese Communist Party, 1942–1944*, Armonk, NY: M. E. Sharpe, 1994
Dallin, Alexander and F. I. Firsov, *Dimitrov and Stalin, 1934–1943: Letters from the Soviet Archives*, New Haven, CT: Yale University Press, 2000
de Jaegher, Raymond J., *The Enemy Within: An Eyewitness Account of the Communist Conquest of China*, Garden City, NY: Doubleday, 1952
Deane, John R., *The Strange Alliance: The Story of our Efforts at Wartime Cooperation with Russia*, New York: Viking Press, 1947
Dennis, A. L. P., 'The Origin of the "Open Door"', *Current History*, 27, no. 5 (Feb. 1928), pp. 651–3
Department of Overseas Trade, *Economic Conditions in China to September 1st, 1929*, London: His Majesty's Stationery Office, 1930

—, *Trade and Economic Conditions in China, 1931–33*, London: His Majesty's Stationery Office, 1933
Dikötter, Frank, *The Age of Openness: China before Mao*, London: Hurst, and Berkeley, CA: University of California Press, 2008
—, *Crime, Punishment and the Prison in Modern China*, New York: Columbia University Press, 2002
—, *The Tragedy of Liberation: A History of the Chinese Revolution, 1945–1957*, London and New York: Bloomsbury, 2013
Dimitrov, Georgi, *Selected Works*, Sofia: Sofia Press, 1972
Duan Kewen, *Zhanfan zishu* (Autobiography of a war criminal), Taipei: Shijie ribaoshe, 1976
Elleman, Bruce A., *Modern Chinese Warfare, 1798–1989*, London: Routledge, 2001
—, *Wilson and China: A Revised History of the Shandong Question*, London: Routledge, 2002
Esherick, Joseph, *Accidental Holy Land: The Communist Revolution in Northwest China*, Berkeley, CA: University of California Press, 2022
Farmer, Rhodes, *Shanghai Harvest: A Diary of Three Years in the China War*, London: Museum Press, 1945
Farnsworth, Robert M., *From Vagabond to Journalist: Edgar Snow in Asia, 1928–1941*, Columbia, MO: University of Missouri Press, 1996
Farrell, Brian P., 'Twilight in China: Great Powers and the Defence of Shanghai, 1925–1937', in Brian P. Farrell, S. R. Joey Long and David J. Ulbrich (eds), *From Far East to Asia Pacific: Great Powers and Grand Strategy 1900–1954*, Berlin: Walter De Gruyter, 2022, pp. 113–50
Feigon, Lee, *Mao: A Reinterpretation*, Chicago, IL: Ivan R. Dee, 2002
Fenby, Jonathan, *Generalissimo: Chiang Kai-shek and the China He Lost*, London: The Free Press, 2003
—, *Modern China: The Fall and Rise of a Great Power, 1850 to the Present*, New York: Ecco, 2008
Fisher, Harold H., *The Communist Revolution: An Outline of Strategy and Tactics*, Stanford, CA: Stanford University Press, 1955
Fitzgerald, James, *Abandoning an Ally: The Real Story behind 70 Million Killed in China and America's 'Forgotten War'*, self-published, 2016
Fleming, Peter, *One's Company: A Journey to China*, New York: Charles Scribner's Sons, 1934
Fletcher, Joseph, 'The Heyday of the Ch'ing Order in Mongolia, Sinkiang and Tibet', in Dennis Twitchett and John K. Fairbank (eds), *The Cambridge History of China*, Cambridge: Cambridge University Press, 1978, vol. 10, part 1, pp. 375–85

Flory, Harriette, 'The Arcos Raid and the Rupture of Anglo-Soviet Relations', *Journal of Contemporary History*, 12, no. 4 (Oct. 1977), pp. 707-23
Forbes, Andrew D. W., *Warlords and Muslims in Chinese Central Asia: A Political History of Republican Sinkiang, 1911-1949*, Cambridge: Cambridge University Press, 1986
Foreign Relations of the United States, Washington: Government Printing Office, 1943
Franck, Harry A., *Roving through Southern China*, New York: The Century Co., 1925
Galbiati, Fernando, *P'eng P'ai and the Hai-Lu-Feng Soviet*, Stanford, CA: Stanford University Press, 1985
Gansu sheng dang'anguan (eds), *Gansu sheng dang'anguan zhinan* (Guide to the Gansu provincial archives), Lanzhou: Gansu renmin chubanshe, 1997
Gao Hua, *How the Red Sun Rose: The Origins and Development of the Rectification Movement*, Hong Kong: Chinese University Press, 2000
Gao Wangling and Liu Yang, 'On a Slippery Roof: Chinese Farmers and the Complex Agenda of Land Reform', *Études rurales*, no. 179 (June 2007), pp. 19-34
Gao Wangling, *Zudian guanxi xinlun: Dizhu, nongmin he dizu* (A new perspective on tenure relationships: Landlords, peasants and rent), Shanghai: Shanghai shudian chubanshe, 2005
Gao Wenqian, *Zhou Enlai: The Last Perfect Revolutionary*, New York: PublicAffairs, 2007
Garver, John W., *Chinese-Soviet Relations, 1937-1945: The Diplomacy of Chinese Nationalism*, Oxford: Oxford University Press, 1988
George, Brian T., 'The State Department and Sun Yat-Sen: American Policy and the Revolutionary Disintegration of China, 1920-1924', *Pacific Historical Review*, 46, no. 3 (Aug. 1977), pp. 387-408
Glantz, David M., *The Soviet Strategic Offensive in Manchuria, 1945: 'August Storm'*, London: Frank Cass, 2003
Gordon, Joseph, 'China Wins Tariff Independence', *Current History*, 34, no. 4 (July 1931), p. 549
Gray, Jack, *Rebellions and Revolutions: China from the 1800s to 2000*, Oxford: Oxford University Press, 1990
Greene, Robert W., *Calvary in China*, New York: Putnam, 1953
Greene, Ruth Altman, *Hsiang-Ya Journal*, Hamden, CT: Archon Books, 1977
Guillermaz, Jacques, *Histoire du Parti Communiste Chinois*, Paris: Payot, 1975

Han Qitong and Nan Zhongwan, *Huangfanqu de sunhai yu shanhou jiuji* (Damage, rehabilitation and relief in the Yellow River's flooded areas), Shanghai: Xingzhengyuan shanhou jiuji zongshu, 1948
Harmsen, Peter, *Shanghai 1937: Stalingrad on the Yangtze*, Oxford: Casemate, 2013
—, *Storm Clouds over the Pacific, 1931–1941*, Oxford: Casemate, 2018
Harrison, James P., 'The Li Li-San Line and the CCP in 1930 (Part 1)', *China Quarterly*, no. 14 (June 1963), pp. 178–94
Hart, John, *The Making of an Army 'Old China Hand'*, Berkeley, CA: Institute of East Asian Studies, University of California, 1985
He Xiya, *Zhongguo daofei wenti ji yanjiu* (A Study of the Bandit Problem in China), Hong Kong, 1925
Hodgson, John H., 'The Finnish Communist Party', *Slavic Review*, 29, no. 1 (March 1970), pp. 70–85
How, Julie Lien-ying, 'Soviet Advisors with the Kuominchun, 1925–1926: A Documentary Study', *Chinese Studies in History*, 19, nos 1–2 (Winter 1985), pp. 7–103
Hsiao Tso-liang, *The Land Revolution in China, 1930–1934: A Study of Documents*, Seattle, WA: University of Washington Press, 1969
Hsiung, S. I., *The Life of Chiang Kai-shek*, London: Peter Davies, 1948
Hsü, King-yi, 'Agrarian Policies of the Chinese Soviet Republic, 1931–1934', doctoral dissertation, Indiana University, 1971
Huang Kecheng, 'Huiyi Xiangnan baodong' (Recalling the insurrection in south Hunan), *Jindai lishi*, 1980, no. 4, pp. 1–14
Huang, Philip C. C., Lynda Schaefer Bell and Kathy Le Mons Walker, *Chinese Communists and Rural Society, 1927–1934*, Berkeley, CA: Center for Chinese Studies, University of California, 1978
Ishikawa Yoshihiro, *The Formation of the Chinese Communist Party*, New York: Columbia University Press, 2013
Itoh, Mayumi, *The Making of China's War with Japan: Zhou Enlai and Zhang Xueliang*, London: Palgrave Macmillan, 2016
Jacobs, Dan, *Borodin: Stalin's Man in China from Moscow*, Cambridge, MA: Harvard University Press, 1981
Jiangxi sheng dang'anguan (eds), *Zhongyang geming genjudi shiliao xuanbian* (Selection of historical materials on the central revolutionary base areas), Nanchang: Jiangxi renmin chubanshe, 1982
Jin Chongji et al. (eds), *Liu Shaoqi zhuan* (A biography of Liu Shaoqi), Beijing: Zhongyang wenxian chubanshe, 2008
—, *Zhou Enlai zhuan (1898–1976)* (A biography of Zhou Enlai, 1898–1976), Beijing: Zhongyang wenxian chubanshe, 2009
Jones, Robert H., *The Roads to Russia: United States Lend-Lease to the Soviet Union*, Norman, OK: University of Oklahoma Press, 1969

Jordan, Donald A., *The Northern Expedition: China's National Revolution of 1926–1928*, Honolulu, HI: University Press of Hawaii, 1976

Judd, Walter, *What is the Truth about China?*, Washington, DC: U.S. Government Printing Office, 1945

Kataoka, Tetsuya, *Resistance and Revolution in China: The Communists and the Second United Front*, Berkeley, CA: University of California Press, 1974

Kerr, George H., *Formosa Betrayed*, Boston, MA: Houghton Mifflin, 1965

Kryukov, M. V., 'Vokrug "Pervoi Deklaratsii Karakhana" po Kitaiskomu voprosu, 1919', *Novaia i noveishaia istoriia*, no. 5 (2000), pp. 30–43

Ladany, Laszlo, *The Communist Party of China and Marxism, 1921–1985: A Self-Portrait*, Stanford, CA: Hoover Institution Press, 1988

Lai, Sherman Xiaogang, 'A War within a War: The Road to the New Fourth Army Incident in January 1941', *Journal of Chinese Military History*, 2, no. 1 (Jan. 2013), pp. 1–27

Laqueur, Walter, *Guerrilla Warfare: A Historical and Critical Study*, London: Routledge, 1997

Ledovskii, Andrei M. et al. (eds), *Russko-kitaiskie otnosheniia v XX veke: Materialy i dokumenty*, Moscow: Nauka, 1995–2010, 5 vols

Levine, Steven I., *Anvil of Victory: The Communist Revolution in Manchuria, 1945–1948*, New York: Columbia University Press, 1987

Li Jihua, 'Dui Mao Zedong geren chongbai de zisheng' (The propagation of Mao's cult of personality), *Yanhuang chunqiu*, no. 3 (March 2010), pp. 40–5

Li, Michell, 'Inflation in Eastern China during the Second Sino-Japanese War', *Journal of Economics Library*, 6, no. 4 (Dec. 2019), pp. 338–53

Liang Surong, *Da shi da fei: Liang Surong huiyilu* (Memoirs of Liang Su-yung), Taipei: Tianxia wenhua, 1995

Lih, Lars T. et al. (eds), *Stalin's Letters to Molotov*, New Haven, CT: Yale University Press, 1995

Litten, Frederick S., 'The Myth of the "Turning-Point": Towards a New Understanding of the Long March', *Bochumer Jahrbuch zur Ostasienforschung*, no. 25 (2001), pp. 2–44

—, 'The Noulens Affair', *China Quarterly*, no. 138 (June 1994), pp. 492–512

Litten, Freddy, 'Otto Brauns frühes Wirken in China (1932–1935)', *Working Papers*, no. 124, Munich: Osteuropa-Institut, 1988

Liu, F. F., *A Military History of Modern China*, Princeton, NJ: Princeton University Press, 1956

Liu Jianyi, 'The Origins of the Chinese Communist Party and the Role Played by Soviet Russia and the Comintern', doctoral dissertation, York University, 2000

Liu Qingjun, 'Reinterpreting the Chinese Revolution: The Balance between Radical and Moderate Approaches, 1937–1945', *Modern China*, 48, no. 2 (March 2022), pp. 1–35

Liu Tong, *Beishang: Dang zhongyang yu Zhang Guotao douzheng jishi* (A record of the struggle between the Central Committee and Zhang Guotao), Nanning: Guangxi renmin chubanshe, 2004

Long Huanqi, 'Mao Zemin ban Zhonghua wukuang gongsi', in Shu Long (ed.), *Mao Zemin*, Beijing: Junshi kexue chubanshe, 1996, pp. 72–7

Long Yingtai, *Da jiang da hai 1949* (Big river, big sea: Untold stories of 1949), Hong Kong: Tiandi tushu youxian gongsi, 2009

Lü Fangshang (ed.), *Jiang Zhongzheng nianpu changbian*, Taipei: Guoshiguan, 2014–15, 12 vols

Luo Pinghan, *Tudi gaige yundong shi* (A history of the campaign for land reform), Fuzhou: Fujian renmin chubanshe, 2005

Luxemburg, Rosa, *The Essential Rosa Luxemburg*, Chicago, IL: Haymarket Books, 2007

MacKinnon, Stephen R., *Wuhan, 1938: War, Refugees, and the Making of Modern China*, Berkeley, CA: University of California Press, 2008

Misselwitz, H. R., *The Dragon Stirs*, New York: Harbinger House, 1941

Mitarevsky, N., *World Wide Soviet Plots*, Tianjin: Tientsin Press, 1927

Neville, Peter, *Mussolini*, Abingdon: Routledge, 2015

Newman, Robert P., *Owen Lattimore and the 'Loss' of China*, Berkeley, CA: University of California Press, 1992

Nie Rongzhen, *Nie Rongzhen huiyilu* (Memoirs of Nie Rongzhen), Beijing: Jiefangjun chubanshe, 2007

Offner, Arnold A., *Another Such Victory: President Truman and the Cold War, 1945–1953*, Stanford, CA: Stanford University Press, 2002

Pakula, Hannah, *The Last Empress: Madame Chiang Kai-shek and the Birth of Modern China*, New York: Simon & Schuster, 2009

Pang Yong-Pil, 'Peng Pai from Landlord to Revolutionary', *Modern China*, 1, no. 3 (July 1975), pp. 297–322

Pantsov, Alexander V., *Victorious in Defeat: The Life and Times of Chiang Kai-shek, China, 1887–1975*, New Haven, CT: Yale University Press, 2023

Payne, Robert, *Chinese Diaries: 1941–1946*, New York: Weybright & Talley, 1970

Peng Dehuai, *Memoirs of a Chinese Marshal*, Beijing: Foreign Languages Press, 1984

Powell, John B., *My Twenty-Five Years in China*, New York: The Macmillan Company, 1945

Qin Hui, *Nongmin Zhongguo: Lishi fansi yu xianshi xuanze* (Peasant China: Historical reflections and realistic choices), Zhengzhou: Henan renmin chubanshe, 2003

Qing Simei, 'American Visions of Democracy and the Marshall Mission to China', in Hongshan Li and Zhaohui Hong (eds), *Image, Perception, and the Making of U.S.–China Relations*, Lanham, MD: University Press of America, 1998, pp. 257–312

Ransome, Arthur, *The Chinese Puzzle*, London: George Allen & Unwin, 1927

Rowan, Roy, *Chasing the Dragon: A Veteran Journalist's Firsthand Account of the 1946–9 Chinese Revolution*, Guilford, CT: Lyons Press, 2004

Rowe, William T., *Crimson Rain: Seven Centuries of Violence in a Chinese County*, Stanford, CA: Stanford University Press, 2007

Roy, M. N., *Revolution and Counterrevolution in China*, Delhi: Ajanta Books International, 1946

Royal Institute of International Affairs, 'World Communism in Figures', *The World Today*, 14, no. 5 (May 1958), pp. 213–16

Ryan, James, ' "Revolution is War": The Development of the Thought of V. I. Lenin on Violence, 1899–1907', *Slavonic and East European Review*, 89, no. 2 (April 2011), pp. 248–73

Saich, Tony, *Finding Allies and Making Revolution: The Early Years of the Chinese Communist Party*, Leiden: E. J. Brill, 2020

—, *The Origins of the First United Front in China: The Role of Sneevliet [Alias Maring]*, Leiden: E. J. Brill, 1991

— and Benjamin Yang (eds), *The Rise to Power of the Chinese Communist Party: Documents and Analysis*, London: Routledge, 2005

Saint Vincent de Paul Mission, *Annales de la Congrégation de la Mission*, Paris: Congrégation de la Mission, 1929–32

Schama, Simon, *Citizens: A Chronicle of the French Revolution*, New York: Alfred A. Knopf, 1989

Schram, Stuart R., 'Party Leader or True Ruler? Foundations and Significance of Mao Zedong's Personal Power', in Stuart R. Schram (ed.), *Foundations and Limits of State Power in China*, London: School of Oriental and African Studies, 1987, pp. 203–56

Schram, Stuart R. and Nancy J. Hodes (eds), *Mao's Road to Power: Revolutionary Writings, 1912–1949*, Armonk, NY: M. E. Sharpe, 9 vols

Seele, Earl A., *Donald of China*, New York: Harper, 1948

Selden, Mark, 'The Guerrilla Movement in Northwest China: The Origins of the Shensi–Kansu–Ninghsia Border Region (Part I)', *China Quarterly*, no. 28 (Dec. 1966), pp. 63–81

Serge, Victor and Natalia Sedova Trotsky, *The Life and Death of Leon Trotsky*, Chicago, IL: Haymarket Books, 2015

Service, Robert, *Stalin: A Biography*, Basingstoke: Macmillan, 2004

—, *Trotsky: A Biography*, Cambridge, MA: Harvard University Press, 2009

Seybolt, Peter J., 'Terror and Conformity: Counterespionage Campaigns, Rectification, and Mass Movements, 1942–1943', *Modern China*, 12, no. 1 (Jan. 1986), pp. 39–73

Shan, Patrick Fuliang, 'Insecurity, Outlawry and Social Order: Banditry in China's Heilongjiang Frontier Region, 1900–1931', *Journal of Social History*, 40, no. 1 (Autumn 2006), pp. 25–54

Shaw, Henry I., *The United States Marines in North China, 1945–1949*, Washington, DC: U.S. Marine Corps, 1968

Sheean, Vincent, *Personal History*, New York: Garden City Publishing Co., 1937

Sheng, Michael M., *Battling Western Imperialism: Mao, Stalin, and the United States*, Princeton, NJ: Princeton University Press, 1997

Shewmaker, Kenneth E., 'The American Liberal Dream: Evans F. Carlson and the Chinese Communists, 1937–1947', *Pacific Historical Review*, 38, no. 2 (May 1969), pp. 207–16

—, *Americans and Chinese Communists, 1927–1945: A Persuading Encounter*, Ithaca, NY: Cornell University Press, 1971

Shi Zhongquan, *Changzheng xing* (The Long March), Beijing: Zhonggong dangshi chubanshe, 2006

Siegel, Jennifer, *For Peace and Money: French and British Finance in the Service of Tsars and Commissars*, Oxford: Oxford University Press, 2014

Smedley, Agnes, *China Fights Back*, London: Victor Gollancz, 1938

—, *China's Red Army Marches*, London: Lawrence & Wishart, 1936

Smith, Roy C., 'Nanking, March 24, 1927', *United States Naval Institute Proceedings*, 58 (Jan. 1928), pp. 1–21

Snow, Edgar, 'Interviews with Mao Tse-tung, Communist Leader', *China Weekly Review*, 14 and 21 Nov. 1936

—, *Red Star over China*, New York: Grove Press, 1971

Stephan, John J., '"Cleansing" the Soviet Far East, 1937–1938', *Acta Slavica Iaponica*, 10 (1992), pp. 43–64

Stilwell, Joseph W., *The Stilwell Papers*, New York: William Sloane Associates, 1948

Sun Shuyun, *The Long March*, London: HarperPress, 2006
—, *Sun Zhongshan congshu* (Collected writings of Sun Yat-sen), Shanghai: Guangyi shuju, 1928
Sun Yat-sen, *Zhongguo Guomindang diyici quanguo daibiaohui xuanyan* (Manifesto of the first national congress of the Nationalist Party), Guangzhou: Xinmin yinshuguan, 1924
Tanner, Harold M., *Where Chiang Kai-shek Lost China: The Liao-Shen Campaign*, Bloomington: Indiana University Press, 2015
Taylor, Jay, *The Generalissimo: Chiang Kai-shek and the Struggle for Modern China*, Cambridge, MA: Harvard University Press, 2009
Thomson, James C., *While China Faced West: American Reformers in Nationalist China, 1928–1937*, Cambridge, MA: Harvard University Press, 1969
Timperley, Harold J., *What War Means: Japanese Terror in China*, London: Victor Gollancz, 1938
Titarenko, Mikhail L. (ed.), *Kommunisticheskii Internatsional i kitaiskaia revoliutsiia. Dokumenty i materialy*, Moscow: Nauka, 1986
—, *VKP (b), Komintern i Kitai: Dokumenty* (The CPSU, the Comintern and China: Documents), Moscow: AO 'Buklet', 1994–2007
Tong, Hollington K., 'Russian Soviet Would Befriend China', *Millard's Review of the Far East*, 5 June 1920, pp. 24–6
Topping, Seymour, *Journey between Two Chinas*, New York: Harper & Row, 1972
Tsin, Michael, *Nation, Governance, and Modernity in China: Canton, 1900–1927*, Stanford, CA: Stanford University Press, 2000
Tsou Tang, *America's Failure in China, 1941–1950*, Chicago, IL: University of Chicago Press, 1963
Utley, Freda, *The China Story*, Chicago, IL: Henry Regnery, 1951
van de Ven, Hans, *China at War: Triumph and Tragedy in the Emergence of the New China*, Cambridge, MA: Harvard University Press, 2018
Vishnyakova-Akimova, Vera Vladimirovna, *Two Years in Revolutionary China, 1925–1927*, Cambridge, MA: Harvard University Press, 1971
Vladimirov, Peter, *The Vladimirov Diaries: Yenan, China, 1942–1945*, New York: Doubleday, 1975
Waldron, Arthur, 'The Life of Mao Zedong', *Orbis*, 44, no. 4 (Autumn 2000), pp. 637–47
Wales, Nym (Helen Foster Snow), *The Chinese Communists: Sketches and Autobiographies of the Old Guard*, Westport, CT: Greenwood Publishing, 1972
Walker, Michael, *The 1929 Sino-Soviet War: The War Nobody Knew*, Lawrence, KS: University Press of Kansas, 2017

Walker, Richard J., *China under Communism: The First Five Years*, New Haven, CT: Yale University Press, 1955
Wang, David Der-wei, *The Monster That is History: History, Violence, and Fictional Writing in Twentieth-Century China*, Berkeley, CA: University of California Press, 2004
Wang Fan-sen, *Fu Ssu-nien: A Life in Chinese History and Politics*, Cambridge: Cambridge University Press, 2000
Wang Fanxi, *Memoirs of a Chinese Revolutionary, 1919–1949*, New York: Columbia University Press, 1991
Wang Hao, *Shoufu feiqu zhi tudi wenti* (Land problems in the territories recovered from the bandits), Nanjing: Zhengzhong shuju, 1935
Wang Ming, *Mao's Betrayal*, Moscow: Progress Publishers, 1979
Westad, Odd Arne, *Decisive Encounters: The Chinese Civil War, 1946–1950*, Stanford, CA: Stanford University Press, 2003
White, Theodore H. and Annalee Jacoby, *Thunder out of China*, London: Victor Gollancz, 1947
Wilbur, C. Martin, *Sun Yat-sen: Frustrated Patriot*, New York: Columbia University Press, 1976
—and Julie Lien-ying How, *Missionaries of Revolution: Soviet Advisers and Nationalist China, 1920–1927*, Cambridge, MA: Harvard University Press, 1989
Willoughby, Charles A., *Shanghai Conspiracy: The Sorge Spy Ring, Moscow, Shanghai, Tokyo, San Francisco*, New York: Dutton, 1952
Woerner, Zack, 'A Reluctant Imperialist: Justice Elias Finley Johnson and China's May 30th Movement', Senior Thesis, Bryn Mawr College, 2012
Worthing, Peter, *General He Yingqin: The Rise and Fall of Nationalist China*, Cambridge: Cambridge University Press, 2016
—, 'A Tale of Two Fronts: China's War of the Central Plains, 1930', *War in History*, 25, no. 4 (Nov. 2018), pp. 511–33
Wu Aitchen, *China and the Soviet Union*, London: Methuen, 1950
Wu Tien-wei, *The Sian Incident: A Pivotal Point in Modern History*, Ann Arbor, MI: Center for Chinese Studies, University of Michigan, 1976
Wylie, Raymond F., *The Emergence of Maoism: Mao Tse-tung, Ch'en Po-ta, and the Search for Chinese Theory, 1935–1945*, Stanford, CA: Stanford University Press, 1980
Xu Xiangqian, *Lishi de huigu* (A look back at history), Beijing: Jiefangjun chubanshe, 1987
—, *Xu Xiangqian huiyi lu* (Memoirs of Xu Xiangqian), Beijing: Jiefangjun chubanshe, 2007

Xu Youwei and Philip Billingsley, 'Behind the Scenes of the Xi'an Incident: The Case of the Lixingshe', *China Quarterly*, no. 154 (June 1998), pp. 283–307
—, 'Out of the Closet: China's Historians "Discover" Republican-Period Bandits', *Modern China*, 28, no. 4 (Oct. 2002), p. 467–99
Yan Daogang, 'Jiang Jieshi zhuidu changzheng hongjun de neimu' (The inside story of Chiang Kai-shek's pursuit of the Red Army during the Long March), *Wenshi jinghua*, no. 10 (1996), pp. 21–9
Yang, Benjamin, *From Revolution to Politics: Chinese Communists on the Long March*, London: Routledge, 1990
Yang Kuisong, 'Kangri zhanzheng baofa hou Zhongguo gongchandang duiri junshi zhanlüe fangzhen de yanbian' (The evolution of the Chinese Communist Party's military strategy after the outbreak of the war against Japan), *Jindaishi yanjiu*, no. 2 (1988), pp. 105–27
—, *Mao Zedong yu Mosike de enen yuanyuan* (Mao and Moscow), Nanchang: Jiangxi renmin chubanshe, 1999
—, 'Sulian daguimo yuanzhu Zhongguo hongjun de yici changshi' (The Soviet Union's attempt to deliver massive aid to the Chinese Red Army), *Jindaishi yanjiu*, no. 1 (1995), pp. 254–70
Ye Lei, 'Wang Shouhua lieshi shi bei Du Yuesheng huomai de ma?' (Was martyr Wang Shouhua really buried alive by Du Yuesheng?), *Shanghai dangshi yanjiu*, no. 2 (1996), pp. 33–4
Yueh Sheng, *Sun Yat-sen University in Moscow and the Chinese Revolution: A Personal Account*, New York: Paragon Book Gallery, 1971
Zeng Kelin, *Zeng Kelin jiangjun zishu* (Autobiography of Zeng Kelin), Shenyang: Liaoning renmin chubanshe, 1997
Zhang Baijia, 'Zhou Enlai and the Marshall Mission', in Larry I. Bland (ed.), *George C. Marshall's Mediation Mission to China, December 1945–January 1947*, Lexington, VA: George C. Marshall Foundation, 1998, pp. 201–34
Zhang Yongdong, *Yijiusijiu nianhou Zhongguo nongcun zhidu biange shi* (A history of changes in the Chinese countryside after 1949), Taipei: Ziyou wenhua chubanshe, 2008
Zhang Youkun et al. (eds), *Zhang Xueliang nianpu* (A chronology of Zhang Xueliang's life), Beijing: Shehui kexue wenxian chubanshe, 1996
Zhang Zhenglong, *Xuebai xuehong* (Snow is white but blood is red), Hong Kong: Dadi chubanshe, 1991
Zheng Dongguo, *Wo de rongma shengya: Zheng Dongguo huiyilu* (Reminiscences of Zheng Dongguo), Beijing: Tuanjie chubanshe, 1992

Zhonggong Haifeng xianwei dangshi bangongshe (eds), *Hailufeng geming shiliao: 1927–1933* (Historical sources on the revolutionary history of Hailufeng: 1927–1933), Guangzhou: Guangdong renmin chubanshe, 1986

Zhonggong zhongyang wenxian yanjiushi (eds), *Zhu De nianpu* (A chronology of Zhu De's life), Beijing: Renmin chubanshe, 1986

Zhongguo jindai lishi cidian, 1840–1949 (Historical dictionary of modern China, 1840–1949), Nanchang: Jiangxi renmin chubanshe, 1986

Zhongyang dang'anguan (eds), *Jianguo yilai zhongyao wenxuan xuanbian* (Selection of important texts on party history), Beijing: Zhongyang wenxian chubanshe, 1992–2011, 26 vols

—, *Zhongguo gongchandang guanyu Xi'an shibian dang'an shiliao xuanbian* (Selected archival documents on the Xi'an Incident), Beijing: Zhongguo dang'an chubanshe, 1997

—, *Zhonggong zhongyang kangri minzu tongyi zhanxian wenjian xuanbian* (Central Committee selected documents of the national United Front in the war against Japan), Beijing: Dang'an chubanshe, 1985

—, *Zhonggong zhongyang wenjian wenji* (Selected documents from the Central Committee), Beijing: Zhonggong zhongyang dangxiao chubanshe, 1989–1992, 18 vols

Acknowledgements

I acknowledge with gratitude two Hsu Long-sing Research Grants from the Faculty of Arts, University of Hong Kong. I should like to thank a number of people who read and commented on draft versions, or otherwise helped with comments, suggestions and answers to queries, by name Gail Burrowes, Christopher Hutton, and Priscilla Roberts, as well as Walter Cheung, Simon Ertz, Brian Farrell, Paul Gregory, Carsten Holz, Li Nanyang, Freddy Litten and Lin Hsiao-t'ing. In a series of previous publications popularly known as the 'People's Trilogy', I explained that I had received help from friends and colleagues in mainland China, although I preferred not to name them for reasons that seemed obvious enough. Some readers believed that this was overly prudent. Yet here we are, several years later, as caution now extends to Hong Kong, where several of the people who helped me have chosen to stay anonymous, and wisely so.

The staff in the library and archives at the Hoover Institution were unstinting with their help, as always. Digital access to the Stanford University libraries was also a lifeline, not least when working in a city where publications deemed to be politically incorrect are pulled from the shelves of public libraries on a regular basis, including my own books.

I am indebted to my publishers, namely Jasmine Horsey in London and Colleen Lawrie in New York; my copyeditor Peter James, proofreader Catherine Best, plate-section designer Phil Beresford and mapmaker Michael Athanson; as well as Anna

Massardi, Elisabeth Denison, Genista Tate-Alexander, Gurdip Ahluwalia, Mia Butcher and all the team at Bloomsbury. I want to make special mention of Adrienne Vaughan, the Bloomsbury president in New York, who made a huge difference but passed so suddenly and tragically. I would like to convey my gratitude to my literary agents, Andrew Wylie in New York and James Pullen in London. I dedicate this book to the memory of my parents, Françoise Koolen and Gerard Dikötter.

Image Credits

Chen Duxiu: Wiki Commons / Shanghai Archives Authority

Li Dazhao: Alamy / Historic Collection

Henk Sneevliet: Alamy / History and Art Collection

Sun Yat-sen and Chiang Kai-shek: Getty / -

Sun Yat-sen and Soong Ching-ling: Getty / Sovfoto

Wang Jingwei: Getty / FPG

Mikhail Borodin: Getty / Topical Press Agency / Stringer

Zhang Xueliang and Chiang Kai-shek: Getty / Hulton Archive / Stringer

Otto Braun: Wiki Commons / https://commons.wikimedia.org/wiki/File:Otto_Braun.jpg

Bo Gu: Getty / Pictures from History

Mao Zedong and Zhu De: Getty / Michael Ochs Archives / Stringer

Mao Zedong on *Red Star over China*: Getty / Sovfoto

Wang Ming: public domain

Mao Zedong and Zhang Guotao: Getty / Bettmann

Zhou Enlai: Getty / Corbis Historical

Mao Zedong and Kang Sheng: Getty / Universal History Archive

Mao Zedong, Chiang Kai-shek and Patrick Hurley: Getty / Universal History Archive

General George C. Marshall, Chiang Kai-shek and Soong Mei-ling: Getty / Bettmann

Yan Xishan: Getty / Pictures from History

Index

'AB elements', 98–100, 110, 117, 121; see also Futian Incident
ABC of Communism, 33
abduction of foreigners, 86, 96
Academica Sinica, 70
Afghanistan, 271
Agariev, Alexis F., 10
Alaska, 228
Allied Powers, 226, 246, 256
American Communist Party, 63
Amur River, 153, 241, 249
Anguo, 192–3, 197
Anhui province, 106, 186, 197, 201–2
    see also Hubei–Henan–Anhui Soviet
Anyuan, 132
Arcos affair, 59
Argentina, 153
Atkinson, Brooks, 230
atomic bombs, 235, 239–40
Australia, 153
Austria-Hungary, 2, 8, 104
Autumn Harvest Uprising, 76–7, 90
Axis Powers, 223

Bai Chongxi, 55, 59, 61, 80, 185, 200
Band, William, 211
banditry, xv
Bank of Taiwan, 30
Bao'an, 157, 168, 173, 188
Baoding, 83, 190, 197
Barrett, David, 228, 232–3
Bauer, Max, 166
Bavarian Soviet Republic, 137

Bazhong, 122–3
Bazhou, 122–3, 190
Bechamp, Georges 147
Beidaihe, 249
Beijing (Beiping), 17, 27–8, 45, 51, 57–8, 63, 77–8, 94–5, 122, 173, 177, 190–1
    airport, 243
    and Boxer Rebellion, 159
    and civil war, 243–5, 258, 260, 262–8
    falls to Nationalists, 82–4
    and Japanese invasion of Manchuria, 104–5, 126
    and Japanese Operation Ichigo, 227
    and Marco Polo Bridge Incident, 180, 243
    and Sino-Japanese war, 162, 164, 180–1, 185, 210–11
    Soviet agents in, 9–11
    Soviet Embassy, 29, 58–9, 63, 88, 264
    Tiananmen Square, 5, 265
Beiping–Hankou railway, 190
Belden, Jack, 226
Benton, Gregor, 274
Beresford, Lord Charles, 7
Big Sword Society, 131
Billingsley, Philip, 273
Bird, William, 233–4
Bismarck, Otto von, 3–4
black markets, 6, 109, 222, 256, 262
Blagoveshchensk, 249
blockhouses, 127–8, 130, 132
Bloody Wednesday, 27
Blue Express train, 96

Blyukher, Vasily (Galen), 41, 88, 167, 195
Bo Gu, 107, 125, 138, 142, 212
Bogomolov, Dimitri, 162–3, 165–6, 178
Bohai Sea, 126, 180, 241, 257
Bonnard, Abel, 11
Borodin, Madame, 57
Borodin, Mikhail, 21, 23–6, 28, 30, 33–4, 39–42, 44–6, 55–7, 64–5, 114
Bosshardt, Rudolf, 154–5
Boxer Rebellion, 159
Brandler, Heinrich, 22
Braun, Otto (Li De), 137–8, 141–2, 144–5, 149
Britain, xvii, 5–7, 17, 144, 46, 50–2, 58, 60, 160, 166, 196
  distrust of Communists, 210, 230, 233
  leaves gold standard, 104
  and Sino-Japanese war, 201–2, 205
British Communist Party, 63
Brondgeest, Carel, 210
Browder, Earl, 63
Buck, John L., 158
Bukharin, Nikolai, 33, 44, 50, 54, 87
Bureau of Investigation, 179
Burma, 205, 259
Burma Expeditionary Force, 227
Burma Road, 202

Cairo conference, 226–7, 234
Canton (Guangzhou), 5–6, 10–18, 20–1, 24–7, 29, 31–2, 34, 40–1, 43, 46–7, 52, 58, 62, 73, 75–6, 79, 82, 114
  Communist uprising, 68–72
  and civil war, 270–1
  inflation in, 224
  and Japanese Operation Ichigo, 227
  modernisation, 159–60
  and Sino-Japanese war, 184, 187, 194
Canton–Hankou railway, 139
Cao Boyi, 131
'capitalist class', 15, 87, 196
Carlson, Evans, 181, 226
Catholics, 146, 250
Central Bank of China, 262
Central General Study Committee, 217
Central Plains War, 94–5

Central Research Institute, 213
Centrososoyuz, 10
Chahar province, 153, 162, 180, 191, 200, 243
Chamberlain, Austen, 50, 60
Chamdo, 272
Chang Jung, 146–7
Changchun, xx, 104, 246, 248, 258–63, 265, 267
Changsha, 14, 42, 46–7, 49, 51, 63, 76–8, 115, 139, 155, 187
  Communist assault on, 90–3, 95–8
Charles X, King of France, 2
chemical weapons, 187
Chen Boda, 206
Chen Bulei, 140
Chen Cheng, 173
Chen Duxiu, 9–12, 14–15, 18–19, 29, 31, 46, 57, 59, 65, 78, 188
Chen, Eugene, 28, 64
Chen Jiongming, 11, 13–14, 16–17, 20, 24, 72–3
Chen Jitang, 109, 113, 138, 165
Chen Li, 203
Chen Lifu, 42, 167
Chen Qun, 61
Chen Yi, 268–70
Chen Yun, 242
Chengdu, 122, 146–50, 194–5, 202, 272
Chennault, Claire, 205, 263
Chenzhou, 80–1
Chiang Ching-kuo, 34, 178, 241
Chiang Kai-shek, xv–xx, 21–3, 25, 27, 34, 40–3, 114, 123
  and Central Plains War, 94–5
  China's Destiny, 225
  and civil war, 205, 210, 229, 243–50, 257–60, 262, 265, 269, 272
  and financial crises, 221, 223, 255
  and German invasion of Soviet Union, 204
  and Japanese invasion of Manchuria, 103–4, 106, 126, 153
  and Japanese surrender, 239–40
  and Jinan Incident, 82–3
  and Korean War, 267

and Long March, 139–40, 143–4, 148–50, 156
modernisation policies, 127–8
and Nanjing Incident, 52–4
Mao's letter to, 194
meeting with Mao, 240–2
military strategy, 129–32
Moscow visit, 22–3, 68
and Nationalist coup, 55–61, 63–4
portraits, 182, 265
relations with Americans, 226–8, 232–3, 235, 246, 249, 256
secret agreements, 153
and Sino-Japanese war, 160–72, 180–2, 184–6, 189, 191, 194, 196–7, 199, 201–6, 228
and Sino-Russian war, 87–9
takes personal command, 102
and Xi'an Incident, 172–80
Chiang, Madame (Soong Mei-ling), 175–6
Chicherin, Georgy, 13, 22
Chifeng, 255
China Inland Mission, 51, 85
China International Famine Relief Commission, 127
China Press, 131
China Society, 50
China Times, 61
China Weekly Review, xvi, 169
Chinese Air Force, 205, 223
Chinese Communist Party
  archives, xii–xiii, xvi
  Central Committee, xii, 66, 72–3, 76, 89–90, 96, 98–9, 107, 111, 117, 121, 123, 125, 191, 199–200, 208, 215
  congresses, 15–16, 18–19, 235
  Cultural Committee, 215
  currency printing, 221–2
  foundation, 15–16
  Mao appointed Chairman, 219
  membership, xiii–xiv, 89, 113, 122, 211
  membership of Comintern, 18–19
  and New Democracy, xix, 206–11
  'On New Democracy' pamphlet, xix
  Politburo, 44, 100, 107, 142, 150, 208, 212, 219, 240

purges, 99–101, 189
recruitment, 211
Revolutionary Military Council, 98
rival Central Committees, 156, 161, 190
Standing Committee, 100, 208
Chinese Eastern Railway, 8, 14, 19–20, 34–5, 58, 88–9, 103, 199, 235, 239
Chinese Soviet Republic, *see* Jiangxi Soviet
Chita, 10–11, 194, 197, 202
Chongli, 151
Chongqing, 31, 56, 122, 141–3, 149–50, 170, 184–5, 187–8, 194, 196–7, 202, 204–6, 210, 221, 223–31, 234
  and civil war, 242–3, 270, 272
  and Japanese surrender, 239–40
Christmas memorandum, 50–1
Churchill, Winston, 234
Cili, 93, 115
class struggle, 49, 164, 178, 183, 191–2, 214
Clougherty, Father F., 186
collective farming, 124, 225
collective shops, 116–17
Comintern, xii, xvii, 9–10, 13, 15, 18–19, 22–3, 26, 33–4, 44, 49, 53–4, 63, 68, 88–9, 98, 130, 137, 156
  anti-Comintern Pact, 164–5
  blacklist, 212–13, 215
  'Bolshevisation' process, 100
  dissolution of, 142, 218–19, 227
  Noulens affair, 101–2
  resentment of, 204
  and rise of Mao, 193–4
  and Sino-Japanese war, 161–2, 166, 196
  and Xi'an Incident, 174, 178
Communist Manifesto, 22
Communist Youth League, xvi, 53, 117
Confucianism, 192
Confucius, 8
Crane, Charles R., 17

Dabie Mountains, 112, 118, 187
Dadu River, 146
Dalian (Dairen), 7, 235, 245–6, 249–50

Dalta Agency, 11
Dandong, 199
d'Anjou, René, 210
Davis, John, 53
Dayong, 154–5
Dayu, 85
de Jaegher, Raymond, 197
'democratic centralism', 207–8, 225
Democratic League, 249
Deng Wenyi, 165
Deng Xiaoping, 34, 212, 268
Deng Zhongxia, 116
Denham, G. C., 16
denunciation meetings, 97, 118, 190, 217, 259, 266
Dimitrov, Georgi, 161, 167, 173, 193–4, 210, 218
Ding Ling, 215
Dingzhou, 112
Doihara, Major General Kenji, 153
Donald, William Henry, 175–6
Dong Biwu, 118
Donggu, 95–6
Doriot, Jacques, 63
Du Yuming, 245–6, 248, 250, 257, 268–9

East River, 82, 99, 112
Einstein, Albert, 102
Engels, Friedrich, 213, 220
Enshi, 115
enslaved people, 2–3
Esperanto, 10–11
Everson, Edward, 29
Eyuwan Soviet, see Hubei–Henan–Anhui Soviet

Falkenhausen, Alexander von, 167
famine, xx, 110, 125, 127, 158, 260–1
Far Eastern Bank, 28
Far Eastern Republic, 11
Far Eastern Trade State Department, 28
Farmer, Rhodes, 184
Feng Yuxiang (the Christian General), 27, 35, 63–4, 83, 94–5
Finland, xiv, xvii, 5
  Soviet invasion, 197
First Army Group, see First Red Army

First World War, 2, 5, 152, 166, 177
Flood Relief Commission, 117, 128
flooding, 104–5, 117, 161, 185–6, 198
Forman, Harrison, 229
Four Elders, 57
France, xvii, 5, 7, 109, 196, 201, 205, 247
Free China, 187, 221, 223–4, 231
French Communist Party, 63
French Indo-China, 60, 202, 227
French Revolution, xix, 1–3
French Sûreté, 14
Frunze Military Academy, 137
Fu Sinian, 70
Fu Zuoyi, 250, 265
Fujian province, 13, 16, 87, 102, 106, 111, 125, 129, 131
Futian Incident, 99; see also 'AB Elements'
Fuzhou, 111, 129

Gan River, 81, 85, 92, 96–7
Gansu province, xiv, 151–2, 156–7, 162, 168, 176, 182, 197, 216, 271
Ganzhou, 102, 125, 131
Gao Wangling, 255, 301
General Labour Union, 44, 54–6, 59–62, 64, 67–8, 70, 76–7, 259
German Communist Party, 102
German October, 68
German Social Democratic Party, 3, 5, 22
Germany, 2–5, 7–9, 22, 109
  invasion of Soviet Union, 204–5, 221
  Nazi Germany, xiii, 160, 170, 174, 178, 196
  Nazi–Soviet pact, 196
  Tripartite Pact, 202
Gillem, Alean, 248
gold standard, 104
Gorki, Maxim, 102
grain, 47, 49, 77, 87, 97, 107, 109, 115, 117, 123, 126–8, 148, 153, 164, 169, 198, 213, 221, 244, 250–4, 259, 262, 266–7
Grand Canal, 30

INDEX

Great Powers, xvii, 6–7, 17, 24, 28, 50, 105, 193, 234
Great Wall, 35, 104, 126, 180, 199, 240, 243, 245–6, 250, 257, 264
Greece, 233, 257
Gu Dacun, 100
Gu Shunzhang, 100–1
Gu Zhenghong, 29
Gu Zhutong, 178
Guangchang, 130, 132
Guangdong province, 13, 16, 41, 66–7, 79, 81, 99, 109, 112, 126, 138–9, 165–6
Guangxi province, 20, 41, 55, 138–9, 141, 156, 166
Guangzhou Bay, 7
guerrilla warfare, principles of, 86–7, 144, 148
Guilin, 17, 139–40
Guillermaz, Jacques, 196–7
Guiyang, 80, 143, 145, 156
Guizhou province, 138, 140–4, 152, 154–6, 164

Hai River, 126
Haifeng, 72–4, 76, 79
Hailufeng Soviet, 72, 74–6, 82, 99
Hainan Island, 112
Haiphong, 202
Haiti, 2
Hall, Martel, 227–8
Hangzhou, 56, 62
Hankou, 30, 42, 43–6, 51, 54–7, 64, 104, 114, 184–8, 195, 190–1, 201, 227
Hankou–Beijing railway, 83
Hankou–Changsha railway, 77
Hanson, Haldore, 193
Hanyang, 42, 65, 114
Haojiapo, 254
Harbin, 34–5, 88, 105, 153, 239, 248, 250–1
Harriman, Averell, 231
Hay, John, 7
He Long, 66, 68, 73, 90, 92–5, 112, 115–19, 125, 197, 212
  and Long March, 138, 141–2, 153–7

He Yingqin, 84, 94–6, 125–6, 153, 174, 200
Hebei province, 113, 153, 162, 180, 183, 190–1, 196–8, 200
  and civil war, 243–4
Hefeng, 93, 95, 115, 154
Henan province, xv, 63, 183, 185–6, 191
  see also Hubei–Henan–Anhui Soviet
Hengshui 265
Henri I, King of Haiti (Henri Christophe), 2
Heydrich, Reinhard, 251
Himalayas, 146
Hiroshima, 239
Hitler, Adolf, 156, 167, 174
Hokkaido, 235
Hong Kong, xiii, 6, 16–17, 21, 27, 50, 69, 72, 75, 82, 205, 272
  boycott, 32–3, 68
hostages, 6, 91, 96, 154; see also abduction of foreigners
Hsiao Tso-liang, 303
Hu Qiaomu, 213
Hu Shi, 9–10, 31, 54, 175
Hu Zongnan, 151–2, 168, 177, 257
Huai River, 118
Huaihai Campaign, 268–9
Huang Kecheng, 80
Huangpu River, 60, 181
Hubei province, 82, 92–3, 95, 104, 106, 138, 154
  see also Hubei–Henan–Anhui Soviet
Hubei–Henan–Anhui Soviet, 112–18
human-wave tactics, xx, 91, 260, 267
Hunan province, xiv, 42, 46, 49, 85, 89, 91–3, 95, 104, 106, 112, 114, 123, 240
  and Long March, 138–9, 154–6
  South Hunan Committee, 76, 78, 80
Hunan and West Hubei Soviet, 115–8
Hurley, Patrick, 232–4, 240
Hurricane, The, 251–2

illiteracy, 211
Imai, Major General Takeo, 240
Imperial German Navy, 7
Imperial Japanese Army, 83, 183, 187

Indonesia, 205
industrial relations code, 94
inflation, 93, 108, 116, 221–5, 255–6, 269
International Relief Committee, 186
Internationale, 22, 107
Isaacs, Harold, 285
Italy, 5, 60, 196, 202, 247
Ivanov, A. A., 9
Izvestia, 173, 235

Jacoby, Annalee, 220
Jaffe, Philip, 229
Japan, xv–xvi, xviii, 7–8, 11, 13, 47, 51, 60, 73
  American aid, 256
  currency war, 224
  invasion of Manchuria, 103–5, 126, 152–3, 156, 162, 180, 195, 199
  and Jinan incident, 82–3
  Operation Ichigo, 227
  pact with Soviet Union, 204
  secret agreement, 153
  Sino-Japanese war, 160–72, 178–206
  trade embargo, 204
  and Tripartite Pact, 202
  unconditional surrender, 239–40
  wartime atrocities, 184, 187
  withdrawal from League of Nations, 126, 160
Jehol province, 164, 180
Ji'an, 81, 96–7, 111, 132
Jialing River, 149
Jiamusi, 249
Jiang Dingwen, 172–3, 177
Jiangsu province, 201–2
Jiangxi province, 43, 66–7, 77, 84–7, 95, 97, 102, 106, 126–8, 131, 201
  and Long March, 137, 150, 154
  Jiangxi Soviet, xiv, 106–12, 115, 125–7, 129–31
Jiaozhou Bay, 7
Jilin, 258
Jinan, 94, 185
  Jinan Incident, 82–3
Jinggangshan, 77, 81, 84–5, 95, 222
Jinsha River, 145, 156
Jinzhou, 105, 259, 263

Jiujiang, 30, 51, 186–7
Joffe, Adolphe, 18–19, 21

Kaifeng, 244
Kalgan (Zhangjiakou), 35, 63, 240, 245, 250, 264
Kang Sheng, 215, 217–18, 254–5
Karakhan, Lev, 14, 19, 27–8, 88
Karakhan Declaration, 14
Karl Marx University, 112
Kazakhstan, 87
Khabarovsk, 249
Kokand, 6
Kolyma, 228
Komsomolsk-on-Amur, 249
Korea, xix, 7, 13, 103, 199, 235, 239, 267
  North Korea, 249–50
Korean Communist Party, 15
Korean War, xx, 267
Kropotkin, Pyotr, 16
Kuibyshev, Nikolai, 39–41
Kunming, 145, 202, 225, 227, 244, 249
Kwantung Army, 83, 103–4, 126, 153, 160, 162, 164, 180, 195–6, 199, 243

Ladany, Laszlo, 312
Lake Dongting, 139
Lake Poyang, 81
Lampson, Miles, 51, 159
land reform, 85, 125, 141, 208, 252–5
landowners, xix, 26, 46–9, 67, 69, 72–4, 80, 98, 107–8, 110, 115–16, 119–22, 126, 130–1, 154, 183, 208–9, 251–5, 266
Langdon, William, 244
Lanzhou, 151–2, 194–5, 197, 202, 271
Lashio, 202
League of Nations, 8, 105, 126, 153, 160, 197
Leiyang, 79–80, 114
Lend-Lease, 205, 219
Lenin, Vladimir, 4–5, 13, 15–16, 18, 22, 28–9, 35, 43, 109, 218, 220
Lhasa, 146, 272
Li Bai, 121
Li Chai-sum (Li Jishen), 62, 68–9, 73

Li Dazhao, 9–11, 14–15, 19, 25, 58, 63, 264
Li Fook Lum, 31, 70
Li Jishen, see Li Chai-sum
Li Kenong, 163
Li Lisan, 90, 96, 100, 213
Li Weihan, 213
Li Wenlin, 97–9
Li Zongren, 166, 185
Liao Zhongkai, 25
Liaodong Peninsula, 7
Liberation Daily, 213, 220, 251
'Little Lidice', 250–1, 265
Lijiang, 156
Lin Biao, 97, 142, 144, 146, 156, 183, 212, 243, 248, 257–64, 267–8
Lin Boqu, see Lin Zuhan
Lin Yuying, 156, 161
Lin Zexu, 6
Lin Zuhan (Lin Boqu), 25, 53, 182
Lincheng incident, 96
Liping, 141
Lishui River, 155
Litvinov, Maxim, 160, 182
Liu Jianyi, 275
Liu Shaoqi, 191, 194, 217, 219–20, 242, 255
Liu Shiqi, 98
Liu Wenhui, 122, 148
Liu Xiang, 122–3, 143
Liu Zhidan, 152
Lizerovich, Jack, 10
Lolo guerrillas, 146
Lominadze, Besso, 65, 67–8
Longli, 145, 156
Longyan, 87
Louis XVI, King of France, 1
Louverture, Toussaint, 2
Lu Shikai, 10–11
Lubyanka, 100
Ludendorff, Erich, 166
Luding Bridge, battle of, 146–8
Lufeng, 72–3, 79
Luo Zhuoying, 137
Luochuan conference, 182–3, 189
Luoyang, 170
Luxemburg, Rosa, 4

luxury items, ban on, 266

Ma Bufang, 271
Ma Su, 33
MacArthur, General Douglas, 234–5
Macau, 272
Macheng, 118, 187
McHugh, James, 246
Madang, 186
Magadan, 228
Malay States, 205
Malinovsky, Rodion, 241
Manchukuo, 153, 204, 259
Manchuria, xiv–xv, xix–xx, 7–8, 18, 83, 89, 171
  and civil war, 234–8
  grain procurements, 259, 267
  Japanese invasion, 103–5, 126, 152–3, 162, 180, 195, 199
Manchus, 83, 271
Mann, Tom, 63
Mao Zedong
  appointed Chairman, 219
  chairman of Military Council, 98
  and civil war, 242–3, 246, 248, 261
  early career, 9, 14, 25, 40, 73
  and guerrilla warfare, 85–100
  and Hunan War, 76–8, 80–1
  interviews, xvi, 168–9
  and Japanese surrender, 239–40
  and Long March, 138, 140–2, 144, 146, 149–51, 155–7, 165
  and Luochuan conference, 183, 189
  Mao Zedong Thought, 218–20
  meeting with Chiang, 240–2
  and New Democracy, xix, 206–8, 210, 225
  and peasant movement, 46–50
  portraits, 182, 188, 265, 270
  and *Red Star over China*, 188–9
  relations with Americans, 226, 228–35, 248
  retreat to Jinggangshan, 77, 81, 84–5
  rise to power, 189–91, 193–4, 212–23
  and Sino-Japanese war, 161, 163–8, 178, 180, 202, 206

and soviets, 106, 111, 125, 127, 130
subject to criticism, 97–100, 125, 144, 146, 150, 156, 189, 212
views on art and culture, 214–16
and Xi'an Incident, 173–5, 178
Maolin (New Fourth Army Incident), 202–3
Marco Polo Bridge Incident, 180, 205, 243
Marquand, Robert, xvii
Marshall, General George C., 246–9
Marshall Plan, 256
Martov, Julius, 4
Marx, Karl, 3–4, 15, 22, 89, 182, 213, 218, 220
Marxist Research Society, 10
May Fourth Movement, 8–10, 16, 66, 192
May Thirtieth Incident, 29–32
Mensheviks, 4
Mexican Communist Party, 23
Mif, Pavel, 100, 107, 212
Military Council, 98, 140, 144, 156, 167, 178, 232
Millar, K. E. F., 154
Ming dynasty, 264–5
missionaries, 7, 11, 52, 85–6, 96, 121, 152, 154–5, 191, 193, 197–9, 230, 253
  destruction of property, 158
modernisation programmes, 127–8, 159–60
Molotov, Vyacheslav, 89, 231
Molotov–Ribbentrop Pact, 196
Mongolia, xiv, 19–20, 126, 168, 177, 194–5, 205, 240, 255, 271
monks, 79, 106
Mougong, 149–51, 157
Mukden (Shenyang), 7, 105
  Mukden Incident, 104, 106, 125
Münzenberg, Wilhelm, 102

Nagasaki, 239
Nanchang, 43, 52, 73, 79, 87, 102, 111, 126, 128, 143, 201
  Communist assault, 91–3
  Nanchang Uprising, 66–7, 92, 118

Nanjiang, 122
Nanjing, 57, 62, 64, 71, 80, 82–3, 89, 94–5, 97, 114, 122, 132, 140, 152, 173
  and civil war, 247, 250, 252, 257–8, 264, 267–70
  flooding, 105
  Japanese atrocities, 184
  and Japanese surrender, 240
  modernisation, 160
  Nanjing Incident, 52–4, 56, 60, 182
  rival capital, 62, 162
  and Sino-Japanese war, 162, 164–7, 169, 178–80, 184–5
  and Xi'an Incident, 176–8
Nanking University, 52
Napoleon Bonaparte, 2
National Assembly, 8, 207
National Labour Congress, 26
National Salvation Association, 188
Nationalist Army, 39–43, 51, 53–4, 65
Nationalist Party (Kuomintang)
  archives, xvii
  Central Executive Committee, 24–5, 40–1, 43, 56
  Central Supervisory Commission, 57
  congresses, 24, 40, 165
  coup, 55–64
  Joint Conference, 56
  Organisation Department, 25
Neumann, Heinz, 68–9
New Democracy, xix, 206–8, 210, 225, 230
New Fourth Army Incident, 202–3
New Youth, 9–10, 46, 66, 78
Nikolsky, Vladimir, 15
Nineteenth Route Army, 106, 125, 129
Ningdu, xiv, 85, 102, 125, 132, 142, 212
Ningxia province, 168, 182, 197
Nomonhan Battle, 195–6
Normandy landings, 227
North-China Herald, 114, 123, 141
North-east Anti-Japanese United Army, 199–200, 241
Northern Expedition, 17, 41–3, 55–6, 60, 64–5, 79–80, 82, 84, 92, 94, 114, 187
North-west Federation, 150

Noulens, Hilaire, 101–2, 182

Office of Strategic Services, 233
On New Democracy, 206
One Third system, 207–8, 211, 216, 231
opium, 6, 81, 123, 222–3
'opportunism'
   'left opportunism', 80, 212–13
   'right opportunism', 142, 146

Pan Hannian, 167, 175–6
Papandreou, Georgios, 233
Paris Peace Conference, 5, 8
Pearl Delta, 16
Pearl Harbor, 196, 205, 223
Pearl River, 25, 32
Peasant Affairs Department, 26
Peasant International, 49
peasant movement, 46–50
Peasant Movement Training Institute, 26, 46, 73
peasants
   'middle peasants', 108, 115, 127, 252–4
   'poor peasants', 126, 198, 209, 251–2, 266
   'rich peasants', 85, 98, 107–8, 110, 115, 120–1, 125–7, 130–1, 208, 252–3
Peck, Graham, 226
Peking University, 9–10, 46
Peng Dehuai, 85, 90–2, 94–5, 97, 99, 146, 182, 271–2
Peng Pai, 73–6, 79
Peng Zhen, 242–3, 246
People's Consultative Conference, 247
People's Liberation Army, 80, 248, 265, 267–8, 270, 272
People's Political Councils, 188, 209, 207
petty bourgeoisie, 84–5, 207, 215
Philippines, 205, 235
Pingshi, 79
Pingxingguan, 183
Pioneer Corps, 152
Poland, Soviet invasion, 196
Polevoy, S. A., 9
Port Arthur, 7–8, 103–4, 235, 240–1, 245, 250

Potapov, A. S., 13
Pravda, 33, 90, 173
Prideaux-Brune, Sir Humphrey, 230
priests, 74, 147, 251
Profintern, 26, 101
prostitutes, 74
'protected village' programme, 199
'protracted war', 102
Pu Yi, Emperor, 153
Public Security Bureau, 259

Qing dynasty, xvii, 5–8, 11–12, 46, 83, 94, 153, 242, 271
Qingdao, 7–8, 171–2, 243
Qinghai province, 151, 271
Qinhuangdao, 245
Qu Qiubai, 25, 29, 65, 67–9, 90
Quanzhou, 139–40

Radek, Karl, 64, 100
Rectification Campaign, 215–20, 229, 242
Red Army, xvi, 13–14, 17, 25, 65–8, 76, 81, 85, 87, 90–2, 127, 129, 157, 213, 236, 240, 246
   Eighth Route Army, 182–3, 189–91, 193–4, 196–8, 201, 241–3, 249, 252
   First Red Army, 90, 112, 125, 130, 149–52, 156–7
   Fourth Red Army, 81, 87, 91, 97, 112, 118, 120–3, 142, 149–50, 157
   and Jiangxi Soviet, 108, 110–12
   and Long March, 138–42, 146–9, 156–8
   New Fourth Army, 182, 197, 201–3, 220
   renamed People's Liberation Army, 265
   reorganisation, 182–3
   Second Red Army, 90, 92–3, 112, 116, 141, 153, 155, 157
   and Sino-Japanese war, 167–9, 172, 174, 178–80
   Third Red Army, 90, 200
   warning letter, 200–1
Red China, 112
Red Cross, 145

Red Guard Army, 110–11
Red Guards, 65, 69–70
Red Lake, 115, 117
Red Pioneers, 148
'Red Professors', 213
Red University, 179
reformatories, 128
Republic of China, 12, 17, 223, 232, 234
   constitution, 207
Rockefeller Foundation, 159
Roosevelt, Franklin D., 202, 205, 226–8, 231–2, 234–6
Rosta, 11
Rudnik, Jakob, 101
Ruijin, 106–7, 109–10, 112, 123, 132, 137–8
Russia, see Soviet Union
Russian Empire, 5
Russian Social Democratic Labour Party, 4
Russo-Japanese War, 34, 103

St Petersburg, storming of the Winter Palace, 4
Sakhalin Island, 235
Salazar, António de Oliveira, xiii
salt, 84, 97, 108–9, 111, 116, 124, 260
Sangzhi, 93, 118, 154
Sanson, Charles-Henri, 1
Schama, Simon, xix
Schramm, George, 85–6
Scotland, 23
Seeckt, Hans von, 167
Semeshko, Gregory, 10
serfdom, 3, 47, 120
Service, John Stewart, 228
Shaanxi province, xvi, xix, 113, 122, 151–2, 156–7, 162–4, 170, 179, 182, 185–6, 209
Shameen (Shamian), 32–3, 70, 270
Shameen Incident, 32–3
Shandong province, 5, 7–8, 51, 82, 94, 113, 180, 183, 185, 191, 197, 201
   and civil war, 241, 243–4, 268
Shanghai, 5–6, 15–16, 18, 28–31, 34, 42, 45, 76, 89, 93, 97–9, 117–18, 124, 130, 143, 153, 177
   American Club, 270
   and civil war, 258, 264, 270
   Commercial Press Club, 60
   Communist purge, 101–2
   French Concession, 15, 60, 62, 101
   inflation in, 224
   International Settlement, 4, 30, 54–5, 60–1, 64, 101, 106
   and Nationalist coup, 51–2, 54–6, 58–63, 68, 71
   Shanghai Commune, 55, 59, 61
   and Sino-Japanese war, 171, 180–1, 184
   Soviet agents in, 10–13
   Soviet Consulate, 28–9
   surrender of foreign concessions, 159
Shanghai Intelligence Bureau, 13–14
Shanghai Life, 10
Shanghai University, 29
Shanhaiguan, 104, 126, 180, 241–2, 245–6, 258
Shantou (Swatow), 16, 66–7, 73, 75, 79
Shanwei (Swabue), 72–3, 76
Shanxi province, 94, 163, 165, 168, 171, 176, 180, 183, 191, 193, 197, 243, 254, 267
Shashi, 93
Sheng Shicai, 271
Shenyang (Mukden), 104, 241–3, 246, 248, 258–9, 262–4, 269
Shi Yousan, 197
Shipping and Godown Workers' Union, 11
Short, Philip, 286
Siam, 205
Siberia, 14, 100, 195–6, 199, 202, 204, 228, 241, 249
Sichuan province, 56, 78, 93, 106, 162, 164
   and Long March, 138–40, 142–6, 149, 152, 154, 156
   Sichuan soviet, 121–5
   and Sino-Japanese war, 185–6
Singapore, 205
Sino-British War (Opium War), 6
Sino-Soviet Treaty, 58, 240, 245
Sino-Soviet War, xv, xvii, 87–90, 167

INDEX

Siping, 248, 257–8
Smedley, Agnes, 102, 289
Sneevliet, Henk, 15, 17–19, 68
Snow, Edgar, xvi, 102, 168–9, 188–9, 226
Soong Mei-ling, 227
Soong, T. V., 41, 175–6, 233, 255
Sorge, Richard, 230
South China Sea, 72
South Manchuria Railway, 103
Soviet Union (Russia)
  agents in China, 9–13
  Bolshevik revolution, 2, 4–5, 7, 25, 33, 44, 47, 73, 106
  border with China, 150, 153, 160
  and Chinese civil war, 234, 251, 257, 272
  civil war, 13–14
  and democracy, 211
  diplomatic relations, 27–9, 35, 88, 153
  enters Pacific War, 235
  German invasion, 204–5, 221
  Great Terror, 215
  invasion of Finland, 197
  invasion of Poland, 196
  Karakhan Declaration, 14, 19
  Left Opposition, 22, 33, 64, 87
  and Manchuria, 239–40, 245–6, 248–50
  Nazi–Soviet pact, 196
  pact with China, 164, 182, 204
  pact with Japan, 204, 235
  and Sino-Japanese war, 153, 160, 163, 166, 178–9, 184, 187, 194–6, 199, 202, 204–6
  and Xi'an Incident, 173
  see also Sino-Soviet War
Soviet Writers' Congress, 214
soviets, 112–33, 154–5
  Chinese Central Soviet, 150, 154, 169
  see also Jiangxi Soviet
Spassk, 195
Special Movement Corps, 129
Stalin, Josef, xviii–xix, 22–3, 33, 35, 49–50, 54, 56, 64–5, 68, 100, 107, 156, 217, 220
  and Chinese civil war, 241, 245–6
  dissolution of Comintern, 218–19
  Great Purge, 212
  and invasion of Soviet Union, 204
  and rise of Mao, 194
  and Sino-Japanese war, 160–1, 164, 167–8, 178, 189, 191, 195, 228
  and Sino-Soviet war, 87–90
  views on art and culture, 214
  and Xi'an Incident, 175
  relations with Americans, 231, 234–5, 239–40
Stalin Prize for Literature, 252
Stalingrad, battle of, 218, 241
Stam, John and Betty, 291
Stein, Günther, 230–1
Stilwell, Joseph, 164, 166, 183, 226–7, 231–2, 246–7
Stopany, Vadim, 10
strikes, 3, 5, 16–18, 26, 29–32, 41, 44–5, 49–50, 54–5, 58–63, 66, 68, 94, 105–6, 111, 162, 171, 224
Suiyuan province, 171, 180
Sun Chuanfang, 43, 52, 55
Sun Fo, 15, 44–5
Sun Shuyun, 147
Sun Tzu, xx
Sun Yat-sen, 11–24, 26–8, 31, 33, 35, 39, 41, 43, 46, 53, 70, 73, 118, 182, 225, 270
  Manifesto to the Foreign Powers, 17
Sun Yat-sen, Madame, 44–5, 64, 102
Sun Yat-sen University, 33–4, 64, 100
Sungari River, 248–9
Suoli people, 200
Suzhou, 184
Sze, Alfred Sao-ke, 51

Tai'erzhuang, 185
Taiping Rebellion, 6
Taiwan (Formosa), xx, 7, 234, 256, 272
Taiyuan, 163–4, 267
  battle of, 183–4
Taku Forts, 264
Tanggu, 258
Tariff Revision Conference, 51
Tashkent, 11
taxes, xviii, 21, 26, 45, 47–8, 84, 108–9, 116, 123–4, 128–9, 143, 150, 198, 221, 223–4, 226, 256, 265–6, 269

Taylor, General Maxwell, 267
Thailand, see Siam
Tian Songyao, 123, 143
Tianjin, 8, 66, 113, 126, 180, 185, 190–1
  and civil war, 243–4, 257, 263–4, 267
  surrender of foreign concessions, 159
Tianjin–Nanjing railway, 190–1
Tianshui, 267, 271
Tibet, xiv, 271–2
Tibetans, 150–1
Timoshenko, Semyon, 201
Timperley, Harold, 184
Tongguan, 173, 179–80, 185
Tongjiang, 122–4, 149
Tongmenghui, 11–12, 22, 118
Trans-Siberian Railway, 8, 195
Trappists, 199
Treaty of Versailles, 8, 14
treaty port system, 5–6, 30, 159
Treaty Powers, 21, 32, 51
Tripartite Pact, 202
Trotsky, Leon, 4, 14, 16, 22–3, 25, 33, 63–4, 87
Truman, Harry S., 246–7, 249, 257
Truman Doctrine, 257
Tsuji, Masanobu, 196
Tucheng, 142
Tung, S. T., 47
tungsten (wolfram), 109, 138, 271
Tunisia, 218
Turkey, 23, 257

Uhlmann, Georges, 210
Uighurs, 271
Umezu, Yoshijirō, 153
unemployment, 20, 45, 60
United Front, 18–19, 56, 63–6, 156, 161–3, 165–9, 172, 175, 182–3, 187–9, 191, 194, 196, 200, 203, 211, 251
  International United Front, 205–6
United Nations, xx, 230, 267
United States, xvii, 7, 83, 86, 104, 106, 109, 152, 159, 188, 196, 225
  arms embargo, 257
  communist membership, xiii–xiv, xvii
  and Sino-Japanese war, 201–2, 206
  and Second World War, 205
  support for Communists, 226–31
US Congress, 256
US Seventh Fleet, 245
US State Department, 229
University of Hong Kong, 21
University of Nanking, 158
Urumqi, 271–2

Valentin, Father, 147
village life, 48–9
Vladivostok, 7, 9–11, 66, 153, 195, 202, 239
Voitinsky, Gregori, 13–15

Waldron, Arthur, 274
Walker, Michael, xvii
Wall Street Crash, 89
Wallace, Henry A., 227–8, 231
Wang, C. T., 105
Wang Fanxi, 31
Wang Jialie, 143
Wang Jiaxiang, 193–4, 219
Wang Jingwei, 24, 28, 39–41, 43, 56–7, 59, 64, 95, 173
Wang Ming (Chen Shaoyu), 100, 107, 117, 120, 161, 165, 173, 189–90, 193–4
  blacklisted in Yan'an, 212–13, 215, 217–19
Wang Shijie, 234
Wang Shiwei, 215
Wang Shouhua, 55, 62
war bonds, 110, 224
'warlord era', end of, 95
Washington Conference, 51
Wayaobao, 152–3, 161, 165, 168
Wedemeyer, General Albert, 232, 240
Wei Lihuang, 259
Weihaiwei, 7, 51
Weizhou, 168
Wellington Koo, V. K., 51, 58
Western Hills, 39–40
Whampoa Academy, 25–6, 31–2, 40–1, 58, 66, 97–8, 151, 167, 176
White, Theodore, 220, 226, 230
White Terror, 256

Williams, John, 52
women's suffrage, 2–3
Workers' Supervisory Corps, 55
world revolution, 22–3, 25, 45, 63, 90, 161
Wu Peifu, 18–19, 42–3, 52, 114
Wu Zhihui, 57
Wuchang, 12, 22, 26, 42–3, 114, 118, 184
Wuhan, 42–4, 53, 63–4, 66, 71, 82, 90–3, 114–15, 118, 184, 270
  flooding, 104–5
Wuxi, xiii

Xia Xi, 117
Xiamen, 62, 87
Xi'an, 182
  Xi'an Incident, 170–80
Xiang River, 91, 139
Xiang Zhongfa, 90, 101, 107
Xiang'exi Soviet, see Hunan and West Hubei Soviet
Xiao Ke, 117, 154–5
Xie Juezai, 221
Xingning, 81
Xinjiang province, 151–2, 182, 184, 189, 271–2
Xiong Shihui, 127
Xiwanzi ('Little Lidice'), 250–1, 265
Xu Haidong, 152
Xu Kexiang, 76–7
Xu Ming, 197
Xu Xiangqian, 121–2, 149, 191, 212, 267
Xu Youwei, 273
Xuzhou, 185–6, 267–9, 271

Yalta Conference, 234, 239–41
Yalu River, 103
Yan Xishan (the Model Governor), 94–5, 163–4, 197–8, 245, 264, 267
Yan'an, xix, 152, 177–9, 182, 189–90, 194–7, 202–3, 206, 210–18, 220–1, 223–4, 235, 251
  and American visitors, 226–8, 230–4, 248
  and civil war, 241–2, 257
Yan'an Forum on Literature and Art, 214

Yang Hu, 61
Yang Hucheng, 162, 170, 172, 176–7
Yangjiang, 82
Yangtze Rapid Steamship Company, 52
Yangtze River, 5, 30, 42, 45, 48, 56–8, 60, 64–5, 81, 91, 93–5, 104, 115, 122, 141–3, 149, 169, 180, 184–6, 201–2, 224, 268, 270
Yangzhou, 83
Yanjiaping, 199
Yantai, 241, 244–5, 268
Ye Ting, 66–9, 72–3, 201–2
Yellow River, 7, 113, 151, 157, 164, 168–9, 179, 185, 243–4
Yellow Sea, 268
Yenching University, 211
Yingkou, 245, 248, 258
Yongxin, 81, 95
Yorke, Gerald, 112
Young, Rev. Edward, 85–6
Young Pioneers, 64, 74
Yu Youren, 29
Yuan Shikai, 12, 78, 94
Yuanbao, 251–4
Yumen oilfields, 271
Yunnan province, 20, 41, 140, 143–5, 149, 156

Zeng Kelin, 241–2, 245
Zeng Zhongsheng, 120
Zetkin, Clara, 102
Zhang Fakui, 66, 69–70, 73, 75
Zhang Guotao, 25, 67, 120–5, 182, 187, 190, 201
  and Long March, 138, 142–3, 149–51, 156–7
Zhang Huizan, 97
Zhang Junmai, 257
Zhang Qun, 143
Zhang Tailei, 68–9
Zhang Wentian, 130–1, 142, 156, 190, 213
Zhang Xueliang (the Young Marshal), 83, 88–9, 95, 103–4, 126
  and Sino-Japanese war, 162–4, 166, 170, 172
  and Xi'an Incident, 173–7

Zhang Zuolin, 18, 34–5, 42, 57, 63, 82–3
Zhao Shangzhi, 199–200
Zhdanov, Andrei, 214–15
Zhejiang province, xiii, 21, 30, 113
Zheng Dongguo, 260, 262
Zhengzhou, 63, 185–6
Zhijiang Airfield, 240
Zhongshan, 40
Zhou Enlai, 25, 40, 66, 68, 79, 92, 101, 107, 125, 182, 190, 194, 197, 210, 217, 232, 312
   and civil war, 242, 269
   and Long March, 137–8, 141–2, 156
   panegyric for Mao, 219–20
   and Xi'an Incident, 173–7
Zhou Fengqi, 59, 61
Zhou Libo, 251–2
Zhou Yang, 215
Zhu De, 78–9, 81, 84–7, 90–2, 95, 97, 99, 111, 115, 168, 173, 193
   and civil war, 243, 247
   and Eighth Route Army, 182, 201
   and Long March, 140, 149–50, 155
   and Luochuan conference, 182, 189
Zhu Shaoliang, 217
Zhukov, Georgy, 195
Zunyi, 141–4, 150, 160
Zunyi conference, 141–2

A Note on the Author

Frank Dikötter is the Milias Senior Fellow at the Hoover Institution, Stanford University. He is also Chair Professor of Humanities at the University of Hong Kong. His books have changed the way historians view China, from the classic *The Discourse of Race in Modern China* to his award-winning People's Trilogy documenting the lives of ordinary people under Mao. He lives in Palo Alto, California.

A Note on the Type

The text of this book is set in Linotype Stempel Garamond, a version of Garamond adapted and first used by the Stempel foundry in 1924. It is one of several versions of Garamond based on the designs of Claude Garamond. It is thought that Garamond based his font on Bembo, cut in 1495 by Francesco Griffo in collaboration with the Italian printer Aldus Manutius. Garamond types were first used in books printed in Paris around 1532. Many of the present-day versions of this type are based on the Typi Academiae of Jean Jannon cut in Sedan in 1615.

Claude Garamond was born in Paris in 1480. He learned how tocut type from his father and by the age of fifteen he was able tofashion steel punches the size of a pica with great precision. At theage of sixty he was commissioned by King Francis I to design aGreek alphabet, and for this he was given the honourable title ofroyal type founder. He died in 1561.